Thought and Behaviour in
Modern Japanese Politics

THOUGHT AND BEHAVIOUR IN
Modern Japanese Politics

By

MASAO MARUYAMA

Edited by
IVAN MORRIS

London
OXFORD UNIVERSITY PRESS
NEW YORK   TORONTO

Oxford University Press, Ely House, London W. 1

GLASGOW NEW YORK TORONTO MELBOURNE WELLINGTON
CAPE TOWN SALISBURY IBADAN NAIROBI LUSAKA ADDIS ABABA
BOMBAY CALCUTTA MADRAS KARACHI LAHORE DACCA
KUALU LUMPUR HONG KONG

First published 1963
Reprinted 1966

PRINTED AND BOUND IN ENGLAND BY
HAZELL WATSON AND VINEY LTD
AYLESBURY, BUCKS

Editor's Preface

Among the spate of books about Japan that have appeared since the war in English and other European languages one type is almost conspicuous by its rarity: namely, studies by Japanese scholars about their own country. Several bookshelves could be filled with works by Western experts dealing with the history, politics, economics, religion, art, and literature of the country. When it comes to translation of what modern Japanese writers have to say about their own land and its people, however, we have been limited largely to fiction. During the past fifteen years a remarkable number of translated novels, plays, and short stories have been published in the West, and cumulatively they give a vivid and authentic picture of life in these distant islands which, though they can now be reached by air in a matter of hours, still tend in many ways to be inaccessible.

Yet, valuable as these translations of fiction may be, both in their own right as literature and for the understanding they provide of Japan past and present, they hardly obviate the need in the West for scholarly studies by Japanese scholars who have systematically examined different aspects of their country. A translation of essays by Professor Maruyama Masao* may help to fill at least a small part of the gap. Both the Japanese themselves and those few Westerners who read their language generally regard him as one of the most creative and stimulating writers who have been at work during the past few decades. He has been mainly concerned with Japanese intellectual history, and is perhaps best known for his studies on the influence of neo-Confucianism and on the development of nationalist thought in the modern period. His interests, however, are by no means confined to the history of his own country, and the present volume includes essays on general questions like political power and on specifically non-Japanese matters like de-Stalinization. Even in the essays that are focused on Japan he usually broadens

* Here and throughout this book names are given in the Japanese order, i.e. with family names first.

his discussion by suggesting significant parallels or contrasts with developments elsewhere. In examining Japanese nationalism, for example, he frequently refers to modern Chinese history, and his study of Japan's wartime leadership owes a great deal to provocative comparisons with Nazi Germany.

Although Professor Maruyama is far from being an easy writer, his books and articles are enormously popular (his recent *Intellectual History of Japan*, and earlier works also, are bestsellers), and they have undoubtedly had considerable influence in Japan, particularly on the generation that has reached maturity since the war. Most of the essays in this volume have been widely read, discussed, and criticized by those Japanese who are seriously concerned with politics and with the intellectual development of their country.

The essays devoted to the Japanese political scene cover a wide range of topics. All of them, however, share a certain general approach that Professor Maruyama had defined as follows. In the first place, he has tried to analyse Japanese politics not so much by studying its legal, institutional setting (the more conventional method) but rather in terms of the general cultural context and the pattern of interpersonal relationships, paying particular attention to the impact of non-political behaviour and activities in politics. Secondly, he has made an effort to define the underlying values of the Japanese (especially of the members of the ruling *élites*) that were not formalized into any doctrinal or theoretical pattern, and to show how such systems conditioned the leadership and decision-making process of Japanese politics. In examining contemporary politics on a world scale, Professor Maruyama has been particularly guided by the belief that contemporary ideological tensions, notably those associated with the Cold War, have been aggravated by the tendency of the 'isms' on both sides to refuse to recognize that there are features of political dynamics common to all societies, which, in a given situation, make certain patterns of behaviour inevitable, regardless of ideology.

Without wishing in any way to prejudge the validity of this approach, or its success as it applies to the essays in the present volume, I would nevertheless suggest that it has in general made for a most original type of analysis. Professor Maruyama's writing can be challenging, provocative, sometimes even infuriating; it is rarely banal. Among his most valuable contributions is to have called into question certain conventional theories about Japanese politics, for instance the idea that a slow but steady progress towards democracy was rudely, and more or less fortuitously, interrupted in the 1930s by the 'militarists' and that since the war Japan has returned to her normal course.

One reason for the liveliness of Professor Maruyama's writing is his readiness to express emotions and value judgements of a type that Western scholars nowadays tend to eschew when dealing with subjects of this kind. A propensity towards such value judgements seems to have been prevalent among Japanese scholars in the social sciences, especially since 1945. As Professor Dore points out, this may be the effect of the almost endemic sense of crisis in post-war Japan, which has prompted an urgent sense of personal involvement among Japanese intellectuals, exacerbated in some cases by a feeling of guilt at not having been sufficiently committed to do anything effective to prevent the success of militarism in the 1930s.

Whatever justification there may be for the introduction of value judgement in scholarly writing (and Professor Maruyama cogently argues the case in his essay on 'Politics as a Science'), the practice is bound to shock many Western readers, especially since his values are often different from ours. One difference may arise from the fact that, like so many modern Japanese intellectuals, Professor Maruyama is deeply conversant with Hegelian dialectics and influenced by Marxist ideas and terminology. This is certainly not to suggest that he is a committed member of any extreme political group. Even a cursory reading of an essay like 'A Critique of De-Stalinization' will indicate how far Maruyama is from being an orthodox Marxist. Indeed his approach to contemporary politics cannot be classed in any ready-made category. His point of view on most questions is thoroughly individual and has the merit of incensing members of both political extremes.

Where the intellectual history of his country is concerned, Professor Maruyama writes with erudition and authority. Yet the reader should remember that his conclusions are often hotly disputed by eminent Japanese colleagues. If Maruyama's position is to be classified, one would presumably describe him as an independent member of the left. Inasmuch as the left-wing intelligentsia nowadays exerts an influence in Japan out of all proportion to its numbers, and since it is generally recognized that the West should try to maintain a dialogue with the non-communist left in Asia, we have a good deal to learn from these writings by one of its most talented and creative representatives. It remains, perhaps, to be added that the views expressed in these essays are not necessarily shared by the respective translators or by the editor.

*   *   *

The editor's aim has been to present these translations in as free a style as was possible while still accurately preserving the sense of the original. Maruyama's ideas tend to be complicated and the language he uses does nothing to make them appear any simpler than they are. The Teutonic style has had a major influence on Japanese scholars, and it is particularly pronounced in the writing of Maruyama, who has been greatly influenced by German writers. The length and complexity of his sentences and his penchant for abstract words and curious turns of phrasing make his work difficult even for educated Japanese readers. To put this into fairly readable English has involved taking considerable liberties with the structure and phrasing of the original. Professor Maruyama, however, has thoroughly checked each of the translations (occasionally making amendments to the original text), and the editor feels confident that if violence has been done to the author's thought it is only very rarely and in minor matters.

Professor Maruyama's notes appear at the bottom of each page and the translators' notes at the end of each essay. The glossary at the back of the volume contains explanations of all the important proper names occurring in the nine essays, and of many less important names also. The editor would like to express his thanks to Kaoru and David Titus and to Paul Varley for their help in preparing this glossary, as well as the index. I should also take this opportunity to thank the teams of translators (whose names appear in the list of contents) for their faithful co-operation, and the following people for the assistance they have given at one stage or another in the preparation of this volume: Professor George Totten (University of Rhode Island); Dr. Ronald Dore (London School of Economics); Mr. Richard Storry (St. Antony's, Oxford); Professors James Morley and Herschel Webb, Miss Miwa Kai, and Mr. Shumpei Okamoto (Columbia University).

IVAN MORRIS

Author's Introduction to the English Edition

The essays included in this volume were published over a period of somewhat less than ten years. The earliest were written almost immediately after I was demobilized and transformed once again from an infantryman into an assistant professor of political science. The most recent is already more than six years old.

Given the tempo and scale of political change throughout the world since the last war, there are probably few students of politics who can re-read with unmixed pride and equanimity their contemporary comments on the controversial problems of a decade ago. The sense of embarrassment is enhanced for one who, like the present author, finds himself writing a preface for a reading public whom he had never anticipated when writing these essays, and whose cultural tradition has been very different from his own.

It would take too long to explain fully to the reader the social and intellectual climate in which we Japanese started—or rather *re*-started—the practice of our profession after a long period of isolation from the Western intellectual world. Here I will confine myself to anticipating what now seem to me the probable reactions of doubt and criticism on the part of a reader unfamiliar with the intellectual context in which these essays were written, and adding a few words in explanation— and perhaps in self-defence.

In the first place, the reader may well wonder, particularly in those essays dealing specifically with modern Japan, at the tones of denunciation in which my criticism of Japanese politics and society—even of the Japanese academic and literary worlds—is couched. It may seem that I have an obsessive concern exclusively with the pathological aspects of my own society. Some may see in this a typical expression of the despairing self-denigration supposedly traditional to Japanese intellectuals.

I certainly would not deny that in these essays my analysis of Japanese society leans towards the pathological rather than the physiological approach. But in view of the post-war situation, this was not unnatural. Social scientists were animated in their inquiries by one big question: what were the *internal* factors which drove Japan into her disastrous war? How was it that Japanese intellectuals, who for decades past had been absorbing Western scholarship and techniques and ways of life, who were more familiar—or at least believed themselves more familiar—with Western than with Japanese or Asian traditions, proved in the end so willing to accept, or at least so impotent to halt, the onrush of a blindly nationalistic militarism inspired by the crudest beliefs in the mythology of a uniquely Japanese 'Imperial Way'? This, the *academic* point of departure for workers in all fields of the social sciences after the war, was also their *practical* response to their sense of social responsibility as citizens. It will be apparent that, however unsuccessful the performance, my conscious intention, at least, in these essays was to expose myself and the body politic of my own society to a probing X-ray analysis and to wield a merciless scalpel on every sign of disease there discovered.

In this I can claim no originality, for this was the posture adopted by most of my intellectually active colleagues in the immediate post-war period. If there is something distinctive to be found in my own approach, it lies in my attempt to broaden the perspective of my Marxist contemporaries. Marxist methods of critical social analysis, which had been responsible for much of the seminal work in the social sciences in the early thirties and which had brought on its practitioners the most vigorous official oppression, saw an enormous revival in the new freedom of the post-war years. As a consequence, under Marxist influence the study of Japanese society and culture tended naturally to become 'a class analysis of the power structure of the Emperor system' or an analysis of 'the socio-economic infrastructure of imperialism'. By contrast my intention was to throw light on these same problems from a somewhat different angle: to examine the nature of Japanese culture in a wider sense, and analyse the daily behaviour of the Japanese people and the nature of their thought processes, including not simply consciously-held ideologies but more especially those unconscious assumptions and values which in a fragmentary way reveal themselves in the actions of daily life. In short, these essays represent a contrapuntal mixture of two themes. On the one hand I seek to expose the *pudenda*, the parts of shame of Japanese society, which the events of the thirties and forties were bringing ever more clearly into view but which had been an inseparable feature of the Japanese body politic throughout the period of Japan's 'remarkable advance' from a feudal society to a ranking industrial power. In this I sought to counter the tendency—most apparent in Japan since the Korean war but present ever since the surrender—to explain the catastrophic events after 1930 simply as resulting from the external international environment or as a temporary response to severe internal problems, but in any case as a contingent and fortuitous deviation from the 'natural' trend of Japanese political development, and as such best put out of mind. The other theme was the attempt to stand out against the flood-tide of the vulgarized, dogmatic Marxism which was swamping the Japanese intellectual world and to work for the development of a broader and more diverse approach. For a Western reader this attempt to fight a war on two fronts may seem a curious manifestation of ideological confusion. So be it. My purpose here is not to win the reader's agreement, only to gain his understanding.

One word, however, about the Japanese intellectual's famous 'self-denigration'. I cannot help recalling, when I hear this discussed, the remarks of Karl Löwith, the Heidelberg philosopher who taught for a time in pre-war Japan. In his postscript to the Japanese edition of *European Nihilism*, an acute piece of cultural analysis, he contrasts the European spirit of self-criticism with the Japanese spirit of 'self-love'! So much for the contrast between pre-war and post-war Japan, but what of the Japan of 1963? To be sure, I cannot deny that my own present interests in the history of Japanese political thought— my evaluation of the importance of problems and my motives for study—have changed somewhat since the decade in which these essays were written. On the other hand, when I read Japanese newspaper reports of the 'Japan boom' supposedly spreading not only through America but also in parts of the communist world, and when I observe the growing conviction

of the Japanese government and people that things Japanese—
everything from the astonishing post-war growth-rate of the
economy to Zen Buddhism, Judo, and flower arrangement—
are winning the universal admiration of foreigners, I cannot
feel altogether happy. The notes may be new, but the shape of
the melody is familiar. Japanese 'self-love', reflecting as it does
a preoccupation with Japan's reputation in foreign eyes, is
something rather different from a proper sense of self-respect
and independence, and I must confess that—though my tone
might not today be as strident as in these essays—recent events
have hardly impelled me to abandon my concern with the
pathological aspects of Japanese society.

A second aspect of these essays which may strike the reader—
particularly one who has some acquaintance with Japan—as
somewhat odd, is the stress which runs through them on the
specific peculiarity of Japanese politics and of the cultural
patterns which underlie them. To some extent, of course, this is
part and parcel of the diagnostic and therapeutic intentions
outlined above. A good doctor should be concerned with the
particular physical characteristics of his particular patient.
Generalizations to the effect that 'all men have occasional
fevers, and all fevers produce such-and-such symptoms' make
for the easy writing of prescriptions—but certainly not of good
ones.

There is, however, the further reason of personal predilection.
By temperament I am less interested, in the analysis of men and
institutions, in discerning those characteristics which they
share in common with other men and institutions, than in those
special characteristics which differentiate them. Immanuel
Kant once remarked that all students of nature could be divided
into two groups, those who were more concerned with principles
of homogeneity, and those who leaned towards specification.
One group, according to Kant, seem to be 'almost averse to
heterogeneousness and always intent on the unity of *genera*';
others 'are constantly striving to divide nature into so much
variety that one might lose almost all hope of being able to
distribute its phenomena according to general principles'.* If the
same classification may be applied to social scientists, I must
own my membership of the latter category. But as Kant himself

* *Critique of Pure Reason*, Muller's translation, Vol. 2, pp. 561f.

goes on to say, both approaches are necessary. The exponents of neither approach can claim a monopoly of the truth; they should supplement, rather than arrogantly reject, each other.

Thirdly, the reader may find the conceptual framework underlying these essays somewhat odd or outdated. In part, I suppose, the essays reflect fairly faithfully the epistemological assumptions and the currency of academic discourse shared by Marxist and non-Marxist scholars alike in the immediate post-war period. Indeed, the careful reader who notes the respective dates of these essays may discern a subtle shift of tone and language which reflects the rapid growth of intellectual communication between Japan and the West since the war and the increasing differentiation of vocabularies and assumptions between Marxists and non-Marxists which has resulted. The preference for a substantialist view of concepts which characterize my earlier essays and the tendency to define certain categories rather rigidly in terms of a theoretical scheme of historical development give way in the later ones to a more nominalistic approach.

There is, however, something more idiosyncratic and personal in this which can best be explained in terms of my own intellectual background. My earliest views of the world were formed under the strong influence of my father, a political journalist who remained to the last a typical representative of Japanese intellectuals of the nineteenth-century positivist generation. He had an inbuilt resistance, which was almost instinctive, towards any attempt to order the intricate detail of the events of history into the conceptual strait-jacket of any grand theory. The idea of any political process as a struggle between 'isms' was alien to him. That the acting individual was the ultimate reality in society seemed to him a self-evident truth.

Thus it was only at the university that I first encountered German idealism, more specifically when I attended the seminar of Professor Nambara in which he used Hegel's *Vernunft in der Geschichte* as a textbook. Hegel attracted me enormously (though Professor Nambara himself, as a neo-Kantian, was highly critical of Hegel's philosophy) and it was largely under the stimulus of such works as *Phaenomenologie des Geistes* that I wrote my pre-war articles on the intellectual history of Tokugawa Japan.

The opposing attractions of these two contradictory modes of thought have been tugging me, now this way now that, ever since. And if there *is* stronger evidence of a nominalist approach in my later essays this is perhaps not so much an entirely new departure as a resurgence of those elements of my thought and temperament which I owe to my father. Still, I cannot go all the way; in the field of social and political studies the thinkers who take a middling position between German 'historicism' and English 'empiricism', men like Max Weber, Hermann Heller, and Karl Mannheim, are the ones whom I have always found most sympathetic and most stimulating.

However wavering and unfixed my methodological standpoint may seem as a consequence, these two opposing elements in my background have at least set boundaries to the presuppositions which I have been able to adopt. For example, great as has been the influence of Marxism on my thought, full acceptance has always been checked by my inbred scepticism of any 'grand theory' as well as by my belief in the force of ideas operating in human history. On the other hand, the pull towards nominalism has never been able to make me forgo entirely any idea of meaningful historical development. I am happy to consider myself a follower of the eighteenth-century Enlightenment who still holds to its 'obsolete' idea of human progress. It was not in his glorification of the state as the embodiment of morality, but in his idea that 'history is the progress towards consciousness of freedom' that I saw the kingpin of Hegel's system, however much he himself was a critic of the Enlightenment.

The reader will find in this book words like 'progressive', 'revolutionary', 'counter-revolutionary', 'reactionary' used in a way to which he is no longer accustomed. If I were writing today I might use such words a little more sparingly. But I have still not given up the attempt to discern certain irreversible trends in history. For me the world since the Renaissance and the Reformation is a story of the revolt of man against nature, of the revolt of the poor against privilege, of the revolt of the 'undeveloped' against the 'West', now one emerging, now the other, each evoking the other and forming in the modern world a composition of harmony and dissonance on the grandest scale. We should be on our guard against any *a priori* attribution to any one political camp of the 'progressive' role of promoter of these revolutionary trends. And we should beware of trying to interpret history as the unfolding of mysterious substantive 'forces'. But I think it would be a pity if we allowed ourselves to be so disgusted with the propaganda use of words that we gave up *all* attempts to distinguish between those events which are pregnant with a further growth in the human capacity and those which have no meaning but of 'turning back the clock' of human history.

However, this is hardly the place for discussion of fundamental philosophical issues, and the reader may safely be left to form his own judgement of the political bias revealed in these essays. I hope he will find them of some interest, less for their academic merits—the majority of them were first published not in scholarly journals but in the monthly political reviews—than as a record of the intellectual development of a Japanese who lived out his youth in the turbulent period of the war and its aftermath.

Finally, I would like to express my deepest thanks to Professor Ivan Morris, who first suggested an English version of this book and undertook the responsibility of translating and editing, to Messrs. Tatsuo Arima, Ronald Dore, Ezra Vogel, and Richard Storry, who have given me useful suggestions on reading proofs, and to all those who have given their help in the translation.

MASAO MARUYAMA

At St. Antony's College,
Oxford,
November, 1962

Contents

EDITOR'S PREFACE   v

AUTHOR'S INTRODUCTION   xi

1   THEORY AND PSYCHOLOGY OF ULTRA-NATIONALISM   1
    Translated by IVAN MORRIS

2   THE IDEOLOGY AND DYNAMICS OF JAPANESE
    FASCISM   25
    Translated by ANDREW FRASER

3   THOUGHT AND BEHAVIOUR PATTERNS OF JAPAN'S
    WARTIME LEADERS   84
    Translated by IVAN MORRIS

4   NATIONALISM IN JAPAN: ITS THEORETICAL
    BACKGROUND AND PROSPECTS   135
    Translated by DAVID TITUS

5   FASCISM—SOME PROBLEMS: A CONSIDERATION OF
    ITS POLITICAL DYNAMICS   157
    Translated by RONALD DORE

6   A CRITIQUE OF DE-STALINIZATION   177
    Translated by PAUL VARLEY

7   POLITICS AS A SCIENCE IN JAPAN: RETROSPECT
    AND PROSPECTS   225
    Translated by ARTHUR TIEDEMANN

8   FROM CARNAL LITERATURE TO CARNAL POLITICS   245
    Translated by BARBARA RUCH

9   SOME PROBLEMS OF POLITICAL POWER   268
    Translated by DAVID SISSON

GLOSSARY AND BIOGRAPHIES   290

CHRONOLOGY   333

SUGGESTED READING   336

INDEX   337

I. Theory and Psychology of Ultra-Nationalism

TRANSLATED BY IVAN MORRIS

This essay was originally published in the magazine Sekai, *May 1946*

I

What was the main ideological factor that kept the Japanese people in slavery for so long and that finally drove them to embark on a war against the rest of the world? Writers in the West have vaguely described it as 'ultra-nationalism' or 'extreme nationalism'; but until now no one has examined what it really is.

Scholars have been mainly concerned with the social and economic background of ultra-nationalism. Neither in Japan nor in the West have they attempted any fundamental analysis of its intellectual structure or of its psychological basis. There are two reasons for this: in the first place, the problem is too simple; secondly, it is too complex.

It is too simple because ultra-nationalism in Japan has no solid conceptual structure. Lacking such a structure it emerges instead in the form of shrill slogans, such as 'The Eight Corners of the World under One Roof' and 'Spreading the Emperor's Mission to Every Corner of the Earth';* for this reason scholars have tended to regard it as unworthy of serious examination.

Here we find a striking contrast to the situation in Nazi Germany, which, for all its emotionalism and illogicality, did in fact possess an orthodox, systematic *Weltanschauung* expressed in books like *Mein Kampf* and *The Myth of the Twentieth Century*. Yet the absence from Japanese ultra-nationalism of this sort of authoritative basis does not mean that it was weak as an ideology. Far from it: ultra-nationalism succeeded in spreading a many-layered, though invisible, net over the Japanese people, and even today they have not really freed themselves from its hold.

* *Hakkō Ichiu, Tengyō Kaikō.*

It is not merely the external system of coercion that determined the low level of political consciousness we find today in Japan. Rather, the key factor is the all-pervasive psychological coercion, which has forced the behaviour of our people into a particular channel. Since this has never had any clear theoretical form or any single intellectual pedigree, it is very hard to grasp in its entirety. We must therefore avoid dismissing slogans like 'the Eight Corners of the World under One Roof' as so much empty demagogy. These slogans are frequently manifestations of an underlying force; and in order to understand the true nature of ultra-nationalism we must grope through such manifestations to discover the common underlying logic.

This is certainly not a matter of exhuming our country's painful past out of some masochistic whim. As Ferdinand Lasalle puts it, 'The opening of a new era finds itself in the acquisition of the consciousness of what has been the reality of existence.' This task may well be an essential condition for any true national reform. Indeed may we not say that a revolution is worthy of its name only if it involves an inner or spiritual revolution?

The following essay, then, is not a systematic explanation of ultra-nationalism, but rather a fragmentary attempt to indicate the *locus* and scope of the problem.

II

The first point is to determine why nationalism in our country evokes such epithets as 'ultra' and 'extreme'. The fact that modern States are known as 'nation-states' suggests that nationalism is no fortuitous aspect of these countries but rather their fundamental attribute. How then are we to differentiate between this type of nationalism, which is more or less common to all modern States, and the 'ultra' form of nationalism?

The distinction that may first come to mind is the presence of expansionist, militarist tendencies. The trouble is that during the period when nation-states first came into being *all* the countries that were under absolutist régimes blatantly carried out wars of external aggression; in other words a tendency to military expansion was an inherent impulse in nationalism long before the so-called age of imperialism in the nineteenth century.

It is quite true that in Japan nationalism was guided by this impulse to a stronger degree and that it manifested it in a clearer way than in other countries. But this is not merely a matter of quantity. Quite apart from any difference in degree, there is a qualitative difference in the inner motive power that spurred Japan to expansion abroad and to oppression at home; and it is only owing to this qualitative difference that Japanese nationalism acquired its 'ultra' aspect.

A comparison with European nationalism will lead us to the crux of the matter. As Carl Schmidt has pointed out, an outstanding characteristic of the modern European State lies in its being *ein neutraler Staat*. That is to say, the State adopts a *neutral* position on internal values, such as the problem of what truth and justice are; it leaves the choice and judgement of all values of this sort to special social groups (for instance, to the Church) or to the conscience of the individual. The real basis of national sovereignty is a purely 'formal' legal structure, divorced from all questions of internal value.

This resulted from the particular way in which the modern State developed out of the post-Reformation wars of religion that dragged on through the sixteenth and seventeenth centuries. The interminable struggle, which revolved about matters of faith and theology, eventually had two converse effects. On the one hand, it obliged the religious sects to give up the idea that they could realize their principles on the political plane. On the other, it confronted the absolute sovereigns of the time with a severe challenge. Until then the monarchs of Europe had brandished the slogan of the Divine Right of Kings, thus providing their own internal justification for ruling. Confronted now with severe opposition, they were obliged to find a new basis for their rule, namely, in the *external* function of preserving public order.

Thus a compromise was effected between the rulers and the ruled—a compromise based on distinguishing between form and content, between external matters and internal matters, between the public and the private domains. Questions of thought, belief, and morality were deemed to be private matters and, as such, were guaranteed their subjective, 'internal' quality; meanwhile, state power was steadily absorbed into an 'external' legal system, which was of a technical nature.

In post-Restoration[1] Japan, however, when the country was

being rebuilt as a modern State, there was never any effort to recognize these technical and neutral aspects of national sovereignty. In consequence Japanese nationalism strove consistently to base its control on internal values rather than on authority deriving from external laws.

Foreign visitors to Japan during the first half of the nineteenth century almost invariably noted that the country was under the dual rule of the Mikado (Tennō), who was the spiritual sovereign, and the Tycoon (Shōgun), who held actual political power. After the Restoration, unity was achieved by removing all authority from the latter, and from other representatives of feudal control, and by concentrating it in the person of the former. In this process, which is variously described as the 'unification of administration and laws' and the 'unification of the sources of dispensation and deprivation',* prestige and power were brought together in the institution of the Emperor. And in Japan there was no ecclesiastical force to assert the supremacy of any 'internal' world over this new combined, unitary power.

It is true that in due course a vigorous movement arose to assert people's rights. Its advocates were soon engaged in a bitter struggle with the authorities, who in their resistance to the new theories tried to 'instil fear into the hearts of the people, brandishing the prestige of the armed forces in one hand and that of the police in the other, thus cowing the populace with power from above'.[2]

Yet the struggle for people's rights was not concerned primarily with the right of ultimate judgement on such *internal* values as truth and morality. All that mattered to the fighters for popular rights was 'to secure the power of the Sovereign and to define the limits of the people's rights'.[3] How frivolously they regarded the question of internalizing morality (a prerequisite of any true modernization) is suggested by the passage in which the leader of the Liberal Party, Kōno Hironaka, discusses the motives of his own intellectual revolution. The liberalism of John Stuart Mill was the decisive influence; yet he describes the process as follows:

I was riding on horseback when I first read this work ['On Liberty']. In a flash my entire way of thinking was revolutionized.

---

* *seirei no kiitsu, seikei ittō.*

Until then I had been under the influence of the Chinese Confucianists and of the Japanese classical scholars, and I had even been inclined to advocate an 'expel the barbarian' policy.[4] Now all these earlier thoughts of mine, *excepting those concerned with loyalty and filial piety*, were smashed to smithereens. At the same moment I knew that it was human freedom and human rights that I must henceforth cherish above all else.*

What really strikes one in reading this description i; how glibly an outstanding Japanese liberal could, from the very outset of his deliberations, 'except' the concepts of loyalty and filial piety —concepts that must be squarely faced before any progress can possibly be made along the road to securing the internal freedom of the individual. Kōnɔ does not show the slightest awareness that the retention of this traditional morality might pose a problem for liberalism.

The 'people's rights' approach, represented by early liberals of this kind, was from the beginning connected with theories about 'national rights'; and it was inevitable that it should in due course be submerged by them. Thus in the struggle for liberalism the question of the individual's conscience never became a significant factor in defining his freedom. Whereas in the West national power after the Reformation was based on formal, external sovereignty, the Japanese State never came to the point of drawing a distinction between the external and internal spheres and of recognizing that its authority was valid only for the former. In this respect it is noteworthy that the Imperial Rescript on Education should have been proclaimed just before the summoning of the First Imperial Diet.[5] This was an open declaration of the fact that the Japanese State, being a moral entity, monopolized the right to determine values.

It is hardly surprising that the clash between Christianity and the policy of national education, which was so important in intellectual circles during the early part of the Meiji Period, should have taken the form of a heated controversy about this Imperial Rescript. Significantly it was at about this period that the word *étatisme* came into frequent use. The controversy was submerged in the wave of nationalist excitement that spread

* Biography of Kōno Hironaka (Banshū), Vol. I. [Unless otherwise indicated, italics in all quoted passages in this and subsequent essays are Maruyama's, not the original author's.]

through the country at the time of the Sino-Japanese and Russo-Japanese wars. Yet the underlying problem was certainly not resolved; only the reluctance of the pro-Christian groups to avoid any open confrontation made it appear as though the issue of free conscience versus the total authority of the State had actually been settled.

Accordingly, until the day in 1946 when the divinity of the Emperor was formally denied in an Imperial Rescript, there was in principle no basis in Japan for freedom of belief. Since the nation includes in its 'national polity'* all the internal values of truth, morality, and beauty, neither scholarship nor art could exist apart from these national values. They were, in fact, totally dependent on them. The dependence, moreover, was less external than internal; for the slogans 'art for the nation' and 'scholarship for the nation' were not simply demands that art and scholarship be of practical value to the country. The essential point was that the final decision about the content of Japanese art, scholarship, and so forth, in other words, the definition of what was actually for the good of the country, was handed down by officials whose duty it was to give loyal service 'to His Majesty the Emperor and the Imperial Government'.†

A natural consequence of this failure to draw any clear line of demarcation between the public and the private domains was the great extension in Japan of the scope of the law. 'Those things', writes Hegel, 'that are free in an interior sense and that exist within the individual subject must not enter into the purview of the law.'‡ It was precisely the sanctity of such an interior, subjective sphere that the Japanese law failed to recognize. On the contrary, inasmuch as the law of the land in Japan arose from the 'national polity', which was an absolute value, it based its validity on inner or contentual, rather than on external or formal,[6] norms and was thus free to operate in all those interior realms from which law in the West had been excluded.

Since the *formal* quality of the national order was not recognized in Japan, it was impossible by the very nature of things for any purely personal realm to exist apart from this order. In our country personal affairs could never be accepted *qua*

* *Kokutai.*   † Public Service Regulation for Officials.   ‡ *Rechtsphilosophie.*

personal affairs. The author of *The Way of the Subject* writes as follows on this point:

What we normally refer to as 'private life' is, in the final analysis, the way of the subject. As such, it has a public significance, in that each so-called private action is carried out by the subject as part of his humble efforts to assist[7] the Throne . . . Thus we must never forget that even in our personal lives we are joined to the Emperor and must be moved by the desire to serve our country.

The ideology reflected in this passage did not emerge in Japan as part of the totalitarian vogue of the 1930s, but was from the outset immanent in the national structure. Private affairs accordingly always involved something shady and were regarded as akin, or even equivalent, to evil. This applied particularly to profit-making and to love.

Since the personal, internal quality of private affairs could never be openly recognized, people tried in one way or another to imbue these affairs with some national significance and thus to dispel the aura of shadiness. In Sōseki's *Since Then*, Daisuke and his sister-in-law have the following conversation:

'And what on earth did [Father] find to scold you about today?'

'That's hardly the point. He always finds something. What really did surprise me was to hear that Father has been serving the nation. He told me that from the age of eighteen until today he has,gone on serving the country to the best of his ability.'

'I suppose that's why he's made such a success.'

'Yes, if one can make as much money as Father has by serving the nation, I wouldn't mind serving it myself.'

Now this father of Daisuke, whom the author presents with such trenchant irony, can be regarded as the typical Japanese capitalist. He represents 'The Road to Success and Prosperity',* and it was precisely when the success motive joined forces with nationalism that modern Japan was able to embark on its 'rush towards progress'. Yet at the same time it was this very combination that led to Japan's decay. For the logic according to which 'private affairs' cannot be morally justified within themselves, but must always be identified with national affairs, has a converse implication: private interests endlessly infiltrate into national concerns.

* Noma Seiji.

III

In Japan, then, we are faced with a situation in which national sovereignty involves both spiritual authority and political power. The standard according to which the nation's actions are judged as right or wrong lies within itself (that is, in the 'national polity'), and what the nation does, whether within its own borders or beyond them, is not subject to any moral code that supersedes the nation.

This formulation will immediately bring to mind the Hobbesian type of absolutism. But there is a clear difference. The authority to which Hobbes refers when he writes: 'It is not the truth that makes laws, but authority' is a purely pragmatic decision and does not connote any value that can be regarded as normative. In his *Leviathan* there are no such things as right and wrong, good and bad, until they are enacted by a decision of the sovereign. The sovereign himself creates the norm; he does not bring into force a system of truth and justice that has already existed. What makes the laws valid in the Hobbesian State is exclusively the *formal* fact that they derive from the orders of the sovereign; and this stress on formal validity, far from involving any fusion of form and content (such as we find in Japanese thinking on the subject), leads to the modern theory of legal positivism. Even in Frederick the Great's Prussia, in which legitimacy (*Legitimität*) ultimately resolved itself into legality (*Legalität*), we can recognize a direct line of descent from the Hobbesian type of absolutism.

Japanese nationalism, on the other hand, was never prepared to accept a merely formal basis of validity. The reason that the actions of the nation cannot be judged by any moral standard that supersedes the nation is not that the Emperor creates norms from scratch (like the sovereign in Hobbes's *Leviathan*) but that absolute values are embodied in the person of the Emperor himself, who is regarded as 'the eternal culmination of the True, the Good, and the Beautiful throughout all ages and in all places'.*

According to this point of view, virtue arises only when this 'eternal culmination', which is in fact the essence of the 'national polity', starts to spread out in waves from its central entity, the

* Araki Sadao, *The Spirit of Soldiers in the Emperor's Land.*

Emperor, to the rest of the world. In the patriotic slogan, 'spreading the just cause throughout the world', the just cause (that is, virtue) is not regarded as something that could exist before the Japanese nation acted, nor is it something that developed afterwards. The just cause and national conduct invariably *coexist*. In order to spread the just cause it is necessary to act; conversely, when the nation acts, it is *ipso facto* in the just cause.

Thus it is characteristic of nationalist logic in Japan that the down-to-earth precept, 'It's always best to be on the winning side', should be subtly blended with the ideology, 'The righteous cause triumphs'. The Empire of Japan came to be regarded *per se* as 'the culmination of the True, the Good, and the Beautiful', and was by its very nature unable to do wrong; accordingly the most atrocious behaviour, the most treacherous acts, could all be condoned.

This point of view about the automatic righteousness of the nation's conduct can also be explained by the interfusion of ethics and power that occurred in Japan. National sovereignty was the ultimate source of both ethics and power, and constituted their intrinsic unity; this being the situation, Japanese morality never underwent the process of interiorization that we have seen in the case of the West, and accordingly it always had the impulse to transform itself into power. Morality is not summoned up from the depths of the individual; on the contrary, it has its roots outside the individual and does not hesitate to assert itself in the form of energetic outward movement. The 'total mobilization of the people's spirit' during the war was a typical manifestation of Japanese morality emerging as outward action.

Owing to this exteriorization of morality in Japan, the 'national polity' could never be discussed without immediately being brought to the level of a political conflict and involving the participants in a political clash. We can see this in the conflict, which has already been cited, of Christianity versus the Imperial Rescript on Education; essentially the same thing happened in the 'Shinto as a primitive religion' case, in the repercussions to Ozaki Yukio's speech about a Japanese republic, and in the Minobe case arising from his 'organ theory' of the Emperor.[8] In all these instances the nationalist moralists carried out their attacks in the name of 'clarifying the national polity', a phrase that, far from implying any self-criticism or need to explain one's position, usually signified a method of putting pressure on one's political enemies.

This identification of morality with power meant that pure inner morality (as opposed to the external type) was always regarded as 'impotent' and therefore worthless. To be impotent meant not to have the physical strength to move other people—a type of strength, of course, that neither ethics nor ideals ever claim to possess.

We find a tendency, then, to estimate morality, not by the value of its content, but in terms of its power, that is, according to whether or not it had a power background. In the last analysis this was because the real *locus* of Japanese morality was not in the conscience of the individual but in the affairs of the nation.

This is most clearly revealed in Japan's relations with other countries. The following passage is significant:

> Our country's determination and military strength made [the principal Allied powers] unable to impose any sanctions whatsoever. When Japan seceded, the true nature of the League [of Nations] was revealed to the world. In autumn of the same year Germany followed our example and seceded, and later Italy took advantage of the Abyssinian question to announce its secession also, so that the League became nothing but an empty name. Thus since the autumn of 1931 our country made great strides in the vanguard of the forces struggling for world renovation.*

Two things set the tone of this passage: unconcealed scorn for the fact that the League was powerless to impose sanctions, and implicit admiration for Italy's dexterity in taking advantage of an opportunity. Neither the 'true nature' of the League nor the behaviour of Fascist Italy was judged according to any intrinsic set of values; the only criteria were real (that is, material) power and tactical skill. Here we see another aspect of the outlook of the Mombu Shō officials, those high priests of Japanese 'education'.[9]

Now, at the same time that morality was being transformed into power, power was continuously being counteracted by

---

* *The Way of the Subject.*

moral considerations. Japanese politicians have never yet given
vent to any open declarations of Machiavellism, nor have they
ever (like some of their Western counterparts) boasted about
resolutely trampling on *petit-bourgeois* morality. Inasmuch as
political power in Japan based itself on ultimate moral entities,
the Japanese have never been able to recognize the 'satanic'
aspect of politics for what it is.

Here we find a sharp difference between the Eastern and
Western attitudes. The German people, as Thomas Mann has
pointed out, have a latent sense that politics is essentially an
immoral and brutal thing; but it is impossible for the Japanese
to recognize this with any real conviction. Accordingly two
types of politician are rarely to be found in our country: the
genuinely idealistic politician who remains steadfastly faithful
to truth and justice, and the Cesare Borgia type of politician who
is prepared fearlessly to trample underfoot all accepted standards
of morality. In Japan we find neither the humble, inward-
looking approach nor the naked lust for power. Everything is
noisy, yet at the same time it is all most scrupulous. It is precisely
in this sense that Tōjō Hideki can be regarded as representative
of the Japanese politician.

This phenomenon, which we may term the diminutiveness of
power or 'power dwarfing', does not apply to political power
alone, but characterizes every type of control that operates
with the State as its background. The ill-treatment of Allied
prisoners during the Second World War provides a good example. (Later I shall discuss the atrocities committed in battle as
involving a slightly different problem.) When one reads the
reports about the beating and other ill-treatment meted out to
the P.O.W.s, one is struck by the way in which almost all the
Japanese defendants emphasized that they had worked to improve conditions in the camps. Of course these men were on
trial and wanted to save their own skins. But I do not believe
that is the whole story. Many of them were sincerely convinced
that they were doing their best to improve the treatment of the
prisoners. Yet at the very same time they were beating and
kicking them. Acts of benevolence could coexist with atrocities,
and the perpetrators were not aware of any contradiction. Here
is revealed the phenomenon in which morality is subtly blended
with power.

Those who have experienced life in a Japanese barracks should have no difficulty in understanding such a state of affairs. The people who exercised power in military establishments found the psychological basis of their control not in any secure self-confidence, but rather in an identification with the power of the nation. When later they were turned adrift and reverted to being lone individuals, no longer able to depend on superior authority, how weak and pitiful they showed themselves to be! At the war crimes trials Tsuchiya turned pale and Furushima wept;[10] but Göring roared with laughter. Among the famous war crimes suspects in Sugamo Prison how many are likely to display the arrogant impudence of a Hermann Göring?

The ill-treatment of prisoners was commonplace in both Germany and Japan. Yet the Japanese type of ill-treatment belongs to an entirely different pattern from the cold-blooded, 'objective' ill-treatment practised by the Germans when, for example, they sacrificed the lives of thousands of prisoners for the sake of medical experiments. In Germany, as in Japan, the State was of course the background against which the atrocities were perpetrated. Yet the attitude towards the victims was different. In Germany the relationship between the perpetrator and his victim was like that between a 'free' subject and a thing (*Sache*). In the case of Japan, on the contrary, the problem of relative position was always involved: in fine, the perpetrator was conscious of the comparative proximity of himself and of his victim to the ultimate value, that is, to the Emperor.

Now this sense of *degree of proximity* to the ultimate value or entity was immensely important in Japan: in fact it was the spiritual motive force that drove, not only the various individual power complexes (the military, the *zaibatsu*, etc.), but the entire national structure. What determined the behaviour of the bureaucrats and of the military was not primarily a sense of legality, but the consciousness of some force that was higher than they were, in other words, that was nearer the ultimate entity. Inasmuch as the formal quality of the national order was not recognized in Japan, it was inevitable that the concept of legality should be poorly developed. The law was not regarded as some general body of regulations that collectively circumscribed the ruler and the ruled, but simply as a concrete weapon of control operating in the hierarchy of authority of which the Emperor was the head.

Accordingly respect for the law mainly took the form of demands directed to those who were below, that is, who were further away from the head of the hierarchy. The application of the complex rules in the Military Service Regulations became increasingly lax as one went up in the hierarchy and increasingly severe as one went down. It is a well-known fact that the people who most brazenly flouted the provisions in the Code of Criminal Procedure regarding arrest, detention, preliminary hearings, and so forth were the Imperial officials themselves. Since the main objective was to preserve and strengthen concrete networks of control, the officials concerned with respect for the law were repeatedly told not to let themselves be hemmed in by 'minor details' in the laws and regulations.

The standard of values, then, that determined a person's position in society and in the nation was based less on social function than on relative distance from the Emperor. Nietzsche characterizes the aristocratic morality as 'the pathos of distance' (*Pathos der Distanz*); for the ruling class of Japan the consciousness of being separated from the 'humble' people increased in proportion with the sense of being near the ultimate value, that is, the Emperor.

Thus the pride of the nobility lay in being 'the bulwark of the Imperial House'; and the very lifeline of the Army and Navy was the independence of the prerogative of supreme command,[11] 'based on the fact that the armed forces are under the personal leadership of His Majesty the Emperor'. What determined the everyday morality of Japan's rulers was neither an abstract consciousness of legality nor an internal sense of right and wrong, nor again any concept of serving the public; it was a feeling of being close to the concrete entity known as the Emperor, an entity that could be directly perceived by the senses. It was therefore only natural that these people should come to identify their own interests with those of the Emperor, and that they should automatically regard their enemies as violators of the Emperor's powers. This type of thinking certainly lay behind the hatred and fear that the leaders of the clan clique[12] felt for the Popular Rights Movement. And it continues to operate even today among the ruling class of Japan.

IV

The identification of morality with power and the constant stress on proximity to the Emperor have an important effect on people's attitudes to their duties. Pride in carrying out one's duties was based not so much on any sense of horizontal specialization (that is, division of labour) as on a consciousness of vertical dependence on the ultimate value. The various pathological phenomena that arose from this state of affairs are perfectly exemplified by the Japanese armed forces. The entire educational apparatus of the military establishment was directed towards cultivating this sort of 'vertical' pride. The primary policy was to identify the armed forces as being the mainstay of the nation, in that 'the military are the essence of the nation and occupy the principal position therein'.* The sense of superiority that the military felt towards the 'provincials' (as they so pointedly described civilians) was unmistakably based on the concept of being an *Imperial* force.

Moreover the consciousness of being under the direct control of the Emperor led them to conclude that they were superior to other members of the community, not only in their position within the hierarchy, but in all values. According to General Araki, for example, men from the armed forces often acquire the reputation of being too honest, 'but such criticism in fact reveals the great discrepancy between the level of morality in the forces and that in society as a whole, which makes it difficult for military men to adjust themselves to society as it is now constituted'.† Accordingly the military are required to 'purify the spirit of society at large and to strive for its amalgamation with the military spirit'.† In the last war it was amply brought home to the Japanese people that there was a 'great discrepancy' between military and general morality—but in the very opposite sense from that intended by General Araki.

The armed forces were thoroughly imbued with this notion of superiority. According to a friend of mine, a pathologist, who was conscripted during the last war and who served for many years as a captain in the Medical Corps, professional medical men in the forces were almost all convinced that the level of medical science was far higher in the military establishment

* Armed Forces Education Order.　　† Araki, op. cit.

than anywhere in the 'provinces', including university medical centres. In fact the situation was exactly the reverse.

This self-centred pride of the military not only determined their attitude towards the 'provincials' but operated between the various branches of the forces themselves. In *Principal Rules of Strategy*, for example, we find the statement, 'Among the various branches of the armed forces the infantry is the main component and constitutes the nucleus of their association.' When I was mobilized to be drafted as a private in Korea, we had to recite this formula daily, and I can still hear the voice of a certain private when he shouted, 'D'you see? The infantry is the main component of the forces—right at the top! It says "main component of the forces", doesn't it? "Forces" doesn't mean just the Army. It includes the Navy too.' I am not suggesting that even this man actually believed the slogan; but a remark of this kind, however exaggerated, certainly reveals a psychological tendency that pervaded military education.

Thus the individual unit was inspired with a sense of superiority towards other units, the company towards other companies, the administrative squad towards other similar squads; at the same time the N.C.O.s insisted on the gulf that separated them from the 'soldier's nature', and the officers emphasized their superiority to the 'character of the N.C.O.'. Such an approach was the basis of the appalling reputation for self-righteousness and sectionalism that the armed forces acquired during the war.

This sectionalism was rampant not only in the Army and Navy but throughout the entire structure of the Japanese government. It has often been described as 'feudalistic', but that is an oversimplification. The feudalistic impulse to defend one's own particular sphere of interests had its origins in the efforts of each unit to entrench itself in a closed, self-sufficient world. Japanese sectionalism, however, derived from a system according to which every element in society was judged according to its respective connexion, in a direct vertical line, with the ultimate entity. This involved a constant impulse to unite oneself with that entity, and the resultant sectionalism was of a far more active and 'aggressive' type than that associated with feudalism. Here again the military provide a perfect example: while they relied at each point on the fortress provided by their prerogative of supreme command, they tried (in the name of total warfare) to interfere in every single aspect of national life.

We are faced, then, with a situation that might be described as the rarefaction of value. The entire national order is constructed like a chain, with the Emperor as the absolute value entity; and at each link in the chain the intensity of vertical political control varies in proportion to the distance from the Emperor. One might expect this to be ideal soil for the concept of dictatorship, but in fact it was hard for this concept to take root in Japan. For the essential premise of a dictatorship is the existence of a free, decision-making agent, and this is precisely what was lacking in our country: from the apex of the hierarchy to the very bottom it was virtually impossible for a truly free, unregulated individual to exist. Society was so organized that each component group was constantly being regulated by a superior authority, while it was imposing its own authority on a group below.

Much has been made of the dictatorial or despotic measures exercised by the Japanese military during the war; but we must avoid confusing despotism as a fact or a social result with despotism as a concept. The latter is invariably related to a sense of responsibility, and neither the military nor the civilian officials in Japan possessed any such sense.

This emerges in the question of responsibility for starting the war. Whatever may have been the causes for the outbreak of war in 1939, the leaders of Nazi Germany were certainly conscious of a *decision* to embark on hostilities. In Japan, however, the situation was quite different: though it was our country that plunged the world into the terrible conflagration in the Pacific, it has been impossible to find any individuals or groups that are conscious of having started the war. What is the meaning of the remarkable state of affairs in which a country slithered into war, pushed into the vortex by men who were themselves driven by some force that they did not really understand?

The answer lies in the nature of the Japanese oligarchy. It was unfortunate enough for the country to be under oligarchic rule; the misfortune was aggravated by the fact that the rulers were unconscious of actually being oligarchs or despots. The individuals who composed the various branches of the oligarchy did not regard themselves as active regulators but as men who were, on the contrary, being regulated by rules created elsewhere. None of the oligarchic forces in the country could ever become absolute; instead they all coexisted—all of them equally dependent on the ultimate entity and all of them stressing their comparative proximity to that entity. This state of affairs led one German observer to describe Japan as *Das Land der Nebeneinander* ('the land of coexistence'), and there is no doubt that it impeded the development of a sense of subjective responsibility.

During the Eighty-First Diet session,[13] when the extension of the Prime Minister's power was being considered by the Committee on Special Wartime Administrative Legislation, the Prime Minister, General Tōjō, was asked by Mr. Kita Sōichirō whether such power should be regarded as a dictatorship. He replied as follows:

People often refer to this as a dictatorial government, but I should like to make the matter clear . . . The man called Tōjō is no more than a single humble subject. I am just the same as you. The only difference is that I have been given the responsibility of being Prime Minister. To this extent I am different. It is only when I am exposed to the light of His Majesty that I shine. Were it not for this light, I should be no better than a pebble by the roadside. It is because I enjoy the confidence of His Majesty and occupy my present position that I shine. This puts me in a completely different category from those European rulers who are known as dictators.*

It is highly suggestive that the Prime Minister who spoke these words should have held greater power than any of his predecessors. For Tōjō's statement provides a candid revelation of the psychology of a timidly faithful Japanese subject: what instantly came to his mind was a proud feeling of superiority, based on the knowledge of being close to the ultimate authority, and a keen sense of being burdened by the spiritual weight of this authority.

In the absence of any free, subjective awareness the individual's actions are not circumscribed by the dictates of conscience; instead he is regulated by the existence of people in a higher class—of people, that is, who are closer to the ultimate value. What takes the place of despotism in such a situation is a phenomenon that may be described as the maintenance of

* *Asahi Shimbun*, 6 February 1943.

equilibrium by the transfer of oppression. By exercising arbitrary power on those who are below, people manage to transfer in a downward direction the sense of oppression that comes from above, thus preserving the balance of the whole.

This phenomenon is one of the most important heritages that modern Japan received from feudal society. It has been aptly interpreted by Fukuzawa Yukichi as the result of 'attaching too great importance to power',* which, as he says, 'has been the rule in human intercourse in Japan ever since the beginning'. Fukuzawa continues as follows:

[The Japanese] make a clear distinction between the moral codes that apply to people above and to people below, and an equally clear distinction in the field of rights and duties. As a result every individual is in one capacity the victim of coercion, while in another capacity he metes out coercion to his fellow-men. He both suffers and perpetrates oppression; in one direction he yields, in another he boasts . . . Today's joy compensates for yesterday's shame, and thus dissatisfaction is evened out . . . Peter is robbed to pay Paul.†

This too is reminiscent of military life. But, though the psychology described by Fukuzawa was most intensively expressed in the Army and Navy, it was not limited to these quarters; it was, in fact, embedded in every nook and cranny of the Japanese national order. For what happened in the Meiji Restoration[14] was that by the union of authority with power the preponderant role of force in feudal society was systematically incorporated into the structure of modern Japan.

With the emergence of our country on the world stage the principle of 'transfer of oppression' was extended to the international plane. This can be seen in the campaign in favour of invading Korea, which flared up directly after the Restoration,[15] and in the subsequent dispatch of troops to Formosa. Since the latter part of the Tokugawa Period Japan had never ceased to be conscious of the close and heavy pressure of the Great Powers, and as soon as the country was unified it used its new strength to stage a small-scale imitation of Western imperialism. Just as Japan was subject to pressure from the Great Powers, so she would apply pressure to still weaker countries—a clear case of the transfer psychology.

* *Kenryoku no henchō.*   † *Outline Theory of Civilization,* Vol. V.

In this regard it is significant that ever since the Meiji Period demands for a tough foreign policy have come from the common people, that is, from those who are at the receiving end of oppression at home. Again, when we examine the atrocities committed by Japanese forces in China and the Philippines, we are confronted with the unhappy fact that, whoever may have been ultimately responsible, the direct perpetrators were the rank-and-file soldiers. Men who at home were 'mere subjects' and who in the barracks were second-rank privates found themselves in a new role when they arrived overseas: as members of the Emperor's forces they were linked to the ultimate value and accordingly enjoyed a position of infinite superiority. Given the nature of Japanese society, it is no wonder that the masses, who in ordinary civilian or military life have no object to which they can transfer oppression, should, when they find themselves in this position, be driven by an explosive impulse to free themselves at a stroke from the pressure that has been hanging over them. Their acts of brutality are a sad testimony to the Japanese system of psychological compensation.*

V

In the psychology of ultra-nationalism what, then, is the real status of the Emperor? Inasmuch as he is the centre of all authority and the fountainhead of all virtue, occupying the apical position in a hierarchy where each element from bottom to top relies progressively on the values belonging to a superior rung, would we be correct in concluding that he alone enjoyed subjective freedom? A comparison with absolute monarchs in the West will provide our answer.

In the early stages of modern European history the absolute monarch was freed from the limitations based on medieval natural law. No longer subject to the control of any contract, he was able to raise himself from being a mere protector of order (*Defensor Pacis*) to being its creator (*Creator Pacis*), and thereby he emerged as the first 'free' individual in the modern period.

What happened at the beginning of modern Japanese history (that is, in the Meiji Restoration) was very different indeed.

---

* Acts of brutality committed towards the end of the war as a result of the psychology of defeat and the thirst for revenge belong to a different category.

The amalgamation of spiritual authority with political power[16] was regarded not as any new departure in the concept of sovereignty, but simply as a return to 'the ancient days of the Jimmu Foundation'.[17] Though the Emperor was regarded as the embodiment of ultimate value, he was infinitely removed from the possibility of creating values out of nothing. His Majesty was heir to the Imperial line unbroken for ages eternal and he ruled by virtue of the final injunctions of his ancestors. The Imperial Constitution, granted to the people in 1889, was not regarded as having been created by the Emperor himself; rather it was a document that 'transmitted the immutable law according to which the land has been governed'.

Thus the Emperor too was saddled with a burden—in his case a tradition that derived from the infinitely remote past. It was only because his existence was inextricably involved with the ancestral tradition, in such a way that he and his Imperial Ancestors formed a single unit, that he was regarded as being the ultimate embodiment of internal[18] values. The situation can be represented by a circle in which the Emperor is the centre and in which all the people, whose function it is to 'assist' the Emperor, are situated at their respective distances from the centre; now in this diagram the centre is not a single point but an axis of ordinates (the time dimension) running perpendicular to the plane of the circle. The endless flow of value from the centre towards the circumference is assured by the fact that the axis is infinite, as expressed in the familiar phrase, 'the prosperity of the Imperial Throne coeval with heaven and earth'.*

We are now in a position to have a clearer and fuller picture of the world from the standpoint of Japanese ultra-nationalism. Within Japan the standard of values is relative proximity to the central entity; by extending this logic to cover the entire world, the ultra-nationalists engendered a policy of 'causing all the nations to occupy their respective positions [*vis-à-vis* Japan]'. Japan, 'the suzerain country', placed each other country in an order that was based on social status. Once this order was secured there would be peace throughout the world. As one ultra-nationalist writer expressed it, 'The meaning of world history is that the august virtue of His Majesty should shine on all the nations of the world. This will indubitably be accom-

* Imperial Rescript on Education.

plished as a manifestation of the martial virtues of the Empire'.*

In such a scheme, where everything is based on the idea of an absolute central entity, there is no room for a concept like international law, which is equally binding on all nations. 'When the light of His Majesty's august virtue comes to illuminate the entire world in accordance with the ways of the Divine Land, there can be no such thing as international law.'†

The contemporaneousness of the myth of the national foundation has been expounded by Professor Yamada Takao: 'If we cut across the time axis, the events that occurred 2,600 years ago constitute the central layer . . . The happenings in Emperor Jimmu's reign are therefore no ancient tales but facts that exist at this very moment.'‡

Here we find a truly skilful expression of ultra-nationalist logic according to which the extension of the axis of ordinates (time factor) represents at the same time an enlargement of the circle itself (space factor).

The fact of being 'coeval with heaven and earth' guaranteed the indefinite expansion of the range in which the ultimate value was valid, and conversely the expansion of the 'martial virtues of the Empire' reinforced the absolute nature of the central value. This process spiralled upwards from the time of the Sino-Japanese and Russo-Japanese Wars, through the China Incident and until the Pacific War. August 15 1945, the day that put a period to Japanese imperialism, was also the day when the 'national polity', which had been the foundation of the entire ultra-nationalist structure, lost its absolute quality. Now for the first time the Japanese people, who until then had been mere objects, became free subjects and the destiny of this 'national polity' was committed to their own hands.

POSTSCRIPT

In this essay I concentrated on the configuration of Japanese nationalism during the Pacific War when it reached its most extreme form; and I tried, in as unified and consistent a way as possible, to identify within the post-Restoration structure of our

* Satō Tsūji, *The Philosophy of the Imperial Way.*
† *Chūō Kōron.* Dec. 1943, symposium, 'How We Must Face Our Country's Danger'.
‡ Ibid., Sept. 1943, 'The Mission of Divine Japan and the Resolve of Her People'.

country the various forces that governed the development of this nationalism. The result is an abstraction derived from historical facts. Accordingly I have deliberately avoided discussing the various stages in the development of the Emperor ideology and the relationship between constitutional and absolutist elements.

I leave it to the reader to decide whether or not the *schema* is arbitrary; but I have little doubt that an abstraction of this sort can be useful in measuring the degree to which the Emperor ideology was 'atomized' after the war, a question that I discuss in a subsequent essay.

* * *

In 1933 the *Mainichi* newspaper, in co-operation with the War Ministry, produced a film called *Japan in Emergency*. The film included a speech by General Araki, the War Minister; and a chart outlining the structure of the Imperial Way was shown by way of illustration. Since I later discovered that this chart agreed entirely with the theory suggested at the end of my present essay, I append it here.

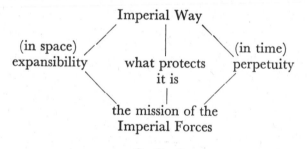

* * *

Some readers may conclude from reading this essay on its own that I have overlooked all the progressive momentum and universality in the development of Japan since the Meiji Period and in nationalist thought as an ideology. I would certainly not wish to give the impression that I have discounted these aspects or that I have dismissed them as being 'pre-modern' or 'special' cases. In my lecture entitled 'Japanese Thought in the Meiji Period'* and in *Kuga Katsunan: The Man and His Thought* I made

* Delivered at the seminar sponsored in October 1946 by the Historical Research Society, included in *Historical Investigation of Japanese Society* (*Iwanami Shoten*).

an effort, albeit quite inadequate, to discuss these forward-looking and positive elements in Japanese society and thought.

I am resigned to the criticism that the abstraction in this essay is one-sided. On the other hand, I certainly cannot accept the view (expressed in typical form by Professor Tsuda Sōkichi) that the pathology I have outlined in discussing the spiritual structure of the Emperor system is merely an 'exceptional phenomenon' produced by the frenzy of an 'emergency period'. This is not the place to enter into such a complex question, and by way of replying to this line of objection I shall for the time being simply quote the following passage from Hegel's philosophy of history:

> The corruption [of the medieval Church] was not an accidental phenomenon; it was not the mere abuse of power and dominion. A corrupt state of things is very frequently represented as an 'abuse'; it is taken for granted that the foundation was good—the system, the institution itself faultless—but that the passion, the subjective interest, in short the arbitrary volition of men, has made use of that which in itself was good to further its own selfish ends, and that all that is required to be done is to remove these adventitious elements. On this showing the institution in question escapes obloquy, and the evil that disfigures it appears something foreign to it. But when accidental abuse of a good thing really occurs, it is limited to particularity. A great and general corruption, affecting a body of such large and comprehensive scope as a Church, is quite another thing.*

TRANSLATOR'S NOTES

1. See Glossary: *Restoration*.
2. Quoted from Iwakura Proposal (*Iwakura Kō Jikki*) by the Meiji statesman, Iwakura Tomomi (1825–83).
3. Joint statement by the Meiji leader, Itagaki Taisuke (1837–1919), and others.
4. See Glossary: *Revere the Emperor, Expel the Barbarian*.
5. In 1890. See Glossary: *Education Rescript*.
6. 'Formal' in this essay is used as the antonym of 'contentual', not of 'informal'.
7. See Glossary: *Assistance*.
8. See Glossary: *Kume, Ozaki, Minobe*.

* *Philosophie der Weltgeschichte*, Lasson Ausg., Vol. II, pp. 871–2. The English translation is taken from J. Sibree, tr., *The Philosophy of History* (New York, 1956).

9. See Glossary: *Education Ministry.*
10. Tsuchiya and Furushima were Class C war criminals charged with atrocities against Allied prisoners of war. (When this essay was written, the major war criminals had not been brought to trial in Japan.)
11. See Glossary: *Prerogative of supreme command.*
12. See Glossary: *Clan clique.*
13. This session lasted from December 1942 to March 1943. The façade of constitutionalism was maintained throughout the militarist period.
14. See pages 3–4 above.
15. Only four years after the Restoration there was a split in the government concerning relations with Korea. One important group, led by Saigō Takamori, was in favour of sending a punitive expedition to the peninsula on the pretext that Korea had refused Japan's offer to establish relations. After a fierce controversy the 'peace' party won and Saigō and some of his supporters resigned from the government. However, two years later (in 1874) the government sent a small force to Formosa to deal with the aborigines who, it was alleged, had ill-treated Japanese sailors. The mission was successful.
16. See pages 3–4 above.
17. See Glossary: *Jimmu.*
18. See page 8 above.

II. The Ideology and Dynamics of Japanese Fascism

TRANSLATED BY ANDREW FRASER

This essay is an adaptation of a lecture delivered at Tokyo University in 1947

I. INTRODUCTION

In any analysis of fascism we should distinguish between fascism as a State structure and fascism as a movement. This essay is concerned chiefly with fascism as a movement and with the ideology that this movement sustained. A complete explanation of Japanese fascism demands a concrete structural analysis of the respective places of the military and of the bureaucracy in the State structure, their social foundations, and the way in which these powers were intertwined with Japanese monopoly capital (*zaibatsu*). These questions are beyond the scope of the present study, though I shall refer to them occasionally. Again, when I speak of ideology, I refer to ideology that is more or less connected with the fascist movement; I shall in general not deal with ideology that served to rationalize the militarist régime. Accordingly, to raise one by one the fascist or pseudo-fascist arguments in academic circles and journalism, for example, is outside my subject.

When we deal with this subject, the meaning of the word 'fascism' becomes an important problem. The first objection that can be raised in this regard is as follows: 'You speak of Japanese fascism, but did Japan actually experience fascism in the true sense of the word? What is the substance of the fascism you speak of?' This is a significant objection, but to answer it at the outset would involve a general discussion of fascism, including its various possible definitions, which I wish to avoid here.

I shall refer to a particular period that lasted for ten years in Japanese history as the fascist period. In examining this period I hope to clarify what I mean by Japanese fascism without having recourse to any abstract *a priori* definition.

The next objection that arises may be phrased as follows: 'Surely the study of such a fascist movement and its thought is a subsidiary concern. Is not the most important matter an analysis of fascism in the State structure and social institutions?' This is quite true, and our ultimate objective is certainly to understand Japanese fascism in terms of the social system as a whole. An essential premise for such an analysis, however, is to study the fascist movement that preceded and precipitated the 'fascization' of the total system.

What is called Japanese fascism, especially as a State structure, collapsed on 15 August 1945. But this by no means precludes the possibility that a fascist movement may arise in Japan in the future. Therefore it is necessary for us to get a firm grasp of the distinctive characteristics of fascist dynamics in the past with a view to comparison with future problems.

II. PERIODIC DIVISIONS IN THE JAPANESE FASCIST MOVEMENT

The development of the fascist movement in Japan may be divided broadly into three stages. The first stage is the *preparatory period*, which extended from about 1919, just after the First World War, until the time of the Manchurian Incident of 1931. This may be called the period of right-wing movements among civilians. The second stage is the *period of maturity* extending from the Manchurian Incident until the February Incident of 1936. In this period what had been simply a movement among civilians became concretely linked with segments of military power; the military became the driving force of the fascist movement, gradually coming to occupy the core of the national government. This was also a period in which conspiracies or plans for a *coup d'état* were disclosed and in which one right-wing terrorist incident followed another—first those like the March Incident and the Imperial Flag Incident, which were shrouded in obscurity; then the Blood Pledge Corps Incident, the May 15 Incident, the Heaven-Sent Soldiers' Unit Incident, the Officers' School Incident, and the Aizawa Incident; and finally the February 26 Incident, which shook the entire nation. This may be called the mature period of radical fascism.

The third stage extends a little longer, and is the period from the army purge carried out after the February Incident until the end of the war on 15 August 1945. We may term this the *consummation period* of Japanese fascism, in which the military, now the open supporters of fascism from above, fashioned an unstable ruling structure in coalition with the semi-feudal power of the bureaucracy and the Senior Retainers on the one hand, and with monopoly capital and the political parties on the other.

The Manchurian Incident is often said to be the boundary line for Japan's entry into the fascist era, but there was a considerable preparatory period prior to it. For example, on looking into the formation of so-called right-wing groups (excluding for the moment those like the Dark Ocean Society and its descendant, the Amur River Association, which were formed in the early Meiji era), the birth of groups related to the fascist movement suddenly becomes very prolific from about 1919. The demand for democracy that grew widespread after the First World War was simultaneously and rapidly radicalized under the influence of the Russian Revolution. Labour and tenancy disputes suddenly rose to prominence owing to radical changes in the business cycle. It was against this background that movements for resisting 'bolshevization' emerged one after another in the period until 1925. In 1918, for example, the Taishō Sincerity League and the Imperial Way Principles Association were set up. These were followed by the Great Japan National Essence Association and the Kantō National Essence Association in 1919; the Anti-Red Corps in 1922; and the Great Japan Political Justice Corps in 1925. Various shades of difference existed between them, but all aimed at positive resistance to the left-wing movement. Acting in concert with the Amur River Association or *rōnin* associations of the same stream, they functioned chiefly as strike-breakers or conducted violent assaults on left-wing labour unions, peasant unions, and the Levelling Society.

Since these groups had no positive programme for domestic reconstruction, it may be better to call them simply reactionary bodies rather than fascist organizations. Their membership was also bolstered by the 'lobbyist' groups[1] of the established political parties and there were many building contractors among their central figures. The platform of these associations was deeply imbued with feudalism. For example, the platform of the Great

Japan National Essence Association states: 'This association is a body sustained by the Heart and dedicated to chivalry.' The Great Japan Political Justice Corps intones,

> The master is like the parent; the follower is like the child. The comradeship of followers is like that of brothers in a family. The orders of the master must be obeyed through thick and thin. The brothers are to assist each other in mutual affection and must not forget the rules of courtesy.

Movements close to fascism in the true sense of the word were also set afoot at this time. For example, it was in 1919 that Kita Ikki, who may be called the ideological father of Japanese fascism, inaugurated the Society of Those Who Yet Remain, together with Ōkawa Shūmei and Mitsukawa Kametarō. Kita's *General Outline of Measures for the Reconstruction of Japan*, which was widely regarded as the ideological source for the February Incident, was the *Mein Kampf* of this association. Its platform included 'the construction of a revolutionized Japan', 'the co-ordination of reform movements', and 'the emancipation of the Asian Peoples'. Thus it was not simply an anti-Bolshevist movement like the previous groups, but displayed a truly fascist ideology that combined domestic reforms and international demands. Shortly afterwards Ōkawa Shūmei and Mitsukawa Kametarō became opposed to Kita, and in 1924 they set up the Society to Carry Out Heaven's Way on Earth, with Yasuoka Masaatsu, Nishida Zei, and others.

Many of the later right-wing groups were the offspring of these two associations. The National Founding Association, which wielded great influence among the right-wing groups, was organized in 1926 by Tsukui Tatsuo, Atsumi Katsu, and others, with Akao Bin as its leading figure. It was later joined by Amano Tatsuo and Maeda Torao of the Heaven-Sent Soldiers' Unit Incident. The president of the association was Uesugi Shinkichi; Tōyama Mitsuru and Hiranuma Kiichirō acted as advisers. The advocacy of national control of industry in the platform of the National Founding Association is to some extent anti-capitalist. But this was a common characteristic of right-wing groups in the first and second periods, and among them the National Founding Association was not particularly anti-capitalist. Its practical activity was chiefly centred on the struggle with the proletarian political parties. At this time the Communist Party was of course operating underground. The National Founding Association put its chief efforts into the struggle with the Labour-Peasant Party and the Japan National Council of Trade Unions, which appeared to be closest to the Communist Party line, and it was active in breaking up May Day celebrations.

A less powerful group was the Statesmanship League of Dr. Uesugi Shinkichi and Takabatake Motoyuki, which was also organized at this time. It had the complexion of a research group rather than a political movement, but it is noteworthy as an association formed by leading intellectuals of the day. We should also note the Great Reform Association set up in 1920 by Iwata Fumio. Thus from about 1919 we can recognize a clear growth in right-wing groups.

Moreover it must be noted that the various activities of radical fascism which became frequent after the Manchurian Incident had already taken fairly concrete shape before 1931. Sagoya Tomeo, who mortally wounded the Prime Minister, Mr. Hamaguchi, at Tokyo Station in 1930, was a member of the Blood Pledge Corps, and this incident is linked closely to the Blood Pledge Corps Incident, which took place *after* the Manchurian Incident. There was also the attempted *coup d'état* of the young officers six months *before* the Manchurian Incident, the so-called March Incident. This affair, born in the dark and buried in the dark, was a secret plot to establish a military government under General Ugaki. The *coup* was planned by radical officers of the time, such as Koiso, Tatekawa, and Nagata Tetsuzan, and was to be carried out by the radical faction of the Army gathered in the clandestine Cherry Blossom Association and by civilian right-wingers like Ōkawa Shūmei. It came to a premature end, but its aftermath trails from the May 15 Incident right up to the February Incident.* Thus, while there

* The *General Survey of the Situation*, issued by the office of the Army General Staff in 1930, not only treated military operations, but also included for the first time a discussion of State reconstruction. This was the result of the views of influential members of the Cherry Blossom Association such as Hashimoto Kingorō and Nemoto Hiroshi of the No. 2 Section of the General Staff (Memorandum of Major Tanaka Akira). Also various clandestine associations that were organized prior to the Cherry Blossom Association, such as Nishida Zei's Heavenly Sword Party in the Army and Fujii Hitoshi's Imperial Warriors' Association in the Navy, sent forth the 'reformist' officers of later years.

is no doubt that the Manchurian Incident acted as a definite stimulus to Japanese fascism, it must be emphasized that the fascist movement was not something that suddenly arose after 1931.

The second stage, from the Manchurian Incident to the February Incident, is a coherent period which requires no detailed explanation. The energy of radical fascism stored up in the preparatory period now burst forth in full concentration under the combined pressure of domestic panic and international crises such as the Manchurian Incident, the Shanghai Incident, and Japan's withdrawal from the League of Nations. Above all, this was the period in which the question of fascism was brought to the attention of the nation. Since our present object is to consider the fascist movement, this is therefore the most important period; and, of the historical materials we shall handle, those that belong to this period are naturally the most numerous. The right-wing movement, which in the first period was still the fanciful novelty of a small group, now linked itself to the military, especially the young officers, and rapidly came to wield actual political power.

In this sense, the creation of the All-Japan Patriots' Joint Struggle Council and the Great Japan Production Party immediately prior to the Manchurian Incident marks an epoch in the history of the right-wing movement. At this point the effort to transform the fragmentary right-wing movement into a more unified political power first took clear shape. At the same time, the fascist movement escaped from its negative role as simply an anti-leftist movement and displayed the characteristics of a positive social movement. I shall avoid giving a detailed explanation of the first of these two associations. Its aim was to amalgamate into a single body all groups affiliated with the Society of Those Who Yet Remain, the Statesmanship League, and the old Dark Ocean Society. Although it was short-lived, its aims were taken over by the Jimmu Association set up in 1932. Under the presidency of Ōkawa Shūmei and supported by funds contributed by Ishiwara Hiroichirō, a leading member of Ōsaka business circles, the Jimmu Association absorbed right-wing elements over a wide field. Having gained the support of the military, it engaged in extremely vigorous activity.

The Great Japan Production Party was formed largely by the absorption of right-wing groups in the Ōsaka region round the nucleus of the Amur River Association. Especially in having labour unions in its sub-organization, it displays an advance from the traditional *rōnin* right-wing movement. The practical character of this party is revealed in the fact that the Heaven-Sent Soldiers' Unit Incident was overwhelmingly mounted by men affiliated with it. The use of such left-wing style names as the All-Japan Patriots' Joint Struggle Council also reveals that fascism in this second period was most imbued with elements from the lower strata of society. Its platform clearly states: 'We intend to overthrow capitalism by the establishment of sovereign authority over industry.' The Great Japan Production Party also put up slogans such as 'Fundamental reform of the capitalist economic system, which is ruinous to the country', 'State control of financial organs', 'Guaranteed right to work', and 'Guaranteed rights of land cultivation'. Of course these demands and the social significance of the movement are quite separate questions; they have the same meaning as the anti-capitalist platform of the Fasci di Combattimento and the initial stages of the Nazi Party. The absence of such a radical programme in the third period, however, testifies to the character of the fascist movement in this second period.

A further striking phenomenon in this period is the fascist movement from within the proletarian political parties. This began with the national socialist movement of Akamatsu Katsumaro and others within the Social Mass Party. Eventually in April 1932 the Akamatsu faction broke away from the social democratic faction of Katayama Tetsu and Matsuoka Komakichi and organized the New National Socialist Party together with Koike Shirō and Hirano Rikizō. At the same time Matsutani Yojirō and others in the National Labour-Peasant Mass Party made moves in positive support of the Manchurian Incident. Finally, Akimori, Imamura, and other old campaigners left the party and joined Akamatsu and Hirano to form the Japan National Socialist Party.

Running parallel to this movement and in slight rivalry with it was that of Shimonaka Yasaburō. Together with Sasai Itchō, Kondō Eizō, and Amano Tatsuo, he set up the New Japan National League, relying on Gondō Seikyō and Kanokogi Kazunobu as advisers. The confluence of the pure right-wing and the socialist stream is revealed in this list of names.

Within the amalgamated proletarian political parties, elements opposed to this extreme trend towards fascism set up a united front under the slogan of the 'three antis' (anti-capitalism, anti-fascism, anti-communism), and formed a grand alliance for a Social Masses Party. But eventually within this group also there appeared the movement of Asō Hisashi, Kamei Kanishirō, and others for close relations with the military. Thus the tide of fascism gradually seeped into the proletarian movement.

A third trend to be noted in this period is the formation of political associations within the bodies of the reservists and bureaucrats. The Higher Ethics Association formed round General Tanaka Kunishige in 1932 was the most outstanding of such movements among reservists, and later played an active part in the series of incidents related to Dr. Minobe's organ theory. Another such group is the Imperial Way Association formed in 1933 when Major-General Todoroki and others joined forces with the Japan Peasants' Union led by Hirano Rikizō.

Among movements centred on bureaucratic groups the most prominent were Baron Hiranuma's National Foundation Society, Yasuoka Masaatsu's Golden Pheasant Academy, and the National Prestige Maintenance Association, in all of which the 'new bureaucrats' became the nucleus. In themselves such groups cannot be called political groups with a clear ideology. But, since men occupying leading positions in military, bureaucratic, and business circles were gathered within them, lateral connexions within the ruling class were naturally strengthened, and consequently such groups played no small part in preparing for the dominance of fascism from above in the third period.

Thus this period marks the conspicuous emergence of right-wing groups. They attracted public attention, since most of the people concerned in the Blood Pledge Corps, the Heaven-Sent Soldiers' Unit, the May 15 and the February Incidents came from among them. These right-wing movements, however, never succeeded in forming a united, powerful front. Constant attempts were made to organize a grand coalition of right-wing movements; such were the All-Japan Patriots' Joint Struggle Council, the Joint Council for Solving the National Crisis, the Joint Association for the Defence of the National Polity, the All-Japan National Socialist Council, and the Council for a

Union of Patriotic Movements. But they were always short-lived, and, in spite of being aided by the external situation, they constantly united and divided, ending finally in mutual strife. Ideologically speaking, this may be attributed to the split between the national socialist policy and the pure Japanism policy. As manifested in opposing views on the organization of a practical movement, it may be seen as the result of the conflict between advocacy of mass organization and advocacy of élitism. But I think that the deeper causes lie in more basic points, and I shall return to this question later.

The third period is from the February Incident until the end of the Pacific War. When we treat fascism as a State structure, this period is not only the most important, but appears to be divided into several separate stages. Great international events, such as the China Incident, the war in Europe, the Japan-Soviet Non-Aggression Pact, the Tripartite Pact, and the Pacific War sealed the fate of Japan and mark successive epochs in the fascist transformation of the domestic structure. Prince Konoe's New Order Movement and the Tōjō Assistance Election are also, of course, important landmarks.

Nevertheless, when fascism as a movement is the central consideration, the February Incident is the great dividing line. For this was the occasion that brought the movement of radical fascism from below to an end, and clearly determined that Japan's course towards fascism would not take the shape of a fascist revolution and *coup d'état* as in Germany and Italy. Hence, though its development takes a zig-zag course, a formation finally occurs within the existing political structure that may be termed the strengthening of State control from above.*

From the time of the Pacific War the Tōjō dictatorship reduced political freedom as far as possible, in fact almost to the zero point. Yet the essential conditions for such a state of affairs had all existed previously; so far as fascist evolution is concerned, this period was simply a development in volume and did not

---

* The Konoe New Order Movement raises a problem. Inasmuch as it involved popular reorganization, this movement appeared, if only momentarily, to represent elements from the lower strata of society; the result was its immediate reform under the counter-attack of the old powers, so that it ended as a completely official and formal affair.

differ in quality from the previous period.* Since the memory of the Tōjō dictatorship is still fresh in our minds, it is easy to fall into the danger of overestimating its significance as an historical stage. Failure to note this point makes people less critical towards those out-and-out fascists who came forward after the war posing as democrats on the sole grounds of having been opposed to Tōjō.

III. DISTINCTIVE CHARACTERISTICS IN THE IDEOLOGY OF THE FASCIST MOVEMENT

In analysing the fascist movement, I shall first discuss its superstructure, that is to say, its ideological character, and then take up the question of its social support.

The ideology sustained by the fascist movement became especially prominent in the first and second periods as defined above. On reaching the third period, fascism was transformed into an actual State structure, and fascism as a movement could no longer be the main-stream. It was in the first and second periods that the fascist movement made its appearance, brandishing a fascist ideology and demanding reforms that extended into the domains of politics, economics, and culture. The representative literature of fascism also appeared mainly at this time. As a result, the ideology of the fascist movement in these periods became the chief object of study thereafter.

The Japanese fascist movement naturally had elements in common with the fascist ideology current in the world, and to save space I shall avoid any comprehensive discussion of such ideologies. Japanese fascism, for example, shared the ideology of

---

* I have fixed the February Incident as the dividing line in order to focus attention on the organization of the fascist *movement*. When the *total structure* of Japanese fascism is the object, a more detailed division becomes necessary. Important events in a detailed description of this third period would be the dissolution of the political parties and the labour unions at the time of the establishment of the Imperial Rule Assistance Association and of the Serve-the-State-through-Industry Association (1940). These events are significant dividing lines, both negatively as marking the destruction of the sources of opposition to the régime, and positively as steps towards conformity to the Assistance system. This process was completed by the Tōjō Assistance Election of April 1942, which followed the promulgation of the Law for the Emergency Control of Speech, Publication, and Association on 19 December 1941, after the formation of the Tōjō Cabinet. Also the contracting of the Tripartite Pact by the second Konoe Cabinet played a large part in petrifying domestic relations by ending discussion of choices in foreign policy, which had continued until then, if only to a slight extent.

its Italian and German counterparts in such matters as the rejection of the world view of individualistic liberalism, opposition to parliamentary politics which is the political expression of liberalism, insistence on foreign expansion, a tendency to glorify military build-up and war, a strong emphasis on racial myths and the national essence, a rejection of class warfare based on totalitarianism, and the struggle against Marxism. Again, there is a great similarity between Eastern and Western fascism in the way of thinking that lies at the root of these concrete demands. For example, Ōkawa Shūmei provides the following estimate of capitalism and socialism:

> The struggle between capitalism and socialism is not one of principle. Both stand on the same principle, and the struggle concerns simply its practical realization. . . . On the one hand, pure capitalism attempts to limit the possession of material wealth to a smaller number of people, that is, to the small number of people called the capitalist class. On the other hand, socialism attempts to distribute material wealth among a large number of workers. Both are attempts to cause this cherished material wealth to be owned on the one hand by a small circle, on the other by a large circle. Both agree in setting an extreme value on material matters, in finding the true happiness of mankind in material pleasures and hence in considering the object of mankind to lie in the abundant possession of material things.*

Ōkawa goes on to say,

> If the way of thought that places material things above the human personality is not reformed, nothing good can be expected from attempts to overthrow the capitalist economic system and to transform it into a socialist system.†

This is the essence of his criticism: since both capitalism and socialism stand on the same materialist basis, socialism is incapable of providing any real relief from the defects of modern civilization; both socialism and Marxism are beasts from the same den as capitalism. This closely resembles the ideology of Nazi and Italian fascism, which says the same thing in different words.

The stress on 'idealism' and 'spirituality' as against materialism in the fascist ideology signifies in reality an attempt to

---

* *The Way of Japan and the Japanese (Nihon oyobi Nihonjin no Michi).*
† Ibid.

divert the eyes of the people from the fundamental contradictions of the social structure; in place of real structural reforms,
they aim at reforms within the minds of men, that is, reforms in
the way of thinking. This provides the real explanation of why
fascism eventually performed the role of serving monopolistic
capital, despite its having displayed a certain anti-capitalist
appearance at the outset. None of these points can be called
distinctive characteristics of Japanese fascism, and I shall not
enter into them here. Instead I shall raise two or three distinctive
points that are especially emphasized in the fascist ideology of
Japan.

In the first place, there is the family-system tendency: that is,
the family system extolled as the fundamental principle of the
State structure. The basic characteristic of the Japanese State
structure is that it is always considered as an extension of the
family; more concretely, as a nation of families composed of
the Imperial House as the main family and of the people as the
branch family. This is not merely an analogy as in the organic
theory of the State, but is considered as having a substantial
meaning. It is maintained, not as an abstract idea but as an
actual historical fact, that the Japanese nation preserves un-
altered its ancient social structure based on blood relationship.
It is true that the idea of a nation of families, and the idea
(derived from it) of the conformity of the two virtues of loyalty
and filial piety, had been the official ideology of the absolute
State since the Meiji era, and are not the monopoly of the
fascist movement.* The fact that this ideology appears con-

---

* Because the military and the right-wing movements were able to make the
'national polity' idea into a veritable Imperial standard, rival groups and forces,
with the exception of a small number of communists, were deprived of a legitimate
basis on which they could risk a frontal assault against the right. The very fact,
however, that this idea was logically implicit in the system (see 'Theory and Psychology of Ultra-Nationalism') meant, ironically enough, that it also became a
major ideological factor inhibiting the development of the Japanese right-wing
movement. The spell-binding power of the 'national polity' as an ideology and as
a principle of organization resulted from its all-embracing supra-political character,
and the attempt by the right-wing movement to give this vaporous 'national polity'
a solid form was the tragi-comedy of the right wing. Considered from the point of
view of the development of fascism, this paradox can perhaps be compared with
the path taken by McCarthyism in post-war America. After making a rapid
advance in the atmosphere of the Cold War on the simple sale of 'anti-communism',
it withered away as an individual influence when anti-communism became, as it
were, a built-in structure in the American political scene.

sistently and conspicuously in a fascist movement that stresses the 'national polity' as a political slogan is a distinctive characteristic not found in the fascism of Germany and Italy. This is so important that it defines the social context of Japanese fascism. Among numerous possible examples, we may note the following statement by Tsuda Kōzō, chief secretary of the Japan Village Government League:

In the family-system principle of Japan the keynote of society is not the demand for individual rights, as in the modern countries of the West, but service to the family as a whole. Socially each family is an independent animate body, a complete cell in itself. The individual is no more than a part or an element of this complete cell. Our nationalism should be the extension and enlargement of this family-system principle. This is perhaps because our nationalism is nothing but the union of these families at the national level. The Emperor is the sovereign, family head, centre, and general representative of the State as a united body.*

From the outset this Village Government League had a strong colouring of provincialism and agrarianism, and this was another reason for its special emphasis on the family system. On the other hand, Kita Ikki's *General Outline of Measures for the Reconstruction of Japan*, which has the strongest centralizing tone and is most tinged with European nationalism, also calls Japan 'an organic and indivisible great family'. This point was in fact common to all the factions of Japanese fascism. Of course, a similar notion existed among the Nazis, the idea of the *Volksgemeinschaft*. But this was definitely not considered as a mere extension of the family principle. Similarly, *Blut und Boden* is not in any sense a concept based on the family, but is clearly a public and political idea. Accordingly Hitler as the *Führer* was regarded not as the head of the family or the clan, but as a public, *öffentlich* leader. The insistence on the family system may therefore be termed a distinctive characteristic of the Japanese fascist ideology; and it is connected with the failure of Japanese fascism as a mass movement.

The next distinctive characteristic of Japanese fascist ideology is the prominent position occupied by the idea of agrarianism. There is a tendency immanent in fascism towards the streng-

* *The Present State of Japanese Fascism (Nihon Fassho no Genjō).*

38   *Thought and Behaviour in Modern Japanese Politics*

thening of State authority and the exercise of a powerful control over all aspects of industry, culture, and thought by means of a centralized State authority. But it is an important feature of Japanese fascist ideology that this tendency was checked by a counter-movement that demanded autonomy for villages in an attempt to put a stop to the expansion of the industrial productive power of the cities. Ōkawa Shūmei among rightists was the most deeply influenced by European education and culture, and people said that there was a 'smell of butter'² about him. Yet in the platform of the Society to Carry Out Heaven's Way on Earth, which he founded after breaking with Kita Ikki, we find the statement,

We must without question reject a capitalist economic policy which stresses commerce and industry in gross imitation of Western ways and must establish a national economic policy according to agrarianism.

The platform also insists on 'decentralization rather than centralization; local autonomy rather than a central Diet; the promotion of the villages rather than the predominance of the cities'.

On the one hand, there is a tendency towards an ever-greater strengthening of absolute State sovereignty focused on the Emperor; on the other, a tendency to centre the conception of Japan on provincial rather than on State affairs. In this respect the right wing may be divided into two sections: those who advocated an intensive development of industry and who wished to increase State control for this end, and those who flatly rejected the idea and thought in terms of agrarianism centred on the villages. Many members of the right wing held both these views, mingled in confusing eclecticism.

The purest representative of provincialism is perhaps Gondō Seikyō, who, after leaping into the limelight with the May 15 Incident, provided the ideological background of the Rural Self-Help Movement of 1932–3. His ideas as expressed in *Self-Government by the People* and *Treatise on Rural Self-Help* are thoroughly provincial and even display an anti-nationalist outlook:

Generally speaking, there have since ancient times been two principles in the administration of States. One is to allow the people a life of autonomy, in which the sovereign hardly goes beyond setting examples, thereby giving the people a good standard. In the other the sovereign takes everything on himself and directs all State affairs. If the former may be termed the principle of autonomy, the latter may be termed *étatisme*. Japan was founded in complete accord with the former principle, and this was the ideal of all the ancient sages.*

What is meant by *étatisme*? Its objectives are to mark out an area for a group called the State, to defend itself from external economic or military invasion, and to control other areas by means of its own economic and military power. In order to increase the prestige of the State, the mass of the people are treated as building materials and as machines to create public funds; all organizations are set up solely for administrative convenience, and the rulers exert enormous authority by controlling the masses through laws and ordinances. All public officials are given a privileged status; the spirit of sacrifice is made the supreme morality; and it becomes necessary to curb the expression of all thought. A detailed study reveals that *étatisme* and autonomy are of an entirely different nature.†

The villages, having been sacrificed to this centralizing nationalism since the Meiji era, are now gasping in the nadir of stagnation and depression:

In the present state of fear and apprehension the villages suffer most. Our villages are the foundation of the country and the source of our habits and customs. At present the farmers form one half of our total population; they utilize the greater portion of the land; and they produce a large proportion not only of the staple foodstuffs of the nation but also of its industrial raw materials and commercial goods.

However:

Tokyo and the other cities have expanded out of all proportion to the villages, and are replete with great buildings that are the last word in comfort and elegance. But, with the Great Depression, the villages are everywhere in financial difficulties. What is the reason for these widespread hardships?

After we have observed the present state of local autonomy, the drift of political party government, and the morale of civil and mili-

* *Self-Government by the People*, Vol. II, Chap. 2.
† Ibid.

tary officials, it becomes perfectly clear that it is the *impasse* of bureaucratic government based on Prussian nationalism that has produced these abnormal phenomena.*

I have quoted these passages in some detail because they most clearly represent the anti-official, anti-urban, and anti-big-industry viewpoints in agrarianism.†

The ideal State that Gondō Seikyō wished to establish was based on the native village community in opposition to Prussian nationalism, and was a State structure built up from the bottom like a pyramid. Hence he upholds the conception of the 'community' (*shashoku*) against the 'nation' (*kuni*). One feels that there is even a tinge of agrarian anarchism here. For example,

If the whole world became Japanese territory, the conception of the Japanese State would become unnecessary. But the conception of the community can never be discarded. The word 'State' is used when one nation is opposed to another. It is a word representing divisions of the world map, and signifies the progressive formation of solidarity between villages, districts, cities and finally a country, in response to the need of men to live together. Even if all countries should remove their boundary lines, the conception of the community would not be destroyed as long as mankind exists.‡

* *Treatise on Rural Self-Help.*

† In a discussion meeting for *A Critique of Criticisms of the Doctrines of Gondō* (*Gondō Gakusetsu Hihan no Hihan*) held by members of the peasant movement with an affinity for Gondō's theories, the following statement is made against criticism from the left wing; it is a good illustration of the character of the Rural Self-Help Movement: 'In the first place it is absurd of them to make the problem of the village a problem of landowners and tenants. While this may be true for the landowners and tenants of Britain in Marx's time, the position of landowners in Japan at present is completely different. In Japan today, since being a landlord is a minor question of legal rights of ownership and since as a rule there is little to choose between landlords and poor farmers in actual economic status, it is no answer to the village problem to try to solve it by a class-warfare movement. It is a larger and more fundamental problem than this. It is a problem of *the village as a whole*.' From this point of view the following argument naturally emerges: 'We certainly do not reject the culture possessed by the cities of today. But we must reject absolutely today's fashion for cities to be mere organs for the ruling class. We know that the city proletariat contains many elements that support the ruling class for economic reasons. This is why we cannot join hands with the city proletariat simply from the principle of class warfare.' (Ifukube Takateru, *The Judgement of Yamakawa Hitoshi on the New Village Movement, and his Errors* (*Yamakawa Hitoshi Shi no Shin Nōson Undō ni tai suru Ninshiki to sono Gōbyū*), attached with the discussion meeting quoted above as an appendix to Gondō Seikyō's *Advocacy of Joint Government by Ruler and People* (*Kunmin Kyōji Ron*).)

‡ *Self-Government by the People*, loc. cit.

This is an example of agrarianism pure and simple. Though it does not always go this far, the tendency against cities, industry, and central authority is immanent to a greater or lesser extent in all Japanese fascist ideologies. Indeed this may be called a consistent tradition of the Japanist-nationalist movement since the Meiji era. Exactly the same thought appears in the Japanism of Miyake Setsurei and Shiga Jūkō, which in early 1887 was the first nationalist movement in modern Japan. For example, in an open letter to the Prime Minister, Count Kuroda, in *The Japanese* (*Nihonjin*), the newspaper of his group, Shiga Jūkō, writes as follows:

There is only one thing we would ask of your administration. That is that the principle of preserving the national essence should be adopted as the national policy of Japan. ... In this connexion, although you are a man of affairs, we simply ask that when you go hunting with your dogs on official holidays or after work, you should get off at Hasuda or Koga stations and take a look at the wretched condition of the local inhabitants. You would then feel how all wealth and ability have been concentrated in Tokyo, how Tokyo has increasingly flourished and prospered while the localities have grown increasingly impoverished, as if Japan belonged to Tokyo and not Tokyo to Japan. Passing on to the seats of prefectural offices such as Utsunomiya and Fukushima, you will find that they are like smaller Tokyos, in which all the wealth and ability of the prefecture or province appears to be concentrated. Thus Japan is made up of one big Tokyo and scores of smaller Tokyos, without which it would not exist. Unfortunately the prosperity of Tokyo is in direct proportion to the decay of the countryside. Only when the people of all the provinces of a nation are rich can the nation as a whole be rich; only when the nation is rich can its army be strong. It is putting the cart before the horse to allow the strength of the inhabitants of the provinces to decline, and yet to hope to enrich the nation; or to try to strengthen the army without first enriching the country.*

This is typical of the way in which early Japanese nationalists criticized the disparity in development between Tokyo and the provinces. In opposition to the Prussian nationalism of the clan clique, they advocated development of villages and cultivation of the strength of the people. The actual substance of the 'Europeanization' that they attacked consisted of the rapid

* *Complete Works,* Book I.

establishment of capitalism by means of State authority from above, and it will be noted that their arguments correspond word for word with those of Gondō.

The development of Japanese capitalism was always attained at the sacrifice of agriculture; and the development of industry was lop-sided, since capitalism developed by the concentration of specially favoured capital allied with State authority. Hence the thought that represented local interests left behind by this rapid central development came out consistently against modernization from above. The important point here is that this tradition eventually merged with fascist thought; in this respect their thinking provides an interesting comparison with that of the Narodniks in Tsarist Russia.

There are, of course, considerable variations in the degree to which rightists manifest this agrarianism. Kita Ikki's *General Outline of Measures for the Reconstruction of Japan* probably represents the palest colouring of the agrarian principle and is the most thoroughly based on centralized national control. His book advocates sweeping changes in governmental and economic organs centred on the authority of the Emperor, and can in fact be regarded as an expression of pure centralized authoritarianism. It includes suspension of the Constitution by the supreme authority of the Emperor; dissolution of the Diet; a *coup d'état* carried out by a national reconstruction Cabinet; restriction of individual private property to one million yen and confiscation of the surplus by the State; limitation of land ownership to a value of one hundred thousand yen; nationalization of enterprises with a capital of ten million yen or more, to be managed by Ministries for Banking, Navigation, Mining, Agriculture, Industry, Commerce, and Railways. This work has the strongest colouring of centralized national socialism, and constitutes something of an exception in right-wing thought.

Tachibana Kōsaburō, who with Gondō Seikyō provided the ideology behind the May 15 Incident, writes as follows in his *Principles of Japan's Patriotic Reformation*:

According to a common expression, Tokyo is the hub of the world. But in my eyes it appears unhappily to be nothing but a branch shop of London. At all events, it is undeniable that the villages are being destroyed in direct proportion to the expansion of Tokyo. The farmers have never been so despised as now and the value of the villages has never been so disregarded.

Here we find the strong animosity against the centre and the cities which he shared with Gondō. Tachibana praises the life bound to the soil in the following words:

Man's world will be eternal so long as the bright sun is over his head and his feet are planted on the ground. Man's world will be peaceful so long as men remain brothers to one another. . . . What is tilling the soil if not the very basis of human life? It is a matter of fact that 'everything that destroys the earth must also perish'. . . . Only by agrarianism can a country become eternal, and this is especially the case with Japan. Japan never could, and never can, be herself if she is separated from the soil.*

Tachibana thus displays a kind of Tolstoyan enthusiasm for the pastoral life. His position is not so thoroughly opposed to urban commerce and industry as that of Gondō, and he recognizes the merits of large-scale industry:

I do not say that large-scale industry and big business should be disregarded. I simply hold that, in view of the great objective of constructing a new Japan based on the principle of self-government, large-scale industry should be controlled and managed according to the principle of a welfare economy. At the same time I insist that we must not be thrown into that most dangerous of errors: the rash dream of immediately establishing a new society and creating a new culture and a great revolution in world history merely by means of the expansion of large-scale industries and the application of their productive power to achieve the level of the most advanced nations.†

This last point refers to Marxist socialism. In contrast, the ideal society advocated by Tachibana was a system of self-government and local autonomy based on the Kingly Way (*Ōdō*). As far as possible, production was to be controlled by popular co-operative organizations based on local jurisdiction. This may be called a compromise between the Kita Ikki and the Gondō Seikyō types. Such a compromising attitude was common in fascism, and it is this point that makes the claims of fascism extremely illogical and fanciful.

* *Principles of Japan's Patriotic Reformation* (*Nihon Aikoku Kakushin Hongi*).
† Ibid.

For instance, the basic platform of the Great Japan Production Party declares:

The socialist reform policy attempts to establish a centralized socialist system in contradiction to a centralized capitalist system. They differ from each other only in so far as the one is based on capitalism and the other on socialism. Both are the same in being centralized systems. The policy of the Great Japan Production Party, on the other hand, aims at the autonomy principle. Autonomy does not mean rendering the central organ of the State completely powerless. While great importance is attached to State control, this will not require a strong centralized authority designed for the purpose. The excellence of the autonomy principle lies in this point. ... Further, the Great Japan Production Party is flatly opposed to the anarchistic economic system of liberalism. Accordingly the Great Japan Production Party adopts the autonomy principle on the one hand, and on the other the principle of national control to the extent that it does not conflict with the former.*

It is a confusing explanation; but in this respect too it is a typical fascist argument. Japanese fascism presents this confused appearance because the tendency towards the concentration of powerful authority and the strengthening of state control, which was common in world fascism, was limited in Japan by the ideology of agrarianism. It should be remembered, however, that the predominant position of this ideology in Japanese fascism did not rest simply on romanticism but was built on a definite social foundation.

As we have seen, the most important social cause for the sudden acceleration of the fascist movement in 1930–1 was that the world depression of 1929 caused, above all, a severe crisis in Japanese agriculture. The crisis that overtook capitalism in Japan naturally brought the heaviest pressure to bear upon the agricultural section of the economy, which was structurally the weakest. In the farm crisis of 1930 the price of rice fell to sixteen yen in October, and in June raw silk at 670 yen showed the lowest price since 1897. The terrible hardships of the farmers of north-east Japan as reported in the daily press are still fresh in one's memory. The extreme poverty of the villages forms the positive background for the acceleration of

* *Reconstruction Front* (*Kaizō Sensen*, No. 8).

the fascist movement, and especially for the acts of right-wing terrorism that occurred continuously after 1931.

For instance, it is reported that just after the assassination of the Finance Minister, Mr. Inoue, Konuma Tadashi of the Blood Pledge Corps (which initiated this terrorism) told investigating officials: 'The extremity of the villages is unbearable to see; it is the result of the bad policies of the former Finance Minister.'* In reporting the thought of the defendants after the May 15 Incident, the prosecution states:

The political parties, the *zaibatsu* and a small privileged group attached to the ruling class are all sunk in corruption. They conspire in parties to pursue their own egoistic interests and desires, to the neglect of national defence and to the confusion of government. As a result national dignity is lost abroad, while at home the morale of the people collapses; the villages are exhausted, and medium and small industry and commerce have been driven to the wall.

Among domestic problems the exhaustion of the villages is given first place. That this was the direct motive which specially turned the young Army officers to radicalism is easily understandable in the light of the fact that many of these officers were the sons of lesser landowners or small independent cultivators. Moreover, the peasants, particularly those of the north-eastern provinces, were regarded as the mainstay of the Army. Gotō Akinori, one of the Army defendants after the May 15 Incident, testified in court as follows:

The impoverishment of the farming villages is a cause of grave concern to all thoughtful people. It is the same with the fishing villages and the small merchants and industrialists. Among the troops the farmer conscripts make a good showing, and the farmers of the north-eastern provinces provide the Army with model soldiers. It is extremely dangerous that such soldiers should be worried about their starving families when they are at the front exposing themselves to death. In utter disregard of poverty-stricken farmers the enormously rich *zaibatsu* pursue their private profit. Meanwhile the young children of the impoverished farmers of the north-eastern provinces attend school without breakfast, and their families subsist on rotten potatoes. I thought that to let a day go by without doing anything was to endanger the Army for one day longer.

* *Tōkyō Asahi*, 10 February 1932.

This statement amply demonstrates the social foundation of radical fascism. In the neat phrase of Tokutomi Sohō, 'The farming villages were the electoral districts of the Army.' The impoverishment of the villages thus gave a most important stimulus to Army interference in politics.

The prominence of agrarian ideology in Japanese fascism is, however, clearly contradictory to the realistic side of fascism: the demand for the expansion of military production and the reorganization of the national economy round the armament industries. As fascism descends from the realm of ideas into the world of reality, agrarianism is bound to turn into an illusion. This was the fate of the right-wing ideology, particularly that of the military. For instance, in the sixty-ninth session of the Imperial Diet (May 1936), one of the members, Mr. Muramatsu Hisayoshi, made the following inquiry:

From the standpoint of national defence in a broad sense the necessity for a speedy solution to the problem of the villages is self-evident. We are quite willing to approve an increase in military expenditure so far as it is necessary to cope with the emergency. Indeed until now we have always given our approval. It is the result that concerns us. Since the manufacture of munitions depends largely on heavy industry, the funds expended for their manufacture flow mainly into industrial and commercial fields. This makes the armament industries flourish and brings about a lop-sided prosperity which results in the concentration of wealth and capital in the big cities and in the hands of big industrialists and merchants. In view of the expected future increase in the costs of national defence, unless steps are taken to remedy this concentration of wealth in the cities from military expenditure, its increase will result in the anomaly of even greater impoverishment of the villages and consequent injury to national defence in the broad sense. I should like a firm answer about whether the Army recognizes that military expenditure draws wealth and capital to the big cities and to the big industrialists and merchants and, if so, how they propose to correct this and promote the basis of national defence.*

The War Minister, General Terauchi, replied as follows:

From the viewpoint of national defence in a broad sense, the Army is greatly concerned about the impoverishment of the villages. We admit that at present, owing to the location of barracks and

* Diet Records.

armament factories, the disbursement of military expenditure tends to be made in the cities. *We feel this to be unavoidable in the present state of industrial development.* In the disbursement of appropriated funds, however, the Army is doing its best in difficult conditions to give relief to the impoverished villages and to assist small and medium industries.

It was a rather lame reply. Despite the Army's wishful thinking, conditions grew progressively worse. As the armament industries developed, the burden fell more and more on the villages. The Army could not brush aside the practical problem of this excessive pressure on the villages, which supplied the best recruits. Patent uneasiness about this contradiction continued until the time of Tōjō. Much later, during the eighty-first session of the Diet (1943), the following question was put by Mr. Hata Bushirō, a member of the committee on the Bill for Special Regulations for Wartime Administration: 'Are not the villages of Imperial Japan being endangered by the absorption of their labour power in the armament industries?' Premier Tōjō replied:

This is a point that truly worries me. On the one hand, I want at all costs to maintain the population of the villages at forty per cent of the total population. I believe that the foundation of Japan lies in giving prime importance to agriculture. On the other hand, it is undeniable that industry is being expanded, chiefly because of the war. It is extremely hard to reconcile these two factors. However difficult it may be, I am determined to maintain the population of the villages at forty per cent. But production must be increased. A harmony must be created by degrees between the two requirements. But, in creating this harmony, care must be taken to avoid making havoc of the Japanese family system. I must confess that things are not proceeding at present in an ideal manner. In the need for a rapid expansion of production large factories have been set up in various places; their workers have to be hired from among farmers, who naturally have to give up work on their farms. Although things are not proceeding ideally, I still believe that a method can and will be found to establish a proper harmony in the Japanese manner.

This anxious and pitiful answer reveals the contradiction between the structural characteristics of Japanese capitalism and the absolute necessity of increasing productive power. It also reveals the acute anxiety of the ruling class in the midst of the unprecedented turmoil of total war to preserve the village as the foundation of the Japanese family system. This is, of course, bound up with the problem of the traditional methods of agricultural enterprise. But the important point is that in the relentless march of history agrarian ideology as a positive force becomes an illusion, gradually receding from reality. On the other hand, it constantly acts as a check on government concern for the welfare facilities of the industrial workers.

This is an extremely important point, and it may well constitute the decisive difference between Japanese fascism and that of Nazi Germany. Of course, the Nazis also attached great importance to the farmers, as the expression *Blut und Boden* indicates; and they tried to bind them to the soil by such steps as the land inheritance law. But the Nazi Party was after all a 'Workers' Party' (*Arbeitspartei*). The Nazis concentrated their energies on how to separate the working class from the power and influence of the social democratic and communist parties, and on how to convert them to Nazism. While the farmers formed one wing of the Nazi movement from the outset, it was extremely difficult to convert the organized workers to Nazism. The Nazis mobilized the industrial workers into *Arbeitsfronten* and took the greatest pains to get them to support Nazism by conciliatory measures such as *Kraft durch Freude*.

In the fascist ideology of Japan, however, the industrial workers were always slighted in comparison with the small and medium merchants and farmers. This was already so in the radical fascist movement, which came closer to representing the lower social stratum. The official report on the May 15 Incident mentions only 'the exhaustion of the villages, the extreme poverty of small and medium shopkeepers and owners of small factories'. No reference is made to the industrial workers. The pamphlet entitled *The True Meaning of National Defence: its Consolidation Advocated* (*Kokubō no Hongi to sono Kyōka no Teishō*), published by the War Ministry in October 1934, displays the typical military ideology of the second period. This is the pamphlet that begins with the famous sentence, 'War is the father of creation and the mother of culture', and that became such a great issue in the Diet. It declares: 'At present the most pressing problem of national welfare is to give relief to the farming, mountain, and fishing villages.' It presents the problem under the heading, 'City versus Village'. Of course, this does not mean that the authors of such pamphlets purposely made no reference to the industrial workers. When they spoke of the poverty and distress of the life of the people, they must have included the industrial working class in their thoughts. But the fact that they all mention only the farmers and the small and medium shopkeepers and factory-owners reveals the insignificant place occupied by the industrial proletariat in their minds.

The notebook of Muranaka Kōji, a leader of the February Incident, states: 'It must be realized that the Shōwa Restoration cannot be brought about until the military clique and the bureaucrats are crushed by the power of the common soldiers, the farmers, and the workers.'* A specific reference of this kind to the concrete agents of change is unusual in nationalist writings; yet it will be noticed that even here the industrial workers are put in last place. In the world of fascist ideas this was already so. Indeed in actual practice this tendency is far more openly displayed. It is well known that during the war the welfare facilities of the workers were far inferior even to those of the Nazis.

Japanese fascist leaders consistently harboured a deep-rooted pessimism regarding the value of industrial workers and the possibility of their spiritual and physical improvement. For example, during a committee meeting on the Bill for Special Regulations for Wartime Administration in the eighty-first session of the Diet (1942–3), Mr. Kawakami Jōtarō made the following demand:

I do not deny that the villages are a source of sturdy soldiers. However, if the factories are incapable of supplying sturdy soldiers, this is a defect and must be remedied. In the past the villages and the cities have been opposed to each other. I think it necessary that measures should henceforth be taken to do away with this opposition and to enable the factories as well as the villages to supply sturdy soldiers.

In a lengthy answer Tōjō replied,

Ideally, both the villages and the factories should be sources of sturdy soldiers. But I must say with regret that at present the factory workers are inferior to the men from the villages in everything, not

* *Untitled Papers* (*Mudairoku*).

only in physique. I may arouse anger by saying this, but it is an incontestable fact that farm workers are of firmer character. To that extent, the factory workers are inferior in present circumstances. . . . In short, I agree with your view that both the villages and the factories should supply sturdy soldiers and that our policies should be aimed at this objective. I should like to proceed in this direction, but I think that at present there is regrettably a great discrepancy between them.*

A pessimistic view of the industrial workers runs consistently through this answer, demonstrating how agrarian ideology put a brake on a positive policy that would accept the factory workers. From this ensued the ill-treatment of the drafted factory workers, their surprisingly poor lodgings and pay, and the indifference of the authorities to their situation. The result was large-scale demoralization. The authorities then tried to remedy the situation by a combination of abstract 'pep talks' and severe punishments.

The divergence between Japanese and German fascism in this respect is clearly revealed in the difference between Japan's Serve-the-State-through-Industry Movement and Nazi Germany's *Kraft durch Freude* movement. This does not mean that the Nazis had the independence and initiative of the workers at heart; in giving them holidays and sending them on coach trips once a year their object was to divert the workers' attention from oppressive reality. Nevertheless in its careful consideration of the workers and in its welfare measures German fascism cannot be compared with the Japanese version. Of course, this is also connected with the degree of capital accumulation in the two countries. But an important factor was that in the case of the Japanese factory workers there was no strong feeling that one would have liked to improve their conditions if only the materials had been available. Such coarse treatment was regarded as justified especially when it applied to drafted factory workers. Although this certainly reflects agrarian ideology, it must be noted that agrarianism alone did not bring about such a result. More fundamentally the cause lay in the difference between the strength of the proletariat in the two countries. The strength of the democratic movement prior to the fascist structure determined the extent of democratic

* Diet Records.

trappings within fascism. In the case of the Nazis the experience of the November Revolution and the baptism of Weimar democracy made their case decidedly different from that of Japan.

The third distinctive characteristic of Japanese fascist ideology relates to the emancipation of the Asian nations on the so-called Greater Asia Principle. The ideal of the emancipation of the Asian peoples from European colonialism, a task which had been upheld since the days of the Popular Rights Movement[3] in the Meiji era, flowed strongly through Japanese fascism. But it became inextricably tied up with the idea that Japan should seize hegemony in Asia in place of European imperialism.* Because of Japan's historical position as the first Asian country to construct a modern State and to check 'the thrust of Europe towards the East', the ideology of Japan's continental development always contained this side-issue of the emancipation of East Asia. As time passed, of course, this side-issue became more and more a mere decoration for imperialist war. But that this type of idea had deep international roots may be gathered from its present-day influence on the nationalist movements in Burma and Indonesia. This point demands careful attention since it has a bearing on future problems.†

IV. DISTINCTIVE CHARACTERISTICS IN THE PATTERN OF THE JAPANESE FASCIST MOVEMENT

We have already noticed that the main driving-force in the advance of Japanese fascism was supplied by political powers

---

* Cf. the development from advocacy of an East Asian Community to that of a New Order in East Asia.

† The relation between the 'rise' of modern Japan and Asian nationalism, the connexion between the continental agents of the Black Ocean and Amur River Societies (which were its distinctive expression) and the Chinese Revolution, and the influence of the 'Great East Asia' war on South-East Asian racial movements are all extremely important and interesting themes, in both their historical and present-day significance. Here I am discussing Asianism simply as a characteristic of Japanese fascist ideology; there is no room for a full treatment of the broader questions. Besides, at the present time (1947) Occupation policy strongly restricts discussion of this question, and I thought that to argue from half-facts would give rise to error. Particularly in relation to Japan's role in the independence movements of South-East Asia there is a need for an analysis based on concrete historical materials. The right-wing movement in Japan since the war is still perplexed by the dilemma of this traditional Asian fellow-feeling and the need to rely on the West against communism.

within the existing State apparatus. That is to say, the influence of the civilian right wing did not expand of itself, but was able to become an important factor in Japanese politics only when it joined hands with the military and the bureaucracy in the second period. Of course the Italian fascists and German Nazis also received the support of the military in their respective countries. But they clearly differ from Japan in having won State power from outside the administration, chiefly by mobilizing the strength of civilians.

What mainly characterizes the formation of the Japanese radical fascist movement from the Blood Pledge Corps Incident until the February Incident is that until the very last its practical managers had no mass organization and showed no particular zeal for organizing the masses. Rather they made it from first to last a movement of a limited number of 'patriots'. The heroism, or the consciousness of the 'patriot' bound up with the Japanese fascist movement, acted as a check on its development on a mass basis. For example, Tachibana Kōsaburō in his *Principles of the Japanese Patriotic Reformation* writes as follows:

> What I now emphasize, and ask you all to engrave on your hearts, is the cardinal fact that a nation-wide social reformation can be initiated only by a group of patriots who are capable of pursuing the great aim of saving the country and relieving the people in accordance with the will of Heaven. . . . Needless to say, the number of patriots who can be found to initiate this great task at the sacrifice of their lives will never be large. But it is also a fact that scattered among all classes of society there are patriots who can carry out the will of Heaven if it chooses them to do so. . . . People who call for reformation must be willing to sacrifice their lives for the people. Only a group of patriots who would sacrifice their lives for the great aim of saving the country and relieving the people can be the leaders of a national reform movement. In view of the present state of Japan, such patriots can be found only among you military men, and it is above all the farmers who will respond to your call. This is why I must ask you to contemplate deeply and to make an iron decision.

In this way Tachibana whipped up the strong patriotic spirit of the military class, which was already imbued with what Nietzsche called 'the pathos of distance'.

Because of this basic idea the movement naturally developed as the visionary idealism of a minority and failed to organize and mobilize the masses. This was allied to other distinctive characteristics of the Japanese fascist movement, such as its extreme fantasy, abstraction, and lack of plan. The radical fascist movement was always governed by the mythological optimism that, if patriots led the way by destructive action, a future course would become clear. For instance, the thought of Inoue Nisshō, the leader of the Blood Pledge Corps Incident, is described in the court judgement as follows:

To overthrow the old system of organization is a destructive or negative act. To establish the new system of organization is a constructive or positive act. Without destruction, however, there can be no construction. Since ultimate denial is the same as genuine affirmation, destruction is itself construction, and the two are one and inseparable.*

During the trial Inoue himself stated: 'It is more correct to say that I have no systematized ideas. I transcend reason and act completely upon intuition.' He deliberately rejected any theory for constructive planning after the rising.

Again, the May 15 Incident was the first relatively organized act of violence of radical fascism, and fairly detailed plans were prepared for the uprising. Let us take, for example, the plan for the first stage by the Navy group. One section was to attack the Premier's residence and Count Makino, and promulgate martial law with the support of Admiral Tōgō. A second section was to attack the Industrialists' Club and the Peers' Assembly Hall, enter the Premier's residence, and begin the task of national reconstruction with the support of Gondō Seikyō. A third section was to attack the headquarters of the Minsei Tō and the Seiyū Kai, and following that to release the Blood Pledge Corps men from prison. Thus a fairly detailed programme was drawn up; yet it is not at all clear what concrete reforms were to be made, other than that Gondō was to be the brains of the new government. On this point Lieutenant Koga declared in court:

We thought about destruction first. We never considered taking on the duty of construction. We foresaw, however, that, once the destruction was accomplished, someone would take charge of the

* Inoue was a Nichiren priest and the present proposition is derived from Buddhist philosophy.

construction for us. We had no guiding principle, but thought to set
up a military government after first proclaiming martial law. . . .
When I called on Major-General Araki in Kumamoto in December
1930 with the late Major Fujii, he told us that the deadlock in the
national situation must be broken by the Yamato spirit. At that time
I trusted and respected Major-General Araki. In 1932 key positions
in the Army such as Director of Military Police and of Civilian
Defence were filled by men of Araki's following. We believed that,
if we could create a situation requiring martial law, a military
government would be set up round Araki as War Minister, and a start
made upon the path of reconstruction.*

Thus, because of the idea that 'We should just destroy; afterwards something will emerge, and someone else take over the
construction', the plan went no further than setting up a
military government.

Here, however, there is a difference of views between the
Army and the Navy defendants. The Army group had not
thought even as far ahead as setting up a military government
under martial law. For example, an Army cadet, Ishizeki Sakae,
stated: 'It is said that the Navy group had thought in advance
of the martial law edict, but we wished to die fighting and did
not think of the results beforehand.' Here the lack of realism is
much more extreme.

This same characteristic may be seen in the Heaven-Sent
Soldiers' Unit Incident. This was a rising planned chiefly by
Amano Tatsuo and Maeda Torao of the Patriotic Labour
Party and Kageyama Masaharu and Suzuki Zenichi of the
Great Japan Production Party, assisted by Lieutenant-Colonel
Yasuda Tetsunosuke of the Army and Yamaguchi Saburō of
the Second Naval Air Command. It ended abortively, but in
the original plan, 3,600 men were to be mobilized at 11 a.m. on
7 July 1933. First, the person responsible for the air attack
(Yamaguchi) was to drop bombs on the Premier's residence, the
residence of the Privy Seal, Count Makino, and the Metropolitan
Police Headquarters. Leaflets were also to be distributed, and
the plane was to land in front of the Imperial Palace in exact
timing with an attack on the Metropolitan Police Headquarters
by the ground forces. The ground forces were then to divide
into several sections. One section, armed with pistols and swords,

* *Tōkyō Asahi*, evening edition, 29 July 1933.

was to attack the Premier's residence and kill any surviving Cabinet Ministers. Other sections were to attack the residences of Count Makino and of the Presidents of the Seiyū Kai and the Minsei Tō as well as the Japan Industrialists' Club and the Headquarters of the Social Masses Party. Another section was to break into armouries and seize arms and ammunition. After the attack on the Metropolitan Police Headquarters the main section was to occupy the Industrial Bank of Japan. From this stronghold they were to fight to the death against the police units of the entire city, while exerting themselves in propaganda activities. Much thought went into this plan, but it ended in death in battle. It is striking that the planning did not go beyond battle strategy.

Finally we come to the February Incident. This was the radical fascist movement in its largest production, with a well-planned and organized character rarely seen in Japanese uprisings. According to the prosecution indictments and the judgement reports, this rising was aimed at realizing Kita Ikki's *General Outline of Measures for the Reconstruction of Japan*. But the accused officers unanimously denied this. For instance, in his *Sincere Record** Muranaka Kōji states:

> By 'Restoration' we meant our desire to uphold a spiritual reformation of the people and to make material reconstruction subsequent to it. . . . How could we fellow-patriots have been able to carry out this scheme if we had nourished political ambitions or indulged in private fancies about the actual structure of the government?

In response to the question, 'Is not destruction without construction pure recklessness?' he replied:

> What is destruction? What is construction? . . . To destroy the wicked is to reveal the path of righteousness. Destroying the wicked and revealing the path of righteousness are one and inseparable, like back and front. The punishment of evil men and restoration are the same thing.

He concludes with the same 'logic' as Inoue's: 'Once the great moral cause is clarified, and the hearts of the people rectified, the Imperial Way cannot fail to be promoted.' These words from Fujita Tōko's *Kaiten-shi Shi* were often quoted by the defen-

---

* *Sincere Record (Tanshinroku), Papers in Prison (Gokuchū Shuki).*

dants of the February Incident as the common object of the uprising. They were extremely abusive about plans like those of the March and October Incidents, which involved setting up a military government and reforming the State, and also about the Hitler-Germany type of régime of Control Faction leaders like Nagata and Tōjō, which they regarded as contrary to the spirit of the Restoration patriot.*

Thus the pattern of the radical fascist movement was almost invariably characterized by fantasy and lack of realism. This is best revealed by the fact that the mobilization of one thousand six hundred troops in the February Incident resulted in nothing more than the murder of a few elderly men.

This point also marks a clear difference between fascism in Japan and Germany. As a result of the strong survival in its ideology of a medieval Bakumatsu patriotism of the type exemplified by Kumoi Tatsuo, this sort of patriotism came to appear in the concrete fascist movement as well. Democracy was flatly rejected by Japanese fascism, but not by the Nazis. The Nazis decried Weimar democracy, but not democracy in general. Rather the aim of the Nazis was to stigmatize Weimar and Anglo-American democracy as a Jewish plutocracy and to proclaim themselves a 'true' Nordic democracy. Of course this claim was simply 'the democratic disguise for dictatorship', to borrow the words of Professor Miyazawa. However, the fact that it was constrained to appear in a democratic disguise reveals that even in Germany democracy had already struck ineradicable roots in the political ideology of the nation.

---

* The objective significance of the conduct of the rebellious officers in the February Incident (in contrast to their motivations) consisted in an attempt to set the Imperial prerogative in motion against a background of military power, and thus to 'reform' the domestic and foreign policy of the government into the policies they desired. This means that they had fallen into extreme self-deception. Nevertheless their 'logic', as reported above, cannot be regarded as an *ex post facto* justification. Why, then, did these young officers decide to mobilize troops on their own initiative, while on the other hand they were so indignant at the behaviour of the upper echelons of the military and attacked them as 'transforming the Imperial Army into a private Army'? What the young officers had in mind when making their decision was the article in the Essential Rules of Military Tactics that allows the commander on the battlefield to act solely on his own judgement and decision in case of emergency. Thus they could insist with subjective consistency that, should their actions be punished as violations of the Imperial prerogative, the measures taken by General Honjō at the time of the Manchurian Incident must also be punished for the same reason.

Hitler was strongly opposed to the monarchism of some Junkers, and was himself fundamentally a republican. In *Mein Kampf* he sharply distinguishes monarchic patriotism from the patriotism that loves the Fatherland and the people, and he ridicules the tendency to worship State power for its own sake as animalian worship. He maintained that 'States exist for men, and not men for States'. Such a way of thinking is accepted as a matter of course only after the experience of a *bourgeois* democratic revolution. This naturally gave the Nazi movement a clear mass character from the outset. Again, it is stated in *Mein Kampf* that 'the previous Pan-Germanism was splendid as an ideology but failed because it did not possess a mass organization'.

But the Japanese fascist movement from below remained to the last a movement of a small number of patriots—visionary, fanatic, and lacking in plan. These are the striking tendencies in the formation of the Japanese fascist movement. Of course mythological elements and the idea of an *élite* are common to all fascist ideologies. The differences in the degree to which these were held in Japan, however, are so marked as to amount to qualitative differences.

V. DISTINCTIVE CHARACTERISTICS IN THE SOCIAL SUPPORT OF JAPANESE FASCISM

If the military and the bureaucracy were the driving forces of fascism, which social classes showed a positive sympathy towards its development? In Germany and Italy, as everywhere else, fascism was a movement of the lower-middle class. With obvious exceptions a large proportion of the intellectuals were also positive supporters of Nazism and fascism.

Roughly speaking, we can say that the middle strata provided the social support for the fascist movement in Japan as well. But in the case of Japan a more elaborate analysis is necessary. The middle or petty *bourgeois* stratum in Japan can be divided into the following two types: first, the social class that comprises small factory owners, building contractors, proprietors of retail shops, master carpenters, small landowners, independent farmers, school teachers (especially in primary schools), employees of village offices, low-grade officials, Buddhist and Shinto priests; secondly, persons like urban salaried employees, so-called men of culture, journalists, men in occupations demanding higher knowledge such as professors and lawyers, and university and college students. The distinction between these two types is especially significant when we consider the fascist movement in Japan.

In Japan it is mainly the first type that provides the social foundation of fascism. If the second group represents intellectuals in the proper sense, the first group might be called the pseudo- or sub-intellectuals. It is the pseudo-intellectuals that create the so-called voice of the people. Of course among Japanese intellectuals of the second type the number of people who persisted in an openly anti-fascist attitude to the last was comparatively small. Most people adapted themselves to the process of fascization and followed in its wake. On the other hand, they were certainly not positive advocates or the driving force of the fascist movement. Rather their mood was generally one of vague antipathy towards it, an antipathy that amounted almost to passive resistance.*

* In my description of the part played by the intelligentsia, too much concern with their mental posture towards the fascist movement can lead to an over-estimation of so-called negative resistance. The need at present is rather for a detailed study of the process by which, though the actions of the intelligentsia of the time were varied, they were all alike in moving towards an acquiescent acceptance of the ruling structure. A view of the intelligentsia more or less common to radical fascists can be seen in the *Prison Papers* (*Gokuchū Shuki*) of Yasuda Masaru, a defendant in the February Incident. In an analysis of the existing state of Japan, under the heading 'A Discussion of the Mental Decadence of the Middle Class', he stated: 'The learned classes timidly take refuge in the pursuit of personal happiness and lack the courage to act faithfully according to their beliefs, which are largely confined to the gospel of Marx. The ordinary *petit bourgeois*, on the other hand, are indulging in sensual pleasures. This must be considered a great cause in misleading the country.' An inquiry was carried out in 1943 by the Tokyo Thought Measures Study Association (Tōkyō-to Shisō Taisaku Kenkyū Kai) into the thought of teachers and secondary school boys in the city of Tokyo. According to this inquiry, the attitude of teachers towards the wartime education system could be broadly divided into attitudes of approval or of criticism *vis-à-vis* existing conditions. The latter could again be divided into the way of thought (which the inquiry calls a 'radical attitude') which complained that educationalists were not fully aware of the present situation, that a wartime educational system should be more positively promoted, and so forth; and the one (which the inquiry calls a 'conservative attitude') that was opposed to the 'extremes' of the system as a whole, saying that teaching was at present excessively controlled, that it would lapse into formalism, that miscellaneous duties were too numerous and prevented study, and so forth. Leaving aside those who approved of the existing conditions (about 50 per cent of those investigated), we find that among those with a critical attitude the radicals were comparatively numerous among the younger stratum of normal school instructors (over 55 per cent).⁴ The 'conservatives' were most numerous among the

This is an important characteristic of Japanese fascism: the Imperial Rule Assistance organizations never succeeded in getting control of the urban salaried employees. The fashion for 'culturism' during the war may be considered an expression of passive resistance to fascism by the intelligentsia of the second group. In Germany and Italy the learned class positively hoisted the banner of fascism, and the university students played a major role. Not so in Japan. Of course, some students participated in the right-wing movement; but among those there were many who by education and intelligence should rather be assigned to the first group. The intelligentsia student class as a whole never supported the fascist movement. There is an incomparable difference between this and the extent to which it was caught up in the whirlwind of Marxism and the socialist movement in the late twenties and early thirties. In Tokyo Imperial University the Student Union organized itself in the late thirties on lines similar to the Nazi student movement, but despite the seemingly favourable situation at the time it made almost no progress and was greeted by the majority of the students with indifference and even ridicule.

For one thing this was because in Japan the intelligentsia is essentially European in culture and, unlike its counterpart in Germany, could not find enough in traditional Japanese culture to appeal to its level of sophistication. In the case of Germany to exalt nationalism meant also to take a pride in the tradition of Bach, Beethoven, Goethe, and Schiller, who at the same time provide the culture of the intelligentsia. These conditions did not exist in Japan; inasmuch as the European culture of the Japanese intelligentsia remained a culture of the brain, filling only an ornamental function, it was not deeply rooted in thinking or feeling. Hence it largely lacked the moral courage

younger stratum of middle school teachers (over 37 per cent) and fewest among primary school teachers. In general the 'radical' group could raise few concrete criticisms; for example, abstract and generalized items such as 'liberalism must be blotted out' and 'wartime morale is not being sufficiently stimulated' were numerous. In contrast it must be noted that 'conservative' criticisms of excesses and faults based on experienced and concrete observations are comparatively numerous. This may be considered as a general reflection of the behaviour of the first and second middle-class groups I am discussing here. Although they were all teachers, primary school and normal school teachers had a strong inclination towards radical fascism and the 'assistance' ideology, while the middle school teachers of the former system had a strong affinity with the intelligentsia and salaried employees.

to make a resolute defence of its inner individuality against
fascism. On the other hand, its European culture would never
permit it to respond to the low tone of the fascist movement and
to its shallow intelligence. Such a lack of thoroughness, coupled
with the intellectual detachment and isolation of the intelligentsia in general, drove it to a hesitant and impotent
existence.

In contrast the first group substantially formed the backbone
class of the nation and was far more practical and active.
Besides, its members held positions of leadership in small local
groups such as workshops, stores, public offices, agricultural
associations, and schools. Because of the patriarchal structure of
Japanese society, such persons exercised paternal authority over
the members of their groups, over the assistants, clerks,
labourers, craftsmen, servants, tenants, and other subordinates.
It is precisely these pseudo-intellectuals who directly controlled
the thought and sentiment of the 'masses'. From the viewpoint
of the Japanese political and social structure as a whole, they
clearly belonged to the class of the ruled. Their standard of
living was not very high, being scarcely different from that of
their subordinates. Nevertheless they were the undisputed rulers
of their own microcosms, in which they had the authority of
petty emperors.

The most stubborn opponents of all progressive trends, such
as attempts by the masses to organize themselves by means of
their social and political rights of expression, were accordingly
found in this group. More important, since in their manner of
life and their everyday existence they were almost identical
with their subordinates, it was these men who could most effectively control the masses. Measures of State control and
ideological indoctrination from the ruling class never reached the
populace directly but were transmitted and even reinterpreted
by them to the masses at the bottom of the social scale. The
mediation of these members of the first group of the middle
stratum was vitally necessary. These small 'bosses' and 'masters'
also served as the executives of town and village councils,
agricultural, religious, educational, youth, and reservist associations, acting as transmitters of local opinion distilled in these
places.

David Hume once said: 'Any government, however despotic,

is based upon people's opinions'; and to be sure, the most despotic government cannot exist without a minimum of voluntary co-operation from the ruled. In wartime Japan it was the middle stratum in this first sense that ensured this minimum of voluntary co-operation. It is here that we can find a 'public opinion' which really moves society, not in newspaper editorials or magazine articles.

The reason that the opinions of journalists are apt to be removed from the people in Japan is because they are primarily generated by the second group of the middle stratum and attach too much importance to the isolated concerns of that group.* Let us consider, for instance, the controversy about the organ theory of Imperial sovereignty[5] that arose early in 1935. This had grave significance for the development of Japanese fascism and almost brought down the Okada Cabinet. The reason that such an academic theory became a great political and social question was that it affected the opinion of the first group of the middle stratum. Once the organ theory had been raised in the House of Peers, it aroused a great storm, since the reservists took it up throughout the country and carried on a large-scale campaign against it. The upper levels of both the government and the military at first took the attitude that the organ theory was a purely academic question.

The answers of the War and Navy Ministers when it was debated in the House of Peers are evidence for this. The Navy Minister, Admiral Ōsumi, declared: 'The matchless dignity of our national polity makes even discussion of it awe-inspiring. I should like you to acknowledge that I say this in all sincerity and not as a reply about an academic theory of the constitution.' The War Minister, General Hayashi, stated: 'Dr. Minobe's academic theory has been expounded for a number of years, and it is not true to say that it has had a bad influence on the military forces.'

Thus even the military authorities did not make a serious

* This state of affairs has markedly changed since the war as a result of the metamorphosis and disintegration of the pre-war intelligentsia, which formed a more or less distinct 'class' before the war. At any rate all the large newspapers have clearly moved in the direction of standardized mass-media methods in an 'equalized' mass society of the American type. The plainest sign of this is the relative decline in the special character that the *Asahi Shimbun* maintained before the war in contrast to the other great newspapers.

issue of it. It became a major political issue because the Seiyū
Kai used it as a lever to overthrow the government, initiating
agitation for the clarification of the national polity in conjunction
with Minoda Muneki and other civilian fascists. But it was the
power provided by the activity of the reservist associations over
the whole country that swept the agitation throughout society.
Nothing exposed the intellectual gulf between the intelligentsia
and the general populace more clearly than this incident. An
academic theory accepted as common sense for many years not
only by specialist scholars and men of learning but by civil and
judicial officials was received by society at large as an improper
and even blasphemous way of thinking.

The part played by the middle class of the first group is just
like that played by the non-commissioned officers in the Army.
While non-commissioned officers belong essentially with the
troops, they are conscious of being 'officers'. The Imperial Army
made deft use of this consciousness to control the troops, for it
is the non-commissioned officers who live with them and in
practice control them. Commissioned officers have little direct
control of camp affairs. Therefore a company commander must
at all costs control the non-commissioned officers in order to
control the troops. In just the same way, it is impossible to
control the masses without controlling the first group of the
middle stratum. The determining factor in Japanese politics
(now as in the past) is the people or political power controlling
the masters of these local microcosms.

The discrepancy between the culture and way of thinking of
the first and second groups of the middle stratum is probably a
characteristic distinctive to Japan. In Britain and America, and
even in Germany, there is more cohesion between the intellectuals and the rest of society. The extreme difference in culture
between the two groups in Japan, the close approximation in
culture between the first group and the labouring masses under
their control, and the pseudo-intelligentsia's understanding of
the language, feelings, and morals of the masses—all these
factors enabled the first group to gain a firmer psychological
control over the masses than could the real intelligentsia.

My use of the term 'pseudo-intelligentsia' refers also to two
things that divide these people from the masses pure and simple:
first, their desire to be accepted as members of the intelligentsia,

secondly, their fragmentary and hearsay knowledge of social problems, ranging from world politics to local affairs, and above all their own self-image as opinion leaders on the local level. We have all met men in barbers' shops, bath houses, and railway carriages who treat those about them to their lofty opinions on inflation or the American-Soviet question. These men are what I call the pseudo-intelligentsia, and on asking them their occupation, we find that they mostly belong to this first group of the middle stratum.

The intellectual and cultural isolation of the second group of the middle stratum is also symbolized by 'composite magazines',[6] the strange term 'pure literature', and the so-called 'Iwanami culture', all of which spring from the isolated character of the intelligentsia. For example, in the American magazines *Time* and *Newsweek* popular features and fairly educated comment on political and economic affairs appear side by side. Why are there no such magazines in Japan? The trouble is that, although there is an Iwanami culture, the 'non-commissioned officer' class of society belongs rather to the Kōdan Sha culture.*

It is only to be expected that the fascist ideology of Japan, based as it was on the positive support of such a class as the pseudo-intelligentsia, should be far inferior in quality and even more absurd in content than those of Germany and Italy. This was another reason why the intelligentsia of the second group were driven into a more and more negative attitude. In Germany leading scholars and professors laid the foundations for Nazism. But what happened in Japan? Of course there were scholars who shouldered the banner of militarism or fascism. But it seems that in most cases the feeling that fascism was stupid prevailed in their minds, if not on the surface. It was

* Since the war the situation has become fluid, and the cultural dislocation of both groups has been fairly continuous. More precisely, the equation between the university-educated salaried employees and the intelligentsia has broken down. On the one hand the salaried man has moved towards mass standards; on the other a new type of intelligentsia has arisen from the uneducated working class through union activities and so forth. Again, the pre-war intellectual journalists have now been drawn into a broader category of 'men of culture'; this has led, on the one hand, to the elevation of the artisan and entertainer to the status of 'man of culture' and, on the other, to the lowering of the critic and journalist to the artisan or entertainer level. The new tendency towards fluidity is symbolized by the change of the *Bungei Shunjū* into a popular, rather than a 'composite', magazine and by the flood of weekly magazines.

because this first group was used as an intermediary that the end-product of wartime control became so fanatical and absurd.

For example, it was these local leaders who became the actual advocates of the bamboo spear principle.[7] However ignorant the military might have been, the top level of the Army could not seriously have believed that highly developed military weapons could be resisted with bamboo spears. Insistence on the bamboo spear ideology was an attempt to cover material deficiencies with spiritual power, and the Army was in general well aware that it was mere propaganda. But, when this ideology permeated downwards and circulated among the masters of the microcosms, it was accepted at its face value. In all earnestness they provided instruction in the bamboo spear principle. The absurd instructions given in air-raid exercises are still fresh in our memories. Such inanity was in no small sense due to the fact that all decrees and instructions from above had to be 'interpreted' by the first group of the middle stratum. Much of the tragi-comedy in Japan's wartime leadership arose here.

The participants in radical fascist uprisings and the leading members of right-wing groups were drawn largely from the class of primary school teachers, petty officials, Buddhist and Shintō priests, masters of small workshops, and small landowners. This is connected with what we have already observed about the importance attached in fascist ideology to small shopkeepers and factory owners, and to peasants rather than to urban industrial workers. Not only the leaders in the villages, but men like local city bosses were largely of rural origin, and many of them maintained some link with the villages. As a result agrarianism was their common concern. This stratum was also united in the traditional demand for local autonomy against central administration. What they called local autonomy consisted in a demand for the elimination of interference by the central bureaucracy in the microcosms where these small masters held sway. Antipathy to bureaucratic control and to the *zaibatsu* is most intense in this class.

In addition the international position of Japan closely resembled the social position of this stratum within the country. In international affairs, Japan was for ever conscious of the pressure of the advanced capitalist countries, yet in the Far East it acted as a relatively advanced country. Japan was thus both bully and bullied. This was why the pseudo-intellectual class felt an inner sympathy for the continental development of Japan. They regarded the pressure of the advanced capitalist countries in the same way as that of the *zaibatsu*. The resistance of the East Asian peoples to Japanese imperialism aroused the same psychological reactions among them as the resistance of their subordinates in the shops, work-places, and other groups under their control. Thus they became the most ardent supporters of the China Incident and the Pacific War.

VI. THE HISTORICAL DEVELOPMENT OF JAPANESE FASCISM

The distinctive characteristic in the development of Japanese fascism was, as we have seen, that it never took the form of a fascist revolution with a mass organization occupying the State apparatus from outside the administration. The process was rather the gradual maturing of a fascist structure within the State, effected by the established political forces of the military, the bureaucracy, and the political parties.

Yet it should not be suggested that the activities of the civilian right-wing movement and of the revolutionary young officers were therefore of no great historical significance. The trend towards fascism in the lower strata of society and the spasmodic outbursts of the radical fascist movement were a continual stimulus to the advance of fascism from above. The important point is that the fascization of the ruling structure developed step by step, with the military and the bureaucracy as its axis and with the social energy of this radical fascism as its springboard. For example, the October Incident took place immediately after the Manchurian Incident; at about the same time the movement towards fascism from within the established political parties also became marked in the movement of the Home Minister, Mr. Adachi, for a coalition Cabinet.

The May 15 Incident put an end to the short history of political party government in Japan. A coalition of the military, the bureaucracy, and the political parties first emerged in the Saitō Cabinet (May 1932). Again, the right of the military to a voice in politics was advanced a step further after the Heaven-Sent Soldiers' Unit Incident. On the occasion of the Grand Army Manoeuvres in Kyūshū in November 1933 the Joint

Council for Rural Policy was organized by the Agriculture Minister, Mr. Gotō Fumio, the War Minister, General Araki, and key officers of the General Staff; and it was from that time that the military as a whole began to take a more positive interest in the question of the villages.

The reform movement of the young officers extends like an unbroken chain from the Officers' School Incident through the Aizawa Incident and on to the February Incident. Regardless of the intentions of the participants, each of these incidents expanded the political domain of the top section of the military. The February Incident above all proved to be a turning-point. This was of course the final and biggest of the successive fascist *putsches*. Thereafter the fascist movement from below, led by young officers or the civilian radical right wing, retires into the background.

As the Army purge got under way, the Imperial Way Faction was overwhelmed at a single stroke by the Control Faction, or rather, by an anti-Imperial Way Faction coalition.* Hegemony was taken from Araki, Mazaki, Yanagawa, and Obata, and grasped by Umezu, Tōjō, Sugiyama, and Koiso.

The powers forming this new direction group thereafter carried out a thorough purge within the Army. While suppressing the influence of radical fascism, they successively realized the political demands of the military, using the menace of radical fascism as a decoy for outsiders. When General Terauchi joined the Hirota Cabinet just after the February Incident, he imposed conditions from the outset, refusing admittance to the Cabinet of persons he regarded as tinged with liberalism. On his appointment as War Minister, Terauchi issued a frankly fascist declaration for 'the renovation of general administration; the renunciation of liberalism; the establishment of a totali-

---

* Since the names of these two factions became the most popular of the terms for factions within the Army, all disputes tend to be classified under the heading of Imperial Way Faction or Control Faction [or the Pure Army Faction (*Seigun Ha*), which supported the Control Faction]. But in reality the situation is much more complicated. The conflict between these two factions was most marked during the period from the appointment of Araki as War Minister in the Inukai Cabinet until the February Incident. The groups that controlled the Army after the February Incident were not necessarily an extension of the previous Control Faction. Only in the case of the Imperial Way Faction is there some kind of coherence. With this reservation these terms are used for convenience from the period after the February Incident.

tarian system'. He presented political demands that would limit the franchise through a revised electoral law and that would maim the Diet by abolishing control of the legislature over the executive. While suppressing fascism from below, then, this fascism from above made rapid progress. The fate of Kita, Nishida, and the young officers of the February Incident is justly expressed in the Chinese proverb, 'when the cunning hares have been killed, the hunting dogs go into the cooking pot'.

The circumstances of this period may also be understood by comparing the punishments awarded after the May 15 Incident with those of the February Incident. The military defendants of the May 15 Incident all received light punishments. Gotō and the ten other military defendants were sentenced to four years' imprisonment; all were subsequently pardoned and discharged from prison in 1936. In the case of the Navy defendants, Koga Seishi and Mikami Taku as the ringleaders received the heaviest sentences of fifteen years' imprisonment; of the others, one was sentenced to thirteen years, three to ten years, one to two years, and one to one year of imprisonment. By 1940 all had been pardoned and set free. These were the punishments for an incident in which armed groups burst into the official residence of the Premier in broad daylight, assassinating him and terrorizing the capital. Yet the War Minister, General Araki, in a public statement just after the May 15 Incident, declared:

We cannot restrain our tears when we consider the mentality expressed in the actions of these pure and naïve young men. They are not actions for fame, or personal gain, nor are they traitorous. They were performed in the sincere belief that they were for the benefit of Imperial Japan. Therefore, in dealing with this incident, it will not do to dispose of it in a routine manner according to short-sighted conceptions.

The Navy Minister, Admiral Ōsumi, stated: 'When one considers what caused these pure-hearted young men to make this mistake, it demands the most serious reflection.'

One can understand, then, how much the military as a whole was in sympathy with this incident. In contrast, Kōda Kiyosada and sixteen other military ringleaders of the February Incident were all executed. And by a judgement some months after the February Incident Lieutenant-Colonel Aizawa was sentenced to death for his assassination of Nagata, the Director of the Military Affairs Bureau, in a previous incident in which he alone had been implicated.*

These cases are sufficient to indicate the sudden change in the attitude of the military towards incidents of this kind. At a special conference after the February 26 Incident the War Minister, General Terauchi, made the following statement:

If we put together the declaration of their motives for rising and their reported statements, it appears that the motive behind this incident was an attempt to clarify the national polity and to carry out a so-called Shōwa Restoration. We admit that in the present state of the country, which has driven them to act in this way, there are many matters requiring correction and renovation. We are, however, unfortunately obliged to note that at the root of their guiding principle there lies an idea of national reformation which is harboured by a group of extremists outside the Army and which is totally contrary to our national polity.

By 'an idea of national reformation harboured by a group outside the Army', Terauchi is presumably referring to the ideas of Kita Ikki. In any case his categorical condemnation of the uprising as an act incompatible with the national polity reveals the extent of the sudden change in the attitude of the military leaders since the May 15 Incident. The 'New Control Faction', which grasped hegemony after the February Incident, included many officers who as members of the Cherry Blossom Association had stood for reform by *coup d'état*. Now that they were in power, however, they declared an Army purge, rejecting the participation of military men in politics except through the War Minister and suppressing radical tendencies.

Just after the war the Imperial Way Faction maintained that it had been largely opposed to Tōjō. But the struggle between the Imperial Way and Control Factions was not simply

---

* It should also be noted that in these incidents the civilians were always punished with far greater severity than the military defendants. For example, the heaviest punishment imposed on a military defendant in the May 15 Incident was fifteen years' imprisonment. In contrast, Tachibana Kōsaburō as a civilian defendant was sentenced to life imprisonment. In the case of the February Incident Kita Ikki and Nishida Zei were both executed although they cannot be considered to have been greatly connected with the actual operations.

one between those who stood for a principle and those who resorted to conspiratorial devices. It had much more the character of a struggle between factions and cliques. The February Incident merely gave the New Control Faction the opportunity to suppress the Imperial Way Faction linked with the radical young officers and to establish their own hegemony. According to Terauchi, the February Incident was an action contrary to the national polity. But, according to the young officers, 'The reconstruction plan [Kita's plan for the reconstruction of Japan] is in complete accord with the national polity. Indeed, it is the manifestation of the national polity as a State organization and as an economic system.' In their opinion, the members of the Control Faction, while repeating the word 'national polity', were constantly trying to exploit the authority of the Emperor in order to carry out their own political ideology. According to the furious denunciations of the young officers, it was Staff members of the Control Faction who did not hesitate to come forth with statements like: 'If the Emperor does not agree, we will make him listen at the point of a dagger.'

This is an extremely interesting point: the actions of the Imperial Way Faction, such as mobilizing troops and starting uprisings, were apparently very radical. But the content of their ideology was extremely vague and abstract, being the principle of accepting the absolute authority of the Emperor and submitting humbly to his wishes.* One of the reasons that the participants' plans covered only the violent stage of the operation and were not concerned with the aftermath is that their thoughts were based on the principle of the absolute authority of the Emperor.' In other words, any attempt at formulating plans of reconstruction would be tantamount to surmising the will of the Emperor and thus an invasion of the Imperial prerogative. This leads to a mythological sort of optimism according to which, if only evil men could be removed from the Court, if only the dark clouds shrouding the Emperor could be swept away, the Imperial sun would naturally shine forth.

In comparison, the men of the Control Faction may be regarded as more rational, and they may be blamed for consciously using the Emperor in order to realize their own plan

* *Shōshō-hikkin.*

from above.* As a result the political process after the February Incident was the 'rationalization' of Japanese fascism, which ceased to take the form of radical uprisings but advanced steadily by legal means from within the governmental apparatus. During the seventieth session of the Diet (1936–7) Mr. Hamada Kunimatsu put a question to the War Minister, General Terauchi, which incidentally provoked the so-called hara-kiri exchange between them. In the course of this question he stated: 'We cannot suppress our regret at the appearance of

* Nagata Tetsuzan, who was called the brains of the Control Faction, often asserted that the whole Army would be made the 'flawless' driving force of State reconstruction. His *rapprochement* with the Senior Retainers and the new bureaucrats emerged from this grand conception of his. The ideology of the Imperial Way Faction was extremely idealistic, but its one concrete proposal was that war with Russia should be the cardinal principle in foreign policy. This was not simply a choice from the strategic point of view, but a 'logical' outcome of their exaltation of the principle of the national polity. In this respect it cannot be overlooked that among the demands to be made on the War Minister drawn up by the mutineers just prior to the February Incident one item was 'the appointment of General Araki as Commander of the Kwangtung Army in order to coerce Russia'. A feeling of urgent crisis was more or less common among them. The following statement is typical: 'In case of war between Japan and Russia have we after all any hope of success? How will it be to receive the enemy both within and without? If the right wing is thoroughly liquidated, there remain only the neutrals (that is to say, the impotents) and the left wing. How can we express our extreme regret?' (*Testament of Nakahashi Motoaki*). Hence we can only begin to understand the radical character of the actions of the young officers of the Imperial Way Faction on the premise of this feeling that a war with Russia was imminent.

However much the young officers were actually spurred by structural contradictions in the social system, since their basic idiom was confined to optimism of the 'manifestation of the national polity' kind, personal idioms such as 'evil men at Court' obstinately precluded reflections on questions of structure and organization. Advancing a step further, since any attempt to reform the structure not proceeding from the initiative of the Emperor was against the national polity (this was the basis of the young officers' attack on 'Staff Officer fascism'), we find that the principle of humble submission to the will of the Emperor operates in real politics as absolute conservatism. The natural conclusion of this ideology was the contribution of generals like Yanagawa and Obata of the Imperial Way Faction (who later joined voices with veterans of business circles in finding the 'evil hand of the reds' in all aspects of government control of economic activities) towards taking the backbone out of the 'New Order' (the transformation of the Imperial Rule Assistance movement into a non-political moral campaign, as they described the process). This logic is common to the attack of the young officers on the March and October Incidents and on 'Staff Officer fascism'. It is impossible to overlook this paradoxical amalgamation of radicalism and conservatism and to understand the ideology of the young officers simply in terms of 'national polity plus socialism'. There was not only a conflict of subjective intentions and objective roles; the most important point was that within the ideology itself, since its radical character was limited to the unlawful *means* they used, there existed an inherent difficulty in raising positively and concretely the question of structural reforms.

a new political evil: as the Army purge progresses, the reformed Army is strongly asserting itself as a driving force in politics.' This was a keen verbal thrust at the paradoxical effect of the Army purge.

Soon after the suppression of radical fascism, a closer alliance of the military, the bureaucracy, and the *zaibatsu* was consolidated and an advance was made towards a 'completed' form of fascism. In the financial policy of Baba in the Hirota Cabinet the slogan was 'national defence in the widest sense'. It was against the background of the troubled social atmosphere after the February Incident that such a slogan was raised; and the budget for unemployment grants and agrarian relief was coupled with increased military expenditure. This extremely inflationary policy gave rise to great apprehension in financial circles. So in the Yūki economic policy, which succeeded it and which was backed by financial interests, a reversal was made to 'national defence in the narrow sense' of military expenditure alone. The grants in Baba's policy for the financial regeneration of the villages were all cut down and grants for local government finance were cancelled. At this time Mr. Yūki came out with the famous words: 'Henceforth I wish to proceed in close embrace with the military', and the term 'close-embrace finance' arose from this.

As an example of this state of affairs, we may note the memorial drawn up by the standing committee of the Japan Economic League on 3 March 1937:

> Recent internal and external conditions make increased national expenditure centred upon military expenditure unavoidable. But an over-rapid expansion of government finance would lead to an insufficiency in domestic productive power and to a rise in prices. There is no way to avoid this contradiction except by restricting government expenditure to necessary and indispensable items. Therefore any increase in administrative expenditure apart from military expenditure should be restricted as far as possible, and at the same time the budget should be drawn up for the next three years on the policy of giving priority to national defence expenditure.

This is representative of opinion in business circles at that time. Thus the interests of business groups and the military drew nearer, and a 'close-embrace' structure of Japanese fascism came to completion.

The fascist movement from below was completely absorbed into totalitarian transformation from above. Thereafter, as the international situation intensified for Japan on the outbreak of the China Incident, the 'unity of the entire nation' became an absolute demand. In the name of national polity a triangular formation was established consisting of the bureaucracy, which had no footing among the people, the military, which called itself the driving force of reformation but which would never assume any political responsibility, and the political parties, which were constantly wrangling and yet had already lost their fighting spirit for a struggle against fascism. Between the Hirota and the Tōjō Cabinets, the Hayashi, first Konoe, Hiranuma, Abe, Yonai, second Konoe, and third Konoe Cabinets were organized in quick succession. Every change in the balance of power between the three powers resulted in a Cabinet change. There arose here the freak phenomenon that the more a 'strong Cabinet' became the watchword, the harder it was to find a nucleus in government.

But this does not imply any slackening in the move towards fascism. It should not be forgotten that in this period important steps were taken one after another in the direction of outright fascism. In late 1937 and early 1938 there was the general round-up of professors close to the Labour-Peasant Faction, the leaders of the National Council of Trade Unions, and those of the Japan Proletariat Party. Also in 1938 there was the ordinance for the permanent prohibition of May Day and the promulgation of the National General Mobilization Law. In March 1939 Japan withdrew from international labour organizations. In 1940 there occurred the dissolution of all the political parties, beginning with the Social Masses Party, the dissolution of the Japan Federation of Labour, the inauguration of the Imperial Rule Assistance Association and of the Great Japan Serve-the-State-through-Industry Association, and the conclusion of the Tripartite Pact. Rome was not built in a day, and the Tōjō dictatorship did not come into existence all of a sudden.

Konoe's New Order Movement throws valuable light on these developments. It aimed at strengthening political leadership by organizing the people, and sprang from an awareness that the existing political instability was due to the lack of a popular foundation. The motivation of the New Order Movement is extremely complex and cannot be described in a few words, but this was at any rate its original intention. However, the movement ran up against the stumbling-block of the absolute Emperor system, and was suspected by the national polity faction of being a kind of Shogunate. As a result it became an emasculated and formalized bureaucratic organ. This was the so-called 'transformation' of the Assistance Association from a political to a moral movement. At the outset it was said that the Association was designed to 'transmit the will of the authorities to the people, and to articulate the will of the people to the authorities'. Soon, however, the expression, 'the will of the people', was being criticized as being contrary to the national polity, and it was revised to read, 'making the conditions of the people known to the authorities'. This should suffice to show how much even the faintest tinge of popular initiative was disliked.

In January 1942, as a supplement to the formalized Assistance Association, the Imperial Rule Assistance Young Men's Corps was set up, but this too was not a political society. Since its basic aim was to act as a subordinate organization of the Assistance Association, it was incapable of vigorous activity. In some districts troublesome issues arose between the Assistance Association and the Young Men's Corps. In April 1942 the so-called Assistance election was carried out, and in the May of that year the Imperial Rule Assistance Political Association was formed as the sole political association in existence. But this was a conglomeration of existing political influences of all kinds, in which radical fascist groups, members of the previous political parties, right-wing idealists, and converted members of the proletarian parties were all gathered together. As a result it became completely vacuous as a political movement.

These meanderings trace the course of the efforts that were made to build the political structure of Japan on the organized masses as in Germany and Italy. But all such movements ended in complete absorption within the bureaucratic hierarchy. Japanese fascism was never able to achieve a firmly organized popular foundation. The Central Co-operative Assembly, set up in conjunction with the Assistance Movement, was a purely advisory organ simply for 'making the conditions of the people known to the authorities'. The drafts of proposals expressed within it had no legal binding power. The government merely 'noted' them. At the time, the Assistance Association brought out a pamphlet entitled 'About the Co-operative Assembly' in which the following statement is made:

> The various questions presented to this Assembly will be heard by the government and by the Assistance Association, and will be promptly adopted or rejected after serious consideration. The important thing is to handle government policy with the sweet and harmonious co-operation that prevails in a family. . . . In short, we think that this Council, in being adaptable and unobstructive, extra-legislative and without legal functions, is of great political value. Its fragile constitution seems at first sight to be its weak point, but it is precisely this fragility that gives it its charm.

This is an apt illustration of the way in which the authorities thought during this period.

Finally, with the outbreak of the Pacific War, we come to the Tōjō dictatorship. Neither the Imperial Way Faction nor the Control Faction any longer existed. All influences troublesome to Tōjō were singled out and all opposition groups suppressed by new measures such as the Law for the Emergency Control of Speech, Publication, Meeting, and Association, and the Special Law for Wartime Crimes. Even the right-wing groups, who prided themselves on their traditions, were forcibly dissolved into the Assistance Association and the Asia Development League. Tōjō himself, being Premier, War Minister, War Supplies Minister, and Chief of Staff, wielded unprecedented authority. Now for the first time a strong dictatorial government approaching that of Hitler and Mussolini seemed to emerge.

But the foundation of its strength lay chiefly in the military police net spread out over the whole country. Japanese fascism never possessed a distinctive popular organization like those in Germany and Italy. It met the catastrophe of 15 August 1945 with the bureaucratic leadership and the sham constitutionalism of the Meiji era still intact.

In the final stages of the war the civilian right wing, which had been deftly used to consolidate fascist leadership from above, ironically emerged as a fierce critic of the Tōjō dictatorship. For instance, in the committee considering the draft of the

Special Law for Wartime Crimes in the Eighty-First Diet (1943) the following statement about the Assistance Association was made by Akao Bin, an early leader of the National Founding Association:

With regard to the ideological content of the present Assistance Association, its members consist of liberals who want to maintain the *status quo*, national socialists, Japanists, and the extreme nationalists of radical terrorism ... the opportunists are also strongly entrenched. Exactly where is this conglomeration of guiding spirits supposed to lead us? ... Large groups have been assembled and merely given an outward form and organization, while the genuine Japanist associations which have produced good results up to the present day have all been dissolved. The Assistance Association lacks a soul because it is an attempt to collect opportunists and bureaucrats with neither faith nor ideals and to launch them all on a spiritual venture with government money.

In the same committee meeting Mitamura Takeo, a member of the Nakano Seigō faction, put the following question:

The character of the present government of Japan is indeed government centred upon officialdom. Another name for this is bureaucratic government. In short it is government without criticism. If criticism is hazarded, it is labelled as liberalism. If to be critical is to be liberal, I should like to ask what is meant by liberalism. Where there is no criticism, there is no hard application; where there is no hard application, there is no progress or development ... There are occasions when what is bad for the government and the officials is not necessarily bad for the country ... In a world in which deceit and flattery are on the increase, society is definitely not in a desirable condition for the country.

This is a bitter thrust at the true character of the Tōjō dictatorship. To say that where there is no criticism there is no hard application, and where there is no hard application there is no progress or development, is the very voice of orthodox liberalism.

Thus ironically it was the civilian right-wing groups, which had acted as the vanguard of Japanese fascism, that took the most determined anti-government stand in the Diet and that were the most openly critical in the final stages. This was the basis for the reappearance of the Imperial Way Faction immediately after the war, when even outright fascists came back as 'democrats' simply because they were opposed to Tōjō. It may truly be said that history had come full circle.

Why in Japan did fascism from below, the fascist movement that arose among civilians, fail to grasp hegemony? This is a crucial question and any answer must emphasize the following point. In the process of fascization the strength of influences from the lower stratum of society is prescribed by the extent to which a democratic movement has taken place in the country concerned.* In Italy before the March on Rome the Socialist Party was the leading party in the Assembly. In the case of Germany we note again the powerful influence of the Social Democratic and Communist Parties just before the Nazi revolution. Both the Nazis and the Fascists could draw in the masses only by flaunting themselves as the exponents of true socialism and as the party of the workers. This bespeaks the power of the mass movement in Germany and even in Italy, and is the reason that popular bases had to be preserved to some extent in the fascist organization, if only for deception.

How does this compare with the situation in our country? Of course in Japan too the labour movement had made an unprecedented advance from about 1926, and, because of the crisis in rural tenancy disputes, had increased rapidly year by year. As we have seen, the Japanese fascist movement flourished in the background of these conditions and appeared on the scene as a reaction to the left-wing movement. In this respect it can be said to follow the rules. But today it is quite clear to any observer that the left-wing movement did not in fact permeate to the workers and farmers to a degree comparable with that in Germany and Italy. It would be going too far to suggest that the overwhelming influence of Marxism was a phenomenon confined to the educated class—to the lecture platforms and journals that this class supported; its power was felt in many other areas also. Yet it is doubtful whether the menace of bolshevism in Japan was ever as real as the ruling class and the conservative circles proclaimed.†

* This is not the only cause that determines the type as 'from above' or 'from below' in the process of fascist advance. See below, 'Fascism—Some Problems'.

† 'Bolshevization' was felt by the ruling class to be a profound menace to Imperial Japan, but it is quite another question whether the material conditions existed for a proletarian revolution. The nervous reaction to 'bolshevization' occurred in the first place because it was tied up with the image of infiltration by the influence of

The progress of Japanese fascist transformation was very gradual. There was no March on Rome and no 30 January 1933; this suggests the weakness of resistance from below. There were no organized labour or proletarian parties to be smashed. Here we should note the form of Japanese monopoly capital itself.* When we consider the population structure in 1930, neighbouring Russia. (In this sense the credit for bringing out the symbol of 'indirect aggression', long before the American Secretary of State, Mr. Dulles, did so, goes to the Japanese ruling class.) The reason that the young officers were out-and-out anti-communists despite their resentment against the *zaibatsu* was their conception of the national polity (discussed above) and their almost instinctive sense of vocation which made it impossible for them to separate their thoughts on communism from their military-strategic standpoint towards Russia. A second factor that contributed to the fears of the ruling class was that 'bolshevization' was believed to be penetrating the sons of prominent men, the intelligentsia and the university students, who formed the true *élite* of Imperial Japan or who would do so in the future. In the *Summary of Incidents* (*Shojiken Gaiyō*), the investigation of the Police Bureau of the Home Ministry into the causes of right-wing terrorism, it is stated: 'We see the importation of socialist and communist thought influenced by the Russian Revolution . . . After the Great Earthquake [1923] graduates from colleges and high schools, the so-called educated class, were most susceptible to the baptism of bolshevist thought, and finally we see the succession of members of the Japan Communist Party who even advocate the overthrow of our splendid national polity. This has even appeared within the Imperial Army.' A situation in which the organization of the workers and farmers was so slight as to present no problem, but in which the *élite* and educated class had become 'bolshevized', is completely abnormal according to the laws of Marxism, and it is ironical that this abnormality should have been regarded as a fearful menace by the ruling class of Japan. As we see in the *Konoe Memorial to the Throne* (*Konoe Jōsō Bun*), what gave the rulers of Imperial Japan nightmares until the last was the 'bolshevization' of the State from within rather than revolution from below. Moreover, even the so-called bolshevization of the educated class and of children from good homes had certainly not gone far enough to be alarming from the point of view of the system as a whole. The question must therefore be carried forward to the spirit and structure of Imperial Japan, which gave rise to immediate allergic reactions to the phenomena of ideological dissemination. On this point see above, 'Theory and Psychology of Ultra-Nationalism'.

* Any systematic treatment of this subject must examine the distinctive characteristics of the Imperial government structure and the mechanism of the process by which loyal Imperial subjects were fostered, a process of intense homogeneization and de-politicization. In Imperial Japan the two supports of structural stability were de-politicization at the bottom of society (government by men of repute, which was the basis of 'good morals and manners', and the Japanese version of local self-government, which ensured it) and trans-politicization at the apex (the transcendence of the Emperor and his officials over all political rivalries). There was a powerful inclination to regard as dangerous all trends towards political and ideological diversity that might interfere with the homogeneity of the community (the 'spirit of harmony'). This tendency becomes strong in direct proportion to the acceleration of a sense that the structure is in danger. In this sense the pet saying of the fascists and national polity advocates, that 'liberalism is the hotbed of communism', has a special validity. It is a general law of fascism that it always con-

directly before the Manchurian Incident when the Japanese fascist movement suddenly became vigorous, we find that the number of labourers employed in workshops of five or more people was 2,032,000, and the number of casual workers 1,963,000. In contrast, employees in commerce numbered 2,200,000, government officials and company employees 1,800,000, and small traders 1,500,000. One understands how small in numbers the true proletariat was compared with the medium and small businessmen and the salaried class. As another example, in the *League of Nations Statistical Yearbook* for 1926 Japan's industrial population (including domestic industries) is given as 19·4 per cent of the total population. When this is compared with, for example, Britain (39·7 per cent), France (33·9 per cent), Belgium (39·5 per cent), Holland (36·1 per cent), and Germany (35·8 per cent), it becomes clear how inferior the industrialization of Imperial Japan was compared with that of the European capitalist nations.

At the peak of the Japanese social structure stood monopoly capital, rationalized to the highest degree. But at its base were crammed together minute-scale agriculture with production methods that had scarcely changed since feudal times and household industries almost entirely dependent on the labour of members of the family. The most advanced and the most primitive techniques existed side by side in a stratified industrial structure. Production forms of different historical stages overlay and supplemented each other. This was a decisive obstacle to the growth of an organized democratic movement in Japanese politics. On the one hand there was the stubborn rule of absolutism, on the other the development of monopoly capital, both in agreement and reinforcing each other.

This may also have determined the fate of the Japanese fascist movement as we have observed it above. Here is revealed the internal weakness of the fascism from below in Japan. In the Japanese right wing, pedigrees ranged from the most advanced

centrates its attack on marginal ideologies in concrete situations. But since the first task of fascism—i.e. the destruction of the vanguard organizations of revolution—had already been effected in Japan under political party Cabinets, the Japanese right-wing and national polity movements were bound at an early stage to change the chief target of their attack from communism and socialism to liberalism (the 'hotbed'). This distinctive character was extremely significant in Japanese political and social processes after 1932–3.

Nazi type to the almost pure feudal *rōnin* type distantly connected with the Dark Ocean Society. Few of them had ever received the baptism of modernity. The dominant type was not so much fascist as Bakumatsu *rōnin*.[8] As Freda Utley points out in *Japan's Feet of Clay*, the right-wing leaders were a cross between the *rōnin* of the feudal period and Chicago gangsters.

The character of the right-wing movement is epitomized by the fact that a personality like Tōyama Mitsuru was one of its most prominent figures. If we compare the way of life of Hitler and Mussolini with that of Tōyama, we should find that the factor of rational planning in the lives of the former was lacking in Tōyama's case. *A True Portrait of the Venerable Tōyama Mitsuru** records various statements by Mr. Tōyama; the following is written about his younger days:

That was when I was about twenty-six, in the prime of my youth. Coming up to Tokyo, I rented a house with five or six companions. Starting with umbrella and shoes, gradually everything disappeared. Even the bedding disappeared. But I was the only one who went naked; the others had to have something on. I took a lunch-box and ate it. I didn't pay. So the waitress from the lunch-box shop came to dun me. When I came out of the cupboard stark naked, she jumped with fright and withdrew. Even if I didn't eat for two or three days, I thought nothing of it.

He feels a kind of pride in not returning borrowed money and in repulsing people by such methods. He also speaks of warding off high-interest money-lenders in this way. However we may regard him, he does not belong in the category of the modern man. There is no trace of modern rationality here. In this respect Tōyama is typical of rightist personalities.

When we look at the internal construction of right-wing groups, we find that they mostly have a paternal boss organization. As we have seen, a united front never emerged from the right-wing movement in spite of fairly advantageous conditions. Unity was constantly intoned, but as soon as they had joined together, they split and exchanged abuse. Since they were associations centred on a paternal boss, they could only be small-scale; each struggled to elevate its own deity. Many groups emerged, each centred on its small master. Among them were gangs of ruffians in disguise. In the case of the Nazis, too,

* *Tōyama Mitsuru Ō no Shimmemmoku.*

the storm-troops were strongly tinged by the gang element; still, for better or for worse, they had organizational rationality and did not constantly unite and divide as in Japan.

This pre-modern character may be attributed not only to the right-wing groups but to the reforming officers who joined them and played important roles. The base in which they fabricated their plots was almost always a house of assignation[9] or a restaurant. While drinking saké and bewailing the depraved state of the country, they no doubt secretly cherished in their hearts the image of the Bakumatsu patriot who sang: 'Drunken, I lay my head in a beautiful girl's lap. Waking, I grasp the power of the whole realm.'

In the final analysis it was the historical circumstance that Japan had not undergone the experience of a *bourgeois* revolution that determined this character of the fascist movement. From a different angle it reveals the marked continuity between the period of party government and the fascist period in Japan. The pre-modern character of right-wing leaders and organizations is a characteristic that can also be found to a lesser extent in the established political parties. The Japanese political parties, instead of behaving as the champions of democracy, had from an early date compromised with the absolutist forces, adapted themselves to it, and were contented with a sham constitutional system. Hence the oligarchic structure that had existed since the Meiji era was able to transform itself into a fascist structure without the need for a fascist 'revolution'.

When the Nazis got control, they eradicated not only the socialist political parties but also the Central Party and all other existing political forces. But in Japan the forces that had previously held sway were not eradicated (*gleichschaltet*). The previous political forces were mostly left as they were and absorbed into the fascist structure. As we have seen, almost all the established political parties were absorbed into the Imperial Rule Assistance Political Association. This is why those who were purged after the war included so many members of the established pre-war political parties and the bureaucracy.

It cannot be clearly stated from what point of time the fascist period began. The totalitarian system gradually came to completion within the framework of the State structure determined by the Meiji constitution. The established political parties had neither the spirit nor the will for an all-out war against fascism. Instead they frequently performed the role of actively promoting it. For example, the Seiyū Kai Cabinet of April 1927 to July 1929 headed by General Tanaka Giichi was supposed to be a purely political party Cabinet. Yet in domestic policy it put severe pressure on the left-wing movements and further restricted freedom of speech, publication, and association by revising the Law for the Maintenance of Public Peace in the form of the Emergency Decree. Abroad it adopted the Tanaka 'positive diplomacy', dispatching troops to China on the occasion of the Tsinan Incident. Until it collapsed after getting entangled in the assassination of Chang Tso-lin, its course of action almost appears to be that of a fascist government. These domestic and overseas measures are extremely significant in the light of the later domination of fascism. Thereafter, the Seiyū Kai also pressed the Hamaguchi Cabinet fiercely on the issue of the infringement of the supreme command involved in the London Disarmament Treaty. Again, when the organ theory of the Emperor became an issue, the Seiyū Kai President, Mr. Suzuki, personally led the movement for the clarification of the national polity in the House of Representatives.

It is no exaggeration to say that the Seiyū Kai made important contributions to the fascist transformation of Japanese politics; for it is well known that the issue of the infringement of the supreme command was a great stimulus to the fascist movement. Again, in the circumstances described above, the issue of the organ theory implied a denial of the theoretical basis of party government. For a political party to take the lead in rejecting the theory was nothing less than suicide. Such was the tragi-comic role of the established political parties.

The Hamaguchi and Wakatsuki Minsei Tō Cabinets, which succeeded the Tanaka Cabinet, have the strongest complexion of *bourgeois* liberalism in the recent history of Japanese politics. Yet they crumbled just after the Manchurian Incident because of fascist trends from within the Cabinet in the form of the coalition Cabinet movement by the Home Minister, Mr. Adachi, and his supporters. Needless to say, the anti-fascist stand of the Minsei Tō does not suffice to draw a clear line between it and the Seiyū Kai. For example, when the Anti-War Pact was ratified by the Tanaka Cabinet, the Minsei Tō as the party in opposition joined the right-wing groups in a vigorous attack on the government on the grounds that the words 'in the name of the people' were incompatible with the national polity.

It seems that the Seiyū Kai took its revenge over the issue of the London Disarmament Treaty. Both parties stopped at nothing in the struggle for political power, and joined hands with any forces to overthrow a government of the other party. This greatly encouraged the growing political influence of the various semi-feudal forces which were already strong and independent of the Diet. The part played by the right wing of the Socialist Party in Germany and Italy was played by the Seiyū Kai and the Minsei Tō in Japan.

Of course in Japan too one cannot overlook the significance of the conversion to fascism within the proletarian movement. As I have said before, this was performed by the Akamatsu and Kamei group in the Social Mass Party and groups like Asō's, which led the Labour-Peasant Party and its successors. But from the point of view of the political parties that controlled the Diet, Japan must be regarded as having diverged one stage from Germany and Italy. With the decline of party politics in Japan the social elements that had made up the lobbyist groups largely flowed into the right-wing societies. On the other hand, in Italy for example, it was the supporters of anarchism and syndicalism who later became the centre of fascist organization.

Thus we can see that a major characteristic separating Japanese fascism from the European form was the gradation of its development. Fascism did not burst on the scene from below as it did in Italy and Germany. The leaders of Japanese fascism were not obliged to manipulate or counter any strong proletarian movement; and, in the absence of a *bourgeois* democratic background, they were able to effect a comparatively smooth consolidation of State power from above by amalgamating supporting groups that were already in existence.

To see in the political developments of the 1930s a sudden, fortuitous break, an historical perversion, in the 'evolution towards democracy' is not only to overlook the fundamental continuity with the preceding period of 'party government'. Such a view fails to take into account the distinctive undercurrent in thought and social structure that had existed in Japanese

political life since the Meiji Restoration and that sanctioned the
advance of Japanese fascism.

EDITOR'S NOTES

1. See Glossary: *Lobbyist group.*
2. The term 'butter-smelling' (*bata-kusai*) is used to describe
   Westerners; butter plays no part in the traditional Japanese diet.
3. See Glossary: *Popular Rights Movement.*
4. The pre-war system called for six years of compulsory elementary education. Beyond this the students had various choices,
   one of which was to attend middle school (five years) and then
   to proceed either to higher school or to normal school. The
   social status of the latter tended to be considerably lower.
5. See Glossary: *Minobe Tatsukichi, Minoda Muneki.*
6. See Glossary: *'Composite magazine', Iwanami Publishing Company,
   Kōdan Sha.*
7. See Glossary: *Bamboo spear principle.*
8. See Glossary: *Bakumatsu Period, rōnin.*
9. See Glossary: *House of assignation.*

III. Thought and Behaviour Patterns of Japan's Wartime[1] Leaders

TRANSLATED BY IVAN MORRIS

This essay was originally published in the magazine Chōryō, *May 1949*

I. LOCUS OF THE PROBLEM

The question of why Mikado, Führer, and Duce opened war on the United States in the midst of Zhukov's successful counter-offensive before Moscow admits as yet of no definite answer. The choices of desperate madmen, imbued with fanaticism and megalomania, are less readily explained in terms of diplomacy and strategy than in those of psychopathology.[*]

So writes Professor Schuman in his analysis of world conditions at the time of the attack on Pearl Harbour.[†] It would be a mistake to dismiss this as being simply a typical comment by a writer belonging to the Chicago school with its Freudian orientation. When we recall the trends in Japan that led to the outbreak of the Pacific War—trends that were brought out in such detail by the war crimes trials in Tokyo—we become sharply aware that the conditions in which Japan decided to attack the West defy all rational understanding, and we can see why Professor Schuman came to the conclusion that he did.

The declaration of war against the United States did not result from any careful analysis of the world situation or from any study of comparative productive capacities and internal conditions. On the contrary, the fateful decision was taken by

[*] Frederick Schuman, *Soviet Politics at Home and Abroad*, p. 438.

[†] When Mr. Schuman's book was written it was not yet clear to what extent Japan, Germany, and Italy had reached prior agreement about declaring war against America, and Professor Schuman probably regarded them as being equally responsible for the decision. In fact, it was Japan that took the entire initiative for the Pearl Harbour attack. What made this particularly strange was that at the time Japan was being guided by Germany. It is said that the German Foreign Minister, Herr von Ribbentrop, was 'wild with joy' when he received the report about Pearl Harbour.

men who were surprisingly ignorant of international affairs (even of matters like the Munich Agreement and the concentration camps),* by men who were in a desperate state of mind, as is revealed by Tōjō's remark, 'Sometimes people have to shut their eyes and take the plunge.'²

During the war Allied observers generally assumed that, since Japan had deliberately embarked on a large-scale war against the two most powerful countries in the world, she must have set up an organization and formulated plans based on a reasonably clear forecast of the future. It is no wonder, then, that the Allies should have been more and more amazed as the truth of of the matter dawned on them. The real nature of the Japanese decision was a riddle even to members of the Prosecution at the war crimes trials in Tokyo. Thus we have the statement of the Prosecuting Attorney, Mr. Golunsky:³

> There are very many intelligent people who are astonished, and not without reason, at Japan daring to attack both the United States and Great Britain, having the unfinished war with China on her hands, and preparing an attack on the Soviet Union. This puzzling problem cannot be solved if we lose sight of this implicit faith of Japanese rulers in general, and military leaders in particular, in German power and inevitable German victory. They hoped that Moscow and Leningrad would fall any day, that the collapse of the Soviet Union long ago promised by the Germans would not be long in coming.†

And in his final address Mr. Keenan, the Chief Prosecutor, candidly recognized the difficulty of grasping the true nature of the Japanese 'conspiracy' to wage aggressive war: 'One of the difficulties in relation to the analysis of this conspiracy is that it was of such breadth of scope that it was difficult to conceive of it being undertaken by a group of human beings.'‡

If the Prosecution was prepared to admit this difficulty—a difficulty that to a greater or lesser extent puzzled all the Allies —it is hardly surprising that the Defence should have brought it into their case against the existence of the alleged conspiracy. In fact the American members of the defence counsel used it as

* General Tōjō's reply to Mr. Keenan.
† International Military Tribunal for the Far East (hereafter IMTFE), no. 85, p. 7275, 8 Oct. 1946.
‡ IMTFE, no. 371, p. 19 of Summation of Prosecution, 11 Feb. 1948.

the very basis of their argument. Thus Mr. Blewett expressed in his closing plea what must certainly have been the honest feeling of an American when confronted with the irrationality of the Japanese decision to attack the West. Adducing the annual aircraft production figures of the Japanese Army, he refuted the Prosecution's claim about 'overwhelming military expansion':

To American counsel who represent a nation which produced fifty thousand planes or more in one year it is an allegation which is not ludicrous but downright tragic in a case where the lives of conscientious public officials are at stake. No one but a Don Quixote would start to conquer the world with a handful of aircraft—not in this day and age.*

Allied propaganda had pictured Japan as a typically 'absolutist' country, belonging to the same category as Nazi Germany. It was only natural therefore that the Americans and others should have been astonished to discover how great was the split among the leading groups in Japan and how unstable its political situation, especially when compared with Nazi Germany. This is brought out by Mr. Brannon, speaking for the Defence: '. . . between the accused in the dock there existed no accord, no sameness of political philosophy and no co-operation that rivalled or excelled the great war efforts of other powers during this tragic era of modern history.'†

And later he argued:

What is the real evidence concerning the government of Japan itself? It is simply that during the period covered by this indictment fifteen separate cabinets rose and fell in Japan . . . The evidence reveals that in the rise and fall of these many cabinets composing the government of Japan there were twenty-one prime ministers, thirty foreign ministers, twenty-eight home ministers, nineteen war ministers . . . Rather than to establish an agreement or common plan or conspiracy, the purpose of which was to dominate the world or any other objective, the evidence definitely reveals the absence of leadership or of a centralized group committed to a common design or purpose of any kind.‡

Unlike the Allies, who looked at Japan from the outside, the Germans, being in the position of associates, had a more inti-

* IMTFE, no. 391, p. 43240, 11 March 1948.
† Ibid., no. 255, p. 26412, 21 Aug. 1947.
‡ Ibid., no. 386, pp. 42388–9, 4 March 1948.

mate view of the country's wartime structure. They had been dismayed for some time by the unsettled foreign policy that resulted from pluralism at the top level of Japanese political power. Thus the Foreign Minister, Herr von Ribbentrop, in his conference in July 1940 with the former Foreign Minister, Mr. Satō, and the Ambassador, Mr. Kurusu, said that 'although he himself knew well what Germany wanted to do, he was regretful that he did not possess any definite knowledge regarding Japanese intentions, so he was eager to know in concrete form what Japan really hoped . . .'* And this a mere two months before the conclusion of the Tripartite Pact!

Another example of the German attitude emerges from the testimony of Admiral Wenneker at the Tokyo trials. He referred to a certain German officer stationed in Japan who was amazed by the extent to which the Army and Navy were at loggerheads and who even undertook a mission of reconciliation himself.[4]

Confronted with the illogical realities of the situation, we must avoid trying to interpret them according to any preconceived idea about the inevitability of the historical process that operated through the Manchurian Incident and up to the Pacific War. Looking at the developments from a wide-range or macroscopic point of view, we can, to be sure, discover a consistent sequence of cause and effect in the development of Japanese imperialism during this decade. Viewed microscopically, however, it appears rather as the result of a vast accumulation of illogical decisions. We must not underestimate this irrationality of Japanese politics or dismiss it as being unworthy of serious attention. Instead we should do our best to recreate the actual patterns of thought and behaviour, however blind and irrational they may appear, and synthesize them in a wide historical rationale.

The war crimes trials were, as we have seen, marked by a sharp clash between the 'joint conspiracy' view of the Prosecution and the argument of the Defence, which stressed the absence of any real planning. From the standpoint of jurisprudence these two approaches were no doubt irreconcilable. This, however, does not necessarily apply in the case of historical analysis.

* According to the telegram of 10 July 1940 from Kurusu to the Foreign Minister, Mr. Arita. IMTFE, no. 106, p. 9694, 6 Nov. 1946.

The men in the dock at the Tokyo trials had unquestionably been motivated by a common aspiration: the desire to establish a Greater East Asia Co-Prosperity Sphere, to build up a new order with the 'Eight Corners of the World under One Roof', to proclaim the Imperial Way throughout the world. Not one of the defendants ever indicated that he regarded this as a mere quixotic dream. Some of them, it is true, were inhibited by intellectual scruples from openly voicing their dream, while others, though firmly believing that the dream would eventually come true, placed the happy date rather further in the future; and even the most fanatic among them, as they gradually drew near to the windmill, were momentarily daunted by its size when compared with the puny lances in their hands.* Yet all of them were driven ahead, as if by some invisible force. Trembling at the possibility of failure, they still thrust their way forward with their hands over their eyes. If we ask, 'Did they

---

* The testimony of Lieutenant-General Suzuki Teiichi provides a good example of the attitude of Japan's civilian and military leaders as the final hour approached. He is referring to a meeting in October 1941 between Prince Konoe, the Prime Minister, General Tōjō, the War Minister, Admiral Oikawa, the Navy Minister, Admiral Toyoda, the Foreign Minister, and Lieutenant-General Suzuki himself, the Director of the Cabinet Planning Board. It was held at the Teki-gai Villa (Prince Konoe's private residence), and the time was the fateful period determined in the Imperial Conference of 6 September (1941) when it was resolved that: 'If by the early part of October there is no reasonable hope of having our demands agreed to . . . we will immediately make up our minds to get ready for war against America and England and Holland.' At the war crimes trial Suzuki explained the meeting as follows:

'It became quite clear as the result of this conference where the thorny question lay. The Navy really thought that the war with America was impossible but did not desire openly to say so. The Army did not necessarily desire war, but vigorously objected to the withdrawal of troops from China. The Foreign Minister was firmly of the opinion that without consenting to the withdrawal of the armed forces from China the negotiations with America offered no prospect of success. The only way for the Prime Minister to avoid war was, therefore, either to make the Navy formally declare its real intentions, or to make the Army understand the unexpressed intentions of the Navy and agree to the withdrawal of the armed forces. I saw that the Prime Minister was in a predicament because personally he felt himself unequal to the task of persuading the Navy or the Army.' (IMTFE, no. 333, p. 35206, 12 Dec. 1947.)

In fine the three principal parties adopted stands that had the effect of mutually checking each other into inactivity. Tōjō was adamantly opposed to withdrawing from China and he finally brought down the Cabinet; yet even Tōjō, for all his toughness, was seriously concerned by the possibility that the prestige of the Imperial family might be used to suppress the military advocates of strong foreign policy (i.e. by the formation of a Cabinet under Prince Higashikuni).

want war?' the answer is yes; and if we ask, 'Did they want to avoid war?' the answer is still yes. Though wanting war, they tried to avoid it; though wanting to avoid it, they deliberately chose the path that led to it.

Unplanned and disorganized though political power was, these patterns of thought pointed unswervingly in the direction of war. Or rather, if a paradox may be permitted, it was precisely because of the lack of planning that Japan's leaders hurried forward so energetically with their 'joint conspiracy'. Here we are confronted with the underlying pathology of Japan's 'structure'. The mountainous records of the war crimes provide an exhaustive illustration of this paradox.*

It was not only so-called Class A war criminals who appeared in the Tokyo courtroom. The Prosecution and the Defence summoned several hundred witnesses; and men representing almost every significant element appeared on the stand—

* There are various possible objections to my having relied so greatly on depositions and statements made during the public hearings of the IMTFE in my attempt to abstract the patterns of thought and behaviour of Japan's wartime leaders. In particular: (i) Quite apart from the political quality of the IMTFE itself, how much credence can we attach to the material presented at the trials and placed on public record? (ii) The depositions and replies were made under very abnormal conditions by defendants who were charged with crimes involving a definite possibility of capital punishment; to what extent are we justified in using this material to deduce their normal modes of behaviour?

These two doubts are quite reasonable. At the time that this essay was written, however, the records of the IMTFE had an epochal significance: voluminous material about political, economic, and social developments in Japan since 1930 that had been hidden from us until then was brought to light at a stroke, so that even today this remains the most complete collection of its type. With these records at hand, I was strongly impelled to use the material in some comprehensive manner, rather than simply to examine certain specific historical points. So far as the credibility of the material is concerned, I agree that it would be dangerous to rely uncritically on the records in drawing a complete picture of the political structure and economic development or in checking detailed questions of fact. My interest, however, was in the mental structure and modes of behaviour of our ruling class, and for the purpose of this type of study such divergences as may exist in the evidence should not represent too great an impediment.

In view of my particular aim, the second objection (i.e. limitations resulting from the abnormal condition of being a defendant) also loses some of its force. The crux of the matter is whether the characteristic modes of behaviour abstracted in this essay were special phenomena that emerged because of the particular conditions in which they were established by the defendants at the IMTFE and which would not be likely to reappear. I would rather interpret it as a case in which political processes belonging to normal modes of behaviour—processes that were so ubiquitous in Japan that they usually passed unnoticed—were spotlighted by the sharp glare of an international trial.

members of the Imperial Court circle, Senior Retainers, Army officers, politicians, to mention only a few. From their respective angles they shed light on the complex, unmethodical pattern of Japanese politics.

In examining their statements we should not pay attention only to the factual content. Hardly less important is the *manner* in which they made their replies in Court; for this vividly reflects the mental and behavioural modes of Japan's ruling class.

What I attempt in the present essay is to use this evidence as a clue to understanding the ethos of Japan's wartime system. It is, of course, a very broad problem and I shall touch on only a few aspects. The principles that I have deduced from my study of the material are extremely commonplace, and perhaps belong more to the realm of daily observation than to that of scholarly analysis. If this is indeed so, it provides a further example of the way in which commonplace circumstances can give rise to the most momentous results. Our knowledge of this important fact must never grow stale and should inspire us with the greatest caution.

II. COMPARISON OF JAPAN'S WARTIME LEADERS WITH THOSE OF NAZI GERMANY

One does not have to be an adherent of Freud to recognize that fascism is invariably linked with an abnormal psychological condition and to a greater or lesser extent accompanied by symptoms of hysteria. In this respect there is no particular difference between its Western and Eastern varieties. There is, however, a quite remarkable gap between the actual forms in which this abnormal psychology expressed itself in Nazi Germany and in wartime Japan.

First and foremost, the background of the Nazi leaders differed diametrically from that of our own criminals. Most of the top Nazis had enjoyed very little formal education and, until they actually seized power, few of them had held any position worthy of the name.* The prisoners in the dock at

---

* Göbbels (with his title of D. Phil. from Heidelberg) was an exception that proved the rule. Most of the others, far from being ashamed of their humble origins, regarded their lack of social status and education as a cause for pride, and used it successfully to suggest how close they were to the masses. Directly after seizing power Hitler addressed the workers in a Berlin factory as follows:

Tokyo, however, were all 'prize students' who had attended the foremost educational institutions or the military colleges, and who after graduation had travelled along the smooth highway of advancement until they came to occupy the highest official positions in the Empire.

There was also a significant difference in personality. The Nazi leaders were a collection of freaks, including drug addicts, sexual perverts, and alcoholics.* By and large they were beyond the pale of normal society: they were, in fact, essentially 'outlaws'.

Among our defendants too there were some genuine psychopaths like Ōkawa and Shiratori, and others like Matsuoka who were borderline cases. Yet, however obscure and irrational their political judgement and behaviour may have been, as a group they can hardly be considered to have been mentally abnormal. Far from being excluded from normal society, they usually enjoyed the most enviable positions, either basking in the reflected glory of impressive ancestors or having been cut out since their youth to become ministers or generals. As regards personality, none of them was a pure outlaw.

To be sure, some members of the military clique, especially certain Army officers, were not entirely lacking in the 'outlaw' aspect;† but even they were guided in equal measure by a timid, bureaucratic mentality, which became more and more pronounced as they rose in the hierarchy.

The true outlaw type did play an important part in Japanese fascism. But, as the name *rōnin* suggests, one of their characteristics was precisely that they did *not* attain any influential position; instead this eerie gentry operated behind the scenes, scurrying in and out of the offices of the men in power, and receiving an unfixed income in return for such services as they

'*Deutsche Volksgenossen und Volksgenossinnen! Meine deutsche Arbeiter!* If I speak today to you and to millions of other workers, I do so with greater right than any other. I have myself come from your ranks. I have been among you for four and a half years in war, and I speak now to you to whom I belong . . . I lead the struggle for the million-masses of our brave, industrious workers and our labouring people . . . I need no title. My name, which I earned by my own strength, is my title.' (Frederick Schuman, *The Nazi Dictatorship*, p. 259.) Even if Tōjō had wanted to make such a speech, he could never have done it.

* E.g. Göring, Himmler, Ley.

† Note, for example, the behaviour of Itagaki and Doihara on the Continent at the time of the Manchurian Incident, and of men like Hashimoto in the March and October Incidents.

could render.* This Japanese type of outlaw differed entirely from his Nazi counterpart.†

The Class A war crime suspects in Japan, far from being the prime movers, can rather be regarded as pathetic robots, manipulated by outlaws (some big and some small, some belonging to the government and some outside) on whom they looked down from the height of their positions. Here we are confronted with a most important contrast between the Western and Eastern manifestations of fascism, a contrast noticed by the Prosecuting Attorney, Mr. Tavenner, when he wound up his closing address to the Court as follows:

> These men were not the hoodlums who were the powerful part of the group which stood before the tribunal at Nuremberg, dregs of a criminal environment thoroughly schooled in the ways of crime and knowing no other methods but those of crime. These men were supposed to be the élite of the nation, the honest and trusted leaders to whom the fate of the nation had been confidently entrusted . . . With full knowledge they voluntarily made their choice for evil . . . With full knowledge they voluntarily elected to follow the path of war, bringing death and injury to millions of human beings and hate wherever their forces went . . . For this choice they must bear the guilt.‡

It is clear, then, that the defendants in Tokyo cannot themselves be regarded as mentally abnormal. Their thought and behaviour are relevant to the psychopathology of fascism only to the extent that they were infected by people, in Japan and abroad, who were abnormal. There is no doubt that they were influenced by the upsurge of Nazism in Europe. The operative

---

* The methods and routes by which these *rōnin* obtained their income varied greatly, as did the amounts. Exact information is hard to come by, but there is no denying that, as one *rōnin* himself put it, 'The words and deeds of the rightists were in no small measure connected with their alimentary canals.' In the inquiry into the February 26 Incident it was brought out that Mr. Ikeda Seihin, the managing director of Mitsui, had from time to time given funds to the following among others: Messrs. Kita Ikki, Nakano Seigō, Matsui Kūka, Iwata Fumio, Akiyama Teisuke, Akamatsu Katsumaro, Tsukui Tatsuo, Hashimoto Tetsuma. Of course the rightists were also greatly dependent on the secret Army fund, so that there was an almost exact correspondence between the fluctuations in this 'blood transfusion' and the rise and fall in their activity.

† Cf. my previous essay, 'The Ideology and Dynamics of Japanese Fascism'. A vivid example of the type of outlaw who was active in the Japanese fascist movement can be found in Inoue Nisshō's autobiography, *One Man, One Killing*.

‡ IMTFE, no. 416, pp. 48410–12, 16 Apr. 1948.

factor, however, was not so much Nazism itself as the low resistance of Japan to infection from foreign sources.

Scholars have already examined the socio-economic basis of the differences between the two countries. My approach to the problem will be a more direct one, namely, to compare the words and actions of the wartime leaders in Germany and Japan.

German and Japanese fascism left the same trail of destruction, chaos, and destitution in the world; but there is a striking contrast between the situation in Germany, where thought and behaviour were entirely consistent, and that in Japan, where the two were remarkably at variance. On 22 August 1939, the day before Hitler's decision to invade Poland, he addressed his generals as follows:

> I shall give a propagandist reason for starting the war—never mind whether it is plausible or not. The victor will not be asked afterward whether he told the truth or not. In starting and waging a war it is not right that matters, but victory.[5]

What an inexorable conclusion, and how uncannily it reveals what Karl Levitt refers to as 'active nihilism'!

No class of militarist in our country ever dared voice so categorical a view. Much as they believed in private that 'he who wins is always in the right', they lacked the boldness to state this openly as the guiding principle of their decisions. Instead they always tried to find some way to conceal or moralize it.* Thus the suppression of foreign peoples by Japanese military might was always 'the promulgation of the Imperial

---

* See 'Theory and Psychology of Ultra-Nationalism'. My purpose here is to compare general trends in mental structure; if one were to compare certain specific individuals, one might well find cases in which the roles were reversed as between Germany and Japan. The type of cynical realism in question occurred relatively often among the 'outlaw' type. The informal conversation of Army officers and others also frequently revealed a degree of cynicism that belied all their talk about justice and morality. A former colonel in the Finance and Accounting Bureau of the War Ministry has furnished me with a good example. The Army was split over the question of how to occupy French Indo-China, the Military Affairs Bureau favouring 'peaceful' occupation, as opposed to the forcible approach of the General Staff. During a discussion of this question a member of the Bureau is said to have remarked: 'There's a stiff penalty for outright robbery. Let's see if we can't manage it by fraud this time.' This blunt sort of approach, however, was reserved for private conversations; when giving explanations in formal conference or for the general public, they dressed up their statements in the finest moralistic style.

Way' and was regarded as an act of benevolence towards the foreigners in question. The attitude was unconsciously caricatured in a speech by General Araki in 1933:

> Needless to say, the Imperial Army's spirit lies in exalting the Imperial Way and spreading the National Virtue. Every single bullet must be charged with the Imperial Way and the end of every bayonet must have the National Virtue burnt into it. If there are any who oppose the Imperial Way or the National Virtue, we shall give them an injection with this bullet and this bayonet.*

Men who could think like this would not be satisfied until they had imbued each individual slaughter with the mystique of the Imperial Way.

Now let us hear what a German leader has to say about the treatment of subject peoples: 'What happens to a Russian, to a Czech, does not interest me in the slightest,' declared Heinrich Himmler on 4 October 1943.

> Whether nations live in prosperity or starve to death like cattle [continued Himmler] interests me only in so far as we need them as slaves to our *Kultur*; otherwise it is of no interest to me. Whether ten thousand Russian females fall down from exhaustion while digging an anti-tank ditch interests me only in so far as the anti-tank ditch for Germany is finished . . .[6]

The S.S. leader's lucidity is nothing short of breathtaking!

The Nazis were of course second to none when it came to disseminating sweet-sounding slogans at home and abroad. They seem to have been perfectly aware, however, of what was reality in their slogans and what was mere propaganda. Our own wartime leaders, on the contrary, were ultimately taken in by the slogans that they themselves had concocted, and as a result their view of reality was hopelessly obfuscated. The cross-examination of General Minami Jirō, the former Governor-General of Korea, provides a good example:

PRESIDENT OF THE COURT: Why did you call it a 'Holy War'?
MINAMI: I used the word because it was in wide currency at the time.
Q. What was holy about it?
A. I never thought about that very deeply. I just happened to use the word because it was in wide currency at that time among the

* IMTFE, no. 270, p. 28370, 12 Sept. 1947.

general public. My idea was that this was not an aggressive war
but one that had arisen owing to unavoidable circumstances.*

The same tendency to be taken in by one's own moralizing
slogan can be seen in the case of General Matsui Iwane, the
former Commander-in-Chief of the Japanese expeditionary
force in Shanghai.[7] In his deposition the true nature of the
China Incident is defined as follows:

> The struggle between Japan and China was always a fight
> between brothers within the 'Asian family' . . . It has been my belief
> during all these years that we must regard this struggle as a method
> of making the Chinese undergo self-reflection. We do not do this
> because we hate them, but on the contrary because we love them too
> much. It is just the same as in a family when an elder brother has
> taken all that he can stand from his ill-behaved younger brother and
> has to chastise him in order to make him behave properly.†

One might imagine that this argument was trumped up for the
occasion, but in fact it appears that the General really believed
his talk about brotherly love. For already in 1937, when he was
about to leave for Shanghai, he told the supporters of the
Greater Asia Society at a farewell party: 'I am going to the
front not to fight an enemy but in the state of mind of one who
sets out to pacify his brother.'‡

The type of psychology according to which one chastises
people because one loves them too much led to atrocities like
the 'rape of Nanking', before which we must cover our eyes in
shame. What our wartime leaders accomplished by their
moralizing was not simply to deceive the people of Japan or of
the world; more than anyone else they deceived themselves.

One of the things that most struck the former United States
Ambassador, Mr. Joseph Grew, who had a wide circle of
acquaintances in the upper strata of Japanese society, was this
self-deception and lack of realism.

> . . . I doubt if one Japanese in a hundred [wrote Mr. Grew] really
> believes that they have actually broken the Kellogg Pact, the Nine-
> Power Treaty, and the Covenant of the League. A comparatively
> few thinking men are capable of frankly facing the facts, and one
> Japanese said to me: 'Yes, we've broken every one of these instru-

* IMTFE, no. 1935, p. 20014, 16 Apr. 1947.
† Ibid., no. 310, 7 Nov. 1947.
‡ Ibid., testimony of Shimanaka Yasaburō, no. 310, p. 32696, 7 Nov. 1947.

ments; we've waged open war; the arguments of "self-defense" and "self-determination for Manchuria" are rot; but we needed Manchuria, and that's that.' But such men are in the minority. The great majority of Japanese are astonishingly capable of really fooling themselves . . . It isn't that the Japanese necessarily has his tongue in his cheek when he signs the obligation. It merely means that when the obligation runs counter to his own interests, as he conceives them, he will interpret the obligation to suit himself and, according to his own lights and mentality, he will very likely be perfectly honest in so doing.[8]

And the Ambassador concluded as follows: 'Such a mentality is a great deal harder to deal with than a mentality which, however brazen, knows that it is in the wrong.'

This conclusion refers precisely to the contrast between the Nazis, who carried out their plan in complete awareness of the meaning and results of their actions, and Japan's wartime leaders, whose inner intentions were for ever being betrayed by their own behaviour. In neither case did any real sense of guilt develop. But whereas the Germans surmounted any incipient guilt feelings by defying them head-on, the Japanese evaded them by constantly moralizing their actions. 'To have wanted good yet to have done evil'—this, in an exact reversal of the Mephistophelean pattern, was the fate of Japan's rulers.

It is hard to determine which of the two countries was the more iniquitous; but what we can certainly say is that one side had a stronger spirit and the other a weaker one. That the weaker should have been infected by the stronger is hardly surprising.

Even when Japan's wartime leaders revealed the same hysterical state of mind as their German counterparts and launched out on the same desperate acts, they were vitiated by a sort of nervous debility, which became aggravated as time went on; and the keynote of their personalities was a sense of inferiority.

With the ultrasensitiveness of the Japanese [writes Grew], arising out of a marked inferiority complex which manifests itself in the garb of an equally marked superiority complex, with all its attendant bluster, chauvinism, xenophobia, and organized national propaganda, the method and manner of dealing with current controversies assume a significance and importance often out of all proportion to the nature of the controversy.[9]

What made the absence of long-term planning and the lack of effective leadership so conspicuous was precisely this inability to regulate the means in terms of clearly perceived objectives. Thus the use of brute force to carry out policy became more and more commonplace, until finally there was no turning back: military power had become an end in itself.

In Germany too a sense of inferiority played an important part in the rise of fascism. There it was manifested by the supporting class, that is, by the lower middle class which helped the Nazis to overthrow the Weimar Republic; the Nazi leaders themselves, far from labouring under any inferiority complex, represented a modern version of the Zarathustran 'will to power'.

In Japan, on the other hand, it was the actual leaders of the government who, despite their superficial air of calm dignity, were in a constant state of nervous tension. As the perfect case of 'weak nerves' most readers will, of course, think of Prince Konoe. His political career certainly provides a wealth of examples of how fatally a weakness of character can operate at important moments.*[10] According to Marquis Kido's evidence, 'Whenever any difficult question arose he frequently said, "I want to give up." '† At the beginning of October 1941, when the negotiations with the United States were nearing their crisis and when the day of decision (as determined by the Imperial Conference of 6 September)[11] was rapidly approaching, he permitted himself the following remark to General Suzuki: 'I want to retire from the world of politics and become a priest.'‡ It is significant too that Konoe should have given shelter in his Teki-gai villa to a typical outlaw and psychotic like Inoue Nisshō: the Prime Minister's behaviour is a clear case of psychological compensation.

Now Prince Konoe's weakness would appear to have been a simple case of individual character, compounded with a type of debility often associated with the aristocracy. But it was not Konoe alone who was weak. When I refer to the weak spirits of Japan's wartime leaders, I am thinking of far more than the

---

* E.g. the spread of the China Incident; the deterioration of the Imperial Rule Assistance movement during his second Cabinet; the resignation of his Cabinet.

† IMTFE, no. 298, p. 31553, 22 Oct. 1947.

‡ Testimony of Suzuki Teiichi (see p. 88 above).

weakness of character exemplified by a man like Konoe. As a different sort of case let us look at Mr. Tōgō Shigenori, Foreign Minister in the Tōjō and Suzuki Cabinets. Tōgō played a leading part towards the end of the war when he advocated the unconditional acceptance of the Potsdam Declaration and put up a good fight against the military. His attitude at this time certainly does not smack of Konoe's type of weakness. Yet, when the war started on the morning of 8 December (Japanese time) and Tōgō, in his capacity as Foreign Minister, summoned the American Ambassador, Mr. Grew, and handed him the memorandum regarding his government's decision to break off negotiations with the United States, he merely thanked the Ambassador for his co-operation during the period of the negotiations and did not say a single word about the launching of hostilities and the attack on Pearl Harbour. It was not until Mr. Grew returned to his Embassy that he learnt that war had started.

Some four years later, when Mr. Blakeney asked him in Court why during the course of the interview he had not mentioned that a state of war existed, he came out with some curious explanations. First, he presumed that the Ambassador already knew about the opening of hostilities from the morning broadcast. Let us accept this for the sake of argument and go on to the second point: since the Imperial Proclamation of War had not yet been issued to the Japanese people, he thought it inappropriate to mention the matter *when it was not necessary*. This already seems rather odd; but what really shocked the Court was his third reason:

Ambassador Grew and I had been acquainted with each other for a long time, and I was very much hesitant about mentioning even the word 'war' between us. And so, instead of talking about or referring to the word 'war', I expressed to him my very deep regrets that the relations between his country and mine had come to such a state that we must part.*

Let us see what this really means. At an official interview between a Foreign Minister and an Ambassador, each representing his country at a most crucial time in their relations, the Japanese party is inhibited by a type of constraint that one

* IMTFE, no. 342, pp. 36140–1, 26 Dec. 1947.

normally associates with dealings between private individuals; this constraint involves a keen sense of awkwardness and embarrassment and makes him hesitate to speak straight out about the situation staring him in the face. Apart from his weakness of spirit, Tōgō may well have been hobbled by a certain sense of shame over the surprise attack on Pearl Harbour. In any case, when sympathy for someone's feelings reaches this point, it is tantamount to the greatest contempt. A perfect contrast is provided by the attitude of the American Secretary of State, Mr. Cordell Hull, during his final interview with the Japanese Ambassadors, Nomura and Kurusu.[12]

A similar case of 'weak spirits' can be found in Japanese domestic politics when the Yonai Cabinet was compelled to resign as a result of its clash with the Army[13] over the Tripartite Pact. The man in the most ticklish position at this time was of course Yonai's War Minister, General Hata, whose letter of resignation to the Prime Minister was the occasion for the collapse of the Cabinet. Some observers believe that he acted entirely on his own initiative, but at the war crimes trials the Defence insisted that he had resigned at the demand of Prince Kanin, the Chief of the Army General Staff, General Anami, the Vice-Minister for War, and certain officers in the Military Affairs Bureau. Whatever the truth of the matter may be, there is no doubting the significance of the following episode told by Yonai:

... after the general resignation of the Cabinet I called Hata to my room and said, as nearly as I can remember: 'I can understand your situation—you have suffered very much. I myself, however, do not blame you at all. I understand. Put your mind at ease and do not worry˙ I shook his hand and Hata smiled a sad smile—a smile of resignation, peculiar to a Japanese. His situation was indeed a pitiful one.*

A fatuous exchange indeed! But what emerges quite clearly is that the dominant consideration was not any concern over the principle of public interest but a private perception of interacting emotions. Whatever Hata's actual role in the resignation may have been, his attitude during the interview with Yonai was probably much as described. General Hata—the Supreme

* IMTFE, no. 391, p. 43337, 11 March 1948.

Commander of the Expeditionary Force to China, the general who as Commander-in-Chief of the Central China Army controlled a huge host of men, the leader who was elevated to the lofty rank of Field-Marshal—what a puny creature he shows himself to be in reality!

This dwarfishness of Japan's wartime leaders was most clearly brought home to the world by the way in which the war crimes suspects with one accord denied their responsibility.[14] It will not be necessary to quote the individual defendants, since their attitude on this point is already well known. The following statement from Mr. Keenan's final address to the Court will serve as an epitome:

> From all the remaining twenty-five accused, including former Prime Ministers, Cabinet members, high ranking diplomats, propagandists, generals, marshals, admirals, and the Lord Keeper of the Privy Seal (the Emperor's adviser), we have heard one common reply: No one among them wanted to bring about this war. This applies to the Manchurian invasion, the subsequent China wars, and the Pacific War, an unbroken course of aggression covering a period of fourteen years ... When they cannot deny the authority, the power and responsibility they held and cannot deny acquiescence in the policy of continuing and expanding these aggressive wars to the extent that the whole world was shaken by them, they coolly assert that there was no other course left open.*

Nowhere does the contrast in attitudes between the German and Japanese defendants emerge more clearly than here. Referring to the Anschluss, for instance, Göring spoke as follows: 'I take one hundred per cent. responsibility ... I ignored even the Führer's opposition and led everything to its final stage of development.'† He was 'wild with rage' about the invasion of Norway, but this was because he had not been informed beforehand; so far as his opinion about the actual attack was concerned, he admitted: 'My attitude was completely positive.' Göring was also against the attack on the Soviet Union; but his opposition was essentially concerned with the timing, being based on the view that until England was subjugated it would be better to postpone operations against Russia. He had no doubt about his motives: 'My ideas were determined exclusively

---

* IMTFE, no. 371, pp. 9–10 of Summation of Prosecution, 11 Feb. 1948.
† Nuremberg Military Tribunal: Judgement.

by political and military considerations.'* What a clear-cut approach! This truly is the lucidity of a nihilist who consciously challenges the traditional European spirit; it is the bluster of the outlaw who defiantly bases his actions on 'evil'.

Compared with this, the answers of the defendants and of many of the witnesses at the Tokyo trials were slippery as eels, hazy as the mist. Instead of replying head-on to the questions of the Prosecution and of the President of the Court, they would evade them or else use their sensitive antennae to anticipate the line of interrogation and thus forestall the questions. Exasperated at the consistent disingenuousness of Admiral Yonai's replies, the President of the Court remarked that of all the witnesses he had heard this Prime Minister was the most asinine,† and this became a newspaper headline. Time after time throughout the trials the defendants and witnesses had to be admonished, 'That is no reply. A suitable answer is either "Yes" or "No".'

The military, whom one would expect from their professional character to give the clearest answers, were in fact the worst offenders in this respect. Lieutenant-General Ōshima, the former Ambassador to Germany, is an outstanding example, as can be seen from the following exchange between him and Mr. Tavenner about the negotiations for the Tripartite Pact in 1938:

TAVENNER. Will you please answer my question? Did you advocate such an alliance or not?

ŌSHIMA. I did not. [In his previous cross-examination he had frequently been cautioned to answer yes or no.]

Q. Did you oppose Ribbentrop's request that such an alliance be entered into?

A. The objection, opposition, came from Japan.

Q. Will you answer my question?

A. I am not trying to evade your questions, but it is not possible to answer yes or no when a question is referring to something of a complicated nature.‡

The Prosecutor now followed up his inquiry into the aims of the Anti-Comintern Pact with the question:

Did Wakamatsu express your views with regard to the result to be obtained by Japan in concluding an anti-Comintern pact with

* Nuremberg Military Tribunal: Judgement.   † IMTFE, no. 275, 19 Sept. 1947.
‡ Ibid, no. 322, p. 34091, 26 Nov. 1947.

Germany when he stated in his cross-examination here that by the conclusion of such a pact Japan could forestall Germany from drawing closer to Russia, obtain the necessary intelligence and new types of weapons from Germany, and also keep Germany from taking sides with China?*

Ōshima evaded this by saying:

I heard what Wakamatsu said here in this Tribunal, but I have not had any occasion to speak of such matters with Wakamatsu. Well, there are various fruits to be obtained by the conclusion of such a pact, but the purpose of the Anti-Comintern Pact is as I have set forth in my affidavit.

Tavenner tried to nail the evasion:

Q. My question was whether or not those views of Wakamatsu were your views also. If you agree with them, say so; if you do not, say you do not.
A. Yes, such fruits would result from the pact.

Similar examples can be found throughout the record.

In examining this vagueness and complexity, we must not overlook the linguistic factor. The characteristic nuances of Japanese, in particular of the Japanese literary language, aggravated the obscurity of the replies and added to the bewilderment of the Court. A 'land in which the soul of language flourishes'[15] can be expected to produce many words lacking concrete contents, words like 'to *protect* (= hold aloft) the Emperor', 'the tranquillity of the Imperial House', 'private reports' to the Throne, 'constant *advice*', 'advocates of a *positive* (i.e. military) policy'. Such expressions appeared especially in relation to the Imperial House and must have done a great deal to obfuscate the understanding of the Bench and of the Prosecution. Thanks to the sorcery of this wording, a personal sense of reponsibility became more and more obscured. It is hardly surprising that when a discussion started about the meaning of the phrase 'greater Asianism', one of the judges should have said: 'The Court is concerned with actions and conduct, not the words with which they were referred to.'† For, as one member of the Defence expressed it,

* IMTFE, no. 322, p. 34080, 26 Nov. 1947.
† Ibid., no. 176, p. 18030, 10 March 1947.

How can we make head or tail of an ideology that changes every-thing about at will, so that the 'Eight Corners of the World under One Roof' means 'universal brotherhood' and the Imperial Way is 'in harmony with the fundamental concept of democracy'?

It would be wrong to conclude that the defendants used words of this kind simply to quibble their way out of their predica-ment. In the last war it was not only the defendants who had an undeveloped sense of responsibility, but the Japanese ruling class in general; and this phenomenon has far too deep roots for us to interpret it in terms of individual moral defects, such as shameless cunning or addiction to the base art of self-pro-tection. For, as we shall see, this is not a matter of the collapse of the individual but a manifestation of the way in which the system itself had decayed.

The best way to understand this point is to analyse the basis on which the defendants in the war crimes trials tried to justify their past conduct. Here we find a reflection of the ethos inherent in the environment in which these men lived and acted.

III. THE DWARFISHNESS OF JAPANESE FASCISM[16] (i)

Through the forest of self-vindication planted by the defen-dants run two clearly marked trails: submission to *faits accomplis* and refuge in one's competence or jurisdiction.

First, what is submission to *faits accomplis*? It is the point of view that because something has happened one is obliged *ipso facto* to approve of it. A line of argument that appears in the replies of almost all the defendants is that they had to conform to a policy once it had been decided, that they had to support the war once it had started, and so forth. When during his interrogation in Sugamo Prison Mr. Shiratori Toshio was asked: 'Were you not from 1931 until the end of the war con-sidered a friend of the military clique that was aggressive in Manchuria and in China?',* he replied: 'I am not a friend of theirs, but I am a Japanese. Being Japanese, I had to side with them; not side with them, but try to cast as plausible and as bright a surface as possible on the things they had done.' Again, when asked by the Prosecuting Counsel, Mr. Sandusky, 'Were you in favour of the so-called China Affair or against it?', his answer was: 'I wanted the China Incident to be settled as

* IMTFE, no. 332, p. 35066, 11 Dec. 1947.

quickly as possible, and as to whether I was for it or against it, since the incident had already begun, I don't think I can appropriately use either expression.'*

Similarly, Ōshima, when asked whether he had supported the Tripartite Pact, said, 'I myself, of course, supported it because it had already been decided as a national policy and was also supported by the Japanese people at large.'†

The important point here is not whether the defendant's argument has any material substance. It is well known that Ōshima was one of the prime movers in the Tripartite Pact, and what is significant is his attitude: here is a man who, having contributed to the formulation of a certain plan, uses the new environment and the new state of public opinion brought about by the realization of that plan as a basis for defending his actions.

Next let us take the case of Marquis Kido. Here again the interrogation concerns the Tripartite Pact:

KEENAN. I would like to know, first, whether you continued to oppose the military alliance with Germany while you were a member of the Hiranuma Cabinet. It seems to me that could be answered generally, 'yes' or 'no'. If it cannot be, why, please tell me.

KIDO. I myself was . . . continued to oppose this alliance, but the matter was investigated thoroughly in the Five Ministers Conference. It was in March that I first heard from the Foreign Minister regarding the progress of these investigations, and I felt that as an actual . . . that practically speaking, it was difficult to oppose this proposed measure since it had now entered the realm of actuality.‡

In the same way, when Tōgō was asked whether or not he had approved of the Tripartite Pact at the time of his appointment as Foreign Minister in the Tōjō Cabinet, he replied as follows:

My own personal feeling was opposed to the Tripartite Pact. But no matter what the subject may be, in human affairs there is also a certain continuity. Once a matter decided on before has become a *fait accompli* it is very difficult to try to change that established fact.§

* IMTFE, no. 332, p. 35088, 11 Dec. 1947.
† Ibid., no. 323, p. 34174, 28 Nov. 1947.
‡ Ibid., no. 297, p. 31480, 21 Oct. 1947.
§ Ibid., no. 340, p. 35989, 23 Dec. 1947. Note that in his earlier deposition Tōgō stated that he had used all his energy to oppose the strengthening of relations with Germany.

The Prosecution then charged him with having made an enthusiastic speech about the Pact in the Eighty-First Diet. He replied:

Well, there was no room in this public speech to include my own personal likes or dislikes . . . It would be more accurate to say that as Foreign Minister of Japan I was in such a position that I had to make a speech of that nature, rather than to say there was no room for truth.*

Let us leave aside the questions of how far Kido and Tōgō were actually opposed to the Pact and of what action they took to counter it. The heart of the problem is the spirit of their replies: where important matters of national policy were concerned, they were not faithful to their own beliefs but repressed them as being 'personal emotions', choosing instead to adapt themselves to the environment; and this they made into their morality.

When we read in the affidavits of the defendants that by and large they had been opposed to the entire succession of political developments and international agreements following the Manchurian Incident, we are overcome by the feeling that this concatenation of historical processes was a sort of natural disaster, a convulsion of nature, eclipsing all human powers. In attacking the affidavit of General Koiso, which was a caricature of this line of defence, the prosecuting counsel, Colonel Fixel, made the point trenchantly and exhaustively:

. . . you tried to prevent the Manchurian Incident; you opposed the Tripartite Pact; you opposed going into a war against the United States; and you tried to settle the China war when you became Premier, and in all of these important matters you were frustrated and prevented from having your ideas and desires prevail. If you disagreed with and were opposed to these events and policies why did you accept one important position in the Government after another whereby you became one of the protagonists of the very matters you now say you so strenuously objected to?†

Koiso's reply was according to form:

The way of we Japanese is that no matter what our personal opinions and our own personal arguments may be, once a policy of State has

* IMTFE, no. 340, p. 36041, 23 Dec. 1947.
† Ibid., no. 37, pp. 32430–1, 4 Nov. 1947.

been decided upon, it is our duty to bend all our efforts for the prosecution of such policy. This has been the traditional custom in our country.

It is evident, then, that for Koiso and the others reality is not something in the process of creation or about to be created; rather it is that which has already been created or, to be more specific, that which has arisen from somewhere in the past. Therefore to act realistically means to be tied to the past.

Similarly, reality is not something'to be grasped by the individual in order to build a new future; it is a blind inevitability flowing from a determined past. In this sense the conversation between Mr. Grew and the Foreign Minister, Mr. Matsuoka, on the occasion of their first meeting on 26 July 1940, is pregnant with meaning:

> Mr. Matsuoka then said that history is based largely on the operation of blind forces which in a rapidly moving world cannot always be controlled. I admitted that blind forces have played their part in history but I added that one of the primary duties of diplomacy and statesmanship is to direct those forces into healthy channels and that I hoped before long to explore with him the present state of American-Japanese relations in the confident belief that he and I approaching the subject in the right spirit would accomplish a great deal in giving helpful directive to the blind forces which he had in mind.[17]

How vividly this conversation brings out the difference in the approach of the two nations! On one side we have the spirit of Japanese militarism, which, having lost its power of autonomy, is led by blind outside forces; on the other, the pragmatic spirit, which is for ever concerned with the balance between ends and means. In 1940, when the Privy Council discussed the Tripartite Pact, Matsuoka said: 'War between Japan and America is inevitable.'* And in an interview with the German Ambassador, General Ott, concerning the Tripartite Pact and the Non-Aggression Pact with the Soviet Union he indiscriminately brandished the argument that history is an inevitable matter of fate:

> If Germany should clash with the Soviet Union, it would be impossible for any Japanese Prime Minister or Foreign Minister to keep our country neutral. Under such circumstances Japan would

* IMTFE, no. 76.

be impelled *with natural inevitability* to attack Russia on the side of Germany.*

How, then, does Nazi Germany compare with Japan in this respect? On 23 May 1939, Hitler had this to say about the Polish question:

> The solution of this problem calls for courage. We cannot permit the approach in which one tries to avoid the solution of a problem by adapting oneself to the existing state of affairs. Rather we must make the state of affairs conform to our wishes. This can be done only by invading foreign countries or attacking their territory.†

For all its Machiavellism, this attitude is in one important respect closer to the type of Western pragmatism expressed by Mr. Grew than to the fatalistic approach that emerges from Mr. Matsuoka's utterances: the subject is recognized as a free, active agent who need not submit himself to the environment but can mould existing circumstances to serve his objectives. In this sense it represents a clear expression of political leadership. Thus the invasion of Poland was a deliberate policy adopted on the initiative of the Nazi leader after a proper study of the strategic situation.

It is quite true, of course, that the Nazis often made mistakes in their assessment of the situation and that, especially as the war in Europe entered its later stages, cold calculation increasingly gave way to desperate resolve. The fact remains that at no point can they be regarded in the same light as Japan's wartime leaders, who were always being dragged along by the 'objective situation' and by the 'force of circumstances' until finally they slithered into the depths of defeat. In this respect, as we shall see, wartime Japan can better be compared to Imperial Germany or Tsarist Russia during the First World War than to the Third Reich.

We are now in a position to understand the psychological basis of a phenomenon noticed earlier:[18] namely, that the men who held supreme power in Japan were in fact mere robots manipulated by their subordinates, who in turn were being manipulated by officers serving overseas and by the right-wing *rōnin* and ruffians associated with the military. In fact the nomi-

---

* Telegram no. 107 from Ott to German Foreign Ministry. IMTFE, no. 76.
† Nuremberg Military Tribunal: Judgement.

nal leaders were always panting along in a desperate effort to keep up with the *faits accomplis* created by anonymous, extra-legal forces. During the entire period under discussion there were endless Imperial Conferences, Liaison Conferences (between the Government and the Imperial Headquarters), and Conferences of the Supreme Council for the Direction of War, all aimed at laying down supreme national policy. Yet the only impressive thing about these conferences was their names; and even now when we read the minutes of the discussions we are struck by how empty they were.*

The fact of the matter is that the agenda for discussion had been prepared in advance by the conference 'secretaries'.[19] General Mutō and other witnesses claimed that these secretaries were mere liaison and clerical assistants, but when we examine the records we find that the posts were occupied by high-ranking military officials, the Chiefs of the Military and Naval Affairs Bureaux and the Vice-Chiefs of the Army and Navy General Staffs. To carry things still further, below these so-called secre-taries was a group of 'advisers' consisting of officials from the Military and Naval Affairs Bureaux and members of the General Staffs, who drafted essential plans put forward in the conferences. And into the offices of the Military and Naval Affairs Bureaux scurried the extreme rightist civilians (men who were truly of the type to which Schuman refers when he speaks of 'burning fanatics' and 'super-paranoiacs'), there to

---

* One of the reasons for this emptiness can be found in the 'weak spirits' (pp. 97 ff.) of Japan's leaders, who put on a bold front by mouthing slogans and clichés in which they did not really believe. It was further encouraged by the fact that the contents of the discussions would promptly leak out via the military authorities present and down to the 'outlaws'. Read in this light, the statements and the man-ner of speaking of the members of the Senior Retainers' Conference held on 5 April 1945, to discuss a successor Cabinet, acquire a new significance. Kido's affidavit provides a good example of how little mutual understanding there was even between the so-called Senior Retainers, and of how hard they had to work to fathom each other's unexpressed feelings. When Marquis Kido had a conference on 13 June 1945 with Admiral Suzuki, the Prime Minister, about the termina-tion of the war, he told him that Admiral Yonai, the Navy Minister, had said: 'The Prime Minister still appears to be very positive [about continuing the war].' At this Suzuki laughed and remarked: 'I thought that Yonai was still very positive. Can I be mistaken about this?' Kido's comment was as follows: 'So *by chance* I learnt that these two men were thinking along the same lines.' Such was the situa-tion between a wartime head of government and his Navy Minister! IMTFE, no. 294, pp. 31153–4, 16 Oct. 1947. (See also Butow, *Japan's Decision to Surrender*, p. 72.)

exchange bombast with field officers of the section staffs, who were half official and half outlaw.

Yet even these people were not always in a position to control the Kwangtung Army and the China Expeditionary Force. How much harder, then, was it for the members of the Cabinet and the Senior Retainers to direct the course of events on the continent! Instead they had to stand there, grumbling away and watching with surprise and anxiety as one event followed another into the realm of *faits accomplis*; and then they had to recognize the inevitability of the 'objective situation'. Thus the shots fired at Liu T'iao River and Marco Polo Bridge reverberated louder and louder until they engulfed the entire continent in war; and the plots of the outlaws were successively ratified by the top officials as *faits accomplis*, so that they came to represent the supreme policy of the nation.*

This brings us to the phenomenon known as the 'rule of the higher by the lower', which paradoxically became more and more pronounced as the anti-democratic, authoritarian ideology, centred on the military, began to make headway on all

---

* The fact remains that, if the *faits accomplis* created by the 'lower echelons' or 'local agencies' had actually run counter to the interests and sense of values of the upper strata of the ruling class, or to the fundamental direction of Japanese imperialism, they would never have reached the stage of becoming national policy. This involves the problem of the underlying forces behind pre-war developments in Japan. It is unhistorical to regard the totalitarian tendencies in domestic policies and the progressive military involvement abroad as representing the 'steady realization of a plot of monopoly capitalism'. On the other hand, if we interpret the history of this period as a process in which the military, the rightists, and other advocates of absolutism succeeded in rejecting the liberalism of the Senior Retainers and of the *bourgeoisie*, we are guilty of a sort of inverted formalism. The crux of the problem is the real significance and the historical context of Japanese 'liberalism'. This is not the place to examine this complex question, but as an example of what pre-war liberalism could involve we might refer to the three points advanced by Mr. Fukai Eigo as the underlying principles of the State. Mr. Fukai was a leading figure in financial circles and later became a Privy Councillor; he was regarded as a 'liberal' in whom the ruling class could put full confidence. These are his points: (i) the individual should serve his country as the supreme existence; (ii) the political and social apparatus must change with the times and so must the individual's attitude to it; we must not adhere to these things in any rigid form; (iii) our constant objective must be to expand the destiny of the nation; we must seize every favourable opportunity to push forward and, if circumstances so indicate, we must accomplish our demands by force. (*Memorandum of Principal Proceedings of the Privy Council*, p. 13.) Mr. Fukai's first and last points are particularly indicative of how far his theory of the State diverged from the essentials of liberalism, and of how little real difference there was between his view and that of the believers in the 'national polity' theory of the nation.

fronts. The fact that the participants in the abortive March and October Incidents escaped without any proper punishment undoubtedly helped to encourage the outbreak of subsequent terrorism. The October Incident, for instance, was an attempt at *coup d'état*, depending on the wide-scale use of terror. It involved the mobilization of the First and Third Infantry Regiments of the Imperial Guards Division, the dispatch of Navy bombers from Kasumigaura, an attack on the Prime Minister's official residence during a Cabinet session, and the assassination of all the participants; in addition the conspirators planned to surround the General Staff Headquarters and the War Ministry and to compel their superior officers to proclaim martial law. The War Minister, General Minami, and the Vice-Minister, General Sugiyama, were powerless to control the insurgents and they had to request General Araki, whom the plotters had selected as the next Prime Minister, to bring the situation under control. Though they succeeded in putting the ringleaders in protective custody, they were not in a position to mete out any condign punishment, and the entire Incident ended in a fade-out.*

In March of the following year, when Major-General Nagata, Director of the Military Affairs Bureau, was asked about the circumstances of the Incident by Marquis Kido and Prince Konoe, he replied:

> In principle this may be a matter that should be judged according to Army criminal law, but it would be better to settle it by administrative measures, having due regard for the motives of the participants and also taking into account the prestige of the Japanese armed forces.†

What a stark revelation of how the armed forces had really lost their prestige! Instead of punishing the conspirators like the

---

* An interesting sidelight on this Incident is that many of the most active participants, like Colonel Hashimoto Kingorō and Major Chō Isamu, had spent a good part of their days and nights since the Manchurian Incident in houses of assignation, where they would frequently invite young lieutenants and captains and 'give parties to stir up their martial spirit'. ('Notebook of Major Tanaka Kiyoshi', in Iwabuchi Tatsuo: *Genealogy of the Military Clique*, p. 67.) Incidentally, this Major Chō was a fanatic outlaw type who was always ready to draw his sword at the slightest provocation. The plotters in the October Incident had arranged that after they had taken over political power he would become Chief of Police. If this had succeeded, a Nazi-type fascist régime might well have come into being in Japan.

† IMTFE, no. 292 (Kido Diary).

gangsters they were, they had to approve of their illegal *faits accomplis* and make a suitable compromise.*

Now this decline in vertical authority within the armed forces was used to great effect by the military when it came to imposing their will in horizontal relations. Thus, when the War Minister wished to advance or oppose a certain measure in a Cabinet meeting or at an Imperial Conference, he would invariably argue: 'In that case the Department (i.e. the military) won't put up with it', or: 'In that case I can't guarantee to keep the forces under control.' When the Abe Cabinet resigned at the beginning of 1940, for example, the military favoured Prince Konoe as the next Prime Minister and rejected both General Ugaki and Mr. Ikeda Seihin. Prince Konoe expressed the following view to General Hata: 'They say that Ugaki is unsuitable and I suppose we have to accept that because of his background. But I really don't see what's wrong with Ikeda. Can't you stop them [i.e. the Army]?' 'With my feeble strength,' replied the General to Konoe's amazement, 'I am hardly in a position to do any stopping. If I tried interfering, I am afraid we might have another February Incident on our hands.'†

Gradually this type of logic was shifted downwards in the hierarchy. Beginning with 'the Director of the Military Affairs Bureau won't put up with it', one moved down through 'the

---

* Marquis Kido's observations about the Incident are significant. After he had exchanged relevant information with Prince Konoe, Baron Harada, Mr. Shiratori, and others, he made the following entry in his diary:

> 'The plan, which evidently dated from about 1927, was aimed at overthrowing the political parties and conducting the country's affairs by a type of "dictatorship" . . . If this plan should ever be realized, I doubt whether it would harm the basis on which our nation is built. The important thing for us is to guide the movement into the proper channels so that 1.0 unnecessary harm will be done; and this means that we must travel along a truly hard road.' IMTFE, no. 292 (Kido Diary).

Here is adumbrated in almost standard form the way in which men of the Senior Retainer level were to deal with reformist trends among the military. They travelled along a 'truly hard road' such as Kido had predicted, striving on the one hand to guide the extreme fascism of the military into the proper channels (that is, into the established order of the Emperor system) and on the other to keep the extremism itself within bounds (ref. 'The Ideology and Dynamics of Japanese Fascism'); yet all the while the fundamental structure of Japanese fascism was taking shape.

† Konoe, *My Work for Peace (Heiwa e no Doryoku)*, pp. 137–8. The episode incidentally provides an insight into the true nature of the so-called Army purge that followed the February Incident.

officials in the Military Affairs Section . . .' and 'the officers in
the field . . .' until finally one came to 'the people won't put up
with it'.* 'The people', of course, referred to the set of rightists
who were always in and out of the Military Affairs Section, and
the ex-servicemen's associations and similar local groups, which
constituted the rightists' background in the provinces.

It is true that the military often made use of the rightists and
of the rightist press, and that they did their best to intensify
xenophobia and fanatical Emperor-worship in these quarters.
Yet, conversely, 'public opinion', which they had helped to stir
up, had the effect of restricting their own freedom of movement.
And thus they made Japan slither further and further into the
morass of crisis.

This emerges particularly in the sequence of events from the
Tripartite Pact until the breakdown of the American-Japanese
negotiations. Already by October 1941 the military had been
forced into a position in which, out of regard for 'the people',
they were no longer able to beat a retreat. In the negotiations
with the United States the greatest barrier to an understanding
was the question of withdrawing troops *from* China; this suggests
what a predominant role *faits accomplis* played in Japanese
decision-making. When Tōjō dispatched Mr. Kurusu to the
United States as Ambassador, he stressed again and again that
this matter of withdrawal was the one point on which there
could be absolutely no backing down; if Japan were to compromise on this, 'he [Tōjō] would never be able to sleep facing
the Yasukuni Shrine'.† And in an article in the magazine *Pan-
Asianism* General Matsui did his part in drumming up sentiment
against any possible concession:

---

* In May 1939, for example, General Koiso, the Overseas Minister, spoke as
follows to Baron Harada about strengthening the tripartite defensive alliance:

'A German-Italian-Japanese defensive alliance must be concluded to bring
the war to a quick end. The officers and men in the field are extremely dissatisfied about the aid that England and France have been giving to Chiang Kai-
shek. We should try to appease them by drawing closer to Germany and Italy.
Subsequently we can use England and France to solve the China problem.
Otherwise the officers and men in the field aren't going to obey us.'
Harada's gloss on the General's remarks was: 'This is typical of how Army men
express themselves.' *Prince Saionji and the Political Situation (Saionji Kō to Seikyoku)*,
Vol. VII, pp. 364–5.

† Kurusu Saburō: *A Chronicle of Thirty-Five Evanescent Years (Hōmatsu no Sanjū-
gonen)*, p. 27.

If we were now to settle the [China] Incident by compromising with England and America and co-operating with the Anglo-Saxons, how would we be able to face the myriad spirits of our war dead? Ultimately it is for the sake of the myriad spirits of the war dead that we are so adamantly opposed to any compromise with America.*

Leaving behind the rationale of 'the people won't put up with it', Japan's leaders had now finally come to the point of saying: 'The spirits of the war dead won't put up with it.' Here the *bond with the past* reaches its apogee.[20]

At this stage, however, we are confronted with an apparent difficulty. In a previous essay I spoke of the 'transfer of oppression' as being one aspect of the psychology immanent in Japanese society.[21] This is the system in which people preserve the total spiritual balance by progressively transferring downwards the pressure that they incur in their daily life from those above them. How does this relate to the 'rule of the higher by the lower', which as we have seen is such a prominent feature in the structure of Japanese fascism? Are they incompatible? Far from it: the two principles, 'lower rules higher' and 'pressure transfer', are the opposite side of a single coin, the former being the pathological manifestation of the latter.

The principle known as 'rule of the higher by the lower' is, in effect, an irrational explosion of irresponsible, anonymous power, and can occur only in a society in which power from below is not officially recognized. It is, so to speak, an inverted form of democracy. In a true democracy, where those in power enjoy the self-confidence of having been officially and institutionally chosen from below by means of elections, leadership, far from being weak, assumes a most powerful form. On the contrary, a society that is governed exclusively by power from above always entails the danger of 'power dwarfing', when the rulers, instead of acting confidently and positively, edge forward with fear and trembling, guided by their subordinates and by other people who are theoretically subject to their rule. As a result such a society is ultimately propelled by the inclinations of outlaws or irresponsible agitators belonging to the lower strata.

* 'The American Problem and the Solution of the [China] Incident' (*Jihen Shori to Taibei Mondai*), in *Pan-Asianism* (*Dai Ajiya Shugi*), July 1941.

Where the pressure-transfer principle operates, the frustrations of those on the lowest rung of the hierarchy have no place to which they can be transferred, and so they are inevitably directed outwards. People in an undemocratic society are consequently liable to become the slaves of fanatic xenophobia, the frustrations of their daily lives being effectively sublimated into jingoism. The rulers of such countries are only too ready to encourage these tendencies in order to counter the backwash of dissatisfaction from below; yet in time of crisis they are themselves mastered by this irresponsible type of 'public opinion' and end by losing their autonomy of decision.* The 'lower rules higher' tendency in the armed forces and the rampages of the outlaws (which were closely related to this tendency) became intense from the time when the question of armament reductions[22] and the Manchurian problem began to colour the international scene, that is, from the moment when Japan entered a period of crisis; and there was nothing fortuitous about this timing.

In his study of *raison d'état* in modern history Meinecke pointed out certain important consequences resulting from the emergence of the masses and from the development of military technique, both of which were the fruit of the machine civilization.† One of these consequences was that politicians became unable to control the movement of the masses. A second consequence was that the military establishment, which in principle was a tool of politics, came to develop its own dynamic as a sort of satanic force. Meinecke went on to argue that 'national necessity' (*Staatsnotwendigkeit*), which had operated during the second half of the nineteenth century as a clearly defined concept, had been replaced by a nebulous 'people's necessity'

---

* On 3 November 1941, Mr. Grew sent the following report to the State Department: 'In Japan political thought ranges from medieval to liberal ideas and public opinion is thus a variable quantity. The impact of events and conditions beyond Japan may determine at any given time which school of thought shall predominate.' And he adds the comment: 'In the democracies, on the other hand, owing to a homogeneous body of principles which influence and direct foreign policy and because methods instead of principles are more likely to cause differences of opinion, public opinion is formed differently.' Grew, op. cit., p. 467. The Ambassador's report provides a simple explanation of why foreign policy in a democratic country is (contrary to what one might expect) comparatively settled and co-ordinated.

† F. Meinecke, *Die Idee der Staatsräson in der neueren Geschichte* (1924), pp. 527–9.

(*Volksnotwendigkeit*), and this he described as the 'crisis' of *raison d'état* (*Staatsräson*). Although Meinecke was thinking primarily of the example of Germany in the First World War, his conclusions would appear to have a general bearing. At any rate there can be nothing fortuitous about the remarkable resemblances between the state of Germany before 1914 and that of Japan during the 1930s. In both countries we find an irresponsible demand from the people for a tough foreign policy, and a sort of superpolitical auto-propulsion among the military. This is related to the facts that both these empires had an authoritarian hierarchical structure on the social as well as on the national level, and that in both cases political leadership was thoroughly dwarfed.

IV. THE DWARFISHNESS OF JAPANESE FASCISM (ii)

The second main line of argument that the defendants used to clear themselves of responsibility at the war crimes trials was that the charges against them referred to matters beyond the scope of their formal competence as government officials. The statements of the Defence were remarkably consistent on this point.

It is hardly surprising that out-and-out bureaucrats like Mr. Kaya and Mr. Hoshino should have been defended on the grounds that 'he was merely an administrative official' and 'all his life he has been nothing but a public servant'.* What is significant is that the same sort of vindication should have been used on behalf of men belonging to a completely different category. Thus General Ōshima's attorney stated: '. . . the acts complained of in regard to the accused Ōshima were committed in the lawful exercise of his function as the agent of a sovereign nation . . . He was simply in charge of transmissions and decoding signals via the foreign affairs organization.'†

Similarly Vice-Admiral Oka's attorney argued:

It is suggested that all the evidence introduced concerning [the defendant] shows that his position was at all times that of a secretary and of a liaison officer, and that he never did attain a position which would place him on a policy-making level. Messages conveyed by

* IMTFE, nos. 291 and 277, 13 Oct. and 23 Sept. 1947.
† IMTFE, no. 161.

him or prepared by him or his subordinates contained the decisions
of his superior officers; and there is no substantial evidence to indicate that he at any time influenced such decisions.*

And even General Mutō was defended on these grounds:

The evidence plainly shows that throughout the greater part of his
military career he has held subordinate positions, in the sense that
those above him were the ones to determine policies; and that his
duty, by every recognized concept of the military throughout the
world, was to carry out the orders of his superiors.†

These arguments were not the invention of the respective
defence attorneys, but reflected the thinking of the accused
themselves. The report of General Mutō's cross-examination
about the atrocities perpetrated by Japanese troops in Nanking
and Manila provides a good example. After the General had
explained that this shocking type of behaviour by Japanese
soldiers dated from the time of the Siberian Expedition, that
various plans for improving the quality of the soldiers had been
discussed by the Army officers, and that, since he (Mutō) had
for a long time served in the Inspectorate of Education, he was
deeply concerned with the true education of the forces, the
interrogation took the following course:

Q. In order to correct these various defects which you say you had
   noticed cropping up from time to time since the Siberian Expedition in 1918, what sort of reform did you subsequently make in the
   training and education of young men entering the Army?
A. When the Japanese Expeditionary Force went to Siberia I was
   a mere sub-lieutenant, so that even if I had known about these
   matters I could have done nothing about them.
Q. But when you became adjutant-general in charge of troop
   training and had all the power that this post involved, what steps
   did you take to correct the weaknesses that you had noticed ever
   since 1918?
A. There was nothing I could do even after I became a lieutenant-
   general, because I was not a divisional commander. To carry out
   anything one had to be a divisional commander.
Q. And when you became Director of the Military Affairs Bureau—
   what happened then?
A. The Director of the Military Affairs Bureau is merely a subordi-

* Ibid., no. 161, p. 16501, 28 Jan. 1947.
† Ibid., no. 161, p. 16488, 28 Jan. 1947.

nate of the War Minister. He does not have the authority to issue orders about such matters.

Q. Well, assuming that you were a divisional commander, or that you were in charge of education and indoctrination in a [military] school, would you have issued orders to correct the weak points that you had recognized since 1918?

A. Yes (the witness laughed).*

No doubt it was embarrassment that made Mutō laugh when answering the last question in the affirmative.

It was not only in their Tokyo offices that the defendants found themselves hemmed in by 'rules' and 'authority'; the same hesitations applied when they were in the field. The following exchange is between the Prosecuting Attorney, Brigadier Nolan, and General Matsui, and here again the subject of the cross-examination is the Rape of Nanking:

Q. You said something a moment ago about discipline and morals being the responsibility of a subordinate commander to yourself.

A. The responsibility of the divisional commander.

Q. You were the Commander-in-Chief of the Central China Area Army, were you not?

A. Yes.

Q. Are you suggesting to this Tribunal that that power of command did not carry with it the power to enforce discipline on the troops under your command?

A. As Commander-in-Chief of the Central China Area Army I was given the power to command operations of the two subordinate armies under my command, but I did not have the authority directly to handle the discipline and morals within these respective armies.

Q. No, but you had the power to see that discipline and morals were maintained in the units under your command?

A. It would be better to say, and more correct to say, obligation rather than authority—obligation or duty.

. . .

Q. And that is because there is an army commander in the units under your command, and you carry out disciplinary measures through your army commanders?

A. I myself did not have the authority to take disciplinary measures, or to hold court martial; such authority resided in the commander of the army or the divisional commander.

* IMTFE, no. 159, 24 Jan. 1947.

Q. But you could order a court martial to be held either in the army or in the division?

A. I had no legal right to issue such an order.

Q. Well then, how do you explain your efforts to show that you ordered severe punishment meted out to the guilty for the outrages in Nanking, and that you did everything in your power as Commander of the Central China Area Army to give severe punishment to the guilty?

A. I had no authority except to express my desires as over-all Commander-in-Chief to the commander of the army under my command and the divisional commanders thereunder.

Q. And I suppose a general officer commanding expresses his desires to those subordinate to him in the form of orders?

A. No, that would be difficult in the light of the law.*

A careful reading of these questions and answers might well give one the impression that in General Matsui's fatherland a more modern rule of law applied than in the country to which the prosecutor belonged. The officer in supreme command of the Japanese forces in the field—forces whose *ultima ratio* was the Imperial mandate, 'Obey the orders of your superior officers as though they were Our orders'—is here revealed as having been in mortal fear of committing the slightest violation of the rules and regulations; in fact General Matsui becomes a timid petty bureaucrat who, when dealing with matters beyond his direct competence, does not, even with his subordinates, dare go any further than to express a 'desire'.

This common stand of the defendants can certainly not be dismissed as a ruse thought up on the spur of the moment to wriggle out of responsibility. Most of the men in the dock had actually been officials in the Imperial Government and, however politically they may have behaved, the 'bureaucratic spirit' (Max Weber's *Beamtengeist*) invariably lurked in the back of their minds. Accordingly, when things went badly, they could always represent themselves as having been 'specialist officials' (*Fachbeamte*), who could function only within the professional limits strictly laid down by the rules and regulations.

In applying this device, the defendants made full use of certain aspects of the Meiji Constitution, notably: the distinction between the prerogative of supreme command and the preroga-

* IMTFE, no. 320, p. 33873, 24 Nov. 1947.

tive of administration; the provision according to which each respective Minister of State 'advises' the Emperor;[23] and the overlapping system of Ministers of State and Departmental Ministers. The crucial role of the Military and Naval Affairs Bureaux is now well known to students of Japanese politics. These Bureaux brought the supreme command (administration) into direct contact with the affairs of State (politics), thus providing an ideal medium by which the military could meddle in political matters. In this sense General Mutō's definition of the functions of the Military Affairs Bureau is highly suggestive:

... the War Minister must carry out the matters decided upon by the Cabinet. For this purpose it is necessary to have a political affairs machinery. The Military Affairs Bureau is precisely the machinery that deals with these political affairs. The function of the Military Affairs Bureau consists in carrying on such political affairs and not in politics itself.*

This was Mutō's justification for his blatant political activity as Director of the Military Affairs Bureau. Since his work was *political* administration, he could meddle in politics; since it was political *administration*, he was free from political responsibility.

It is natural that there should have been a good deal of overlapping in jurisdiction between the system of military administration (War Minister — Vice-Minister — Military Affairs Bureau) and that of the high command (Chief of General Staff —Vice-Chief—Staff Headquarters), and the defendants in the Tokyo trials frequently exploited this in order to foist responsibility on to each other.† In particular, when the War and Navy Ministers were questioned about their responsibility for drawing up defence plans and for extending operations in the field, they invariably adduced the fact that they were unable to interfere with the prerogative of supreme command. Representatives of the General Staff, on the other hand, explained their position as follows:

Plans of operation are [normally] drawn up on the basis of national policy. But things have now come to the point that the War Ministry had taken over all defence policy. Not only that, but everything related to national defence had come under the War Ministry. The

---

* IMTFE, no. 313, p. 33122, 13 Nov. 1947.
† E.g. responsibility for the rules governing the treatment of P.O.W.s.

Chief of General Staff was in charge of defence tactics ... Both in theory and in practice it is impossible to formulate tactical plans independently from national policy and questions of national defence.*

And so the locus of responsibility remained as nebulous as ever.† A further factor that made it difficult to assign responsibility to specific individuals was the old Cabinet system established under the Meiji Constitution. This system did a great deal to encourage the diversity of political power and thus to weaken Japan's wartime potential; there were various efforts to overcome this handicap by rationalizing the system, but they proved abortive. This point has already been clarified by Professor Tsuji, and requires no further analysis here.‡ The war crimes trials, however, produced some interesting evidence about how the organization of a type of inner Cabinet to integrate political power failed in the end to change the 'spirit' of the Ministers of State. Mr. Tavenner summarized the claims advanced by various defendants regarding this point:

> The members of the potent Four Ministers' and Five Ministers' Conference, like Hirota, Hiranuma, Itagaki and Kaya, assert that they were powerless without the acquiescence or approval of the other members of the Cabinet, and that nothing they did was of any importance unless approved by those other members. On the other hand, the Cabinet members who were not members of the conferences,

---

* IMTFE, no. 159, 24 Jan. 1947.

† The Harada Diary provides a good example of how the differentiation between Ministers of State and Administrative Ministers was used to evade responsibility. Baron Harada is here discussing the attitude of the War Minister, General Itagaki, at the time of the Five Ministers' Conference in August 1939:

> 'In the final analysis the Army's contention was that the situation had changed in such a way as to make an offensive-defensive alliance with Germany essential. However, they said that as a first step we should continue with the established policy and that when this became impossible we should go ahead with the second stage, that is, we should conclude the alliance. When the Prime Minister [Baron Hiranuma] asked the War Minister: "What is your real opinion about this?" Itagaki replied: "In one capacity I am a Minister of State, in another I am War Minister. As Minister of State I of course agree that we should pursue the established policy, but in so far as I represent the consensus of the Army I also think that we must go ahead with the second stage." ' *Prince Saionji and the Political Situation*, Vol. VIII, pp. 42–43.

‡ Tsuji Kiyoaki, 'The Difficulties Experienced by Organs of Government in Maintaining Their Spheres of Influence' (*Kakkyo ni Nayamu Tōji Kikō*), *Chōryū*, May 1949; included in *A Study of the Japanese Bureaucratic System* (*Nihon Kanryōsei no Kenkyū*).

like Araki and Kido, contend that they are not liable because these matters were not reported to them for action or if they were reported, that they accepted them solely on the expert advice of the members of the conferences. Thus, *within the cabinet itself we have no one who has responsibility for some of the most important actions taken during the course of execution of the common plan.**

In short, no amount of 'bureaucratic spirit' will produce anything that can properly be called political integration. Instead mountains of documents and circulars pile up, laws and ordinances follow each other in bewildering confusion, and new governmental organizations are for ever being set up.

Very interesting in this connexion is the dispute that occurred in Court about the establishment of a Total War Research Institute. This body came into being as a result of the regulations for government organizations contained in Imperial Ordinance No. 648. It was inaugurated with a great fanfare in 1940, its highfalutin objectives being set forth in the following statement: 'The Institute shall be under the administration of the Prime Minister and shall be responsible for basic research and study in regard to total war and for the education and training of officials and others for total war.'† Students were chosen from the War College, from each of the Ministries, and from business circles. Research at the Institute was predicated on the hypothesis of war with the United States, and various planning assignments were given to groups of students. These ranged from pure military strategy to total mobilization, including politics, economics, education, and culture. Quite understandably the Prosecution regarded this Institute as important. But what was the true state of affairs? According to one of the witnesses, a Mr. Horiba, who was a student at the Institute,

Although the governmental official regulations governing the Institute mentioned the Prime Minister as head of the Institute and therefore it was within the jurisdiction of the Prime Minister, the Prime Minister himself, if he attended the Institute at all, attended it only at the time of the opening of the school and the graduation or commencement exercise and he gave no personal direction or guidance of any kind to the Institute. I was associated with the Institute for one year and during that time hoped very much that

* IMTFE, no. 416, pp. 48370–1, 16 Apr. 1948.
† Ibid., no. 100, p. 8198, 29 Oct. 1946.

the Prime Minister would show a little more conscientious interest in the Institute itself but, generally speaking, it was more or less left alone, left to itself. That is a fact. When the Institute itself was opened up it did not know what to do and therefore members who were assigned to the Institute from various departments just got together and started to do something in order to create some appearance that it was doing something . . . Students gathered together and there was a question about what to teach these students and for that reason much of the effort that was supposed to have gone into study and research was neglected for this . . . and during this time there were no orders, no direction, no advice from the government.*

The witness may have been exaggerating things slightly, but for us Japanese, who know what the term 'office work' can involve in our country, it is only too easy to picture what the realities must have been. The Prosecuting Counsel, Mr. Lambert, tried to rebut Mr. Horiba by saying:

Are we really expected to believe that in September 1940 Japan wasted time and effort on a mere academic debating society? . . . Can it seriously be suggested that at a time like this such an important person would have been summoned to Tokyo for inessential work that had no possible practical aim, just in order to waste his time?†

The Prosecutor's doubts are eminently reasonable; yet the fact is that in the world of wartime Japan illogicalities could flourish that cannot possibly be understood by the yardstick used in a democracy.

Charged with war responsibility owing to the fact that Hoshino, Suzuki, and others were all 'counsellors' in the Institute, Mr. Horiba made another significant observation. The following quotation is from the conclusion of his cross-examination by the Defence Attorney, Mr. Kiyose:

KIYOSE. Mr. Witness, you have been a government official for twenty-five years. Do you know whether in our country councillors and advisers, so to speak, have always been just nominal existences?

HORIBA. Although there are exceptions, generally speaking it is my way of thinking that councillors and advisers have been in most

* IMTFE, no. 100, pp. 8836–7, 29 Oct. 1946.
† Ibid., no. 379, 24 Feb. 1948. The 'important person' was Lieutenant-General Iimura, the Chief of Staff of the Kwangtung Army, who was transferred to the Institute as Director.

cases merely figureheads or decorations, or nominal existences, which gave some form to an organization.*

The general question of responsibility is further complicated by the tendency, noticed in an earlier essay,[24] according to which each unit finds refuge in the limits of its authority; since every such attempt involves an effort by the respective unit to link itself vertically with the prestige of the Emperor, the various units (with their limited authority) are transformed into something absolute and their relations with each other become infinitely complex. In such a system a public servant does not have any consistent standpoint or ideology; nor in his capacity as a specialized official is he permitted to have one. Mr. Sakomizu Hisatsune once made the sage observation: 'A public servant must be a deliberate opportunist. Even if he should seem to have a certain ideology, this must be related, not to his personality, but to his "position".'

A good illustration is provided by the opposition between the two factions in the Navy, the Navy Ministry Faction and the Navy Command (Chief-of-Staff) Faction. Their clash at the time of the London Naval Conference provided the spark that set off the rise of military fascism in Japan. Yet what did their opposition really involve? Mr. Mizuno Hironori strikes at the heart of the matter:

> In both factions the important thing was not the men themselves but the seats they happened to occupy. If the roles had been reversed so that Admiral Suetsugu was Vice-Minister of the Navy and Admiral Yamanashi Vice-Chief of Naval Staff, it might well have been the former who would have been accused of selling out his country.†

The same thing applied in varying degree to all the so-called ideological confrontations within the military bureaucracy. This does not mean that there was anything moderate about these internal struggles. Far from it: in proportion as slogans like 'a hundred million hearts beating like one' and 'the whole Empire working together in harmony' became more clamorous, so behind the scenes the horizontal splits among Japan's wartime leaders became even more intense. And, inasmuch as they

---

* IMTFE, no. 100, p. 8863, 29 Oct. 1946.

† 'Kobayashi Seizō, the New Governor-General of Formosa' (*Shin Taiwan Sōtoku Kobayashi Seizō*), *Chūō Kōron*, 1936, no. 10.

arose from a bureaucratic mentality, these splits were for ever being atomized. Thus we find a series of confrontations on progressively lower levels: among the leaders, civilian versus military officials; among the military, Army versus Navy; within the Army, War Ministry versus General Staff; within the War Ministry, Military Affairs Bureau versus Military Service Bureau; and so forth. In the same category is the notorious hostility between officials in the Cabinet Planning Board, the Manchoukuo Government, and the Home Ministry.

What was the role of the Emperor in this situation? Theoretically he was in a position to bring about the ultimate integration of the pluralized political power in his country; yet throughout this period he firmly adhered to the 'competency' of a constitutional monarch—to such an extent, indeed, that Japan's constitutional system, spurious though it was, gave the impression of having attained a very advanced stage indeed. Until our country reached the bitter end of surrender there was scarcely a single occasion on which the Emperor handed down a decision that really emanated from himself.[25]

Thus up to the very day of its destruction the Japanese Empire was constantly prey to clandestine strife. The weak character of the Emperor himself was undoubtedly one of the reasons; a further factor was the counsel of the Senior Retainers close to the Emperor, who had chosen war abroad in preference to class struggle at home, and who were then less afraid of losing that war than of risking revolution.*

* In his post-war memoirs Admiral Okada writes as follows when discussing the headlong course towards war that Japan followed since the February Incident:

'We so-called Senior Retainers have ample reason to be ashamed of the fact that it was impossible to check this [course]. Yet it was no such easy task . . . To check [the course] inevitably implied the use of force and this meant civil war. If it came to civil war, cracks were bound to develop in the foundations of the country or at least in the basis on which Japan had been built up since the Restoration. This was the point that most concerned me and probably everyone else who was in a position of authority at the time . . . And, even though Japan had to experience military defeat, what a blessing it was that at least the country was not split in two and that we are able to share our misfortunes and hardships as members of the same single Japanese nation! When I consider this, I feel what a good thing it is that the situation did not develop into a civil war—and that we never let it develop in that way.' 'February 26: The Day' (*Niniroku no sono Hi*), *Chūō Kōron*, February 1949.

The ideology of the Senior Retainer group would be well worth analysing. It is not, however, the aim of this essay to examine the ideologies of specific groups; I am concerned with the patterns of thinking of the ruling class as a whole.

But the pluralism and irresponsibility of power in wartime Japan has a deep cause. It obeys a law of dynamics common to absolute monarchies everywhere, especially when they have reached their stage of decadence. Max Weber's explanation of the political function of the bureaucracy is most apposite:

A special discovery of the bureaucracy is the concept of professional secrecy, and there is nothing that it guards so jealously. Particularly when the bureaucracy is functioning outside its prescribed limits, the motive that makes it adhere to this concept does not derive from merely functional considerations. In confronting parliament, the bureaucracy fights with a true power instinct, opposing all plans whereby the latter tries in its characteristic way to obtain specialized knowledge from the relevant quarters (e.g. by its right of investigation). It is natural therefore that a parliament becomes more desirable from the bureaucracy's point of view as it ceases to be conversant with conditions and accordingly loses power. Even an absolute monarch—or, in a sense, *especially* an absolute monarch—is impotent in face of the superior specialized knowledge of the bureaucracy . . . A constitutional monarch, inasmuch as he may hold the same opinions as a socially important group of his subjects . . . can often exert more influence on the executive than can an absolute monarch who relies exclusively on the bureaucracy for his information. It was virtually impossible for the Tsar of Russia to carry out any plan consistently if it involved matters about which his officials disagreed or in which their power interests clashed. The ministers who were directly under this absolute ruler . . . were engaged in a secret struggle among themselves; each one had his own private plan, whose ramifications extended into every sphere. In attacking each other they made particular use of 'memorials to the Throne', which were presented to the Tsar in endless succession. The Tsar himself, being a dilettante, was incapable of dealing with the situation.*

This phenomenon is certainly not peculiar to Tsarist Russia. In any system where political integration is dependent on a monarchy we normally find the same type of irresponsible control being exercised by officials directly under the sovereign and, in consequence, the same fragmentation of government.

There are only two (or, at the most, three) exceptions to the rule. One is the case in which the monarch himself is a great personality with a truly charismatic nature (or in which an

* Max Weber, *Wirtschaft und Gesellschaft*, Chap. VI, p. 672.

official directly under the sovereign has such a personality and is therefore no longer a mere official). The other is a country in which parliament has the same substantial power that it enjoys in a democratic republic. The former situation is of course extremely rare. The latter is dependent on very special historical conditions such as obtained, for example, in England; for normally the aristocratic circles centred on the monarch are prompted by their instinctive power interests to check the rise of any democratic legislative body.

Consequently there is a tendency inherent in almost any modern monarchic system for irresponsible anonymous forces to be given free rein. The situation in the German Reich following the period when Bismarck ruled with Kaiser Wilhelm was essentially similar to that in Tsarist Russia:

> Bismarck was the great master of foreign policy, but what was his legacy so far as domestic affairs were concerned? He left a people with no political training and no political purpose, a people wholly dependent on some strong politician who would look after everything for them. He destroyed all the powerful political parties. He allowed no one to possess any independent political qualities. On the debit side of the ledger the result of Bismarck's impressive authority was a fearfully unimpressive, craven, impotent parliament. And what was the consequence of this? It was precisely the situation in which the bureaucracy took over all control.*

Japan's development as an absolutist state was ultimately determined by these same laws. When the leaders of the Meiji clan clique, using every means in their power to suppress the movement for democratic rights, set about constructing an absolutist régime (discreetly covering it with a figleaf of a constitution patterned after that of Prussia), they were in fact laying the foundations for the country's bankruptcy. The various symptoms of political disintegration (e.g. the control of the State by 'their Excellencies the Imperial officials' and the internal corruption of this officialdom, the clandestine struggle between civilian and military officials, the collapse of cabinets owing to the manoeuvres of the military) were certainly not phenomena that made a sudden first appearance in the Shōwa Period.

Political methods that became commonplace for the military

* Marianne Weber, *Max Weber—Ein Lebensbild* (1926), p. 596.

in later years were clearly foreshadowed by developments in the Meiji Period. The refusal of General Ōyama, Admiral Nire, General Kawakami, and the other military leaders to associate themselves with the Matsukata Cabinet at the time of its reorganization in 1892,[26] and the direct appeal to the Throne by the War Minister, General Uehara,[27] when the question of adding two divisions to the Army was being debated in 1912, are only two of the many excellent models on which the military could base their behaviour in subsequent decades.

The Imperial Diet, for its part, could never become the *locus* where consistent political integration might ultimately be carried out. Far from it: since the time when the Diet was first established, Japanese political parties lacked the fighting spirit and true strength that made it necessary for Bismarck to destroy their counterparts in Germany with his iron fist. Modern Japan was thus burdened with its 'original sin': the pluralism of political power.

If these conditions were inherent in Japan's structure, why, it may be asked, did the political bankruptcy of the country not emerge in critical form until relatively recently, and how is it that the Meiji era witnessed a degree of political leadership and unity that could not be matched in the later period? The clue lies in the charisma possessed by Emperor Meiji himself and in two factors that helped to reinforce this charisma: namely, the special type of fusion existing between the clan officials, and the fact that these officials were relatively well developed as politicians.

We read with amusement about how Itō Hirobumi assumed the airs of Prince Bismarck. But the important thing is that he and most of the other clan leaders had undergone the experience of establishing their power with their own strength while the waves of revolution lapped about them. Before being officials they were politicians. Though on the whole they were far from fitting into any democratic category, they did possess their own sense of responsibility and self-confidence as oligarchs. The well-known remark that Admiral Kabayama let slip in the Second Imperial Diet was an outburst of precisely such confidence: 'Is it not thanks to the strength of Satsuma and Chōshū that our country has attained its present strength?'[28]

Later the pride was lost and power took the road that led to its dwarfing. Ex-politician bureaucrats presently became ex-bureaucrat politicians, until finally there was a deluge of bureaucrats-cum-officials, who were not really politicians at all. The autocratic sense of responsibility receded; and no democratic sense of responsibility arose to take its place. During the war Ozaki Yukio was charged with the crime of *lèse-majesté* for having used the expression, 'third generation',[29] in reference to the sovereign. Yet it was not only Emperor Shōwa who was third generation. During the period of crisis the Janus-headed Emperor, with his two faces of absolute monarch and constitutional monarch, was constantly being dwarfed and at the very same time being made into a divinity; and the psychology of the officials below him grew more and more into that of timid vassals.

There is the following story in Aesop's Fables. An elderly man with grizzled hair has two sweethearts, one older than he and the other younger. The younger woman dislikes having an old lover and each time that she visits him she pulls out some of his white hairs. The older woman, on the other hand, wants to hide the fact that she has a lover who is younger than herself, and so she pulls out his black hair. As a result the man ends by being completely bald. Thus the Senior Retainers and Japan's other 'liberal' leaders were afraid that the Emperor or they themselves would be saddled with political responsibility and accordingly they did their best to remove the absolute aspect from the monarchy; on the other hand, the military and the rightists, wishing to 'protect' the prestige of the Emperor and thus to have things their own way, brandished the theory of divine right. In consequence the Emperor not only lost his charisma as an absolute monarch but was steadily divested of the role of constitutional monarch who is close to the people. It was none other than His Majesty's loyal retainers who made the Emperor system bald.

V. CONCLUSION

In this essay I have tried to give a rough sketch of the massive 'system of irresponsibilities' that constituted Japan's fascist rule. Three basic types of political personality can be abstracted from this sketch: the Portable Shrine, the Official, and the Outlaw (or *rōnin*). The Shrine represents authority; the Official, power; the Outlaw, violence. From the point of view of their position in the national hierarchy and of their legal power, the Shrine ranks highest and the Outlaw lowest. The system, however, is so constituted that movement starts from the Outlaw and gradually works upwards. The Shrine is often a mere robot who affects other people by 'doing nothing' (*wu wei*).

The force that 'holds aloft' the Shrine and that wields the real power is the Official (civilian or military). His rule over the powerless people is based on the legitimacy that descends from the Shrine. He in his turn is being prodded from behind by the Outlaw. Yet even the Outlaw does not seriously entertain any particular 'will to power'. He is quite content if he can storm about irresponsibly at the bottom of the hierarchy, uttering great yells of delight and dumbfounding the rest of the community. Accordingly his political fervour can readily merge into the hedonism of the assignation house.

These three types do not, of course, represent fixed categories. Frequently two or three of them will be blended in a single individual. If an Outlaw gets ahead in the world, he may develop into a petty bureaucrat and become more 'moderate'; if he advances still further, he may even in the end find himself being carried on people's shoulders as a Shrine.

The entire hierarchy displays a pattern of mutual relationships of the Aristotelian form-matter kind. The same man may behave as an Outlaw to those above him, but regard those below with the eyes of an Official. Another man may be held aloft as a Shrine by the lower elements, while he serves those above as a loyal, circumspect Official. The important thing is that the formal hierarchy of value is extremely rigid: unless the Outlaw can transform himself so that he becomes like an Official or a Shrine, he has no hope of attaining high rank. Here is one of the great contrasts with the situation in the land of the swastika, in which Outlaws seized power *qua* Outlaws.*

And all this is no fairy tale that happened somewhere once upon a time.

---

* Note, for instance, the peculiar relations between Prince Konoe and Mr. Inoue Nisshō, or again those that connected Marquis Kido to men like Mr. Hashimoto Tetsuma of the Purple Cloud Pavilion and Mr. Matsui Kūka. When Mr. Takuya Dempu of the Politics and Learning Society, who went in for black-mailing Senior Retainers, was arrested in connexion with a certain major incident[30] in the Palace, Marquis Kido wrote in his diary that he felt as if 'a grain of rice

sticking to the sole of my foot' had been removed (3 March 1933). This neatly illustrates what members of the ruling class felt about the lower-ranking Outlaws and suggests the relationship between them.

The three types of political personality and their structural relationship serve to formulate not only the fascist period but the entire political world of Imperial Japan. If we examine the internal structure of the established political parties, for example, we find that the president of the party is the Shrine, the chairman and the secretary-general hold actual power as Officials, and the pressure groups contain the Outlaws. In the total political structure members of the rightist organizations occupy the position of Outlaws; but within each organization we again find the tripartite hierarchy, a man like Mr. Tōyama Mitsuru (to take an obvious example) being a Shrine. The existing parties were limited to these three types and were unable to create any political image or *persona* apart from them. This is further evidence of how divorced they were from democracy. A man like Mr. Mori Kaku can be regarded as belonging to two types: his role in the party was that of supreme Official; but so far as political function and behaviour were concerned he was closer to an Outlaw. His Outlaw mentality clearly emerges in a statement that he made just before his death: 'It has been the great satisfaction of my life that I have been able to contribute to dividing the world into two' (*Mori Kaku*, p. 846).

The Outlaws are at the same time rebels against established society and parasites on that society. Their attitudes to life and their modes of behaviour vary in accordance with environmental and cultural differences—not only national differences but those that exist within a single country between urban and rural backgrounds, or again between upper-class and lower-class provenance. Nevertheless the Outlaws have certain striking features in common that supersede these differences. It is hard to put one's finger on the forms of mental approach that the Outlaws share, but the following are the general characteristics: (i) both lack of will and ability to engage continuously in any given occupation, in other words, a striking inability to stand the routine of normal civic life; (ii) a concern with human relationships rather than with things (*Sache*); for this reason Outlaws are in principle not suited to being specialists, except in the sense that Laswell means when he refers to 'special lists in violence'; (iii) conversely they are in the habit of undertaking exceptional adventures and 'work' of a sensational nature; (iv) moreover they are interested and excited not so much by the aims and meaning of this 'work' as by the actual storm and struggle involved in carrying it out; (v) they do not distinguish between private and public life; in particular they lack any general or functional sense of responsibility; in its place they have a highly-developed specific or private feeling about human obligations; (vi) they are uninterested in making a fixed income by regular work and tend to look down on such a life; as a corollary they are in the habit of supporting themselves by irregular income from outside sources; (vii) morals and modes of thinking appropriate to emergency conditions and crisis become their standard for judging everyday matters; hence their predilection for drawing a sharp line of distinction between good and evil, right and wrong, and for expressing themselves in extreme language with phrases like 'let us deal the finishing stroke'; (viii) a debauched sexual life.

It need hardly be pointed out that in practice there are endless nuances, both in proportion and in degree, in the combination of these elements, so that where real people are concerned any absolute judgement is impossible. All that we can do is to point out that a certain specific case involves a greater or smaller quantity of Outlaw elements. Nevertheless an abstraction of this sort can be effective when it comes to applying the general dynamics of fascism to particular political conditions in a particular country. In examining the composition of communist parties, for example, we find that the greater the proportion of members who are

Lumpenproletariat or defected elements from various social strata and the smaller that of organized workers and specialized intelligentsia, the Outlaw element grows more important and it becomes harder to distinguish between communists and fascists in so far as actual forms of political behaviour are concerned.

TRANSLATOR'S NOTES

1. 'Wartime' in this essay refers not simply to the Pacific War but to Japan's entire militarist period from 1931 to 1945.
2. Konoe Fumimaro, *Ushinawareshi Seiji* (*The Politics That Failed*), p. 131.
3. Quotations from the proceedings of the International Military Tribunal for the Far East (IMTFE) are in almost every case taken from the English text, not from the Japanese translation of the record which was used by Professor Maruyama. Italics, however, are Maruyama's. Wherever possible both the English and the Japanese versions of the IMTFE transcript have been checked and occasional alterations have been made when the English translation seemed inaccurate. Numbers refer to the Japanese record, pages to the English version of the proceedings (they run from p. 1 to p. 49849), dates to the days of the hearings. Thus IMTFE, no. 416, pp. 48410–12, 16 Apr. 1948, means: 'No. 416 of the Japanese record of the International Military Tribunal for the Far East, pp. 48410–12 of the English record, hearing held on 16 April 1948.' The best detailed index of the voluminous proceedings is *Kyokutō Kokusai Gunji Saiban Kiroku—Mokuroku oyobi Sakuin*, prepared by the Asahi Shimbun Research Office (Asahi Shimbun Chōsa Kenkyū-shitsu), 25 March 1953. Another useful reference work is *The Tokyo Trials: A Functional Index to the Proceedings of the International Military Tribunal for the Far East*, by Paul Dull and Michael Umemura (Ann Arbor, Center for Japanese Studies, Occasional Papers No. 6, 1957).
4. 'During my stay in Japan and from my many social and business contacts with various military men, I noticed a decided lack of co-operation even between the Japanese Army and Navy. They were constantly suspicious and jealous of each other and I personally tried to smooth matters over as best I could . . .'
5. Quoted from William Shirer, *The Rise and Fall of the Third Reich*, p. 532.
6. Shirer, op. cit., pp. 937–8.

7. After a period of mounting tension between Japanese and Chinese forces in Shanghai, the Japanese government decided on 15 August 1937 to dispatch two divisions under the command of General Matsui to 'chastise the lawless Chinese troops and to impress upon the Nationalist Government the necessity for reconsidering its attitude towards Japan'.

8. Joseph Grew, *Ten Years in Japan* (New York, 1942), p. 84.

9. Ibid., p. 146.

10. The following exchange provides an interesting view of Prince Konoe's character:

MR. KEENAN. You have described him in your affidavit, and I am using your language, as a weak man. Is that not correct?

MARQUIS KIDO. One of his defects was the weakness of his character.

Q. He was weak in character and he was not robust physically, was he?

A. He was not sick or ailing, but he wasn't especially a robust man.

Q. Did he not complain of illness constantly while he was Prime Minister the first time?

A. Not constantly, but he often caught colds and stayed at home.

Q. And he constantly threatened to resign during his first premiership, did he not?

A. Yes, when any difficult question arose he frequently said: 'I want to give up.'

Q. How many times would you estimate, roughly, during his first premiership that he threatened to resign that you know of?

A. I think about four times, including the time when he actually resigned.

Q. That is, during his first premiership?

A. Yes.

Q. When did you first discover that Prince Konoe had a weak character?

A. Well, I knew this tendency or nature in him from the time we were children.

IMTFE, no. 298, pp. 31552–3, 22 Oct. 1947.

11. 6 Sept. 1941: ref. notes p. 88 above.

12. In his *Memoirs* (II, 1095–6) Mr. Hull describes the Japanese Ambassadors as 'cowering' when he said (concerning the final Japanese note) that in all his fifty years of public service he had 'never seen a document that was more crowded with infamous falsehoods and distortions'.

13. In June 1940 the Army had decided that the Yonai Cabinet must be replaced by one under Prince Konoe, who would take a more positive attitude on concluding a pact with the Axis powers and bringing about a 'new political structure' at home. To accomplish this aim the Army resorted to its old device of obliging the War Minister (General Hata) to resign and refusing to appoint a successor. Hata resigned on 16 July (reluctantly, according to IMTFE testimony) and the Yonai Cabinet duly collapsed.

14. For 'power-dwarfing' see 'Theory and Psychology of Ultra-Nationalism'), p. 11. About denial of war responsibility, see ibid., pp. 16 ff.

15. *Kotodama no sakiwau kuni*, a traditional epithet of Japan.

16. See note 14 above.

17. Grew, op. cit., p. 322.

18. See p. 92 above.

19. See Glossary: *Secretary*.

20. 'Theory and Psychology of Ultra-Nationalism', pp. 20 ff.

21. Ibid., pp. 17–19 ff.

22. I.e. the London Naval Conference, 1930.

23. According to the Meiji Constitution, 'the respective Ministers of State shall give their advice to the Emperor, and be responsible for it' (Art. LV). Ministers of State were to proffer advice (*hohitsu*) on affairs of state; the Imperial Household Minister and the Minister of the Interior advised on palace matters; and the Chiefs of General Staff on the supreme command.

24. 'Theory and Psychology of Ultra-Nationalism', pp. 15–16 *et passim*.

25. But note the views given in Butow's *Japan's Decision to Surrender* (Chap. 9) about the personal role that the Emperor may have played in making the final decision possible.

26. Following the scandalous election of February 1892 the Prime Minister, Viscount Matsukata, forced the resignation of the Home Minister, Mr. Shinagawa, who had been largely responsible for the strong-arm police methods used to obtain a majority for the government. Shinagawa was supported by the military and they showed their annoyance at his removal by refusing to serve in the reconstituted Cabinet; this method, which became commonplace in later years, soon brought about the fall of the government.

27. In 1912 the Army leaders took advantage of the death of General Ishimoto, the War Minister, to press their demands for two new divisions, which were opposed by the Prime Minister, Prince Saionji. General Uehara, Ishimoto's successor, demanded that

the Cabinet agree to the military increase and when they refused he presented his resignation directly to the Emperor. The Army prevented any other qualified General from accepting the post of War Minister and Saionji was obliged to resign.

28. See Glossary: *Clan clique.*
29. See Glossary: *Third generation.*
30. This incident (*Tōgū Hisakuritsu Mondai*) concerned the selection of a wife for the Crown Prince (the present Emperor Hirohito). When the name of the proposed princess was announced in 1919, it turned out that there was a hereditary strain of colour-blindness in her family. The strongly conservative elements in the country, headed by General Yamagata, demanded that the plans be cancelled, since such a marriage might, he averred, lead to a pollution of the Imperial stock. Many rightist personalities were active during the controversy. The pro-marriage group won, however, and the wedding took place in 1924, thus providing a major setback for the Yamagata faction. For details of this curious incident see Itoko Koyama, *Nagako, Empress of Japan* (New York, 1958).

IV. Nationalism in Japan: Its Theoretical Background and Prospects

TRANSLATED BY DAVID TITUS

This essay was originally published in the magazine Chūō Kōron, *1951*

I

Nationalism in Japan has evolved along unique lines; consequently any study of Japanese nationalism involves difficulties of a special nature. To explain the singularity of its evolution we are obliged in the last analysis to focus on the unique pattern of Japan's evolution as a modern state.

Neither practising politicians nor political scientists have yet clearly seen the pattern and direction of Japan's modern social and political development, a fact that suggests how difficult it is to assign Japan a place in world history. It may be argued that the range of ideological conflict in Japan is so great that no clear understanding on this point is possible; but this is to beg the question. The truth of the matter is that each of the groups engaged in the conflict is itself lacking in ideological coherence. Even within the Communist Party, whose strategy and tactics supposedly rest on precise universal principles, we can detect serious differences of opinion on the most fundamental problems, ranging from the historical laws governing the imperial system and imperialism to class relations in rural districts. The most striking feature of the perennial disputes within the Japanese Communist Party after the Cominform criticism of 1950[1] is the disclosure that the Party itself, which pretends to have a complete understanding of the nature of the coming revolution, lacks a unified view on the subject.

Such disunity reveals a serious problem, and one that is not at all peculiar to the Communist Party. The ideological diversity throughout Japan is a result of the confusion that still surrounds the country's position in world history. Ultimately, the complexity of Japanese nationalism originates in this confusion.

The difficulty we confront in trying to understand Japanese nationalism can be attributed to two related factors: its structural content and its pattern of fluctuation.

Structural content is one source of complexity in that Japan's particular social organization, political structure, and cultural patterns have been the primary determinants of Japanese nationalism. This means, on the one hand, that Japanese nationalism has features in common with nationalism throughout Asia in the sense of being distinct from the classical European model. At the same time, however, it has elements sharply different from nationalism as it appears in China, India, and South-East Asia; in this respect Japanese nationalism might rather be regarded as a modification of the European form.

The question of its fluctuation adds yet another complexity. Japanese nationalism reaches a peak on 15 August 1945.[2] This climax separates two periods in its history so different in background and sphere of operation that it is exceedingly difficult to see its evolution as being a single or continuous development.

From these two considerations a delicate relationship can be foreseen between the future character of Japanese nationalism and nationalism in other countries of the Far East. It is no exaggeration to say that Asian nationalism has been a focal point of world attention ever since the Korean War. In China, in India, in South-East Asia, nationalist movements have emerged as great revolutionary forces. Not only are the urgent issues of war and peace at stake in these countries. No matter which course these nations take, war or peace, it is probable that during the next fifty years world politics will revolve about the axis of emergent Asian nationalism. It is here that the future nature and course of Japanese nationalism will have a great bearing on world affairs.

August 15 1945 marks the beginning of a new state of affairs in Japan. After this date Japanese nationalism confronted a task very similar to that of nationalism in other areas of the Far East that were former colonies or semi-colonies. Superficially at least the 'independence of the Japanese nation' has become a slogan common to all political parties, from the Liberal to the Communist, demonstrating that Japan's position in the world is instinctively grasped by a people who have attained a measure of political consciousness.

But why do the Japanese, to say nothing of other people, hesitate to discuss Japan's future nationalism as part and parcel of the problem of nationalism throughout the Far East? The answer becomes obvious when we examine the relationship between Japanese and Asian nationalism. Prior to 15 August Japan experienced the highest phase of nationalism, labelled 'ultra'-nationalism, and its crushing denouement. Among the nations of the East, Japan is the only one to have lost her virginity so far as nationalism is concerned. In contrast to other Far Eastern areas, where nationalism brims with youthful energy and is charged with adolescent exuberance, Japan alone has completed one full cycle of nationalism: birth, maturity, decline.

There can be no complete break in history. Japan's future nationalism, whether it emerges as a reaction against the past, as a compromise with its heritage, or as a revival of the pre-war form, cannot escape being branded by its own past. Depending on which of these forms it assumes, world conditions, or at the very least the situation in the Far East, will also markedly alter the features of the new nationalism. On the one hand, then, there are the known factors of ultra-nationalism; on the other, the unknown elements that will identify the new nationalism with future nationalism in Asia. Since various combinations of these elements are possible, it is very hard to provide any clear forecast of Japanese nationalism at this stage.

Therefore, I should like to limit the problem of nationalism in Japan to certain aspects of its psychological structure that I consider important in tracing the connexions between pre-war and post-war nationalism. This essay is only a rough outline in which the steps that Japanese nationalism has taken since the Meiji Restoration of 1868 will be treated as clues to its future development and configuration.

II

It is well established that modern Japanese nationalism stems from the impact of European power in the closing period of the Tokugawa era. Nationalism throughout the Far East in general arose under similar circumstances. Many characteristics that differentiate Japanese nationalism from that of European countries are consequently found in its genesis; but at the same time the way in which Japan responded to the impact of the West saddled it with a historical task markedly different from that assigned to other Asian nations, particularly China.

Nationalism in the West was conditioned by the ideas and institutions of the society in which it arose. Before the modern nation-state was born, Europe had already established one form of universalism. The foundations had been laid by the Roman Empire, which bequeathed its ideas to the doctrine of a European corporate body—the Corpus Christianum—symbolized by the Roman Catholic (Universal) Church and the Holy Roman Empire. The development of modern nation-states beginning in the Renaissance and Reformation periods was no more than a pluralistic disruption within this world that had originally been one.

National consciousness in Europe therefore bore from its inception the imprint of a consciousness of international society. It was a self-evident premise that disputes among sovereign states were conflicts among independent members of this international society. Precisely for this reason war, since Grotius, has come to occupy an important and systematic place in international law. Even after Europe had dissolved into sovereign states, the tradition of universalism flowed on without interruption. This is apparent from Rousseau's observation that 'the nations of Europe form among themselves an invisible nation'. Fénelon remarks to the same effect: 'All nations which are neighbours and have commercial relations form a great body and a kind of community. For instance, Christendom forms a kind of general republic which has its common interests, fears, and precautions.'*

How does this compare with the so-called Asian world? No matter how one answers the still controversial question of whether 'the East' has ever really existed, it is clear that it embraces three cultural spheres that are highly self-sufficient both historically and traditionally: India, China, and Japan. It is equally clear that the nations of the East have never constituted a corporate body or international society in the European sense, although various forms of diplomatic intercourse

* H. Morgenthau, *Politics among Nations* (1949), pp. 160–1.

have existed among them. Thus the appearance of Western power in the East was more a case where a single entity, 'international society', confronted several more or less closed worlds and forced each of them to 'open the country'. The countries of the East were not themselves aware of being within the international community; rather, they were dragged into it, through force or threat of force, by 'international society'. An elementary form of national consciousness first arose throughout the East when countries like China and Japan reacted against the corporate pressure of European power surging in from the outside.

Those most sensitively aware of the implications of Western power were the privileged ruling classes in the old states. For them 'national consciousness' meant above all defending the traditional socio-political order from the infiltration both of European Christianity and of industrialism.*

'Expel the barbarians' was the most typical expression of nationalism in this early phase, a phase that may be called 'initial-stage' nationalism to distinguish it from the modern manifestation. Two prominent features in this idea were common to China in the closing years of the Manchu Dynasty[3] and Japan in the Bakumatsu Period. First, 'expel the barbarians' was inseparably merged with the aspirations of the ruling class to maintain its social privileges, thus weakening what we would today call consciousness of national solidarity. As a result there was an estrangement from the common people that actually amounted to hostility and that divorced the ruling class from the vast majority of the population. During the Bakumatsu Period, for example, the expression 'wicked subjects and crafty foreigners' frequently appeared in the writings of the Mito School. Such a notion expressed a fear and suspicion that the people were in league with the enemy. In fine, 'wicked subjects' represented in the eyes of the ruling class a problem no less menacing than 'crafty foreigners'.

Secondly, an awareness of equality in international affairs was totally absent. The advocates of expulsion viewed inter-

---

* This attitude stands in contrast to that of the old ruling classes of Europe. In Europe it was the rising *bourgeoisie*, not the nobility, that assumed responsibility for nationalism, and in so doing they pitted themselves against a cosmopolitan aristocracy.

national relations from positions within the national hierarchy based on the supremacy of superiors over inferiors. Consequently, when the premises of the national hierarchy were transferred horizontally into the international sphere, international problems were reduced to a single alternative: conquer or be conquered. In the absence of any higher normative standards with which to gauge international relations, power politics is bound to be the rule and yesterday's timid defensiveness will become today's unrestrained expansionism. Naturally, a psychological complex of fear and arrogance holds sway here as a primitive attitude towards the unknown.

This picture is of course highly simplified. I have omitted various nuances in the conditions surrounding the birth of nationalism in the several countries of the Far East. Moreover the factors I have given are essentially those common to ethnocentrism, the irrational source of nationalism in general. It cannot be denied, however, that Asian nationalism has emerged under different circumstances from those in Europe where nationalism originated in a common normative consciousness. It is largely owing to these differences that nationalism in the countries of the Far East has been obliged to overcome many obstacles in its quest for rationalization, particularly in arriving at a workable balance with internationalism.

The burden of nationalism in its initial stage lay with the old privileged classes. Confronted by the overwhelming superiority of the West in industry, technology, and armament, they were soon compelled to recognize that only by arming themselves with the 'enemy's' civilization could they defend the old world against the new. To do so, however, involved them in a grave dilemma. They could no longer maintain the old world without adopting European civilization; yet, if they adopted it *in toto*, they would likewise destroy the old system and undermine their own power.

There was but one way to escape from this paradox: adopt only European industry, technology, and armament—the 'material civilization' of the West—and restrict the infiltration of various undesirable political influences, such as Christianity and liberal democracy, to an absolute minimum. This solution was the 'differential usage' classically expressed by Hashimoto Sanai ('Acquire mechanical arts from others, retain righteousness, sympathy, and filial piety as our own'), and by Sakuma Shōzan ('Eastern morality, Western arts'—arts here of course meaning technology).

It is readily apparent, however, that difficulties remained in applying this formula. The so-called material civilization of the West could not be extracted so simply from the modern spirit that had fostered it. Even if it were feasible, it would have been next to impossible to prevent modernization in the nation's material life and environment from adversely affecting its thought and consciousness. How the old ruling classes in China and Japan responded to this historical trial by fire caused the structure of nationalism in the two countries to diverge and their historical destinies to separate.

In both China and Japan the more progressive sectors of the ruling class tried desperately to carry out the differential usage under the banner of 'a prosperous nation and a strong military'. Japan, as we all know, succeeded in this endeavour. Having accomplished a successful revolution from above through the Meiji Restoration, Japan became the first centralized nation-state in the Far East. The influx of European power was checked and, with a speed that astonished the world, Japan emerged as an imperial nation with a seat among the Great Powers.

China, however, failed. Even the modernization efforts from above, starting with the 'Foreign Affairs' movement sponsored by Marquis Tseng Kuo-fan and others and ending with K'ang Yu-wei's 'Reform and Restoration' policy, succumbed in the face of powerful opposition from the firmly entrenched conservative forces within the Manchu court. As a result of these failures, Great Power imperialism reached extensively into China during the latter half of the nineteenth century. China lapsed into a semi-colonial condition, into the distressing state of what Sun Yat-sen described as a 'secondary colony'.

There are many reasons, to be sure, why China's destiny should have differed from Japan's in this respect: geographical position, time lag in 'opening the country', the manner in which the old society dissolved, and the historical character of the ruling class, to mention only a few. A discussion of causes, however, is beyond the scope of our problem here. The important thing for us is that differences in point of origin have cast

Chinese and Japanese nationalism into almost diametrically opposite moulds. These points of departure have left an imprint that critically influences the course of events in the Far East even today. It is therefore worth while at this point to take into consideration what some of those differences were.

When the Chinese ruling class failed to modernize by reorganizing the nation's internal structure, China suffered a prolonged period of imperialism led by the Great Powers, including Japan. In reacting against imperialism, Chinese nationalism ironically enough came under an obligation to transform, not preserve, the old socio-political order. Having more or less joined hands with imperialism in order to survive, the ruling class had been forced to 'compradorize'. An extensive anti-imperialist, national independence effort could therefore not emerge from that quarter. The adhesion of the old order to imperialism inevitably inspired the fusion of social revolution with nationalism.

It will not be necessary here to trace this phenomenon through its various stages of development from Sun Yat-sen via Chiang Kai-shek to Mao Tse-tung. Suffice it to say that a consistent union of nationalism with revolution, though classically apparent in today's China, is in point of fact an historical feature common to nationalism throughout Asia in general. It can be seen in the histories of such countries as India, French Indo-China, Malaya, Indonesia, and Korea. Only one nation, the Empire of the Rising Sun, followed a completely different path.

In Japan the powers that overthrew the Tokugawa régime and seized authority in a unified nation were themselves constituent elements of the old ruling class. Spurred ahead by one sole aspiration, to elevate Japan to a position where she could 'stand tall in the world' and 'attain equality with nations abroad', the Restoration leaders swiftly routed the pluralistic feudal powers within the country and brought them together under the authority of the Emperor. The 'differential usage' was then employed with consummate skill and 'a prosperous nation and a strong military' carried into effect. From this standpoint the Meiji leaders scored brilliant successes in their modernization programme. Japan achieved complete independence and entered the company of 'international society'. In no less than fifty years after the country had been opened Great Power status was attained.

At the same time, however, visible deformities developed in all spheres of Japanese society. By subordinating modernization to the one supreme goal of 'a prosperous nation and a strong military' and by pressing this programme forward with lightning speed, imbalances were bound to occur. Although there were a number of corrective tendencies in the theory and practice of nationalism in this initial stage, such efforts to redress the distortions caused by modernization were soon abandoned.

Despite the turns and twists of its early development, nationalist thought and activity generally evolved in such a way as to justify the given course of Japan's imperial expansion. Far from uniting with social revolution, nationalism directed its efforts against revolution, or rather against its latent possibility. The Dark Ocean Society and its successors, the Amur River Society and the Great Japan Production Party, are typical illustrations of such anti-revolutionary thought and action. In certain cases nationalism became the direct force of anti-revolutionary oppression; in others it operated as a transfer mechanism for revolutionary energy, a role it played consistently until 1945.

Japanese nationalists, moreover, knew next to nothing about the happy marriage of nationalism with *bourgeois* democracy and popular sovereignty as seen in classic Western nationalism. On the contrary, Japan allowed the peculiarities of initial-stage nationalism to continue in profusion. The resulting conglomeration was then fused with imperialism as a last-stage degeneration of modern nationalism. Japanese nationalism prematurely abandoned any thought of popular emancipation, popular movements being repressed in the name of national unity. Under such conditions a searching inquiry into what 'national consciousness' or 'patriotism' meant in the context of Japan's 'democratic' and labour movements was indefinitely postponed. Democratic elements and labour were driven willy-nilly into a relatively cosmopolitan bent of mind. These conditions of initial-stage nationalism also fostered a vicious circle which permitted the ruling class and reactionary segments to monopolize the symbols of nationalism.

When nationalism abandoned the cause of popular liberation and sublimated popular nationalism into state nationalism and then ultra-nationalism, much more was involved than how democracy and labour were to exist institutionally. The psychological structure of the entire nation was at stake.

To put it briefly, the rapidity of modernization, made possible by Japan's remarkable success in applying the differential usage, created uneven social development. Modernization in the livelihood of the masses lagged far behind, both in tempo and in degree. The speed of modernization, by divorcing the people from the national purpose as it were, also left a decisive imprint on national consciousness and the intellectual and psychological content of nationalism. The *élite*, standing at the apex of Japanese society, engaged in a ceaseless struggle to reach the pinnacle of world prominence. The masses, however, remained behind. Here at the base of Japanese society the traditional forms of social consciousness were tenaciously rooted. It was this law of structural imbalance that permeated the ideology of nationalism.

On the surface, then, Japan's much paraded nationalism seemed to display a toughness from the fact that it had refused to unite with the forces of democracy. But in this respect Japanese nationalism paralleled the history of the Empire, whose astounding onslaught prepared the stage for a collapse of equally astounding rapidity through serious internal contradictions. The hiatus that arose between popular consciousness and national aims constituted an insurmountable weakness throughout the lifespan of pre-war nationalism. Japan's patriotism, for all that it was vaunted abroad, swiftly vanished from the scene after the war. The people became lethargic and sluttish, nakedly pursuing egoistic ends. The answer to why the Japanese have become the despair of both progressives and old-line conservatives alike in Japan, while the neighbouring peoples of Asia are beating the drums of national passion to fever pitch, lies in the attitude that had taken root in pre-war nationalism.

To begin with, two key features in the psychological structure of pre-war nationalism must be pointed out as the pivots of such attitudes: first, the tendency to symbolize the State as the direct extension of the primary group (family or village) in which the individual is submerged; secondly, love of fatherland, expressed pre-eminently as love of one's native place which in turn is an aspect of love of the environment. Love of environment, of course, is an important factor in tribalism, which is considered to be the beginning of nationalism. But modern nationalism, particularly 'the child of the French Revolution',* is not emotionally dependent on the environment alone. Rather, it is attended by a high degree of popular spontaneity and autonomy. As expressed by Renan, 'a nation's existence is an everyday plebiscite'.[4]

Indeed, this was the most valuable historical product to result from the union of nationalism and the principle of popular sovereignty. (The Popular Rights Movement in the Meiji Period accordingly reveals a certain degree of such unity.) Because of the nature of the Restoration, the Meiji leaders could not rely on the spontaneous and active growth of a consciousness of national solidarity among the people at large. Oppressed by a constant feeling of foreign crisis, the Meiji leaders were propelled into a makeshift form of patriotism devised from above through national education.

Organizationally this programme for patriotism was not carried into effect until the time of Japan's first Education Minister, Mr. Mori Arinori. By then, however, Japan's 'modernization' had already been driven forward by harshly oppressing the Popular Rights Movement. With the democratic front silenced, the Meiji leaders zealously injected national consciousness by a full-scale mobilization of irrational attachments to the primary group. Above all, this meant that feudal loyalty and traditional devotion to the father as family head were centralized in the Emperor, the concrete manifestation of Japan's national unity.†

Among the intellectuals who were in intimate contact with events during the Meiji era a considerable number point out that the effects of this national education under the Meiji leaders have been greatly exaggerated today. They argue that effective and thorough 'national polity' education took place only during the ultra-nationalist stage and that the Meiji Period was by far the most liberal and 'enlightened' in modern Japanese history.

Such a view tends, however, to minimize the problem of

---

* G. P. Gooch.
† There is no need to elaborate here on the idea of 'loyalty to the Emperor and patriotism' or on the concept of a family State with the Imperial Family as its head.

structural imbalance, the incongruity of the social apex and base, that had existed long before ultra-nationalism arrived on the scene. To be sure, national polity education may not have penetrated very deeply into the Meiji intellectual class, the class to which these proponents of Meiji enlightenment themselves belonged. As was the case with the intellectuals of Tsarist Russia, their educational experience was overwhelmingly Western. But the masses, steeped in darkness and groaning at the base of society, were so unrelated to the 'concept of the state' that Fukuzawa Yukichi resolved to devote his life to 'making all the people comprehend the idea of "nation" (*kuni*)'. It was precisely through national polity education in 'obligation' that the people became good Imperial subjects who combined a brave and loyal soul with a minimal knowledge of necessary industrial and military techniques, a combination of what Mr. Frederick Hulse has called 'magical and scientific practice'.[5]

Moreover successive foreign victories and imperial expansion gradually strengthened the national consciousness that had been so efficiently created. Imperial expansion as an emotional projection of the self magnified the insignificant individual and received his fanatic support. Despair deriving from the narrow confines of the citizen's freedom and the straits of his economic life found compensation in the nation's foreign expansion. The age of imperialism from the end of the nineteenth century gave the ruling class good grounds for drumming up a mood of foreign crisis. Mobilizing the fears and insecurities of Japanese life through one of history's most successful state stratagems, the rulers of Meiji Japan were able to nip all indications of social disintegration in the bud. 'The spiritual solidarity of the Japanese people' became a regular first-page feature of almost every foreign study on Japan.

Here again, we should look at the other side of the coin. First and foremost, national consciousness did not result from the conquest of traditional social consciousness, but was implanted by a systematic mobilization of traditional values. Consequently, Japan did not produce *citoyens* able to bear the burden of political responsibility in a modern nation-state. In their stead came quantities of loyal but servile lackeys who, entrusting all things to 'the upper ranks', clung fervently to the decisions of authority.

On the other hand, family and village consciousness could not be extended smoothly to national consciousness. Primary group values tended to foster sectionalism, which in turn weakened national solidarity. Family egoism in many cases hamstrung the 'execution of state policy'. As an example, for some time after conscription was inaugurated government policy exempted the eldest son in deference to the family system. This measure was often utilized against the government; families would send their younger sons into other families for adoption as eldest sons and heirs. 'Do Not Offer Your Life', a famous poem by Yosano Akiko,[6] was not so much an indictment of war as a simple expression of attachment to the primary group. It was shocking precisely because it so boldly exposed an open secret in national life.

Tokutomi Sohō once remarked that: 'Our nation's patriotism, once having been the patriotism of national emergency, never became part of our daily lives.'* This observation should not come as any surprise; we have already seen that national consciousness did not enter the individual's life but remained external, expressed as an emotional projection and compensation of the self. That patriotism should remain superficial was a natural outcome.

When Japan reached the point of total war, which necessitated a complete reorganization of the nation's life, the negative side of Japanese nationalism became more and more exposed as the slogans grew in number and intensity. One need only recall the deep-rooted psychological resistance that met the shrill demands to enforce conscript labour placement, controlled industrial production-distribution, and forced evacuation plans. The resistance stemmed from none other than the family principle, 'agriculture first', and 'love of the village'.

'Down with family considerations! Down with personal interests! Vote in the public and national interest!' Ironically enough, this theme running through the spirit of modern elections was repeatedly hammered home in the picture-story shows[7] that toured every area of Japan on behalf of the Imperial Rule Assistance Association during Tōjō's notorious election of

* *Young Men of Taishō and the Future of the Empire* (*Taishō no Seinen to Teikoku no Zento*).

April 1942. This, however, was the price that the entire ruling class had to pay for neglecting to put nationalism on a rational foundation while exploiting its traditional and irrational sources to the fullest. They first realized how outrageously high the price was when they arrived at the stage of national mobilization. But then it was too late.

III

With defeat the Japanese Empire, once supreme over South-East Asia, the Western Pacific, and half of China, was suddenly compress d into the insignificant island country it had been at the Rest ration. Scathing criticism at home and abroad went to the very heart of the 'national polity' idea, and the national polity was altered. The value of the Imperial symbols that had surrounded it, such as Shintō shrines, the national flag, and the national anthem, plummeted. Having lost its central props, national consciousness collapsed.

In many cases defeat has stirred the flames of nationalism. Outbursts of nationalist feeling occurred in Prussia after the Napoleonic conquest, in France after the Franco-Prussian War, in China after the Sino-Japanese War, and in Germany after the First World War. But in Japan a feeling of stagnation, of prostration so complete that foreigners were astonished, reigned supreme.

To be sure, many important factors are responsible for Japan's post-war disintegration. But from our consideration of pre-war nationalism and in particular the structure of national consciousness we know that such a collapse was no mutation; for the seeds were planted in the pre-war era. The extensiveness of the collapse can be explained by the quality and scope of Japan's concept of nationalism.

Evolving nationalism is generally accomplished by a mission idea that is essential to its appeal and success. 'Proclaiming the Imperial Way', 'Spreading Righteousness and Truth throughout the World', and 'The Eight Corners of the World under One Roof', are all expressions of such an idea. No matter how absurd a ring they have for intellectuals, the irrational logic which supported these slogans wielded a tenacious and mystic sway over the nation's populace in the Japan of the past. In essence this resulted when the concept of hierarchy with the

Emperor as its apex was extended horizontally into the international sphere.*

As a mission idea, Japan's 'Imperial Nation' appears to resemble China's notion of being the 'Central Kingdom'. In point of fact, however, the two are decidedly different: China's mission idea focused on cultural superiority whereas Japan's always rested on military superiority as its indispensable though not its only base. Therefore, although China might be subjugated by barbarians, the Central Kingdom as an idea retained its validity. Japan's notion of being 'flawless like a golden chalice', however, had been supported by the 'historical' facts that the Imperial Army was invincible and that the territory of the divine land had never been defiled by the feet of enemy soldiers. Naturally enough, when Japan was defeated and occupied there was a decisive decline in the value of Imperial symbols.

In this respect it is well worth while to examine Mr. Hashimoto Sanai's formula of the differential usage in relation to the mission idea. Robert Michels distinguishes a mission idea into the integral mission (*Integralmissionsbegriff*) and the partial mission (*Teilmissionsbegriff*). The latter emphasizes a nation's mission in one particular sphere, such as art, politics, or industry.†
In Japan's case it is clear that a typical integral mission idea was created under the differential usage by forging the 'spiritual civilization' of the East with the 'technical-material civilization' of the West and then adding Japan's peculiar 'military spirit'. The 'national polity' amounted to a unified body of values derived from precisely such an integration; that is, an all-encompassing mission idea. If Japan had developed a partial mission idea, the psychological setback caused when it ran aground might have been overcome by transferring the national mission into another sphere. As it was, however, the spiritual vacuum left by the collapse of the 'national polity' was total, just as Japan's mission idea had been total. Along with the new constitution a mission idea with a new look and supported by new rationales entered the post-war scene: 'a nation of peace and culture'. That this idea should have no compelling attraction for the people, that it should appear only as a slogan made

---

* I have discussed the psychological basis of these appeals in 'Theory and Psychology of Ultra-Nationalism'.

† *Der Patriotismus*, pp. 38–39.

inevitable by Japan's defeat, may be paradoxical, but it illustrates how integral was the mission idea of the old Empire.

Consequently, most Japanese still have no satisfactory answer to what possible *raison d'être* a Japan poor in resources, overpopulated, and unarmed has in the world of the future. Yet this is precisely the question that the new nationalism, regardless of its form, must answer. If it fails to inspire a mission idea at least as compelling as that formulated by the old Empire, it is highly unlikely that the new nationalism can develop as a free and independent power.

Another conspicuous aspect of the post-war situation is what might be called the social decomposition of the former nationalist psychology. Constituted as it was by a systematic mobilization of traditional values and *mores*, such as regional sentiment and paternal loyalty, it was only natural that, once the cohesive power at the nation's centre weakened, national consciousness should quickly decompose and return automatically, as it were, to its old haunts in the family, village, and small local groups at the base of the social structure.

This demobilization of national consciousness, so to speak, occurred with lightning speed. Amidst the social and economic turmoil directly following the war, gangsters and black marketeers emerged in droves. Semi-violent gangs of hoodlums and mobsters revived throughout the countryside. These gangs, the Ozu gang in Shinjuku or the Matsuda ring in Shimbashi, for example, assumed the functions of local police by proxy.

The post-war operations of gangsterism are all too well known. Less attention, however, has been paid to the psychological implications of the fact that demobilized soldiers continued to pour into such local groups. Organized along disciplinary lines similar to the military and offering the loyalty relations of *oyabun-kobun*, these 'anti-social groups' were well suited to fill the psychological void left when the central symbols collapsed. By submitting to group hierarchy and regimentation, ex-service men could mitigate their feelings of isolation and helplessness. The mobs became a refuge from the social turmoil engendered by defeat.

Probably related to this phenomenon of reversion is the appearance in astounding numbers of small, shady political parties after the war. Many, however, could be recognized as mere continuations or camouflages of former right-wing groups.

The examples of reversion cited above are more or less abnormal 'translocations' of loyalty to the Emperor and the Empire. The point, however, is that originally the structural base of Japanese society had rested consistently on the family principle. A spiritual demobilization consequently took place in the more 'sincere' groups and places of work, all the more extensive because it was not visible. Members of right-wing societies and former military officers switched over to food production and land reclamation drives and entered local fiscal agencies, repatriation societies, service groups for cleaning Shintō shrines, and so forth. These bodies were intermediate forms between the national military establishment and the primary groups; but they also indicated the direction of spiritual demobilization in Japanese society as a whole.

Horse racing, bicycle racing, and other sporting amusements have become current fashions among the people, providing an outlet for the military psychology of victory and defeat which 'masturbates' in such activities. When the San Francisco Seals arrived for a series of baseball games with Japanese teams in October 1949, Professor Otis Cary[8] had hoped that the Japanese teams would win the matches. After observing the attitude of the spectators and players, however, he said that he had been rather pleased that the Seals won. He also expressed certain misgivings when not only the radio and press but all of Japan went mad with ecstasy over the records set by Furuhashi at the swimming contests of August 1950 held in the United States. 'I seriously questioned whether this was the way things ought to be. The Japanese seemed to feel that they had made a "landing in the face of the enemy" with the instruments of peace.'*

From such evidence it would not be quite right to say that the old nationalism had either died out or qualitatively changed. It would be more precise to say that it had vanished from the political surface only to be inlaid at the social base in an atomized form.

What impact will this decentralized and latent sentiment of traditional nationalism have on Japan's future nationalism?

First, it is quite obvious that national sentiment as it now

* *Young People of Japan* (*Nihon no Wakamono*), p. 283.

stands can never become the mainstay of a new nationalism united with the democratic revolution. Only by destroying the tenacious family structure in Japanese society and its ideology, the very place where the old nationalism ferments, can Japan democratize society from the base up. If the progressive camp is bewitched for an instant by fragmentary forms of the old nationalism, either misjudging them as the buds of future national consciousness or knowingly mobilizing them under the temptation of securing immediate political goals, the effect will be disastrous. The 'new' nationalism will inevitably turn harshly towards reaction and probably revert to its former nature.

The fact that traditional nationalism can inhabit non-political everyday phenomena in an atomized state proves above all that Japan's post-war democratization went no further than institutional and legal reforms in the State machinery. It did not reach the social structure or the people's way of life, much less the mental constitution of the people. So long as democracy remains for Japan a lofty theory, an edifying doctrine, it will continue to be an indigestible import. In order to unite nationalism and democracy effectively, an internal reform in the psychological structure of Japanese society must occur. For Japan to accomplish this union, nationalism must be rationalized in the same degree that democracy is irrationalized.

Secondly, will the old national sentiments that reverted to the social base reappear on the political scene and remobilize around the former symbols of Empire? If there is such a re-mobilization, the structural laws of Japanese society will probably funnel these emotions back into the old channels like water flowing into a ditch. For this reason it is only natural that flying the national ensign, reviving the national anthem, and worshipping at Shintō shrines have become hotly debated subjects. This applies in particular to the recent tendency towards reintroducing the old symbols into national education.

Certain people laugh at the over-sensitivity of someone who reads into every such event a revival of ultra-nationalism or fascism. It would of course be absurd to link the frenzy over the Seals' baseball tour or the Furuhashi swimming records directly to a rising militaristic spirit. Such phenomena lie clearly in the non-political sphere of private life. Even Professor Cary would not have 'misgivings' in such a direct sense. But from the dynamics of political behaviour we know that an accumulation of everyday acts, at first glance unrelated to politics, can suddenly be transformed into great political energy. The horizon on which these storms appear in the political world is extremely hazy. Flying the national colours and reviving the national anthem do not have much import as isolated events. When they are placed beside other events, however, such as the establishment of the National Police Reserve Forces, the augmentation of the Maritime Safety Force, and the debate over rearmament, they acquire a certain significance. To recognize the germination of a familiar political tendency here is far from groundless.

On the other hand, such a tendency cannot be regarded simply as a restoration of pre-war nationalism in its original form. The matter is far more complicated. First of all, it is almost out of the question that Japan can either economically or militarily retrieve the international strength and prestige possessed in the former age of 'Empire'. From the ideological standpoint, too, it would appear all but impossible for Japan to emerge once more as 'the national polity standing first among all nations', regardless of the symbolic power regained by the Emperor, national flag, and national anthem.

Consequently, even if there is a systematic effort to recentralize the dispersed and amorphous national sentiments of today, it does not seem likely that sufficient strength can be mobilized for the resultant nationalism to be an independent political force. In all likelihood the new creation from old fabric will be joined to a higher political force, perhaps to an international power. It will then be permitted to exist only in so far as it serves to further the latter's set political goals.

I have previously pointed out the most striking functions of pre-war nationalism: concealing or repressing all social opposition, restraining the emergence of an autonomous consciousness from among the people, and diverting social discontent towards fixed domestic and foreign scapegoats. If in the future Japan mobilizes the nation's patriotism to secure these external aims, she will abandon the supreme principle of a valid nationalism: popular independence. It will mean inheriting only a gruesome legacy; namely, union with anti-revolution.

Whether or not one still calls such a creature nationalism, each is free to judge. In any case, one thing is certain. If Japan does follow the path of reaction, she is destined to break once and for all with the future of nationalism in Asia.

TRANSLATOR'S NOTES

1. In January 1950 the Japanese Communist Party was attacked by the Cominform for its easy-going strategy in regard to the Japanese revolution. The Party toed the line and abandoned its 'lovable party' policy. Under the discipline of the Cominform the Party's assertion of autonomy gave way to an explicitly international orientation. The Party's prospects of a peaceful transition to a 'People's Government' were denied by the Cominform as unrealistic in view of the impact of the American Occupation. Though the Party's 'main stream' admitted its errors, there has been considerable dissension within the ranks since.

2. On this date the Emperor made his unprecedented broadcast transmitting to the people his decision 'to effect a settlement of the present situation by resorting to an extraordinary measure'. Resolving 'to pave the way for a grand peace for all the generations to come by enduring the unendurable and suffering what is insufferable', the Emperor announced Japan's acceptance of the Potsdam Declaration ending the Pacific War.

3. The Manchu Dynasty dates from 1644 to 1912; its immediate decline may be placed from about 1860.

4. 'L'existence d'une nation est . . . un plébiscite de tous les jours. . . . 'Ernest Renan, 'Qu'est-ce qu'une nation?' (1882), in *Discours et Conférences* (Paris, Ancienne Maison Michel Lévy Frères, 1887), p. 307.

5. Frederick S. Hulse, 'Effects of War Upon Japanese Society', *Far Eastern Quarterly*, Vol. 7, Nov. 1947, p. 24.

6. Yosano Akiko, 1878–1942. Waka poetess and exponent of romanticism. 'Do Not Offer Your Life' was written in 1904 for her brother who was with the Japanese army in China:

> Dearest brother,
> I weep for you.
> Do not offer your life.
> Did our mother and father,
> Whose love for you, last born,

Surpassed all others,
Teach you to wield the sword?
To kill?
Did they rear you these twenty-four years,
Saying:
'Kill and die'?

You,
Who shall inherit the name of our father—
A master proud of his ancient name
In the commerce of this town of Sakai—
Do not offer your life.
Whether Port Arthur falls or not
Is no matter.
Do you not know
That this is nothing
To the house of a merchant?
Nothing?

Do not offer your life.
The Emperor himself does not go
To battle.
The Imperial Heart is deep;
How could he ever wish
That men shed their blood,
That men die like beasts,
That man's glory be in death?

Dearest brother,
Do not offer your life
In battle.
Mother, whom father left behind
This past autumn,
Suffered when
In the midst of her grief
Her son was called away.
Even under this Imperial reign,
When it is heard
That the home is safe and secure,
Mother's hair has grown whiter.

Do you forget
Your forlorn young wife

Weeping,
Hidden in the shadows of the shop curtains?
Or do you think of her?
Consider a young woman's heart when
After less than ten months
Her husband is taken away!
Alas, who else
Than you alone
Is she to rely on
In this world?
Do not offer your life!

7. See Glossary: *Picture-story show.*
8. Otis Cary, American, Assistant Professor of History at Dōshisha University in Kyōto.

V. Fascism—Some Problems:
A Consideration of its Political Dynamics

TRANSLATED BY RONALD DORE

This essay was originally published in the magazine Shisō, *October 1952*

INTRODUCTION

On my desk are two issues of the American journal, *The Nation*: one old, the other recent. The older one, the seventy-fifth anniversary issue (the journal was founded in 1865 immediately after the American Civil War), bears the date 10 February 1940. When it appeared, Europe was already caught in the whirlpool of war and the flower of Hitler's Wehrmacht was drawn up on the Maginot Line in full preparedness for the overwhelming breakthrough that was to come. In the East, China and Japan were still, after two and a half years, locked in a death struggle for which no end seemed in sight. From the West and from the East the forces of international fascism were beginning to press ominously on America, the last remaining continent 'at peace'. The issue contains a special anniversary message from President Roosevelt. *The Nation* had, he said, earned respect for the way in which throughout its long history, though frequently forced into a position of isolation, it had never hesitated to represent minority opinion—sometimes 'mighty unpopular minority opinion at that'. He sent his best wishes in Voltaire's words: 'I disapprove of what you say but I will defend to the death your right to say it.' The editor, Freda Kirchwey, as if responding to the toast, ends her discussion of the nature of the contemporary crisis of democracy by saying:

> We are happy in having as our President a man who so heartily supports the expression of minority opinion . . . But the President is himself under the fire of groups, strongly intrenched in Congress and the country, who are determined to abolish this ancient weapon of democratic change. Against such forces *The Nation* will fight with all its power and vigilance as it has done throughout the years.

Most of the articles that I read in *The Nation* of that period I have long since forgotten, but I do still clearly recall feeling a sudden warmth, as of an electric charge tingling up the spine, when I received this anniversary volume and read this gracious exchange between President and editor.

This was not simply empty rhetoric on Freda Kirchwey's part. There was no mistaking the bitterness with which *The Nation* in those days attacked the forces of international fascism led by Japan, Germany, and Italy. At home, in the struggle against the frantic efforts of big business and its allies to take the teeth out of the New Deal, *The Nation* made the running in the world of journalism. I recall that writers like Laski frequently made brilliant contributions to its pages. Soon, however, as Japanese-American relations rapidly worsened we Japanese readers were forcibly deprived of the chance to hear its bold clarion call. There was still some consolation left as long as we could gaze banefully at its mutilated page cruelly cut by the censor. But soon it ceased to arrive at all.

It was not until after the end of the Second World War that I was able once again to leaf nostalgically through the pages of a copy of *The Nation*. The immense sacrifices of a great war had seen the Axis powers overthrown. But this did not necessarily mean that the force of fascism was spent. In the editorial quoted above Miss Kirchwey had written: 'Fascism may lose the war but win the peace. A basic social change in Europe, not mere readjustments of boundaries, will be required if fascism is not to win', and unfortunately her fears had proved well grounded. The challenge that *The Nation* had been concerned to meet had not lost its immediacy. Far from it; for now, with the defeat of the Axis countries, the forces of reaction had moved their headquarters into Miss Kirchwey's own country.

A difficult time was in store not only for *The Nation* but for all those in the United States who were concerned to defend the liberal tradition. The President who had made Voltaire's dictum an article of faith was dead, and those groups 'strongly intrenched in Congress and the country' who were determined to abolish the weapons of democratic change, the groups that had always made him an object of their attacks, were rapidly spreading a powerful network throughout the nation. In the face of this situation would *The Nation* still be able to preserve its tradition and continue the struggle to represent 'mighty unpopular' minority opinions?

The more recent issue that I have before me—it is dated 28 June 1952—provides the answer. It is a special number on civil liberties, the whole issue devoted to detailed reporting of the nature of the McCarthyite threat in every field: administration, law, labour, science, education, publishing, films, and the drama. Again Miss Kirchwey has an editorial, this time entitled 'How Free is Free?' She deplores the fact that America has failed to learn the profound lessons of two world wars and instead, by making a desperate attempt to bolster up the crumbling old order, has handed over to Russia the leadership of revolution. She urges American liberals to ever greater efforts to resist witch-hunting and compulsory uniformity. *The Nation* and its editor are still in good heart.

But this special number does show clearly with what frightening speed and on what a frightening scale the freedom of the 'land of the free' is being suppressed. Compared with the situation when *The Nation* published its seventy-fifth anniversary volume, it is obvious in every line of this issue that even the body of opinion such as *The Nation* represents—however sharply distinct from communist opinion it may be—now has to face a far more unfavourable climate. Reading the well-documented and vivid accounts of the activities of public and private spy organizations, and of the harrying onslaughts by reactionary groups who attack with all the persistence of a flock of ticks, and reading, too, of the astonishingly weak resistance shown by the general public, I am sure I cannot be alone in thinking 'Alas, has America come to this?' ...

I

Fascism is the twentieth century's most acute and most aggressive form of counter-revolution—just as Jesuitism formed the vanguard of the Counter-Reformation in the sixteenth century and Metternich's principle of legitimacy was the most concentrated expression of the counter-revolution at the beginning of the nineteenth century. A counter-revolution presupposes a revolution. Needless to say, the twentieth-century analogue of the religious Reformation of the sixteenth century and of the French Revolution of the eighteenth is the Russian Revolution.

But this does not mean that the Russian Revolution is the sole pattern of revolution in the twentieth century, nor does it mean that Bolshevism is the century's sole revolutionary ideology.

The twentieth-century revolution is a profound shift in the crust of modern society and modern civilization, and the Russian Revolution itself is best seen as the form that this transformation takes under a particular set of historical conditions. One cannot stress this point too much. A proper realization of it is a necessary antidote for a mistaken notion actively propagated both now and in the past by fascist demagogues and other conservative reactionaries. (Fascism is necessarily reactionary, but conservative reaction is not necessarily fascism.) I mean the view that the rising tide of revolutionary pressure in modern Asia and Europe is to be blamed solely on the Bolshevik revolution and on the external incitement and interference of the country that gave it birth. To borrow the apt metaphor of a foreign critic, that is like blaming the first horse home for the fact that all the other horses are racing towards the finishing line. The other horses may well be encouraged and stimulated by the horse that leads the field. But each is running its own race; it is not necessarily dragged on by the horse ahead. In the twentieth-century revolution Russia has certainly led the field. But what form the revolution will take in other countries and in other regions and what course of development it will follow depend on a most complex combination of factors—the international situation, historical and geographical circumstances, patterns of culture, and ways of life.

Consequently fascism, as the concentrated expansion of the counter-revolution, corresponds to particular revolutionary circumstances, and it need not be framed as a response to communism. The fact that communism and the Communist Party have hitherto been fascism's first and foremost enemy is because, as a matter of historical fact, it has generally been the Communist Party that—actually or potentially—has been the most energetic and most aggressive organizer of revolutionary situations. If in certain circumstances a social democratic party should become the vanguard of social revolution, it would immediately find itself the object of the concentrated attack of fascism.

How much 'tolerance' a fascist shows to social democrats and liberals is not in the least a matter of ideological principle, but of the marginal limits of revolution. If social democracy or liberalism are considered to be 'breeding grounds for red revolution' they will be liquidated or subjected to a process of *Gleichschaltung*; but if on the other hand they function as bulwarks against revolution they will be tolerated or even supported. It follows from this also that the mere fact that 'social democrats' and 'liberals' are allowed freedom of activity in a country is never proof that the ruling power of that country has not become fascist; it always depends on the actual behaviour of the social democrats and liberals in the particular situation.

To oppress liberals who keep silence on vital issues of civil liberty or social democrats whose sole concern is anti-communism (leaving aside the question of whether they still deserve to be called liberals or social democrats) is meaningless from the point of view of the economy of power. This too is the reason why militant liberals are frequently more subject to fascist attack and repression than 'Marxist' social democrats. Moszkowska's definition of fascism as 'a crusade against the whole of the Left'* is in this sense true only in its indication of the mobility of fascism's attack on its enemies. Thus, the characterization given above of fascism as the most acute form of counter-revolution was intended to mean that it is relatively the most militant form in any particular time and place, not to imply that it has any constant organizational form. The concrete forms of fascism change with the concrete circumstances of the revolutionary situation.

Again, whether fascist control implies the formal suspension or destruction of a modern constitution and parliamentary system or whether it preserves these constitutional forms is not a question of principle, but a question of the marginal effectiveness of those systems. If parliamentary institutions should ever become a bridgehead for revolution, then, as in Germany† and

* 'The Resurgence of Fascism', *Monthly Review*, Vol. IV, 3.

† It may be as well to expand a little on this point since the myth that the Nazis achieved power 'legally' under the Weimar Constitution still gains occasional currency. Quite apart from the way in which the civil service under the Weimar régime (especially in the judicial administration) either openly or covertly abandoned the principle of political neutrality to give help to reactionary groups and so eroded the 'rule of law' from within, and quite apart from the way in which the

Italy, they are probably doomed to destruction. However, if a parliamentary system (not simply in the narrow sense of a responsible cabinet system; the same applies to a presidential system) is for a number of political and economic reasons free from this danger, and if the anti-revolutionary forces have an overwhelming parliamentary majority which seems unlikely to be threatened for some time to come, then parliament presents no serious obstacles to the development of fascism.* Of course, if parliamentary principles are fully operative and if the rule of law guaranteed by the constitution is maintained in a relatively pure form, the effective organization of counter-revolutionary forces will meet with considerable difficulties and resistance,

backbone was effectively taken out of the Weimar Constitution during the three succeeding cabinets of Brüning, Papen, and Schleicher, an examination of the passing of the Enabling Act (the *Ermachtigungsgesetz*, which provided the first and decisive legal basis for Nazi dictatorship) and of the events which followed shows how little foundation such a myth can claim. Certainly the law was, in accordance with Article 76 of the Weimar Constitution, passed by a majority of two-thirds of the members present in the Reichstag. But before this happened the Reichstag fire had been engineered to make the Communist Party in effect an illegal organization, and the opening of the Reichstag in March 1933 was preceded by the arrest of all the eighty-one members of the Communist parliamentary group and of a number of Social Democratic members as well. What is more, the law included, in Article 5, a provision that it would lose its effect as soon as there was a change in the cabinet. (It is important to remember that the twelve members of the first Hitler cabinet included only three members of the Nazi Party. President Hindenburg insisted on having his close intimates, Papen, Hugenberg, and Gerecke, in the cabinet, and demanded the inclusion of Article 5 as a means of preventing a Nazi dictatorship.) Before long, however, Hugenberg had resigned, and Gerecke had been arrested on a charge of misusing public funds. Darré, a Nazi, had been made Minister of Agriculture and Hess had started attending cabinet meetings although he was not a member of the cabinet. In this way Article 5 became a dead letter. Furthermore, the Enabling Act was intended solely as a piece of emergency legislation—witness Article 2 which insists that the position of the Reichstag and the Reichsrat shall be preserved, and guarantees the powers of the President. Quite apart from the question of the constitutionality of the law itself with the very wide delegation of power that it entailed, there can be no doubt that even this law was ruthlessly trampled underfoot by the Nazis in building their dictatorship. It was the Social Democrats, not the Nazis, who showed a persistent preoccupation with questions of legality and so permitted the fascist seizure of power. (Cf. F. Neumann, *Behemoth* (1944), pp. 52–54; and F. Schuman, *The Nazi Dictatorship* (1936), pp. 217–22.)

* I should make it clear that I am not suggesting that countries in which *bourgeois* parties have a semi-permanent majority are *ipso facto* fascist-dominated. Where the development of fascism is of the form that comes 'from above' it usually permeates gradually, so that whether or not one can describe the whole of a country's form of political control as fascist depends on a comprehensive assessment of all kinds of other social symptoms. This is not an easy assessment to make, and opinions tend to differ. I hope to indicate what these symptoms are as the argument develops.

and hence it is in reality unlikely that fascism would develop without any change in modern constitutional forms. Even where this appears to be the case, in actual fact constitutionalism will be undermined in a variety of subtle ways. But the point to be made here is that there is no *a priori* reason for thinking that the existence of legal provisions for a constitution and for a parliamentary system is of itself proof of the absence of fascist forms of control. The political forms of single-party dictatorship or the corporate state are only the clothes in which fascism has chosen to dress itself in particular circumstances—the most effective organizational means it can find for the forcible suppression of revolutionary forces.

II

To say that fascism can take a variety of concrete forms depending on the nature of the concrete revolutionary circumstances is not, of course, to suggest that this is an arbitrary matter; the tempo and forms of its genesis and development are to a certain extent subject to political 'laws'. Fascism is likely to appear only in countries in which, or within the sphere of influence of which, a revolutionary situation has already reached a certain level of tension. Even where there is opposition between revolutionary and counter-revolutionary forces, if this has not matured to a point at which the stability of the established order is threatened, fascism will not appear, or if it does appear will make little headway. The most one is likely to find in such a situation is a *bourgeois* reaction in the broad sense.

Here too, however, it is important to note that the judgement about whether or not the revolutionary situation has reached a point where it threatens existing authority is not simply a matter of objective fact, but has at the same time a subjective dimension. For instance, even if objectively the revolutionary forces have not achieved a degree of organization anything like commensurate with the tension of the revolutionary situation, so that consequently there is no imminent possibility of revolution, should the ruling class or its political subordinates be driven by fear to overestimate the strength of the revolutionary forces then there may well be a rapid growth of fascism. The same may be true when, even if there is internally very little revolutionary tension, there is a great fear of 'infection' from neighbouring countries undergoing revolutionary change.

Thus, for instance, there certainly *were* objective factors which, by disturbing the existing order, hastened the maturing of fascism in pre-war Japan. The conflict was intensified internally by the great depression of 1929–31, and externally by the development of revolutionary movements in China, and particularly in Manchuria, the 'lifeline of Japan'. But one must not overlook the effect of a certain 'hyper-sensitivity', a certain 'over-developed consciousness' on the part of Japan's rulers which made these factors assume in their eyes a much larger importance than they really had.

Generally speaking, the more a society manages, for a variety of historical and social reasons, to preserve a high degree of cultural and ideological homogeneity,* the more sensitively it reacts to the danger of infection from, or infiltration by, 'heterogeneous' elements. In such circumstances the growth of fascism does not necessarily correspond accurately to the 'tenseness of the revolutionary situation'. This is a factor that one cannot overlook when considering the problem of fascism in contemporary America.† To put the matter in another way, in such

* The question of the degree of homogeneity of ways of life and ideology can be separated from the question of class divisions. It is quite possible for class division to reach extreme limits, while homogeneity in these other respects remains comparatively unimpaired.

† The 'American Way of Life' is undoubtedly a very vague concept, but there is no doubt that it plays an important role in guaranteeing a homogeneity of attitudes among the American people. On this point Laski has this to say about the stereotyping of American behaviour patterns:

'No other people can be so easily persuaded to read the same books, to play the same games, to have the same friendly extroversion in human relations. No other people feels the same pain in the sense of separation in outlook from his neighbours . . . and I doubt whether any other people, save one which, like the Germans under Nazi rule, is driven to dumb acceptance of orders, has ever been so slogan-minded.' (*American Democracy* (1948), p. 622.)

This seems a very sweeping criticism, but in fact Laski is only confirming, in the new age of mass communication, the observation of de Toqueville more than a century ago that 'I know of no country which has so little real independence of spirit and freedom of discussion as America'. However, to avoid giving a false impression, I should add that Laski goes on to say that, on the other hand, America *does* have a tradition of non-conformism which resists the lure of conformity and that even at present the educational propaganda of such voluntary organizations as trade unions, churches, and women's organizations is still capable of putting up a lively resistance to the newspaper and radio companies linked with big business, so that 'something always escapes the net [of the mass media] which is thrown about the people'.

societies, the greater the failure of the revolutionary forces and their ideology to become 'acclimatized', the more they are felt as 'foreign' elements incapable of being absorbed into the national way of life. When this happens, and the situation is complicated by the intensification of international rivalries, there is mounting fear, not only on the part of the ruling classes, but also among the masses of the people, a fear which opens the way for fascism to become the cement of a compulsive national unity. 'The temptation of our day is to accept the intolerable, for fear of still worse to come.'* Men who are in the clutches of fear quake before delusions of their own creation. History offers many examples of the illusion giving birth to the reality. Fascism is, *par excellence*, the child of fear—as well as the mother.

III

If these are the conditions under which fascism is born, how does it develop, and in what forms? It is generally accepted that, depending on the existing State structure, there can be two forms—fascism 'from above' and fascism 'from below'. If one looks on fascism as being, for better or for worse, a *new* social and economic system—or at least as a movement towards such a system†—then fascism too becomes a form of social revolution. But if one rejects this view (and I hope it is apparent by now that I do) there cannot in the strict sense of the term be any such thing as fascism 'from below'. Nevertheless, fascism, as a counter-revolution born out of the tension of a revolutionary situation, cannot simply stop at mere traditionalism and negative conservatism; it must to some extent take on the features of a pseudo-revolution. Not only does fascism take over slogans—looking towards its own 'new' order and proclaiming the 'liberation' of the people from the oppression of slavery, but in its more radical forms the fascist's entire processes of thought are, consciously or unconsciously, permeated by those of the revolutionary camp.

Generally speaking, such tendencies are strongest before

* H. Rauschning, *Germany's Revolution of Destruction* (1939), Introduction, p. xi.
† It is natural for this view to be taken by scholars who are sympathetic to fascism or who consider capitalism in its liberal phase as the ideal society, but it is also held by some students of fascism who quite clearly reject both fascism and historical liberal capitalism. See, for example, P. Drucker, *The End of Economic Man* (1939).

fascism achieves power. But it is not always so. For instance, a leading article in the *Frankfurter Zeitung* for 15 December 1940 entitled 'The Sinking World' runs as follows: 'The bourgeois social system was essential for the destruction of feudalism', but now it has completed its mission. 'Within this world ... a solemn roar could be heard for more than a century.' It was 'the roar of the masses living without free light and air ... In England, the Labour Party does not want to overthrow the bourgeois world.' As Franz Neumann comments, so close is its logic to that of Marxism that anyone given this leading article without explanation might well decide that a communist had written it.* Just as God created man in his own image, so fascism often disguises itself in the image of its enemies.

Another important consideration in such cases is the danger of war.† If there is an imminent and critical danger of war breaking out,‡ fascism from above can proceed at a rapid rate, whatever the degree of organization of the revolutionary forces within the country. Since in such circumstances there is insufficient time to create a mass organization to combat the revolutionary forces, national mobilization under military leadership acts in a sense as a substitute. Despite the fact that the army is, in itself, an undemocratic structure *par excellence*, it can, especially when there is compulsory conscription, develop a certain popular base and at least an illusory appearance of democracy. In the process of fascist development one can say that fascist parties and organizations proper are a kind of unofficial army, and conversely the army is a kind of unofficial fascist party.

Of course, this distinction between fascism 'from above' and 'from below' is in the last analysis only a question of degree; for unless the tenseness of the revolutionary situation has reached

---

* F. Neumann, op. cit., p. 59.

† The twentieth century is said to be the century of 'war and revolution'. Certainly in the present age 'war is produced by the conditions which have made revolution necessary, and in turn hastens the consummation of the revolution' (E. H. Carr, *Conditions of Peace* (1942), p. 4). In this sense fascism, as a counter-revolution born of the conditions which make revolution inevitable, is a twin of war. Fascism, as everyone knows, is for both subjective and objective reasons the most fanatic promoter of wars. But since it is obvious that imperialist wars took place long before the birth of fascism, in this discussion I have made counter-revolution, not war, the primary element in the definition of fascism.

‡ This again is a matter not only of the objective facts, but also—and to a large extent—of their subjective assessment; self-deception can play a large part.

a certain level the counter-revolution will not in any case take a fascist form, and even if mass organization does develop from below it is destined, by its very counter-revolutionary nature, to coalesce with the upper-level counter-revolutionary forces. In practice the two always go hand in hand. Nevertheless it is possible, and necessary, to make a distinction between the two types—between fascism that comes mainly as a result of the seizure of power by a fascist party with some kind of mass organization, and fascism that succeeds largely by permeating the existing power structure from inside. Germany, Italy, and Spain are obvious pre-war examples of the former type, and Japan of the latter type. That the tendency towards fascism in contemporary America is also predominantly of the latter type is made clear by Sweezy and others.*

Even when fascism is of the type that comes 'from above', unofficial or semi-official bodies usually act as the vanguard of counter-revolution, the main forces later moving into ground which these advance troops have already 'cleaned'. In pre-war Japan the right-wing groups and terror-gangs—the Army Reservists' Association, the youth groups, and the Imperial Rule Assistance Young Men's Association—come in this category. The so-called 'young officers' do not formally belong to this group, but functionally they were the most militantly effective of vanguards.

There are several points of difference between the type of fascism that comes from above and that which comes from below, but in the nature of their vanguard forces one finds many similarities between the two types. Regardless of the differences arising from historical circumstances, the ideology and campaign methods of these groups, and the personality characteristics and patterns of behaviour of their members, have many points of close similarity that stem from their critical situation, from the fact that as the *élite* troops of the counter-revolution they are in closest opposition to the enemy and the soonest to come into conflict. To give an example, what one might call the orthodox ideology of Japanese fascism was at pains to distinguish itself from Nazism and from Italian fascism, and was in fact of a considerably different breed; but if one looks at the motives and objectives that lay behind the first attempted *coup*

* 'The Meaning of MacArthur', *Monthly Review*, Vol. III, 2.

d'état, the March Incident of 1931, one finds that they were, according to the Kido Diary:*

1. The penetration of communism in recent years has reached serious dimensions, and if nothing is done there is every danger that the State will fall into communist hands.
2. No movement can succeed in Japan unless in some way it puts the Imperial Household at its head.
3. Hence the aim should be to establish national socialism under the aegis of the Emperor and so destroy the existing political parties and bring about dictatorial rule.

Such were the intentions of the group headed by Ōkawa, to which must be added:

4. The Army, in sympathy with these ideas, joined forces with the Ōkawa group to achieve a political structure on the lines of the Italian fascist model.

Here is a clear case where, in Japan too, the radical fascist movement is a response to, and the other side of the coin of, radical left-wing movements. Its ideology, too, is still a Japanese version of fascism in its homeland. (At this time the Nazis had not yet seized power.)

Again, the composition of this radical fascist movement—its core elements were *déclassé* intellectuals, converts from the left wing, and adventurers unable to sustain the routine boredom of *bourgeois* life—is similar to what one finds in the case of the Nazis and the Italian Fascists. As Japanese fascism took shape, however, these elements ceased to play the main theme. They are first relegated to the role of harmonic accompaniment, and then later, as some become guilty of disharmony, they drop out of the chorus altogether. Unlike their German counterparts, the 'lawless adventurers' never succeeded in climbing to the seats of power *qua* adventurers; they merely played a spectacularly violent role in accelerating the growth of fascism from above.[1] The higher up the pyramid one goes, the greater the predominance of more 'gentlemanly', more conformingly civil-servant-like personalities, until at the very peak one finds the 'liberal',

* Kido got this information from Arima Yoriyasu. Arima had, through Shimizu Gyōnosuke of the Great Deeds Society, been invited into the conspiracy of Ōkawa Shūmei, one of the principals in the Incident, and therefore was fully apprised of the details.

'peace-loving' group of palace statesmen, far removed from the usual stereotype of the fascist personality. But this hierarchy, this division of labour between authority, power, and violence, formed a total system that both internally and externally was as fascist in function as anything Nazi Germany could show.

Such was pre-war Japan. *Mutatis mutandis* one can perhaps draw from its example a rough picture of the future progress of fascism in America—assuming, that is, that America *does* take the road to fascism. One would expect America, with its proud record of freedom and human rights, to be far above the level of Japan or Germany with respect to the peacefulness and order-liness of its civil life. Yet even here, the reactionary groups which man the front line of the witch-hunt and of the anti-integration movement, and the behaviour of the people whom they manage to mobilize, show astonishing similarities to their German and Italian counterparts. The following is taken from a detailed eye-witness account of the Peekskill incident in the summer of 1949 —the organized and violent attempt to break up a concert given by Paul Robeson:

The kids grow up in these river towns with no jobs and no future— just a rotten, perverted petty-bourgeois outlook. They get a job at a gas station or a grocery store or a lunch wagon or with the fire department or some other political handout—or they don't work and just scrounge around and live off the few dollars they pick up. They get twisted with bitterness, and they don't know what causes it or where to direct it. Then they hate, and it's easy for the Legion and the local Chamber of Commerce to use that hate.*

Gangs like these could count on the hidden, and sometimes even overt, protection of the district attorney and the state police for their exploits. Fortified by a few drinks, they charged the audience at the concert—including a good proportion of women—armed with pistols, stones, and truncheons, and shouting such slogans as 'God bless Hitler and f——— you nigger bastards and Jew bastards'. They even put themselves to the trouble of giving a repeat performance of the Nuremberg burning of the books, the incident that once made the Nazis notorious throughout the world.

There is, of course, no comparison between the degree and

* Howard Fast, *Peekskill: USA* (1951), p. 71.

skill of their organization and that of their counterparts in Germany in the late twenties and early thirties. The point to be made here is that the social strata which these groups sought to organize, the circumstances of their daily lives and their mental attitudes, are exactly those of the S.S. or the S.A. What they have in common is the frantic sense of frustration that comes from the blocking or the narrowing of opportunities to climb the social ladder, the insecurity and loss of hope that comes from the absence of all positive goals in their lives, and a sense of isolation bred of the collapse of social bonds. Such circumstances only too easily nurture a diffuse hatred and fear directed towards some indefinable and inexplicable object, emotions that provide the perfect driving force for a move towards fascism.

The positive spring of human life is faith, a passionate sense of the reality and significance of life. If that fails them people fall back— they are bound to fall back—upon the negative spring of life, which is fear. Today we are all afraid . . . And let me say this to the people who shout 'Bolshevism' when anyone suggests a new thought about society—they are not proving that Bolshevism is foolish or wicked; they are not helping to prevent Bolshevism spreading; they are merely parading their terror of life and their lack of faith.*

However, it seems likely that these avowedly fascist groups with their Peekskill slogans, 'We're Hitler's boys. We'll finish his job', will find it very difficult to 'finish his job' on the lines of the Nazi Party for all the earnestness of their intentions. At the most they can act as self-appointed underlings of those pressure groups which seek to foster an ever more narrowly orthodox definition of Americanism (the American Legion, the Chamber of Commerce, the National Association of Manufacturers *et al.*) or of the official thought-control organs such as the F.B.I. and the House Committee for Un-American Activities. Their job at the grass roots will be to spread an atmosphere of fear and hate, and so work 'from below' to hasten the process of enforcing ideological homogeneity. And the penetration of fascism at the upper levels will take the form of yielding, in part willingly, in part under protest, to such social pressures. In concrete terms this may, in the words of Schuman commenting on a marked

* John Macmurray, *Freedom in the Modern World* (2nd ed., 1935), p. 213.

feature of the transition from the Roosevelt to the Truman régime, take the form of a tendency for the highest offices of State to 'gravitate increasingly to professional military men and investment bankers', so that the nation is run by 'a combination of pecuniary and military skills'.*

In Germany, where fascism developed from below, the vanguard of the counter-revolution seized power by what at least claimed to be a national socialist 'revolution', and in consequence the characteristics of vanguard extremism remained until the very end. The party leadership, dominated by maladjusted fanatics and nihilistic lovers of violence, was not altogether congenial to the *bourgeoisie*; for the latter, whatever else might be said of them, were at least men who lived by capitalist principles of economic rationality. The fate of Thyssen and Schacht makes this clear enough.† 'Capital's' acceptance of the Nazi 'revolution' was a desperate gamble, a choice between it and socialist revolution. It is true, of course, that the Nazi Party gradually shed its 'anti-capitalist' programme as the fascist régime matured and it is equally true that under the Nazi régime there was a rapid acceleration of capital concentration and increased monopoly control. In this sense a 'fusion' took place between the Nazis and monopoly capital.‡ But this was by no means to the one-sided advantage of 'capital';

* F. Schuman, *International Politics* (1948), p. 208.

† Under the Nazi régime, even before the war, rigid governmental control was imposed not only on wages but also on the specifications, the quantities, and the prices of manufactured goods, and especially in the field of construction materials, boots, and chemical fertilizers enterprises were ordered to produce at prices below costs. The ploughing-back of profits was made compulsory, dividends were limited (at first 6 per cent., later 8 per cent.), and the purchase of government bonds was compulsory. In the summer of 1938 the cream of the labour force was mobilized for the construction of fortifications while their employers not only had to continue their wages, but had to be ready to take them back into employment at any time. (Cf. P. Drucker, op. cit., pp. 148–9.) In exchange for such restrictions the capitalists gained the suppression of all autonomous labour organizations, and consequently freedom from strikes and other forms of conflict. It is not a total error to describe Nazism as a violent form of control by monopoly capital, but such a characterization is far too sweeping. It was not the *bourgeoisie* as a whole, nor even the monopoly capitalists, who were in the last resort the makers of policy.

‡ On this point see especially F. Neumann, op. cit., p. 504, n. 63, pp. 611–14. In the course of his book Neumann develops an analysis of Nazi society which serves as a brilliant refutal of the views of Emil Lederer and Peter Drucker, the former characterizing Nazism as the rule of the mass in which all class barriers have been dissolved, the latter seeing it as a kind of garrison economy (*Wehrwirtschaft*) in which the laws of capitalism no longer apply.

the rationality of capitalist profits was frequently sacrificed to the irrationality of political and military aims.

It is obvious enough that even in Japan, where fascism essentially developed from above, the violence and the anti-capitalism of the radical fascists gave the ruling groups a good deal of trouble. In two stages—the Army purge after the February Incident of 1936, and the compulsory absorption of right-wing organizations into the Imperial Rule Assistance system—they were finally and completely successful in taming the wild horses in the vanguard of fascism.

In this sense one can say that the radicalism and rebellious-ness of the vanguard was at its greatest in Germany and is at its weakest in America, with Japan lying somewhere in between. This is a further indication of the way in which the radicalism of the vanguard is determined by the tenseness of the revolu-tionary situation at the time of the birth of fascism, and in which at the same time its rebelliousness is influenced by the extent to which there is an imminent possibility of war—again at the time of the birth of fascism. (We have already seen that the imminence of war at this stage tends to accelerate the penetra-tion of fascism from above. If Germany had been involved in a war, or in an acute war crisis, in the early thirties before the Nazi seizure of power there is every reason to suppose that fascism would have taken a different form, advancing more 'from above', with perhaps the Wehrmacht playing a central role.)

As these considerations suggest, the forms and tempo of the future development of American fascism will be determined by the most delicate balance between two contradictory forces. The way in which the energies of the fascist vanguard are absorbed by monopoly capital and the fusion of business with the Army suggest that American fascism is starting out in a form which in Germany and Japan was eventually reached only after many twists and turns. In this sense it already contains elements of considerable maturity. When Sweezy, in comparing Japan and America, notes the way in which the Japanese Army and bureaucracy remained relatively independent of monopoly capital, and defines American fascism by contrast as a process of self-militarization of the *bourgeois* class, this is probably the aspect that he wishes to emphasize.

This, however, does not automatically mean that America could more easily be turned into a fascist State than Japan or Germany, or that the process would move at a faster tempo. The weak popular support of the vanguard forces, though it carries the advantage that there is that much less possibility of their revolting against their masters, also means that it is extraordinarily difficult to undermine the trade unions and other voluntary organizations from below. The S.S. and the S.A. certainly did sometimes exhibit a 'radicalism' that embarrassed the Party leadership, but they were an extremely useful weapon to have on hand in order to quash all opposition.

Unless autonomous popular organizations, and especially those of the working class, are shattered into granulated fragments to become part of an amorphous 'mass', it will be impossible to achieve that degree of cemented social unity necessary to eradicate class conflict at home and prosecute wars abroad. However undeveloped the class consciousness of the American unionized worker, it would be no easy task to emasculate the unions and rob them of their autonomy. Unless reliance is placed chiefly on the energies of fascist mass organizations working from below, the only way in which this could rapidly be done is by the crude use of State power to suppress the freedoms of speech, publication, and assembly.

Short of an actual outbreak of war, there seems no real possibility as yet that the American ruling class would choose such direct measures as its major means of exercising political control. Did not Hitler himself say: 'Terrorism is absolutely indispensable in every case of the founding of a new power'? But too much frightfulness does harm. It produces apathy. Even more important than terrorism is the systematic modification of the ideas and feelings of the masses. And this 'is incomparably easier nowadays, with the radio'.* Where the mass media are as firmly in the grip of big business as they are in America today, it is even more likely that chief reliance would be placed on these more delicate means. But to effect the 'systematic modification of the ideas and feelings of the masses' in this way, while maintaining civil liberties, however attenuated, is a lengthy process.

A more important role of America in the present stage of fascism is to act as the international headquarters of the counter-

* H. Rauschning, *Hitler Speaks* (1939), p. 275.

revolution. Since the counter-revolution is but the revolution in reverse, the more the revolution takes on an international character the more fascism is itself forced to organize on an international scale. In this sense the pattern of counter-revolution that America has developed throughout the world is rather like the pyramidal pattern of fascism 'from above' laterally extended. Just as, where fascism proceeds 'from above', the most extremist fascist groups are found in the lower reaches of society, so in the international line-up of the counter-revolution it is in those countries where the revolutionary situation is most tense and where the revolutionary forces are making their most direct challenge that one finds the régimes that adopt fascist methods of rule. In the Far East the régimes of Syngman Rhee, Quirino, Bao Dai, and Chiang Kai-shek are examples; and the same principle explains why the Liberal Party government in Japan, though showing marked tendencies towards fascism, is still more 'moderate' than these régimes.

Greece and Turkey were the first countries to receive large-scale aid under the Truman Doctrine, the policy enunciated in the President's historic speech of 12 March 1947, which aims, as he said then, to preserve from totalitarian oppression the 'free institutions' of 'free people'. But how 'free' were the institutions those countries enjoyed at that time? King George II of Greece was the man who conspired with General Metaxas to establish a fascist dictatorship in 1936, and his brother Paul who succeeded him was formerly head of the Fascist Youth organization. In Turkey, after a long period of single-party dictatorship, the opposition Democratic Party was allowed to participate in elections for the first time in 1946; but these elections were held under martial law and all opposition newspapers had been suppressed. It is not necessary to elaborate on the nature of the Franco régime.

Let it be said, in all fairness to President Truman, that he probably has no positive liking for these blatant fascist régimes in the East and in the West. In exactly the same way the leaders in Washington and in the Pentagon do not necessarily approve of the activities of the more notorious reactionary groups and veterans' associations, even less of blatant violence towards 'reds' or Negroes. But, as we have seen, in the internal and external situation which prevails today even the 'intolerable' can be tolerated out of fear of something worse to follow. We would do well to recall the words of Lloyd George in the House of Commons a year and a half after the Nazi accession to power: 'In the very near future, perhaps within one or two years, conservative elements in this country will come to look on Germany as Europe's bulwark against communism . . . Let us not hasten to condemn Germany. For soon we shall be welcoming her as a friend.' As Schuman remarks, 'The root cause of "appeasement" as practised by the democratic powers towards the warlords of fascism lay in the fact that many members of the propertied *élites* who were most influential in the shaping of policy in the Western capitals, openly or secretly admired fascism as "insurance" against communism.'*

Leaving aside for the moment the McCarthyites among American politicians, let us ask whether the more rational elements, those more loyal to the traditions of European democracy, will learn the appropriate lesson from the mistakes of the pre-war period? Or will they be so seized in the grip of fear that they follow in the footsteps of those representatives of the *ancien régime* in nineteenth-century France who 'learned nothing and forgot nothing'? On the answer to this question hinges the likely course of fascism, both in the immediate and in the more distant future.

CONCLUSION

Fascism is in no sense a new social system, nor does it represent an attempt to move towards one. Consequently it has no positive goals, no unambiguous policies. If it has a single objective, then it is simply that of counter-revolution. Hence its slogans can take only a negative form—*anti*-communism, *anti*-semitism. Hence also the fact that, when it adopts the form of single-party dictatorship, it will attempt to make counter-revolution into a permanent form of government on the ideological level as well as on practical grounds. Moreover, fascism pretends in its propaganda to be the friend of every social stratum. But in modern societies composed of a plurality of conflicting and interlocking interests any proponent of a consistent and positive political programme is inevitably bound to run counter to the interests of some class or other. Hitler, how-

* F. Schuman, op. cit., pp. 626–8.

ever, promised the capitalists the eradication of workers' organizations, while to the workers he pledged the final elimination of all exploitation by capital; for the benefit of the small businessmen he attacked the department stores and the trusts; to the farmers he preached about the decadence and corruption of the towns; to the Roman Catholics he proposed a campaign to suppress atheism and irreligion, and to Protestants he spoke in biting terms of the decadence of the Catholic Church; and everywhere and at all times he proclaimed his message of liberation from Bolshevism and from the Jewish menace. The contradictions of his programmes and policies might well be called the built-in contradictions of fascism. Drucker claims to have heard a Nazi agitator who was addressing a wildly cheering crowd of peasants declaim in all seriousness: 'We don't want lower bread prices, we don't want higher bread prices, we don't want unchanged bread prices—we want National-Socialist bread prices.'*

Nonsense this may be, but it does serve, in almost cartoon form, to bring into relief the deepest essence of fascism. In abstract and 'theoretical' terms, the process of total organization of the counter-revolution can be completed only when, by the compulsory cementing of society, all heterogeneous elements—all actual and potential opponents of the established order—are swept away. But the appearance of these elements opposed to the established order is a consequence of the underlying revolutionary situation, not its cause, and unless there is a halt in the world-wide onward march of social revolution itself, this kind of homogeneization can never in reality be completed. In this sense the work of fascism is eternally 'unfinished';† it can exist only as a *perpetuum mobile* towards the goal of total organization of the counter-revolution.

And this is the ultimate fate of 'activist nihilism' in modern society.

TRANSLATOR'S NOTE

1. See 'Thought and Behaviour Patterns of Japan's Wartime Leaders', pp. 91–92, 129 above.

* P. Drucker, op. cit., pp. 13–14.

† When the Nazi theorist, Carl Schmitt, speaks of the State, the movement, and the nation, as the three elements of national socialism, with the movement (*Bewegung*) as the central core, his words are indicative of much more than he intends.

VI. A Critique of De-Stalinization

TRANSLATED BY PAUL VARLEY

This essay was originally published in the magazine Sekai, *1956*

I

Some three hundred years ago Thomas Hobbes regretfully observed how difficult it was to arrive at infallible conclusions about men, for, unlike lines and circles, the comparison of men almost invariably involves a clash of truth and interest. It is highly significant that Hobbes should have made this lament at a time when the passion fomented by the English Revolution was at its height.

During certain periods of history the stability of the foundation on which people establish their lives is undermined and not simply specific phases but the very principles of society itself are questioned. At such times a fundamental disturbance may cause the simultaneous exposure to attack both of a mode of life, in which conflicting economic and other interests are deeply embedded, and of a sense of values, which people regard as self-evident and beyond question. The resulting condition of chronic instability becomes the characteristic mental climate of the period, and changes that occur in rapid succession before people's very eyes are so bewildering and astonishing that the psychological shock of events temporarily overwhelms them. It is only later that they can attempt to understand the meaning of these events within a wider context.

Today, even though we remind Roman Catholics of such developments in the later Middle Ages as the tyranny of the Inquisition, the corruption of the Papacy, and the brutality of the Massacre of Saint Bartholomew, none of them, however ardent he may be, is likely to flush with anger and speak out in spirited defence. Furthermore a Presbyterian minister would no doubt agree readily to the assertion that the political system that Calvin established at Geneva was an 'absolutist' system and that his burning of Servetus was entirely unbecoming to the spirit of Christianity. Moreover neither a Roman Catholic nor a Protestant today would deny that there is some truth in the words of the English historian who stated that the more one analyses the religious wars the less one sees in them the essential elements of religion.

In the case of the French Revolution we see that even today its historical interpretation is hotly disputed. Yet the period when such an academic debate took on direct political significance has already faded into the distant past. Even people who emphatically denounce the follies and slaughters resulting from the French Revolution and from the succeeding war of intervention acknowledge that the principles of the declaration of human rights, which were the ideals of the Revolution, exist today as axioms throughout the civilized world. At the same time nobody finds it particularly strange that in a country that celebrates the anniversary of the storming of the Bastille as a national holiday, and has as its national anthem the Marseillaise, films are produced that cause people to respond with emotional sympathy to the fate of Marie Antoinette.

Let us now turn our attention to the Russian Revolution and to the chain of events it set in motion. Sufficient time still has not passed to allow the world of today to recover from the psychological shock of these events. While speaking of time, I do not refer simply to the natural period of forty-odd years that has elapsed since the Revolution. Forty years can be regarded as *only* forty years as well as *already* forty years. Rather the problem here is that within this period of time the world (this includes the present socialist world centred on the Soviet Union as well as the non-socialist world) has not provided a satisfactory settlement to the challenge of the Russian Revolution. Consequently the issues created by this event are still very much alive and continue to stir our existence profoundly.

No matter how highly one may regard the achievements of Soviet Russia or Communist China, it does not follow that their methods should be imported into one's own country. At the same time, no matter how frantically one discloses the faults of the Soviet Union or Communist China, it will in no way eliminate those conditions in one's own country that are so sensationally displayed in the newspapers every day—conditions such as the corruption of power, the scandals, and the disasters that bring unemployment and privation. Nevertheless, although it may not be wise either to praise the communist experience too highly or to condemn it too harshly, it is also difficult to remain aloof. As events occur within this 'new world' of communism they evoke the feeling that 'this is not somebody else's business'.

The average person still has not found a point of equilibrium between the two sides of the Russian Revolution (which Laski calls the 'immense gains' and the 'immense costs'). Depending on the impact of the Revolution on their own interests and attitudes, people either psychologically exaggerate the favourable aspects or over-emphasize the unfavourable ones. And, the more international and internal political tensions increase, the more intense the speech and criticism towards both extremes of friend and foe become. Both sides seek to make full propaganda capital out of even the smallest acts that they feel may be advantageous to the 'friend' and disadvantageous to the 'enemy'. Hence, as new aspects of communism and of the socialist system are perceived and evaluated, they are judged first from the standpoint of their social impact on friend and foe rather than from the standpoint of truth or falsehood. At the same time there is speculation about the 'ulterior motives' of those who perceive these new aspects and of those who pass judgement on them. When someone presents a view of the communist world, it is immediately classified as either pro-communist or anti-communist, and while hailed by one camp it is denounced by the other. A political magnetic field is created and even individuals who start out as 'impartial', objective critics are frequently drawn off in one direction or the other. Within each camp alignment proceeds half spontaneously and half forcibly as fear and suspicion of 'utilization by the enemy' continue to affect people strongly.

It is ironical that with intensification of the Cold War both the United States and the Soviet Union have come more and more to resemble each other as they turn their internal organizations into 'garrison-states'. Yet this is only one, albeit a conspicuous, aspect of the wider and more protracted critical situation that exists between the communist and non-communist worlds. Ever since the Russian Revolution there has been a tendency throughout the world for people either wholeheartedly to attack the Soviet system and the principles of communism or wholeheartedly to support them. In other words, in perceiving and evaluating the various aspects of communism, they have taken an absolutist position of opposition or support.

In a strange 'agreement of opposites' the logic of the all-out communists has, at least in one respect, come to coincide with that of the all-out anti-communists; and this is a telling expression of political conditions in the modern world and of the mental climate to which these conditions have given rise. In the first place, the two 'opposites' are alike in failing to regard the development of communist movements in the Soviet Union and elsewhere in terms of the peculiar historical conditions that preceded them, or in terms of the interaction between them and the given political situations; instead they deduce everything from the 'essence' of the Marxist world-outlook, or else ascribe it all to some 'inevitable' process of development. Secondly, the two extremes share the same approach concerning the aims of the leaders in the Kremlin; whether they regard these aims as being based on 'scientific principles', or whether, on the other hand, they lump them together as a 'sinister scheme for world conquest', they agree in regarding the aims themselves as being the overriding factors in the situation.

II

The broad internal 'liberalization' trend within the communist camp, which extended from the policy of 'de-Stalinization' presented at the Twentieth Party Congress to the proposal by the Chinese Communist Party to 'Let One Hundred Flowers Bloom', may prove to be a turning-point in the course of this chronically unstable condition. In general there are two things that any revolutionary force must struggle against: the State structure and the 'old order' of society. In this struggle the old order always has the advantage of being able to mobilize the traditional customs and symbols of society as well as its ingrained cultural forms, all of which we may call the 'unorganized social forces'. Consequently, in order to counter this advantage, it becomes absolutely essential that the revolutionaries establish rigid solidarity and discipline both in their organization and in their ideology. In this way the concentration of power and symbols necessary for leadership are legitimated. The need for such action becomes ever more necessary as the *ancien régime* intensifies its effort to contain the revolutionary forces and as the power relationship between the revolutionary and counter-revolutionary forces changes rapidly and becomes more and more insecure. In this sense, Cromwell's Puritanism and the Jacobinism of the French Revolution bear a physiological and pathological resemblance to communism and are no less 'monolithic'.*

These comments apply to the concentration and distribution of power within the international revolutionary movement, as well as to the internal structure of the revolutionary party. Franz Borkenau, a sharply critical student of the Comintern, observed as early as in the 1930s that it is a great mistake to characterize the communist parties of the world as simply the product of 'orders from Moscow'. On the contrary, 'regardless of the enormous prestige of the Russian Revolution, when relatively strong revolutionary movements exist in areas outside Russia these movements do not necessarily receive instructions from Moscow'. The activities of people like Bela Kun, Rosa Luxemburg, Paul Levi, and the Chinese communist leaders confirm the truth of these words. Borkenau made the equally interesting observation that 'the further the practical chance of the revolution fades into the background, the more *worship* of the revolution that has *already* succeeded in Russia is substituted for it'.†

Group strength creates a corresponding feeling of stability, and the latter, in turn, strengthens among its members a sense of independence—an independence that does not necessarily imply cliquishness. The development of this process diminishes the fear that individual and spontaneous thought and action on the part of members of the group may endanger its unity; and this again encourages development of more diversified patterns of behaviour. Communism and communist countries are no exceptions to this spiralling process. We can note, for example, two significant and related facts that emerged from the Twentieth Congress: first, the leaders of the Soviet State were enjoying an unprecedented feeling of international security; and,

---

* In making this comparison I am not, of course, overlooking differences among the three movements arising from their respective historical and social conditions and from the special ideological weapons used by each.

† *Communist International*, 1938, pp. 416–18.

secondly, by undertaking 'de-Stalinization' they embarked on a 'new course' that startled the world. The self-confidence generated by group strength and independence is further demonstrated by the fact that the two groups within the international communist camp to express the most original as well as the most critical views concerning the Russian way of de-Stalinization were the Italian Communist Party and Communist China. The former is the strongest communist group in Western Europe, while China is generally acknowledged to be the most powerful communist country in the world apart from the Soviet Union.

Under existing international conditions the repercussions of de-Stalinization have spread in accordance with their own political dynamics. The Twentieth Congress itself graphically presented anew to the world both sides of the Russian Revolution, 'the immense gains' and 'the immense costs'. Since this was the first time the Soviet leaders had publicly acknowledged the latter aspect of their Revolution, anti-Soviet, anti-communist forces throughout the world promptly sought to make propaganda capital out of it. The receipt of Khrushchev's secret report by the American State Department and its partial publication on 4 June 1956 were the climax of this drama. Although the Soviet leaders may have carefully considered the political pros and cons of a course of de-Stalinization before boldly pushing forward, subsequent international repercussions caused them more and more to stress defence against 'utilization by the enemy'. This trend was also reflected in communist party papers throughout the world.

De-Stalinization, of course, came as a severe shock to those communists and fellow-travellers everywhere who had deified Stalin and had given unqualified support to the domestic and international policies of the Soviet Union. At the same time it challenged the assumptions of the many anti-communists who had either interpreted communism solely in terms of one given phase of its historical development, or who had persistently attempted to attribute universal 'laws' and tendencies of politics to the principles of the Soviet system and of communism.

The former (the communists and fellow-travellers), initially at least, did not or could not conceal the effects of the shock they had received. For example, there is the statement of the National

Executive Committee of the American Communist Party on 24 June 1956: '. . . [we] are deeply shocked by the revelations contained in Khrushchev's speech . . . We admit frankly that we uncritically justified many foreign and domestic policies of the Soviet Union which are now shown to be wrong.'*

On the other hand, the position of the anti-communists appears to have remained largely unchanged, and they continue to adhere to the theory of the 'essential' immutability of communism. It would be quite unrealistic, of course, to envisage the 'liberalization' of the Soviet Union and the communist bloc as a return to free enterprise and to the parliamentary political system of the West. I shall not enter into a discussion of systems at this point. The important point to note is that this one-sided emphasis on the immutability of communism by the anti-communists has the converse effect of strengthening the communists' own version of the 'immutability theory'.† Such a process gives rise to a vicious cycle of ideological inflexibility on both sides.

An American professor, who was travelling to India and who happened to be in Moscow during the Twentieth Party Congress, received the following impressions from his contact with a wide range of citizens and students:

> Some of them spoke freely, with abandon, 'letting their hair down', behaving as if this was the long-awaited opportunity for talking about things they could not discuss before, for saying all that they had on their minds. Others were formal, restrained, weighing every word and studiously avoiding any 'ticklish' subjects, anything that might be interpreted as an indiscretion . . . as if they were a representative of one power talking to an ambassador of another.‡

These two types characterize the great majority of communist party members throughout the world today; and an alternation of the two attitudes can be found in the Soviet Union's pattern of behaviour in international politics. The problem for the future is which type will become predominant and which course will ultimately prevail; but the solution will not be provided simply by unilateral decisions on the part of the

---

* *Political Affairs*, July 1956, pp. 35–36.
† Those who hold this view limit as much as possible the implications of de-Stalinization on the grounds that the 'quintessence' of socialism has not changed.
‡ Paul A. Baran, 'On Soviet Themes', *Monthly Review*, July–August 1956, p. 84.

communist camp. For this problem is deeply rooted in world politics, and the response of the West and of the non-communists in general will have a significant bearing on whether or not the intellectual meaning implicit in de-Stalinization reaches historical maturity.

Regardless of the specific nature of any future criticism or appraisal of de-Stalinization, one thing is certain: if the motivating spirit is simply a continuation of that spirit which has been bred in the feverish mental climate caused by the polarization of world politics, it will result in an undermining of the historical significance of de-Stalinization. If we are to establish a basis of co-operation for Marxists and non-Marxists to set common scientific problems and to derive therefrom common historical lessons, then a critical examination of the 'critique of Stalinism' must stem from an investigation of thought and behaviour patterns born and bred in the peculiar psychological atmosphere that has become chronic since the Russian Revolution. Otherwise the vociferous international debate surrounding de-Stalinization will simply continue along the two customary parallel lines: on the part of the communists, the usual casuistic debate concerning the interpretation of the Marxist-Leninist 'gospel'; and, on the part of the anti- or non-communists, an attitude that nothing can be expected unless communist self-criticism comes up to the 'Western' level.

With the above observations as a working hypothesis and using as material the literature published on this issue both in the Soviet Union and by communist parties elsewhere, I shall now try an 'epistemological' approach to the political problems contained in de-Stalinization. Such an approach will naturally lead to criticism of Marxist interpretations, particularly in regard to their understanding of political processes. This does not, however, necessarily imply a critique of the Marxist *Weltanschauung* from the standpoint of any particular political ideology, nor an examination of the political and social systems of the Soviet Union and the socialist republics as such. I admit that a certain measure of ideological preference will inevitably enter into my critique, and if the reader so wishes he is of course free to interpret my remarks as bearing on the 'essence' of Marxism and of communism. Nevertheless my intention in this essay is rather to refrain from making a fundamental evaluation of Marxism and its world-view. To use the analogy of photography, I shall try to place communist theories—particularly those of internationally famous communists—concerning the present problem into the 'developing solution' of political maxims that are as universal as possible, and thereby to print a 'positive' that will reflect certain patterns of thought and behaviour.

Thought and behaviour patterns of this sort are not necessarily characteristic of Marxism and communism. Still, in today's atmosphere of ideological polarization between East and West, there is a strong tendency for communist ideas of partisanship combined with the systematic nature of Marxism to express themselves in terms of a complete and closed system. Hence they are liable to take mental attitudes and political measures that belong to the political conditions of a specific historical situation and transfer them to the basic 'world-view' of Marxism, or else to rationalize these attitudes and measures as simply an inevitable necessity of 'struggle'. In any event there can be no doubt that such inclinations on the part of the communists have produced several significant effects: they have blocked the exchange of views among different schools; in the field of practical politics these liabilities have made it difficult for communist leaders to exercise rational control of their own political means, thus lending support to the 'absolutist' views of anti-communists. Herein lies the reason for demanding that the communists first of all recognize that certain 'laws' of politics operate in *any* movement or *any* system, regardless of ideology. This action would indeed be the first step towards liberation—thaw in the true sense of the word—from ideological inflexibility. Moreover this decisive step has already been taken by the communists themselves, whether consciously or not, in the de-Stalinization issue.

III

Among the first steps taken by the Soviet leaders in their de-Stalinization campaign was a complete reversal of the 'cult of personality'. By oversimplifying the distinction between 'good' and 'bad', these leaders attributed to Stalin as an individual such 'bad' aspects of recent Soviet history as the great purges, forcible liquidations, arbitrary decisions, rampant bureaucratism, and failures in military leadership. At the same time they credited the heroic struggle of the Soviet masses concentrated round the Bolshevik Party for such 'good' things as the rapid strides in the development of the Soviet economy and the victory over Nazi Germany. It is absurd to claim that only the individual is responsible for the 'bad' things that happen and that the people have nothing to do with them, while, at the same time, insisting that history is made not by individuals but by the people. Moreover, the Soviet leaders are arguing in a vicious circle when they attribute the growth of the cult of personality to a lack of collective leadership and at the same time blame the cult of personality for the neglect of collective leadership.

The first step towards a more plausible explanation of how a cult of personality arises can be found in an article in the 5 April 1956 issue of the Chinese *People's Daily News* entitled 'On Historical Experience Concerning the Dictatorship of the Proletariat'. The significant observation is made that the cult of personality results from the 'force of habit of millions of people'.

The shock of the secret report on 4 June 1956 forced the leaders of the world's important communist parties, beginning with Togliatti, to examine the causes of the growth of Stalin-worship as having a direct bearing on their own interests. They began with an expression of dissatisfaction over the manner in which the Soviet Union had presented and explained de-Stalinization. So long as all criticism had emanated from the 'enemy', the Soviet leaders had either ignored it or had countered with charges of their own. But now doubts and demands began to pour in from friendly parties, and these leaders had no alternative but to reply. This came in the form of a 'Determination Concerning the Conquest of the "Cult of Personality" and its Various Consequences' issued by the Central Committee of the Soviet Communist Party on 30 June.

The Soviet Communist Party Central Report listed two categories of factors that gave rise to the cult of personality: 1. Objective historical conditions under which socialism was constructed in the Soviet Union; 2. subjective causes connected with Stalin's personal temperament. Let us set aside for the time being an examination of the historical factors that have contributed to the cult of personality, such as the international isolation of the Soviet Union, the centralization of power made inevitable by the threat of internal counter-revolutionary groups and international fascism, and 'restrictions placed on certain democratic forms' by power centralization. The key to the problem of the cult of personality lies rather in the intermediary factors that tie these 'objective' and 'subjective' causes together. Here we can note such vital political considerations as the following: the connexion between the personality of the individual and existing historical situations; the functional relationship between the leader and the led; and the significance of the informal group within the formal organization. When examining not only the cult of personality but any political phenomenon, it is extremely important to consider these intermediary 'linking' factors. Otherwise the examination will be made through two separate approaches: on the one hand, by explaining things from the standpoint of 'macroscopic' historical situations and socio-political systems; and, on the other, by seeking the causes in the inherent character of leaders (the sort of character analysis that in extreme cases can lead to the theory that certain 'rogues' are responsible for all the 'bad' elements of history).

We can see examples of the latter approach in the statements by *Pravda* on 28 March 1956 that Stalin 'lacked personal humility' and by Khrushchev in his Secret Report that he 'lacked even elementary modesty'. Are these statements correct? I shall not pause to examine the nature of Stalin's personality. But from various sources it is clear that Stalin was not excessively vain and that his capacity for self-control was not inferior to that of other dictators in history. This is especially true when we consider the length of time during which he occupied the summit of power as well as his colossal achievements. De Toqueville's appraisal of Louis Napoleon—'He possessed an *abstract respect* for the people, but did not display much good will towards freedom'—applies even more to Stalin. Further, even if we acknowledge the point that Khrushchev raised (that Stalin possessed an 'abnormally suspicious nature'), this refers to a personal characteristic and does not provide any solution to the problem of the cult of personality. Communists throughout the world have preached and are still preaching the urgency of 'revolutionary vigilance'. Yet under the pressure of acute political tensions it is hard indeed to distinguish clearly between the growth of 'revolutionary vigilance' (or 'counter-revolutionary vigilance') and the development of suspiciousness. Not a few Japanese communists must have experienced such difficulties during the schism in their party from 1950 to 1955.

The following statement by Eugene Dennis about the great purges after 1934 appeared in the 18 June 1956 issue of the *Daily Worker*: 'The search for "enemies of the people" took on hysterical proportions *in which virtually all opposition and serious differences of opinion became suspect.*' Dennis also referred to: 'The terrible phenomena of false "confessions" and fabricated "evidence"—*evil products of a feverishly suspicious and hysterical atmosphere* exploited by a Yezhov, a Beria, and other agents of imperialism.'

The psychological atmosphere generated by a tense political situation has its own auto-propulsion. Even after objective conditions have changed, the patterns of thought and action imprinted on men's behaviour by such a psychological atmosphere still remain in effect. We must not forget that the great purges of the Communist Party and other national organs and the reign of terror instituted by Kirov's assassination in 1934 reached their peak *after* the completion of the first Five-Year Plan, *after* the extermination of the Kulaks through agricultural collectivization, *after* the Trotskyites within the Soviet Union had been 'disarmed' and the social base of the counter-revolutionaries had largely disappeared—in short, *after* socialism as a system had consolidated its base. (The promulgation of the Stalin Constitution was a legal confirmation of these processes.)*

The Khrushchev Report stated: '. . . owing to the numerous arrests of party, Soviet, and economic leaders many workers began to work uncertainly, showed *over-cautiousness*, feared all which was new, *feared their own shadows*, and began to show less initiative in their work.' In effect the report recognized that the auto-propulsion of the psychological impact of the purges was, conversely, creating new 'conditions'. But this does not neces-

---

* On the other hand, the increasing threat of Japanese-German fascism after 1933 certainly provided a basis for rationalizing the aggrandizement of power by Stalin and the O.G.P.U.

sarily mean that Khrushchev himself was aware of the *theoretical* significance implied in his report. In any event it is going too far when one attempts to attribute such political dynamics as suspicion, distrust, and fear to the character or mentality of a particular individual. Nor can one necessarily term these factors characteristic of any specific social structure or political system. For example, if we take the above words of Dennis and substitute 'enemy of the Republic' for 'enemy of the people' and 'Senator McCarthy and other China Lobby agents' for 'Beria and other Imperialist agents', they would apply *mutatis mutandis* to the atmosphere of the United States from the late 1940s to the early 1950s.

The self-criticism within the international communist camp occasioned by de-Stalinization was, for the most part, remarkably uniform, and provides a clue to the psychology of communist political behaviour. For example, Eugene Dennis stated in the above issue of the *Daily Worker* that the American Communist Party had often been '. . . intolerant of the critical opinions and viewpoints of many labour and liberal spokesmen. We too often treated criticism from sincere trade unionists and liberals as though it came from the professional anti-communist and anti-Soviet baiters.' James Klugmann of the British Communist Party observed in a similar vein: 'We have been far too prone to brand individuals whose *policy* we consider wrong or even disastrous as personal traitors. Personal intentions are not in fact the issue. There is no such thing yet invented as a "sincerometer" that could measure accurately personal sincerity, and a man with a disastrous policy can be perfectly sincere.'* In their self-examinations these men had tended to categorize indiscriminately any opinion or policy that did not agree with their views as 'evil designs' of the opposition. But certainly the American and British communists were not the only ones to have adopted this attitude.

A statement in the 28 March 1956 issue of *Pravda* reflects a tendency that, for all practical purposes, nearly *all* communists in *all* countries have shared until very recently: 'In this atmosphere (adulation of Stalin) the only one who could develop theory, have it advanced, and state anything original and new

---

* James Klugmann, 'Communists and Socialists', *The Marxist Quarterly*, July 1956, p. 155.

was Stalin. It was considered the function of everyone else to disseminate the ideas pronounced by Stalin and to interpret the formula laid down by him.' Consequently we cannot arrive at a true solution to the problem of this 'flaw' in communism with the evasive charge that it is simply a reflection of the 'low level' of communism in particular countries. Nor can we solve anything by adopting the moralistic attitude that this flaw is due to lack of culture on the part of individual communist party members. As an example of the last point, we can find ample support for the 'moral' that blind obedience to authority is bad both in the self-criticism of the communists and in the critiques of the anti-communists, and it is obvious that blind obedience to authority *is* bad. Nevertheless, the problem is not so simple. One cannot simply alter one's attitude and determine thenceforth to be more independent of authority.

The cult of Stalin was not merely the result of the worship of a specific personality. Rather it was a tendency on the part of the great majority of communists to accept the *theories* advanced by Stalin as gospel truth, not because all communists by nature possess 'authoritarian personalities' but because Stalin's theories functioned as a symbol of the organizational solidarity of the proletariat throughout the world. Accordingly any expression of doubt about his 'theories' within the communist camp would be regarded as a threat to unity and solidarity. And when communists are fearful of a drift away from the party line, there is an increasing tendency for them to synchronize their thoughts and speeches with the upper level of the party hierarchy. The upward alignment proceeds from party member to party leader of each country and from party leader to the 'fatherland of socialism', the Soviet Union, and to the ultimate authority of the Soviet Party. Thus what Sydney Webb once called the 'disease of orthodoxy' comes to prevail. Of course this disease of orthodoxy in the Soviet Union is a direct legacy from Tsarist Russia and can be traced to the traditional union between the Greek Orthodox Church and imperial power. In similar fashion the Japanese Communist Party received a psychological legacy from the 'national polity'[1] orthodoxy.

As I pointed out at the beginning of this essay, however, the communist disease of orthodoxy *on a world scale* stems from two things: the psychological habit of a revolutionary group still aware of its own inferiority in the existing power relationship; and the behavioural response common to both political camps when confronted by the acute polarization of political situations. To clarify the last point, while the communists were suffering from the disease of orthodoxy the corresponding response of the 'liberal' countries was to engage in orthodox *anti-communist* activities such as the loyalty investigations in the United States.

Another type of attitude that commonly accompanies alignment resulting from the disease of orthodoxy can be seen in the remarks of Dennis: 'We refused to believe, and regarded as slander, any news that purported to tell of grave injustices in the socialist countries.'*

Most of the matters revealed by *Pravda* and the Khrushchev Secret Report were already well known in the '*bourgeois* world' and could scarcely be called secret. For example, the famous note left by Lenin in which he cautioned against the installation of Stalin as Secretary-General, the existence of forced-labour camps, and the fact that the Great Purges were carried out with utter disregard even for the legal procedure established by the Stalin Constitution—Western observers were quite familiar with all this before de-Stalinization. However, it was only when the highest responsible officials in the Soviet Union took note of them that the other communist parties in the world acknowledged them one after another.

Despite the oft-repeated maxim 'learn from your enemy', the communists usually make little use of journalistic reports available from non-communist sources except for propaganda purposes. In the field of scholarship too there has been a marked tendency for the rigid Marxist to cite the works of non-Marxist scholars either for the purpose of refutation or simply to confirm his own views. This tendency is most conspicuous in treatments of the social and political systems of the Soviet Union and the People's Democracies. Moreover, such rigidity is generally stronger in those fields where Marxist-Leninist theories are more 'complete', or in those cases where the issues involved are more clearly defined by Marxist-Leninist classics.

This failure to learn from the enemy is not necessarily due to

* Eugene Dennis, 'The U.S.A. and Khrushchev's Special Report', *Daily Worker*, 18 June 1956, p. 2.

the fact that Marxists are by nature narrow-minded or that they inherently lack liberal ideas. Furthermore it is not inevitable that Marxism develop as a closed system. Nevertheless, so long as the psychological atmosphere of a world polarized between communism and anti-communism continues, academic debate and ideological struggle will invariably remain intertwined. And under such conditions there is a strong tendency for Marxism to function as a symbolic 'totality'. The natural result is that within this 'totality' caution against a backslide towards 'revisionism' is always stressed in preference to the bold adoption of non-Marxist contributions.

As we look more closely, we see that the stereotyped patterns of behaviour that Marxists display are all more or less functionally related to prevailing political situations. Consequently these patterns of behaviour do not disappear simply because the communists 'repent'; nor do they exist merely as 'exclusive' phenomena within the communist camp, as so many anti-communists delude themselves into believing.* However, it is precisely because such psychological tendencies are firmly grounded in existing situations that we must constantly isolate and examine them on a clinical basis.

The communists may insist as much as they wish that the studies of '*bourgeois* scholars' and the press reports relating to the Communist Party and the Soviet System are governed by bias and contain only slander and false rumour. But if they rely exclusively on the studies and reports of their own camp, they may turn out to be like the husband who is the only one unaware of his wife's infidelity. The shock of being suddenly faced with harsh reality can be considerable. Above all, this attitude on the part of the communists, while it may make them more sensitive towards ideological affiliations, is of little value in cultivating the ability to judge independently the credibility of certain materials and analytical results.

There is always the possibility that diversity of opinion and multivocal interpretations about vital problems may loosen group solidarity or prove advantageous to the enemy. As the

---

* Actually, there are many examples of Western anti-Marxist scholars who ridicule the communists' academic 'lockout', yet who are 'psychologically' repelled by such phraseology as, let us say, monopoly capital or imperialism. Without sufficiently examining the pertinence of 'formal', these scholars often live serenely in their own 'formalism' in which the Marxist term 'formal' simply equals 'error'.

communist becomes more and more apprehensive of this possibility, his inclination to conform becomes habitual and, even though he may not be authoritarian by nature, he tends to *become* increasingly authoritarian.

We have already noted the stereotyped patterns of behaviour that can emerge from the interaction of political situations and human personalities. This is certainly not an inevitable process. Nevertheless it is important to go beyond particular cases and to try to establish a general theory on how such patterns develop. Otherwise the so-called 'analysis of objective conditions' will simply provide the conclusion that certain things took in certain specific historical situations in the past, and discussions of individual character will result in the moralistic resolution: 'Now let us strive to become good communists!' How can one expect to overcome the pathological phenomenon described above from such a basis of orientation?

When dealing with Stalin's personal defects and the Soviet purges, there is not much to be gained by trying to distinguish between good intentions and bad, or by seeking salvation from these 'bad' things in the 'inherent' righteousness and perfection of system and 'world view'. It makes no sense to say simply that revolutionary vigilance is 'very good' and suspiciousness is 'very bad'. We must investigate, with reference to a concrete political process, under precisely what conditions revolutionary vigilance turns into suspiciousness and at just what point the transition takes place. Only then can the results be made a common heritage. The fitness of the leader, of course, differs according to the nature of the political organization. Furthermore the political functions of leadership change with the phase of organizational development—for example, the transition from the acquisition of power to its stabilization, from the offensive to the defensive, or from crisis to normality. Hence the leader himself is neither 'good' nor 'bad'.

Prominent Marxists have in practice intuitively perceived the importance of this problem, and have realized that analysis of the political personality can link macroscopic objective conditions and the socio-economic process with concrete political decisions. Still, they have persistently treated such problems in terms of practical tactics. Consequently they have not been able to formulate any typology of political behaviour out of the complexity of historical situations. Thus we are confronted with the ironic situation in which Marxists, who claim to be highly conscious of the political character of their own theories, employ opportunistic empirical techniques to deal with urgent political problems. In particular they reject all efforts to grasp the inter-action between personality and situation as 'detestable psycho-logisms' inconsistent with the materialistic approach.

This often leads the communists to a ridiculously simple and unrealistic 'explanation' of the motivations for human be-haviour. For example, in the formal announcements branding Beria and Itō Ritsu as 'traitors', the communists employed nearly identical processes of 'retroactive' logic to explain their treacherous actions. According to this hackneyed logic, Beria and Itō had inherently evil characters and joined the party with bad intentions. Realizing their sinister designs step by step, they succeeded in rising within the system to the highest positions of party and State. Regardless of whether or not Beria and Itō really were traitors, this kind of 'logic' is hardly convincing.

At this point we must examine in a more general context the thought processes that have actually motivated the majority of Marxists.

IV

Applying the 'retroactive' approach to the analysis of per-sonality and behaviour, the communists work backwards from the 'crime' to discover that at a much earlier period the culprit was motivated by evil intentions. If the search is carried back far enough it will result in the revelation of the individual's essential character—in other words the 'essence' of his nature that has determined all of his subsequent actions. Of course in the case of people like Beria and Itō the communists were dealing with an analysis of 'bad' behaviour. But this same approach is applicable also to the growth of class consciousness among the people or to the historical process of the socialist system. The purpose would be to reveal the inherent character of the proletariat or of the system, as though 'dispelling the dark clouds from the outside'.

The logic in this process of revealing the *a priori* inherent quality can be considered logic either of organic development or of natural law. The process cannot, however, be called 'dialectic' unless the momentum of the inside (the subject in question) changes as a result of a shock from the outside (objective conditions) and the 'outside' in turn changes as a result of the 'inside' motion.

As a further illustration of this retroactive process of analysis let us examine the way in which the communists sought to theorize the post-war Occupation policy in Japan. Initially they looked on the United States as an 'army of liberation'. This attitude soon changed, however, and the United States was charged with seeking 'world domination through monopoly capital'. After thus changing their evaluation, the communists with their retroactive analysis explained the post-war demo-cratization policy as having emanated from the 'original and essential aims' of the American ruling class.* Of course there undoubtedly was a certain amount of plain political strategy in this pronouncement, but the fact remains that communists *do* tend to think in such a manner. In fact the foreign policy decision-making of the United States has often been simply a series of opportunistic responses to changing situations. Never-theless the communists have regarded these moves as part of a chess master's grand strategy and have thus ironically over-rated the consistency of America's decisions as well as the depth of her perspectives.

The 'revelation of essence' approach also makes it difficult to analyse satisfactorily the cyclical variations that mass conscious-ness and behaviour describe in response to the vicissitudes of economic and political situations. Instead, this approach often includes the so-called macroscopic perspective that mass con-sciousness will become 'more and more' revolutionary. If the proletariat is by essence revolutionary and, further, if the Com-munist Party is destined to be the vanguard of the revolution, it naturally follows that each failure of a revolutionary move-ment can be attributed only to the 'treachery' of democratic socialist leaders outside the Communist Party. It has been repeatedly stated that one should not attempt to force a high-level programme on the mass level, yet this is precisely what has taken place in practice. The point is that the person who *does* force a programme does not regard it as 'forcing'. Instead he

* Recently this analysis has been revised to a large extent.

feels he is helping to bring forth the revolutionary spirit that rests *a priori* in the masses.

I do not say that *all* communists reason in this manner, nor that this is the sole basis of their actions. Nevertheless from an examination of their past behaviour it seems clear that the communists do tend to act in accordance with this way of thinking. I further believe that this tendency extends through the entire communist camp and cannot be attributed simply to the political and intellectual immaturity of the Japanese communists.

There are several reasons why Marxists generally adopt a distrustful attitude and seek to guard against investigation of the dynamics of political behaviour and personality structure. Apart from the political rationale according to which Marxists condemn any such psychological approach as a surrender to 'decadent imperialist' methods of science, I believe that there are two main reasons. First, because this approach inevitably makes us focus on the irrational aspects of human thought and behaviour, it clashes with the rationalistic assumptions inherent in Marxism. Secondly, Marxists are influenced by what we might term 'the inclination to reduce everything to the basic system'. I shall examine this second point later when discussing the question of organization. In the present section I shall briefly elaborate on the first point.

Generally speaking, the communist countries and socialist parties that embrace Marxism place great emphasis on principles and rules of thought. They formulate their policies and execute them on a firm theoretical basis. This accent on theory is a significant characteristic not seen in the decision-making of the non-socialist world and *bourgeois* political parties. The great majority of politicians and journalists in non-socialist countries tend to survey the events of the communist parties, both within the so-called communist sphere and within their own countries, solely in conventional political terms. They depend on such stereotyped conceptual frameworks as 'aspiration to power and glory', 'power struggle for leadership', and 'mass manipulation'. This tendency to conventionalize, coupled with a lack of historical view and outlook, causes these non-communist politicians and journalists to fall into a type of reverse 'formalism' and 'schematism' which is usually attributed to Marxism.

Thus they often fail to grasp the development of communism within the context of the long-range trends of world history.

On the other hand the communists, especially the intellectuals, are prone to overestimate the importance of theoretical principles in the actual political process. As a result they come to rely on the complacent attitude, 'Among *us* politics is the application of science to real life.' When mistakes and follies occur, the communists attribute them either to ignorance of theoretical principles or to the misapplication of these principles. An individual whose decision-making is ostensibly based on correct theoretical principles may in practice go awry; in such cases the communists either fail to face squarely the problem of why such contradictions between theory and practice arise or else push it off into the sphere of 'literature'.

It is said that Stalin was contemptuous of the principles of collective leadership. Yet he always insisted:

The decisions of single persons are always, or nearly always, one-sided. Out of every one hundred decisions made by single persons that have not been tested and corrected collectively ninety are one-sided. In our leading body, the Central Committee of our party, which guides all our Soviet and party organizations, there are about seventy members. Each one is able to contribute his experience. Were it otherwise, if decisions had been taken by individuals, we should have committed very serious mistakes.*

He was also criticized for his constant distrust of divergent views and opinions. Still, in his *Foundations of Leninism*, Stalin did acknowledge in principle: 'Iron discipline does not exclude the clash of views within the party; rather, it presupposes it', and he admitted: 'It is generally recognized that no science can develop or progress without a conflict of opinion and freedom of criticism.'†

As for the charge that Stalin 'ignored' Lenin's methods of persuasion and education, a study of *Problems of Leninism* will show that he repeatedly preached the method 'Persuasion first —compulsion only when unavoidable'. Hence one can hardly insist, as Khrushchev did in his Secret Report, that this technique of Lenin's 'was utterly alien' to Stalin. Let us grant that the Old Bolsheviks like Stalin engaged in a great deal of activity

* Edgar Snow, *The Pattern of Soviet Power* (New York, 1945), p. 165.
† Joseph V. Stalin, 'On Marxism in Linguistics', *Pravda*, 20 June 1950.

completely unrelated to Marxist-Leninist principles. Perhaps this is proof that the adoption of 'infallible' principles and theories does not, in and of itself, guarantee correct behaviour.

Demonstrating the principle that erroneous theory causes mistakes in practice, the communist parties, headed by the Communist Party of the Soviet Union, gave as the reason for Stalin's mass purges and violations of legal procedure the Stalinist thesis that the class struggle is intensified as the establishment of socialism is carried out. This thesis presumably stemmed from Stalin's desire to do away with the Trotskyist theory of permanent *international* revolution and in its place to carry out a so to speak permanent *internal* revolution of the Soviet Union. Nevertheless I definitely do not think that such a protracted period of tragic purges and terrorism 'flowed' inevitably from this thesis. Personally I feel that the thesis contains an element of truth. Rather, the real danger lies in the union of political faith with the assumption that science controls the political process down to the smallest particular.

In Sartre's drama *Soiled Hands* there occurs the following conversation between an intellectual party member, Hugo, and his wife, Jessica:

HUGO. *Objectively*, he's acting like a class traitor.
JESSICA [*not understanding*]. Objectively?
HUGO. Yes.
JESSICA. Ah! [*a pause*]. And he, if he knew what you are up to, wouldn't he consider you a class traitor?
HUGO. I have no idea.
JESSICA. But isn't that what he would think?
HUGO. What of it? Yes, probably.
JESSICA. But who is right?
HUGO. I'm right.
JESSICA. How do you know?
HUGO. *Politics is a science. You can demonstrate that you are right and that others are wrong.**

The former party chief, Hoederer, who is judged a traitor by a majority of the party executive branch and who in the end falls before Hugo's pistol (although he is later shown to have been in the right), at one time told Hugo:

* Jean-Paul Sartre, *No Exit and Three Other Plays*, p. 214.

They [people like the party member, Olga] get their ideas ready-made, and then they believe in them as in God. With us others, it's not so easy for us to shoot some chap for the sake of a theory, because we're the ones who cook up the theories and we know how they are made. We can never be entirely certain we're right.*

And he criticizes Hugo for loving, not men, only principles.

Hoederer, of course, is not an unprincipled opportunist. He is simply a revolutionary with eyes that see clearly the irrational aspects of political reality and with a heart that 'loves people as they are'. The Shigailov-type of socialism that Dostoevsky satirized in *The Possessed* is unquestionably the spiritual fore-runner of Hugo's creed. This, however, is certainly not the only approach to communism. For example, the thought and prac-tice of the Chinese Communist Party, comparatively speaking, seems to be closer to the Hoederer-type. But this problem requires a more penetrating investigation by the communists; for it is related to the question of why dogmatic practices have repeatedly developed within the communist camp in spite of the constant and unanimous cries for the rejection of 'dogma-tism'.

v

The nature of the Stalin dictatorship revealed by the critique of the 'cult of personality' has also created an important prob-lem in a field other than political psychology—i.e., the problem of organizational patterns. Already in the 1920s Georg Lukacs drew certain conclusions about the way to overcome the mis-takes and defects of leadership through criticism and self-criticism.†

First: to regard what has actually happened in terms of 'abstract' inevitability leads only to fatalistic resignation. *Second:* the 'accidentalist' attitude that attributes success or failure of leadership to the cleverness or ineptitude of particular individuals is not very instructive for future practice. Relying on this approach one simply acknowledges that a certain person was not qualified for a certain position. *Third:* when we inquire into the 'realistic possibilities' of a particular action as well as the realistic potentialities of the fact that a particular leader was

* Ibid., p. 231.
† 'Methodisches zur Organizationsfrage' in *Geschichte und Klassenbewusstsein*, p. 303.

placed in a particular position, we are then confronted with the problem of organization. As Lukacs said, theory is transferred into practice only through the medium of organization. If we debated the validity of a theory without relation to its organizational function, it would be so vague and abstract as to justify any practice.

Presenting his view carefully and trenchantly, Togliatti attacked the Stalin dictatorship from the standpoint of organization. Though Togliatti simply presented the problem and suggested the need for more detailed investigation, his criticism did draw a reaction from the Soviet governing body, which was becoming more and more 'vigilant' towards the growing international repercussions of de-Stalinization.

Togliatti criticized as anti-Marxist the attempt to attribute all the bad aspects of the Stalin dictatorship to the 'cult of personality'. At the same time he pointed out the marked increase in the relative importance of bureaucratic structure in Soviet economic and political life. He stated that the gradual predominance of harmful restrictions on democratic institutions and the rampancy of bureaucratic patterns of organization have their germination in the Party, and concluded that these evils have exerted a baneful influence over the entire Soviet system.

The Soviet Communist Party replied to Togliatti in a resolution of the Central Executive Committee: 'We cannot agree with Togliatti's suggestion that Soviet society is due for "some reforms".' The Russians insisted that the evils of the cult of personality are 'wholly unrelated' to the essence of the social system. They based their argument on such Marxist ABCs as 'the essence of the social system is determined by the pattern of production and the location of the means of production'. Far from developing the points suggested by Togliatti, the Russians adopted a completely opposite attitude.

The Soviet Union may substitute collective leadership for the cult of personality; but, if they do not analyse the organizational theory behind that collective leadership, how can they answer the chorus of sceptical anti-communists who ask: 'If one leader is increased to one hundred leaders, does that become a guarantee against evil?'

In his superb political realism Lenin called for the union of 'goal consciousness and 'natural growth'. However, if the Soviet leaders use this as a hard and fast formula with the Party standing for goal consciousness and the proletariat for natural growth, they will be on their way to a sinister *Führerprinzip* or another cult of personality. Lenin's dialectic did not start with the proposition that the Party existed 'before all else'; nor did it hold that the Party *per se* was the vanguard under all conditions. Lenin constantly tried to show that during the process of leading the proletarian movement the Party becomes, through its organizational activities, the vanguard party. The Chinese communists made skilful use of Lenin's ideas in the epistemology of the 'mass line' which they decided to pursue in 1943. In the above-mentioned article of the *People's Daily News* the Chinese quoted this decision and emphasized that: '. . . it is necessary for us to establish a specific institution in order to guarantee the thorough implementation of the mass line and collective leadership'. These views of the Chinese communists as well as those of Togliatti contrast sharply with the attempt to dispose of the problem of leadership with rank and file moralisms such as: 'There are no institutional guarantees against the cult of personality. The greatest guarantee is the unslackening effort of the Soviet people.'*

Even the Soviet resolution refuting Togliatti acknowledged that the cult of personality impeded the 'development of socialist democracy', and that 'a bad influence was exerted on the development of some democratic forms owing to the demand, in the face of complex internal and external conditions, for iron discipline, for the strengthening of an unwavering sense of vigilance, and for the strictest centralization of leadership power'.

It is unlikely that obstruction to the growth of 'democratic forms' and 'socialist democracy' took place in a vacuum unrelated to the organizational activity of the Party, labour unions, and other national organs. After all, is excessive centralization of leadership power possible without a structural base in the system? In any event those who reacted to Togliatti's questions about system and organization with a nearly physiological show of displeasure, as though the 'essence' of basic socialism

---

* The reply of Kawasaki Misaburō (a leading member of the Japanese Communist Party) in response to the October *Sekai* questionnaire.

were being challenged, revealed a typically 'monolithic' attitude.

We need not limit our discussion to the problem of leadership, for there is a strong tendency throughout Marxist thinking not only to relate but also to reduce things to the 'base' or 'substructure' of the system without considering the different levels above the base. When dealing with individual organizations, Marxists usually treat them as 'ultimately' attributable to the problem of the whole *super*structure. They then reduce the superstructure 'in essence' to the level of the substructure. This 'inclination to reduce everything to the basic system' is also revealed in academic discussions by Marxists on schools other than their own. In viewing the post-war situation, for example, they have categorized the individual approaches of non-Marxist scholars as variations of 'pragmatism'. Pragmatism, by their definition, is a philosophy at the historical stage of imperialism which they have accordingly termed *the* Philosophy of Imperialism. This Marxist method of reduction to the substructure is closely related to the ideological criticism of individual behaviour discussed above. Hence if we trace this logic in reverse we shall progressively work back to the 'essence' as expressed in the process of 'revealing one's character'.

This type of thinking often causes Marxists to view the historical process as a *single track*. By attempting to follow the Marxist order—mode of production . . . relations of production . . . class structure—they channel as much as possible into the basic track and admit the presence of double or multiple tracks in the historical process only when absolutely necessary. Furthermore Marxists regard those events that do progress along one or more additional tracks as phenomena that have 'branched out' from the main track of history. While they have to acknowledge them, Marxists assign these phenomena to a position of inferior or secondary historical importance.

We can observe this approach to historical analysis in the Marxist attitude toward social groups that cut across different classes as well as toward such problems as *Kulturkreis* (for example, the geographic spread of Christianity and Islam) that span many production modes. As the Marxist tendency to make a fetish of 'theory' accelerates, this kind of distinction between the main track and its branches is applied also to the relative values of the various academic disciplines. Thus economics and economic history are sciences of the basic process of history and deal with the substructure. Consequently they are rated as primary and essential sciences in this scale of values. The other sciences simply touch the upper level of the superstructure. They are of value only for analysis of the surface phenomena of history and society and could never be used to penetrate to the 'essence'. A similar attitude prevailed in the Middle Ages when men looked upon theology as the 'queen science' and regarded the other sciences as simply 'servants' of the queen.

Using this single-track analysis of history, combined with the idea of progress, the Marxists rearrange according to historical order the many complex and interrelated problems that exist *simultaneously* and assign them to their respective historical stages according to the law of the development of 'bases'. If two ideologies exist side by side, it is necessary for the Marxists to assume that the one they assign to a *later* historical stage has already passed through the *earlier* stages and has absorbed the preceding ideology. For example, Marxists often divide contemporary philosophies into 'modernism' and Marxism. They look upon the evolution from modernism to Marxism in the light of the evolution of the basic system from capitalism to socialism. We might acknowledge, for example, that pragmatism is part of modernism. But how can we agree to the inclusion in modernism of Catholicism, which is not only a great present-day movement but also has a powerful influence in the academic world? Existentialism, another powerful current of contemporary thought, does not belong in this category either, but should, so far as its intellectual background is concerned, be understood as a rebellion against modern philosophy.

It may appear as if I were extending the scope of this discussion too far, but I feel that it is definitely connected with the problem of de-Stalinization. The communists for many years have neglected the need for constitutional procedures to check the arbitrary use of governmental power. We cannot attribute this neglect solely to revolutionary or emergency situations. Surely another factor is the historical optimism with which the communists have embraced the concept of a one-track evolution from constitutionalism to *bourgeois* democracy to proletarian democracy. This has caused them to regard constitutional guarantees against arbitrary rule as problems of a past stage. Compared to that of the Soviet leaders, the Chinese Communist Party's interpretation of the cult of personality as the 'force of habit of millions of people' seems far more realistic. Yet if we trace this 'habit' to its origin we will find that it too contains the 'single-track' mentality.

The Chinese *People's Daily News* stated on 5 April 1956:

> The cult of the individual is a foul carry-over from the long history of mankind. The cult of the individual is rooted not only in the exploiting classes but also in the small producers. As is well known, paternalism is a product of small-producer economy. After the establishment of the dictatorship of the proletariat, even when the exploiting classes are eliminated, when small-producer economy has been replaced by collective economy and a socialist society has been founded, certain rotten, poisonous ideological survivals of the old society may still remain in people's minds for a very long time.

According to this the cult of personality is *petit-bourgeois* ideology based on 'small-producer economy'. Following this logic, one would expect that in places like France, where the small producer is numerically strong and a typically *petit-bourgeois* spirit prevails, the cult of personality would be popular. But in France, even though 'individualism' is widespread (or rather *because* individualism is widespread), the psychological resistance to a *cult* of the individual is extremely strong.

The cult of personality certainly reflects a 'retarded' consciousness. Yet it has flourished in the Soviet Union, the first nation to establish a dictatorship of the proletariat, to a degree inconceivable in a Western European society worm-eaten to the marrow by *bourgeois* or *petit-bourgeois* concepts. This can hardly be explained by attributing it to a specific historical stage within a given mode of production.

A similar way of thinking is also revealed in the strong reluctance of communists to deal with problems that are more or less common to different systems, such as the role of *raison d'état* in international politics and the relationship between technology and bureaucratization. For example, the communists have been in the habit of saying that the adjustment between the centralization and decentralization of governmental power and the use of 'checks and balances' are problems only in *bourgeois-*

democratic countries. According to them, the socialist nation is basically a nation of the people; hence protective devices like decentralization and the balance of one power against another are unnecessary. If this is true, then why have certain transfers of power from central to regional agencies recently been made in the Soviet Union? And why has the Chinese Communist Party proposed the long-term coexistence of various parties and mutual supervision of each other's affairs?

Of course the problem of power in a communist country is not the same as in a capitalist country, and concentration of power *per se* is not a harmful thing. Nevertheless, if State power belongs 'essentially' to the people and if the Communist Party is 'essentially' a party for the people, the most appropriate attitude towards power is probably that of the Benthamists: 'If power works for a good purpose, why divide it up? If it is used for a bad purpose, why continue it?'*

One of the basic propositions of Marxism is that the *bourgeoisie* 'possess' and use as tools for class control the legislature, courts of justice, and other governmental institutions, as well as the mechanisms for mass communication. When the Marxist methods of reducing everything to the basic system (or in the case of individuals, to the 'revelation of one's true character') and of tracing historical progress along a single track is combined with this proposition, the ruling class and these institutions are 'frozen' into a relationship of 'substance' and its 'attributes'. Consequently there is no room for opening up the objective possibilities of such a 'servant' revolting against his 'master', or for recognition of *Heterogenie der Zwecke*—the phenomenon of something originally formed with goal A developing and coming to serve different goals, such as B or C. Thus the theoretical definition of these institutions belonging 'essentially' to the ruling class exists side by side with the practical consideration of their value for purely tactical purposes. The problem of how the former relates to the latter, however, is ignored.

In the parliamentary system, parliament has developed the dual role of ruling machinery and representative organ, and even the Marxists would have difficulty in proving that it is a 'servant' of the ruling class. At about the time of the Twentieth

---

* Cf. C. Friedrich, *Der Verfassungsstaat der Neuzeit* (1953), p. 197.

Party Congress there was a vociferous debate among the world's communist parties, especially those of Western Europe, about the possibility of carrying out a socialist revolution within a parliamentary system. The British Communist Party's view that parliament is a 'product of Britain's historic struggle' (*British Road to Socialism*) could not be reconciled with the traditional view that it is a 'possession' of the ruling class. The communists were faced with essentially the same problem in their conflicting analyses of the American Occupation policy in Japan. As mentioned above, the interpretation that the post-war democratization simply 'flowed' from the 'essential aims' of the American ruling class coexisted with the view that it was a 'reflection' of the power relationship between antagonistic classes.

In this sense, de-Stalinization is providing the communists with the opportunity to examine *for themselves* parts of their system that have until now either been entirely overlooked or deliberately concealed by the Marxist theory of State. There were especially valuable lessons to be learned from the operation of political weapons such as terrorist organizations and the secret service. We can see this, for example, in a statement by Eugene Dennis about the inflated power of the national security preservation bureau and its abuse of authority:

> Similar to the secret intelligence agencies in our own country, like the F.B.I. and the C.I.A., which have dictatorial powers, flaunt the constitution, and are not accountable even to Congress, Beria and his accomplices obviously were able to perpetrate their crimes against the people under the guise of 'national security'. All this was not the 'fruit of socialism', but a bitter product of contradictions and abuses alien to socialism, which a socialist society could not digest or tolerate.*

Thus Dennis acknowledged the danger of a political police organ arising under *any system*.

In my opinion, however, the latter part of this statement is only partly acceptable. It is quite contrary to dialectic thinking to suppose that a secret service could exist in a society having no connexion whatsoever with the political structure as a whole, or to suppose that it could function like a thrashing tail, completely

---

* Eugene Dennis, op. cit.

dissevered from the body of the State. Such abuses and mal-functions of a secret police organization are of course not pecu-liar to the socialist system; nor is there necessarily any *a priori* factor in socialism that makes the emergence of such an organization inevitable. Nevertheless there is an unfavourable tendency for the abnormal development of a secret police organization to occur within the political system during a certain stage in the establishment of socialism. Furthermore such abuses are almost sure to appear in any system under particular political conditions.

The size and power of the O.G.P.U. increased rapidly during the process of suppressing the *kulaks*, whose resistance to agricultural collectivization and counter-revolutionary activi-ties posed a real threat to the national security. However, '. . . as Soviet society consolidated, the activities of the security services did not contract in proportion: particularly since the war, they tended to be directed more and more against innocent citizens who showed some eccentricity or too much indepen-dence of thought.'* A high degree of secrecy and mobility is absolutely essential for a political police organization. Conse-quently, once such an organization is formed and begins to expand, it becomes exceedingly difficult to abolish or even curb, with the result that *all* political police portend the greatest of dangers to civil liberties and basic human rights.†

On 5 April 1956 the Chinese *People's Daily News* acknow-ledged that '. . . the existence of contradictions between the individual and the collective in a socialist society is nothing strange'. And Togliatti observed: 'The socialist society is not *by itself* guaranteed against mistakes and danger. It would be childishly naïve to think that it is.' Consequently there should no longer be any room for the 'naïve' belief that: 'Since in a socialist society the State embodies the benefit of the workers and of society's greater development and prosperity, the highest moral principles are reflected in the State itself.'‡

It is no disgrace for socialism or for communism that its advocates must now acknowledge the existence of mistakes. On

---

* Bob Davies, 'The New Stage in Soviet Democracy', *The Marxist Quarterly*, July 1956, pp. 190–1.
  † In nearly the same way this holds true for an army.
  ‡ P. A. Charrier, *Communist Morals*, p. 5 (Japanese Edition).

the contrary, it is a great step forward. For the individual as well as for the system, the danger one is unaware of—or insufficiently aware of—is far greater than the danger one is keenly alert to. For example, the 'ritualization' or arteriosclerosis of her own liberal-democratic system are much more of a threat to the United States than communist infiltration. Similarly, the Soviet Union would do well to turn from vigilance towards the 'evil influence' of *bourgeois* ideology to the greater danger of complacency about the historical development of socialism.

If we are to make an unbiased examination of the history of the 'Stalin era', we must acknowledge that the laudable and the disgraceful, the great and the ignoble, the truths and the errors, all stemmed from the same source. In February 1931 Stalin told a gathering of business managers: 'We are fifty or a hundred years behind the advanced countries. We must make good this distance in ten years, or they [the Imperialists] will crush us.' And under his leadership the Soviet Union, isolated and without any help from the outside and while struggling under inconceivably severe and difficult conditions, succeeded in 'making good the distance'. If the Soviet Union had not succeeded, it is difficult to imagine how she could have not only checked but turned back the overwhelming German offensive in a critical phase of the war.

What Soviet Russia had embarked on was the first great experiment in world history of socialist construction without blueprint or historical precedent. During this process the revolutionary dictatorship became a dictatorship of Stalin. Nevertheless, the great changes in Soviet society, such as the rapid rise in productive capacity and the large-scale emergence of modern skilled labourers and technical intellectuals, were the product of the 'Stalin era', and laid the internal groundwork for de-Stalinization. Thus, while Stalin was overcoming the backwardness of a Russia worm-eaten by Byzantium, barbarism, indolence, and inefficiency with appropriately 'backward' methods, he was destined to become the 'gravedigger' of his own absolute authority. At the same time, however, these illegal, brutal, and barbaric methods set in motion by both Stalin and his enemies produced an automatic chain reaction.

At the same time of de-Stalinization, when *Pravda, L'Humanité,* Togliatti, and Dennis examined the series of events thus set in motion and were faced with this confusing pattern of historical plus and minus factors, they labelled the whole era a 'tragedy'. This 'tragedy', however, was threefold: 1. the tragedy of Russia; 2. the tragedy of revolution; 3. the tragedy of 'politics'. Consequently it was not a tragedy peculiar to Russia but one that could have arisen at other times and in other places. The important question is the extent to which these critics truly appreciated the nature of the tragedy. If used too casually, the word 'tragedy', like 'dialectic', loses its full value and becomes an expression either of moralistic sentimentalism or of conventional Machiavellism.

Moralistic denunciation that is made abstractly and without a sense of responsibility on the part of the critic can easily become hypocrisy; moreover it lacks the strength to penetrate to the source of political behaviour. On the other hand, Machiavellian criticism is an attempt to rationalize everything with phrases such as 'it was unavoidable' or 'there were no other means'.

It is impossible to justify evil political behaviour when or wherever it occurs. Such behaviour, however, should not be regarded fatalistically. The chance of averting certain political evils at a particular time and within particular limits may, as a result of the mistakes of leadership and failures of policy, cease to exist in the following period. Conversely, under other conditions the unavoidable evil of one period may provide compensation by producing good results in the future. Moreover evil in one context may function as a preventive against a different kind of evil in a wider context. This of course does not alter the fact that it was entirely evil in the first context. So it seems we must accept the unhappy conclusion that, as Fukuzawa Yukichi[2] put it, politics involves a constant choice among 'degrees of badness'. As the scope of choice broadens and as the choice itself becomes more crucial, this antinomy of political behaviour—especially of political leadership—also expands.

When explaining the historical conditions surrounding Stalin-worship, communist leaders add, as though in previous agreement, 'Simply to explain Stalin-worship and its effects is not to justify it', and thus caution against confusing historical explanation with moralistic rationalization. This is a healthy symptom. The fascists would never speak about actions within their own camp as 'violations of the law and the application of illegal preliminary examination methods which should be morally rejected with disgust' (Togliatti), or have advocated to party members a policy of 're-education to that standard of tolerance indispensable for the uncovering of truth' (Togliatti). This is because the fascists act solely in accordance with 'political necessities' and have no theory nor norm which stand above them and by which they abide.

No matter what doubts may be raised about the position of morals within existing Marxist theory, who would not welcome the communists' keen awareness of tension between theory and practice and the strengthening of the distinction between norm and reality? Imagine the effect this would have on their actions and on their 'world-view'. The rule of world revolution is that it engulfs the revolutionary forces themselves and that the revolutionaries are continually revolutionized in the process. In our present age this is surely the only pattern of revolution worthy of the name 'progress'.

POSTSCRIPT (1957)

Shortly after the original version of this essay was published, the Hungarian Revolt broke out and de-Stalinization in the Soviet Union and Eastern Europe was faced with an entirely new set of conditions. I do not feel, however, that these new conditions have greatly altered the basic views of my original essay. I venture to believe that the essay offers a general forecast of the international repercussions likely to be created by problems such as the Hungarian Incident and the Suez Invasion and of their possible effect on the 'liberalization' of the communist sphere.

Therefore in the present revised version I have deliberately avoided quoting from materials like the Tito-*Pravda* debate over de-Stalinization, which appeared later, and which was clearly kindled by the Hungarian Revolt, or the recent article of the Chinese *People's Daily News* entitled 'Historical Experiences of the Dictatorship of the Proletariat'. I would rather leave to the reader the attempt to explain these events in terms of the method of analysis I have developed in this essay. Still, I feel it is incumbent on me to present my basic views on the question of 'liberalization' of the communist régime, particularly as it relates to the fundamental problem of Marxism-Leninism.

In order to examine the development of liberalization in the Soviet Union and the 'people's democracies', we must draw a general distinction between domestic problems and international relations. Further, we must note that the tempo of liberalization in different spheres, such as politics, economics, and culture, is not necessarily the same.

I believe the reader can tell from statements in the main part of this essay how sensitively the relations between the Soviet Union and the countries in the Soviet orbit reflect concrete situations in world politics and how closely the degree of tension in world politics is tied to the progress or lack of progress in decentralization of the international revolutionary movement (which Togliatti calls 'polycentrism'). A number of changes in communist relations from the time of the return of Gomulka to power in Poland until now are clearly related to changes in world conditions. For example, Communist China, cautioning against 'great-nation chauvinism', promptly supported and encouraged Gomulka's rise in Poland.* Meanwhile the Chinese also gave full support to the Soviet Union during the Hungarian Revolt and vigorously rejected the views of the Yugoslavian Communist Party as disruptive of communist unity.

During his trip to the Soviet Union and Eastern Europe in 1956–7, Chou En-lai joined in a message and declaration that emphasized the struggle against 'international imperialism' and the central role of the Soviet Union in this struggle. Again, at a recent mass meeting the Italian Communist Party chose not to promote the case for polycentrism. Both of these instances show the effect on the world's communist parties of Western reaction to de-Stalinization.

In a dispatch dated 13 January 1957, Nicholas Carroll, the Washington correspondent for the *Sunday Times*, wrote:

The impact on this side of the Iron Curtain of the Suez intervention and the new Eisenhower Doctrine has been truly surprising. The responsibility for encouraging Stalinist reactionaries in party

* According to the 19 January issue of the *New Statesman and Nation*, a copy of Mao's circular telegram opposing Soviet military intervention at that extremely critical time was circulated secretly in Warsaw.

executive meetings throughout the communist world and for bringing on the latest Chinese and Russian hard lines lies precisely with these two policies.

This statement shows that Western correspondents on the spot frankly recognize the grim logic that motivates the international communist movement. So long as the West continues its present course of anxious watching and waiting, and is ready to mobilize into anti-communist campaigns even the slightest aberrations within the communist sphere, 'liberalization' will never develop fully. On the other hand, if the unrest in Eastern Europe remains within manageable limits and if the Cold War should again enter a period of ebb, it will be impossible to stop the socialist countries and revolutionary parties from following the course of polycentrism in both their structures and their functions.

The forced establishment of heavy industry in Eastern Europe during the post-war period was closely related to the *raison d'état* of the Soviet Union; and leadership lay in the hands of cliques of Stalinists within each country who were 'more pro-Soviet than the Soviets themselves'. There was, accordingly, a certain historic irony in the events in Poland and Hungary which demonstrated that the Soviet Union was no longer able completely to control the material and human social changes produced by this heavy industrialization.

For the time being, and in particular so long as N.A.T.O. continues in full operation, 'liberalization' in the East European countries will probably proceed within a three-part framework: 1. support of military alliances with the Soviet Union based òn the Warsaw Treaty; 2. rigid maintenance of existing borders within East Europe as well as borders shared with West European countries; 3. preservation of the socialist system led by the Communist Party.

The tendency to polycentralize on the international level has come to a halt as a result of renewed world tensions. Within the Soviet Union and other socialist countries, however, a 'new line' is even now being steadily advanced. The demand for this kind of internal 'liberalization' arises naturally during a certain stage in the establishment of socialism; it reflects neither a sudden change in attitude resulting from de-Stalinization, nor a temporary piece of international strategy. The Soviet Union itself is a case in point. Nearly all the important aspects of the new line emphasized at the Twentieth Party Congress had appeared before that time. Let us consider, for example, the matter of judicial procedure, which has left one of the darkest blotches on Soviet history. As early as July 1951 punishments for production slow-downs and lags were largely abolished. And after the problem with Beria in 1952 the Soviet leaders decided to strengthen Party control of the M.V.D. As a result the Special Council of the M.V.D., which had the power to banish political offenders without recourse to normal court procedure, was abolished.

The magazine *Kommunist* stated in its July 1955 issue (No. 2):

No one has the authority to issue orders concerning a judge's decision in any trial. Officials of the Government and administrative organs, members of the Justice Ministry staff and social organizations must not interfere in the decisions of individual cases. Interference of local party organs in court decisions represents violation of the principle of judicial independence established by the Soviet Constitution.

Accordingly after the Twentieth Party Congress the continuing process of judicial reform was linked to the widespread abolition of revolutionary law and to the partial transfer of national judicial power to the various republics.

In his statement of resignation Malenkov reported that his administration's policy of emphasizing consumer production had been 'reversed'. Yet, despite disagreements over the precise speed and tempo, even Western observers acknowledged that the post-1951 rate of production increase in light industries and in agriculture had nearly overtaken the heavy industries, and that even the farmer's purchasing power had risen rapidly during the period.

There was also support, prior to the Twentieth Party Congress, for a more positive labour union role in industry, and the words of Lenin were widely quoted, 'Even under the dictatorship of the proletariat, struggle with the bureaucratic perversions of administrative organs is necessary.' And again, from the magazine *Kommunist* (No. 11, 1955): '[between management and labour] there is need for an occasional active dispute'.

We can see from these examples that a 'thaw' had been developing slowly and fragmentarily from about the time of Stalin's death. Its course was not to be controlled by personnel changes in the power structure nor to be 'reversed' by a temporary worsening of the international situation. Consequently the Twentieth Party Congress did not institute a thaw; it simply gave formal recognition to one already in progress.

A distinguished student of the Soviet Union, Mr. Isaac Deutscher, has stated: 'Changes far more thorough and profound than those which normally take place during a half century of the lives of a nation's people have recently been occurring every decade in the lives of the Russian people.'* The great advance of the industrial revolution and the dramatic rise in urbanization (urban population has increased by seventeen million during the past five years) have borne out the truth of these words. How can such advances fail to have an effect on a country's political development?

An American critic, Mr. Marshall Schuman, observed the irony that in Russia the *bourgeois* revolution followed the revolution of the proletariat. This seemingly fatuous remark holds more than a grain of truth. After all, the de-Stalinization campaign 'from above' was effectively launched with support 'from below'—the artistic intelligentsia, the students, the skilled labourers, and the factory and *kolkhoz* leaders. These people, who reap the benefits of the Soviet system and who will produce tomorrow's *élite*, demanded a greater degree of rationality and predictability in the structure and functioning of the government; and there is a close historical parallel between their claims and the demands of the middle classes (composed of entrepreneurs and intellectuals) in the advanced capitalist countries, who came into being after a period of initial capital accumulation.

Like the Soviet Union, the great majority of the countries in the Soviet orbit are faced with the twofold task of imposing socialism and, at the same time, of carrying out an industrial revolution. Their future course may at times alter and veer, but they will probably describe a path not basically different from that of the Soviet Union.

Apart from concrete variations in substance of the political, economic, and cultural 'new lines' of these countries, the devel-

* *Russia Since Malenkov.*

opment and scope of the resulting 'freedom' is prescribed by a universal political dynamism within the revolutionary process.

When a revolutionary force comes to power, its first task is to destroy the traditional institutions that had supported the old system. While dismembering social groups that are in a counter-revolutionary position, such as rural co-operatives, regional organizations, and 'reactionary' associations, the revolutionaries must establish a new national homogeneity at the social base. At the same time they must gain society's consent for a new system of values and for a human 'image' to exemplify these values. The *citoyen* of the French Revolution and the 'people' of the 'people's democracies' are examples of such images.

The smoothness of transition and the length of time necessary to effect these changes will depend on a number of factors, among them historical and social conditions of the revolution, international relations, and the reactions of the old ruling class. In any event, history has shown us that during this process of revolutionary consolidation some restriction of democratic forms is unavoidable. In fact, under certain social conditions it is nearly impossible to use purely democratic means to develop the prerequisites of democracy. Let us take as an example the case of democratization in post-war Japan. How many of the 'steps' to democracy, beginning with the land reform, were carried out through the process of *unqualified* free elections— that is to say, elections held without prior emasculation by extra-legal means of the old power structure? We must not confuse this with the process of revolution 'from the outside' and 'from the inside'. National and social homogeneity determine the extent to which democratic processes develop.

It is precisely this logic that underlies the concept of 'unanimity' in Rousseau's original contract and it is this unanimity that makes majority rule possible. An idea of this sort was also part of the ideological background of the French Revolution. Furthermore this principle was taken over intact by the Chinese communists in their proposal to 'Let One Hundred Flowers Bloom' and in their call for the co-existence of parties. After establishing the principle that 'politically we must clearly distinguish between friend and foe', the Chinese communists authorized the formation of multi-parties and the contention by one hundred schools *within* the revolutionary homogeneity.

They said that 'counter-revolution must be suppressed and overthrown'. At the same time, however, 'people who harbour harmful thoughts against the establishment of socialism are not only free to exist but are also free to debate, so long as they do not engage in reactionary political activity'.* Moreover: 'We advocate expansion of such freedom in proportion to the increase in strength of the people's government.'†

Thus the Chinese communists distinguish between friend and foe and deny freedom to the heretical 'foe'. At the same time, however, they establish the premise that 'foe' is a relative term which shifts according to concrete situations. The purge within the Soviet Union during the 1930s provided ample proof of the fearful results of such a policy when it is rigidly enforced in the political arena or simply 'gets out of hand'. Still, it must not be overlooked that the logic behind this policy is also the driving force for *bourgeois* democracy and will inevitably come to the surface during times of emergency.

Ernest Barker gives the following conditions for democracy:‡ national homogeneity on both the material and social levels; acceptance and observance of certain 'axioms', including the freedom to have different opinions within the framework of 'unanimity' on fundamental issues. According to Barker, 'When unanimity exists exactly as does the atmosphere and is accepted naturally and without question, differences can be tolerated. The emergence of various party factions and the existence of a variety of personal tastes and opinions is acknowledged and can even be expected.'§

The establishment of these preconditions for democracy has a long history even in Western Europe, where democracy is deeply rooted in the customs and traditions of the national system. If these conditions have become valid in Western Europe only as the result of long-term growth, it is clear that we cannot expect the advanced stage when 'unanimity exists exactly as does the atmosphere and is accepted naturally and without question' to be achieved immediately under socialism. The concrete characteristics of 'liberalization' vary according to the degree and scope to which this 'unanimity' has developed

---

* 15 June Kuo Mo-jo Report.   † Lu Ting-i.
‡ He refers here, of course, to Western European democracy.
§ Ernest Barker, *Reflections on Government*.

socially and politically. Consequently it is premature to regard the present stage of limited 'liberalization' as the full extent of socialism's growth potential and thus to reject or rationalize it.

The Chinese Communist Party has already gone considerably beyond the position of Lenin and Stalin even in its definition of dictatorship of the proletariat, the central proposition of Marxism-Leninism. As the 'diverse routes to socialism' dominate political discussions, or, to put it another way, as the exclusive legitimacy of the 'Moscow line' is challenged more and more, the concrete political forms of the dictatorship of the proletariat (or, more precisely, the political forms *attributed* to the general concept of the dictatorship of the proletariat) continue to diversify. Furthermore we can make the same assumption in regard to the common ownership of the means of production. Bernstein once provoked a controversy by stating that capitalism has a capacity for adaptability (*Anpassingsmöglichkeit*) to reality beyond the prediction of Marx. We are now at that point in history when communism must also demonstrate its capacity to adapt on a world scale.

Though it may seem paradoxical, I feel that the most difficult, in fact the central, problem of 'liberalization' within the communist orbit lies in the dimension of the highest level of the superstructure (i.e., the theoretical plane) rather than in the economic and political spheres. The problem is to distinguish clearly between freedom from the standpoint of the world-view of Marxism-Leninism and from the standpoint of socialism. Moreover it is a question as to whether or not the world communist leaders recognized the meaning of the statement: 'Socialism is not tied to a specific world-view. *It is the common conclusion of a variety of different world-views.*'* It was Lenin who said: 'We cannot think of Marxist theory as something perfected, as something inviolable.' The same rule should apply to Leninist theory as well. Nevertheless, as soon as Marxism-Leninism is legitimatized on the basis of State power and is made the officially recognized doctrine of State, it does, in fact, assume the role of 'highest truth' above all learning and art.

No matter how widespread its influence may be, so long as Marxism remains an opposition force without official power, it will display the fundamental characteristics of one school out of

* Gustav Radbruch, *A Cultural Theory of Socialism.*

many. Under these conditions it must constantly contend the validity of its tenets with other schools in the free market of the intellect. Once it assumes power, however, Marxism ceases to be one among many. In any event, if we take the case of the Soviet Union, the situation of the Marxist-Leninist in the seat of power is completely different from that of the president or prime minister of a *bourgeois* nation who by chance may also be, let us say, a Roman Catholic or a Keynesian scholar. So long as its basis is found exclusively in Marxism-Leninism, the concept of a dictatorship of the proletariat will in effect be a 'dictatorship of truth'. As such it will bear internal resemblance to the political rule of Plato's ideal State and to the 'universal' church of Rome in the Middle Ages.

The masses of the capitalist societies continue to decay in an atmosphere of 'free competition' leading to the endless vulgarization of cultural values, where, to paraphrase Gresham, 'bad culture drives out good'. In sharp contrast, this new 'government by philosophers' in our age of mass society certainly offers an epoch-making solution to the problem of raising the *qualitative* cultural level of the working people.* There is, however, another side to the problem. While criticizing the Platonic State, Windelband once warned against the union of a theory (no matter how lofty its precepts), in the exclusive role of highest truth, with political control. According to him the result would be rule by dogma and forced submission of the conscience to a fixed principle. This observation is fundamentally valid in regard to communist countries too. In fact the dangers implicit in a combination of theory and political control are extremely great in the Soviet Union where, as we have seen, there is a long history of union between the Greek Orthodox Church and State power. This does not mean, however, that in practice non-Marxists are not permitted to exist in the communist State, nor that there is no freedom among scholars and artists. We can see an interesting analogy to this situation in a statement by Professor Carl Becker:

Mediaeval universities present us with an arresting paradox: they appear to us to have been singularly bound and yet curiously free. We know that the mediaeval church suppressed heresy with a ruth-

* Apart from the aspect of guarantees of economic life.

less hand, and yet nearly all the great scholars, from Abelard to William [of] Occam, were associated with some university sponsored by the Church and appear to have been quite free to learn what they could and to teach whatever they thought to be true. The key to this enigma is that at that time the common man, the constituted authorities and the fraternity of scholars all accepted the Christian faith—the Christian story of man's origin and destiny—as the necessary basis of all knowledge and all ordered and virtuous living.*

But the real problem of society lies in the tendency to render orthodox in each sphere of learning and culture the 'highest truth' or, since the truth is regarded as a fixed universal, to establish some one theory or doctrine as the embodiment of 'truth' or to set up one form as the 'model' to be followed in every sphere of culture. When hearing Oistrakh and Oborin or when seeing films of Ulanova's dancing, I have been struck by their flawless artistry and its pure and human spirit. At the same time I have been aware that the greatest problem confronting Soviet culture lies precisely in the pursuit of this highly stylized perfection. Is there not, after all, a close connexion between the image of the Soviet nation as the objective embodiment of the 'highest truth' called Marxism-Leninism and the tendency to conventionalize objectively a particular 'model' beauty within the arts?

At this point we should refer again to the proposal of the Chinese Communist Party to 'Let One Hundred Flowers Bloom'. The communist leaders are political realists. Hence liberalization as a practical issue had been initiated on the ideological level before the Soviet Union's de-Stalinization. Besides, the theoretical basis for a 'thaw' had already been provided in literature and other individual fields. However, the public theorizing of 'liberalization' in each ideological sphere by the highest echelon of leaders as reflected in the policy to 'Let One Hundred Flowers Bloom' was an unprecedented step. It is impressive that this should have been taken in a country where just a few years had passed since the acquisition of power by a revolutionary force. This is not the place for a detailed description of the 'Hundred Flowers' campaign. Yet we should

* Carl Becker, 'Freedom and Responsibility', *The American Way of Life* (Vantage Books edition, 1960), p. 66.

note the key fact that it suggests a kind of 'anti-monopoly law' in regard to criticism and controversy in the arts and sciences. That is to say, the campaign made clear that no one is to hold a privileged position in the fields of criticism and controversy; the principle of the minority submitting to the majority is not valid in the field of culture and learning; and no one is duty-bound to express self-criticism. Moreover:

The Chinese Communist leaders are not preparing a *text book of the history of the party*. They are planning only to continue to edit and publish a *record* of important events and *various kinds of documents* of the party. Therefore, scholars should be able to do research *individually* into the various problems of modern history.*

This statement reflects a lesson drawn from the re-writing of Soviet party history under Stalin's aegis. Moreover it is a lesson of great significance if it does in fact imply a rejection of the 'authentic' interpretation of or the 'orthodox' approach to history. Yet, while noting that a communist country has gone this far in openly clarifying the functional distinction between the political and cultural dimensions, we must also observe that as a general rule all the above basic problems remain to be solved. For instance, when it is said that 'differences of opinion can arise concerning art, science, and technology, and we entirely approve of such difference',† does this statement also apply to criticism of Marxist philosophy and theory itself? The governmental authorities claim 'there is freedom to propagate idealism among the people'. Yet the same authorities also speak of 'the struggle against tardy idealism among the people', and predict that 'materialistic thought will overcome idealistic thought step by step'. Consequently, even though they say that victory will be achieved through public debate and not by administrative order, we could hardly call such a debate free and unhandicapped.

Ch'en Po-ta has stated: 'There is no development in learning when conclusions exist from the very beginning.'‡ If taken in their true meaning, these words should apply to the academic justification of Marxist-Leninism itself. I do not wish to emphasize only their faults or to make unreasonable demands of the Chinese communist leaders at the present stage in their

* Lu Ting-i Report.   † Ibid.
‡ A conversation with Ogura Hirokatsu in the August 1956 issue of *Sekai*.

development. It is simply that the problem of legitimatizing a fixed world-view and doctrine by authoritarian means has not been entirely resolved by the 'Hundred Flowers' campaign. Marxist theorists have still not solved this problem. Moreover, a common 'logic of politics' was at work when *bourgeois* democracy at its inception also denied freedom to 'counter-revolutionary enemies'.

While Marxist-Leninism functions politically as a symbol of the international solidarity of the proletariat, any attempt to relativize the validity of world-views is promptly interpreted as suspicion of the socialist system. Therefore we cannot realistically anticipate that the communists will soon abandon their tendency to denounce deviation from the orthodox as surrender to capitalism and counter-revolution. In the event, however, that a course of socialism that deviates from the 'orthodox' world-view—or, more precisely, is not entirely led by a single world-view—should arise and should secure a strong international position, the communist leaders will be obliged by the weight of circumstances to acknowledge sincerely the truth of Radbruch's words.

At the same time, assuming a regular increase in political and economic stability, we can expect the phenomenon of divergence from the ideological monolith of a single world-view to continue to develop gradually within the communist sphere. It is impossible in the world of modern communication to construct a psychological and cultural 'great wall' about a single nation of people. The cultural heritage of the Soviet Union's younger generation already differs markedly from that of the old hard-core Bolsheviks. These young people enjoy reading not only classical world literature but the works of Graham Greene and Ernest Hemingway as well. Moreover they are enthusiastic over music like George Gershwin's *Porgy and Bess*. We simply cannot escape the fact that, regardless of the original aims or plans of the régime, the rise in the intellectual level of the masses will, by means of its own dialectic, continue to have wide repercussions on the entire socio-political process. For example, little has happened since the removal of the virtual ban on Dostoevsky's works. Yet how many people can now predict the latent possibilities of this 'removal of the ban' in the event that Dostoevsky should come to be widely read?

The concrete phases and tempo of 'liberalization' of the various cultural spheres will, of course, vary according to the different countries of the communist sphere. Yet the basic order of liberalization can be fairly well determined by the following three criteria. First, genres that are intimately connected with the individual's innermost feelings are liberated from the orthodox world-view relatively early—religion first, followed by the arts, and, last of all, scholarship. Since Marxism is above all a science of the social system, it is extremely difficult for the communists to make an effective ideological infiltration of those genres, such as religion, that are most deeply embedded in the individual.

After the severance of religion from its union with the political and social systems in Tsarist Russia, the vehement anti-religion campaign of the first stages of the Russian Revolution retreated into the background. All the communist governments in Eastern Europe have had problems with the Roman Catholic Church within their territories, not so much as a result of the conflict between atheism and theology as because of social and political privileges of the Church such as land ownership.

In the field of art and literature, so-called socialist realism is still assumed to be the 'orthodox' creative principle. Despite its omnipotence, however, dialectical materialism can by no means prescribe the actual creative process of writers and artists. Thus the term 'socialist realism' becomes ever more ambiguous. Today it is interpreted to mean simply that art and literature must 'serve the people' and must reflect the 'advancing and constructive' phases of history. For example, there is the well-known case of the *Work of the Artist* in which Ehrenburg provided a theoretical basis for liberation of the artist's inner creative process. Moreover the Chinese communists have publicly announced that realism is only 'one way among many': 'We think that socialist realism is the best creative method. *But it is not the only one.* Assuming that he serves the worker, the farmer, and the soldier, any artist is free to create and compete with others by those methods that he himself considers best.'* Suppose, however, that we were to substitute the phrases 'historical materialism' or 'dialectical materialism' for 'socialist realism', and the phrase 'method of scientific research' for 'creative process'. How

* Lu Ting-i Report.

would the communists regard this? The answer, of course, is that they have never gone this far in recognizing in principle the plurality of approach.

The second criterion for determining the order of liberalization is the degree to which any particular field of culture is related to the Marxist world view or to its political ideology. Comparatively speaking, those spheres in which world-view or political ideology are not directly apparent are liberalized earlier than others. Within the arts themselves, for example, music and ballet may be liberalized before literature. For the same reason, of course, the natural sciences are freer from orthodoxy than the social sciences. This brings us to the third criterion: liberalization tends to be slower in those spheres in which the Marxist outlook has hitherto been theoretically more developed and in which there are more achievements by Marxist scholars. It is therefore a very difficult matter to secure approval of equal rights within the spheres of philosophy, economics, and history for standpoints and approaches outside Marxism. The problem is not simply to be permitted freedom of research and publication. Rather it is a question of whether or not there is to be a mutual exchange of ideas and methods with Marxism under conditions of equality.

To insist upon the need for liberation from the all-embracing view of Marxist orthodoxy is not, of course, to deny entirely the truth contained in Marxism. Though it may sound paradoxical, the Marxists' self-limitation of their world-view actually has the opposite effect of establishing ever more clearly the truth in that world-view. As John Stuart Mill made clear in classic terms, truth is not 'better' without 'error'—on the contrary, truth becomes truth only through error. Though diversity and plurality may be an 'unavoidable evil' from the standpoint of political necessity, for truth they are a constant prerequisite.

Marxism, no matter how lofty its truth and historical significance, could never be the final world-view of mankind. In time it will come to occupy a suitable place in the great chain of intellectual history. Then the truth will become sifted from the dogma within historical Marxism. Along with its constant philosophical ideas (presentation of the problem of man's self-estrangement and of the historical agent who liberates him from it), Marxism's contribution to empirical research will become a permanent legacy for mankind—as have all other classical systems of thought.

TRANSLATOR'S NOTES

1. See Glossary: *National polity.*
2. See Glossary: *Fukuzawa Yukichi.*

VII. Politics as a Science in Japan: Retrospect and Prospects

TRANSLATED BY ARTHUR TIEDEMANN

This essay was originally published in the magazine Jimbun, *No. 2, 1947*

I

With the end of the war many freedoms were officially recognized for the first time. Among them was academic freedom. All at once academic life, which had long been battered by the heavy pressures of existence in pre-war Japan, enjoyed a great revival. Surmounting all sorts of obstacles in material conditions, the resuscitated spirit of learning stimulated vigorous activity in every branch of knowledge. The renaissance of the social sciences was a particularly brilliant spectacle. At a single stroke they were freed of the innumerable taboos that had thwarted their development; all their pent-up energy burst forth in one glorious explosion.

Amid this exciting revival of the social sciences, political scientists alone still flounder about, puzzled over what they should do. Since 'things political', both international and domestic, are now much wider in scope than formerly and are affecting people's lives much more, the sluggish start of political science has become even more obvious.[1] Everywhere during the past few years one has heard such comments as 'Political studies are the most poorly developed field in Japan', or 'Precisely where in Japan is there a person who can properly be called a political scientist?' Whenever I come up against this kind of criticism, my first reaction is an instinctive antipathy. I spare no effort to vindicate Japanese political science, but in the end I am reduced to silence by the element of incontestable truth contained in these criticisms.

On 15 August 1945 an unprecedented reform began, a reform that even now continues before our eyes. It is true that this reform, usually called the 'democratic revolution', is not confined to narrow political changes. It includes fundamental transformations in every sphere of Japanese life, social, cultural, economic. Yet the point of departure for such enormous changes is undeniably *political* reform and the main agent is *political* power. Did any Japanese of the past feel the immense power of politics breathing down his neck in the way that every citizen does today, when every housewife knows that a speech made by an American President thousands of miles away may quite literally be related to her family's next meal? Farmers in the remotest villages have learnt by personal experience that a single decree has the power to transform into worthless scraps of paper savings accumulated through a lifetime of scrimping.* Caught in this great political upheaval, people are asking uneasily: 'What is the true character of these powerful political forces? Where do they come from and where are they going?'

People's interests and hopes are naturally directed towards that branch of learning which dwells on 'politics'. But nothing even faintly resembling an answer can be heard from that quarter. If we take a closer look, we find wriggling there something whose features as a branch of learning are still unshaped. Never before has the public been so clearly confronted with the contrast between the sweeping control exercised over its life by politics and the meagre progress of the discipline that studies it.

There has undoubtedly been a brilliant revival in the other social sciences, but political science in this country, to put it bluntly, really has no tradition worth reviving. For Japanese political science everything depends on what happens in the future.

Extensive self-examination does seem to have taken place in other branches of the social sciences too, once the hollow-sounding tunes heard briefly in the immediate post-war period had subsided. A year and a half after the war ended social scientists were asking themselves whether their sciences could really serve as guiding influences in contemporary reality if they used methods that simply took over lock, stock, and barrel the old ways of formulating problems and that relied uncritically on the categories previously employed. They realized that the problem was not to be solved by merely returning to 'the good old days' and treating the decade of reaction as an historical

* E.g. the Emergency Financial Measure Ordinance, February 1946.

vacuum. Still, for a while such fields as economics and law have been able to use their same old tools to cope with reality. In these fields new wine *can* sometimes be put in old bottles.

When it comes to Japanese political science, however, we find that traditional systems, as well as the way the problems have been posed, cannot provide any guidance in today's political realities. For instance, Japanese political science was long agitated by a methodological debate concerning which should have precedence, the concept of politics or the concept of State. What contribution to an understanding of contemporary politics can such an argument possibly make?

The impotence of political science in this country is no recent phenomenon. The methodologies and conceptual schemes of other disciplines such as law and economics had once been well adapted to their historical situations and the difficulty is that in this age of convulsion they have lost their former validity. The case of Japanese political science is quite different; for in its development it almost never had the corrective experience of shaping and being shaped by political realities.*

Instead of drawing its problems from its own native soil, Japanese scholarship has tended to chase persistently after the passing themes and methods developed in the European academic world. To this may be traced the divorce of our scholarship from reality. Political science in Japan manifests this fatal weakness in an extreme form. Here the dissociation of scholarship from the reality it purports to study is so deep that the gap seems to be almost insurmountable.

II

The sterility of Japanese political science is not to be blamed on either the laziness or the incompetence of individual political scientists. It is essentially an outcome of the political structure established after the Meiji Restoration. It is unreasonable to expect any genuine social science to thrive where there is no

* Among political scientists of the last generation Dr. Yoshino Sakuzō had the greatest influence on his period. His name is inseparably linked with the democratic movement of the Taishō era. Dr. Yoshino's writings on democracy, however, are largely *Zeitkritik* written for the general public rather than theoretical works. His more significant achievement in terms of scholarship lay largely in the field of political history, particularly modern Japanese political history. Yoshino's case is certainly exceptional in respect both of his practical influence and of the direction of his academic interests.

undergirding of civil liberty. It is particularly unreasonable to expect it in the case of political science.

The inseparability of a virile political science and civil liberty is borne out by the political tradition of the West. Behind the political theorists of ancient Greece, the founding fathers of the subject, there stands the brilliant flowering of Greek democracy. It was the political experiences of the City State that furnished them with an inexhaustible wealth of raw material for their theories. The tradition of political liberty in ancient Greece made possible the intellectual development of even a thinker like Plato who was invariably biased against democratic government. This is made quite clear by what followed upon the establishment of the Macedonian hegemony. As soon as the freedom of the *polis* was lost, the intellectual climate made it hard to be concerned with political reality; thinkers concentrated on the problem of how the individual might attain spiritual contentment for himself, e.g., Epicurus and the Stoa. In the Hellenistic age there were no further successful attempts at developing theories in the form of either *politeia* or *politika*.

There was to be no fresh start until the veil of the Middle Ages was torn away and the Italian Renaissance flowered in all its magnificence. In the vigorous environment of Florence, Machiavelli produced his *Prince* and *Discourses*, which became the corner-stone of modern political science. Yet, since the road to modern democratic development was blocked for Italy, no successor to Machiavelli appeared in that country. Thereafter empirical political science developed principally in the Western democracies, in England and America (political science) and in France (*sciences morales et politiques*).* It has been in these countries that the most fruitful results have been obtained.

In Germany, on the other hand, political science evolved almost exclusively as State science (*Staatslehre*), a matter that I shall touch on later. And even State science was swallowed up by the gigantic expansion in the study of public law (*Staats-rechtslehre*) and of public administration (*Verwaltungslehre*). Of course this trend merely reflected the tradition of bureaucratic

* The terms 'political science' and *sciences morales et politiques* are of course very wide in meaning and are not necessarily limited to political science in the narrow sense. I shall not enter into this matter here; the important point is that scholarly works of outstanding value to political science proper have appeared under both these rubrics.

rule and its firm control over whatever sickly political liberty was to be found in the Prussian Kingdom and the German Empire.*

As a rule, the extent to which politics can become the object of free scientific inquiry is a most accurate barometer by which to measure the degree of academic freedom in a country. After all, political power has nothing to hate and fear more than to have its own nakedness objectively delineated. Any political power that is liberal enough to allow itself to be freely studied will certainly sanction the scientific analysis of all other social phenomena. Consequently the degree to which it is possible to study politics will usually suggest what limits are being placed on all forms of academic speculation in a given place at a given time. In a sense political science stands at exactly that point where there occurs the most strained confrontation between politics and scholarship, or, to put it more broadly, between those two great forms of human activity, politics and culture.

When we view the matter in this way, there is clearly no need to ask whether in pre-war Japan there ever existed any foundation on which scholarly disciplines like political science could grow. The collapse of the Tokugawa régime and the succeeding upheavals resulted in the hegemony of absolutist power. The Popular Rights Movement of the late 1870s and early 1880s was ruined by internal weaknesses as well as by repression from above. This historical process determined the road that Japan was to follow in her political modernization. The Meiji Constitution stamped the national polity as 'eternal'; after that the fundamental constitution of the State was no longer a subject that could be freely discussed. Any inquiry into the ultimate source of political power became taboo. The sole basis for the legitimacy of State power lay in the Emperor, the possessor of sovereignty. All legislative, judicial, administrative, and military powers were understood to issue from the exclusive and absolute 'Imperial Prerogative', and no other political rights were recognized as being on the same plane as this 'Imperial Prerogative'.

Consequently the system had by its very nature no place for what in the modern State is ordinarily understood by the term 'political process', namely, *public* competition among diverse

* For conditions at that time, especially for the bureaucratic approach to political matters, see K. Mannheim, *Ideologie und Utopie* (1929), pp. 72 ff.

social groups for the control of a State apparatus that in itself is regarded as neutral. Unlike the legislatures in the Western parliamentary system, the Japanese Diet was not an institution through which the competitive interplay of political groups could ultimately bring into being a unified national decision. From the very beginning the Diet had not been accorded a position strong enough for it to fulfil this function of political integration. As a result, important national decisions were made outside the Diet and were the product of behind-the-scene bargains and compromises among various legal and extra-legal political powers. Thus the struggles and controversies in the Diet were bound to have less and less relevance to public affairs. This applies in particular to the period after the political parties and the clan oligarchs had concluded their hasty working agreement. One can discover no conflict in the Diet that is rooted in and represents a clear differentiation of social strata; nor was there any struggle over different types of *Weltanschauungen*. As the scroll of history unrolled, nothing was to be seen but personal brawling over the sharing of profits and concessions to be derived from control of the government, brawling that grew more scandalous as it became more intense.

Naturally this kind of political squabbling is no incentive to serious scholarly investigation. Given that a strict taboo had been placed on any scientific analysis of the nucleus of State power, and that the warfare in the Diet had become a caricature, what was left for political scientists to study? It was not feasible for them to subject the State to a scientific scrutiny that would help to solve the fundamental problems treated by political scientists in the West, such as the genesis, structure, and legitimacy of political power. It is true that there were conscientious political scientists in Japan who did not wish to make a hallowed mystery of the 'national polity'. Such scholars devoted themselves exclusively to methodological discussions, ultimately indulging in methodology for methodology's sake. Or else they contented themselves with an abstract elucidation of what they had learnt about States and political phenomena from European political science textbooks and they avoided relating these to the realities of Japanese political life.*

* Dr. Onozuka Kiheiji was the founder of political science in the Japanese academic world. At the end of the preface to his *Principles of Political Science* (1903)

The conclusions of Western political science may also be abstract, but behind them lie several centuries of historical development in European politics. There is not a single proposition that did not take shape under the constant check of actual experience. If one unravels these propositions or categories, it will be found that they embody the very political reality through which Europe has lived.

It is true that Japan imported the ideas and institutions of the West. However, these political systems, though similar in form, are animated by quite dissimilar spirits, since the history and fundamental national structure of Japan was so different from that of Europe. Abstract generalities derived from a European context are therefore often highly misleading when it comes to understanding and analysing the hard facts of Japanese political development. Take the political scientist who specialized in methodologies and general propositions based on European experience. If he turned to a problem of everyday politics, he was about on the same level as the political reporter who had not the slightest training in political science, and he was virtually confined to expressing platitudes.

This state of affairs was not really a problem of the scholar's

he has a comment that seems prophetically to epitomize what was afterwards to be the consistent character of Japanese political science:

'I have a number of thoughts and feelings about contemporary domestic and foreign events. However, I believe I should not precipitately engage in political discussions since my scholarship is still shallow and my practical experience is not yet extensive. I prefer rather to stroll in the free world of thought, to sit at ease in the midst of a profusion of books and to converse with gentlemen from all the ages. This book is completely scholarly and includes no political discussion whatsoever.'

In his *Theory of State Structure* (1936), a landmark in the development of the Japanese school of social science, Professor Odaka Tomoo laments 'the lack of co-ordination between thought and action'. When he published the book he fervently proclaimed that in order 'to grasp the soul of the State' he would 'serve as a common soldier in the front line operation of the scholars'. Yet in this very place (Preface, p. 2) he adds: 'My inquiries in this book have no direct relation to any effort to display the special State structure of the Japanese Empire in its practical significance.' When we consider the period in which this book was published, such a statement poignantly recalls how bitterly scholars struggled under the old régime to preserve the academic integrity of State science and political science. Even under such limitations the development of political science was connected with political liberty. This is shown by the fact that the greatest number of books on political science appeared from about 1918 until the late 1920s, during the era of post-war democratic upsurge. Almost all political scientists who are active today began writing in that period.

ability. Basically it can be ascribed to the ambiguous character of Japanese political processes. In Japan, as we have seen, political integration was not achieved through a rational, that is, a commensurable (*berechenbar*), process of open and free discussion, nor was a real decision made by elections or general balloting. A more irrational arrangement prevailed in which decisions depended on fortuitous human relations, psychological coercion by the Elder Statesmen and other 'officials close to the Throne', shifts in the relative strength of cliques, deals among wire-pullers and bosses, assignation-house² politics, and so forth.

Under such circumstances political science was bound to become almost useless, for it presupposes organizational processes in which some degree of *Zweckrationalität* exists. It was thought, and quite correctly, that reading even a hundred volumes on political science would contribute little to an understanding of Japanese political realities. The important thing was to be familiar with the networks of personal relations within the ruling *élites*. The actual conditions prevailing in Japanese politics were more often uncovered through the insights of the newspaper reporter than through the techniques employed by the university professor with his superfluity of learning in political science.*

During the national crisis that developed after the China Incident, several political scientists were unable to endure the excessive gap between reality and their own scholarly work. They left their ivory towers and plunged directly into the vortex of raw politics. Eventually they established personal ties with specific politicians or military men. These scholars were excessively anxious to use such private relations to move political events in the direction they thought desirable.

Such was the tragic fate of political science in Japan.

III

The foregoing has been an evaluation of Japanese political science in the past. Because I have been discussing very broad matters in a short essay, I may give an impression of producing sweeping generalizations about the situation of Japanese politi-

---

* Of course, to some degree the same thing was probably true in other fields of study such as economics, but in no other field was the separation between fact and theory so great as it was in political science.

cal science. It would of course be absurd to suggest that there
is nothing to be learnt from previous work on political science
done in this country. Nor should we disregard the numerous
monographs that have made substantial contributions to the
field. The fact remains that the political scientists of the past
were unable to influence realities, even compared with scholars
in neighbouring disciplines such as law and economics. Being
myself a political scientist, I find this most regrettable; I have
come to the conclusion that we must start by making a fundamental reappraisal of what scholarship in political science
should be. As a first step I have tried to discover why Japanese
political science has until now been so sterile.

The structure of the Japanese State has been undergoing an
historic transformation since 15 August 1945. Now for the first
time it is possible to criticize rationally the very hub of State
power, which hitherto had been shrouded in secrecy. The
groups that were politically powerful under the *ancien régime*
have been liquidated. The complicated process of forming the
national will, which was formerly carried out in obscurity, has
been opened to the public. The Diet has been made the
'highest organ of State power' and the parliamentary cabinet
system has been fully adopted. The Emperor has withdrawn
from his position as source of substantive values and become a
'symbol'. The neutral and formal character of State power has
been proclaimed. At long last a political struggle, in the proper
sense of the term, has emerged, carried on in an open arena
and overtly aiming at control of State power.

Political reality has now been laid completely open to
scientific criticism. A real base has thus been created for the
development of political science. Henceforth political scientists
will not be allowed to attribute the stagnation of their science
to external conditions. We must now make every effort to use
the vast amount of living research material spread before our
eyes. We must do as Aristotle did with the ancient *polis*, as
Machiavelli did with Renaissance Italy, as Hobbes and Locke
did with seventeenth-century England, as Marx did with the
Revolution of 1848 and the Paris Commune, as Bryce did with
the democracies, as Beard, Merriam, Laski, and Siegfried
did in the twenties and thirties. By analysing the complicated
trends that underlie Japanese politics, we must elicit the laws

of political process and behaviour, constantly trying to verify in the actual political situation the propositions and categories thus acquired.

Methodological discussions and definitions of concepts are also, of course, indispensable to a scientific political science. But, as W. Z. Ziegler points out, a logical analysis of political concepts is like an X-ray: 'Even though the bone structure is well delineated, it does not give the slightest notion of the warm living flesh coursing with blood. If the spirit of politics is not alive in us, the most subtle conceptual analysis is of no use.'* Moreover it is characteristic of speculation about politics that problems of methodology are inseparably intertwined with its subject matter. A pure methodology that transcends its subject matter has no meaning in this world.

Another important activity for political science is comparative government. But I suspect that Japanese studies of foreign political systems, unless they are ultimately related to the problem of what to do about *Japan's* politics, are rather in the nature of old men's hobbies. In brief, theory in Japanese political science should be concrete enough to provide a fruitful analysis of political realities in Japan and the world. Only when we have achieved this can we say that we have proved the *raison d'être* of political science to the people, who at present are floundering about in the midst of an unprecedented political upheaval. Nowadays political science must, above all, be a science oriented to actualities (*Wirklichkeitswissenschaft*).

We should, however, constantly bear in mind that, although political science must by its nature be rooted in political realities, this does not mean that it should be directly linked to political parties or groups and become a weapon in political warfare. It is clear that contemporary political strife tends to assume the character of ideological conflict. In both international and domestic struggles ideological armament plays an important role. Under these circumstances there is also a tendency for a scholar's political theories to be mobilized in the service of one or another of the embattled political groups. In a sense, we might say that, if a theory completely lacked this kind of utility value, it would be not only meaningless from a practical standpoint but worth little even as an 'abstract' theory.

* *Einführung in die Politik*, p. 1.

When the political scientist investigates contemporary political phenomena and living political ideologies, however, his interior guide must always be the truth, and that alone. In contrast, the politician usually values a theory in terms of its capacity to mobilize the masses. His criterion is its propaganda or agitation potential rather than its truth. Though both the politician and the political scientist are equally concerned with politics, here there is an ultimate difference in approach.

Naturally, as a citizen, the political scientist must not be indifferent to what kind of political forces might make use of his theory. It is his duty to take into account the social effect of his theory when it is made public. But this is a separate problem from the motive behind his speculations. For instance, imagine a political scientist who belongs to one of the competing political parties and who fights day and night to further the political ideas of his party. Once he turns to the *scientific* analysis of political reality, all his political aspirations, hopes, likes, and dislikes must be subordinated to the requirements of the cognitive process. So long as he is not inspired with this spirit of abstinence, the only difference between his theoretical *magnum opus* and a party pamphlet will be the number of pages. This is one of the greatest pitfalls in the path of political science: too eager to become more realistic as the science of politics, political science may overstep the bounds proper to itself and become the servant of political forces.

It is comparatively simple to protect political science from *directly* subordinating itself to the demands of a specific political party. It is far more difficult to prevent subjective value judgements from insinuating themselves into the cognition of political phenomena. Politics has by its very nature the power to stir human instincts and passions to their depths. As a result prejudices rooted in the observer's irrational likes and dislikes may often come to be mixed with his cognition of political reality.

If we consider this matter further, we are faced with the question: can any cognition of political things ever be totally free from such bias? Here we are compelled to deal with a specific characteristic of speculation about politics: the relation between theory and practice. If we are to establish political science as a *Wirklichkeitswissenschaft*, we cannot evade the difficulty posed by this problem.

IV

Bismarck once called politics 'the art of the possible'. It is characteristic of political investigation that it deals with situations that are not fixed but constantly being shaped anew. Many political scientists in the past have in one way or another realized that its subject matter is essentially dynamic, changeable, filled with unknowns. As we have seen, the development of nineteenth-century German *Staatsrechtslehre* was a process in which the political element was gradually eliminated from the theory of the State; State science ended up as the study of public law.* Yet even here the common tendency was to distinguish political science from the theory of law by relating the former to the 'dynamic' aspect of the State.†

Thus Schäffle makes a distinction between politics and the ordinary life of the State (*laufendes Staatsleben*). The model of the latter he takes to be administration (*Verwaltung*), State acts that are constantly being reproduced in accordance with established law. In contrast he labels as 'politics' a situation in which each decision brings something new into being. According to Bluntschli, theoretical State science deals with the political order when it is in repose (*ruhende Staatsordnung*), while the task of political science is to grasp 'the currents and trends in the life of the State'. In contradistinction to pure State science, whose subject matter is limited to past and present State phenomena, Georg Jellinek conceives of political science— applied or practical State science—as an art (*Kunstlehre*) oriented essentially towards the future. These approaches differ in detail, but they all agree that the distinctive characteristic of politics is a plastic futurity. This interpretation is bound up with the view that political science is not the study of pure being-as-it-is (*das Seiende*) but includes value judgements and thus is the study of being-as-it-ought-to-be (*das Sein-Sollende*).‡

Here there is no need to discuss the ideological implications inherent in these two taxonomic divisions of German State science or their relation with the German bureaucratic State.

---

* The theory that carried this trend to its extreme was the Kelsen theory of pure law.

† For an example of the legal philosopher's approach, see Professor Odaka Tomoo, op. cit., pp. 75, 532.

‡ G. Jellinek, *Allgemeine Staatslehre*, 3rd ed., pp. 13 ff.

If one disregards their unmistakably antipathetic or evasive attitude towards 'things political', it is clear that these scholars are perfectly correct in their intuition concerning the chaiacteristic of political speculation.

Thus, to borrow Landshut's words, it is the destiny of political science to grasp political reality 'from the standpoint of its potentiality for change' (*unter dem Aspekt ihrer möglichen Veränderbarkeit*).* Here an object does not exist in any fixed form prior to the cognitive process. It is through the cognitive process itself that objective reality acquires a fixed pattern. There is a constant interchange between the subject and the object: 'In his whole thought and feeling' the investigator 'belongs existentially' to political reality.† This truth need not, of course, be limited to political speculation in the narrow sense. It is common to all the social sciences, applying equally to any discipline that is concerned with social and cultural reality. Yet clearly this interplay between subject and object is greatest in political science, since that discipline takes as its immediate object of investigation human beings who are acting and struggling to shape the future. In the political world the very proposal of a category or of a formulation for a problem already involves a certain evaluation of the forces at work in the sphere of actual situations.

This is confirmed by the wide variation in the way people see the political and socio-economic crisis that confronts Japan today. Some people start from the problem of capitalism versus socialism. Others consider the basic question to be government control versus freedom. For some the greatest issue is parliamentarianism versus 'direct action'. Still others single out the formation of a democratic front against reactionary forces as the key problem.

Since such presentations of the problem cannot be arbitrarily contrived, they are limited in number. This divergence of approach arises ineluctably from the actual dynamics of Japanese society and the responses thereto by the various social strata. Each approach is tied to the basic interests and demands of a particular social stratum.

Consequently the problem of capitalism versus socialism is

---

* *Kritik der Soziologie*, p. 67.
† H. Heller, *Staatslehre*, edited by G. Niemeyer, p. 53.

often regarded as having no real existence by those who see the issue as one of control versus freedom. In this sense they think of 'capitalism versus socialism' as mere 'ideology'. And of course their presentation of the problem is just as violently repudiated by those who believe in the capitalism versus socialism approach. The reason for this is that to discern a problem is itself to acknowledge the inevitability of a certain course in socio-political change, a truth that also applies to almost all political concepts in use today.

There is no question that the actual way in which a person uses words like 'democratic' or 'reactionary' depends largely on his *Weltanschauung*. 'Order and morality', 'Down with the dictatorship of the minority', 'National independence', and other slogans that sound plausible enough in themselves are phrases that developed from, and can only be properly understood in the context of, specific political circumstances. Each of them is connected with an attempt to shape the course of events either in favour of or against a specific political force. When the investigator tries to organize his perception of political reality round such categories, consciously or unconsciously he has already made an evaluative selection from among existing political trends.

A political scientist must start by frankly recognizing the existence in his own field of this kind of close interrelation between the process of knowing and the object known. In other words, he must recognize that all political speculation, including his own, is existentially bound.* In the political world there can be no observer who is not also an actor. 'Strict neutrality' is also a *political* position. In this sense, when a scholar constructs a theory of political situation, he is *ipso facto* committing himself to a specific political course of action.

By such action every scholar participates in shaping political realities. To close one's eyes to this inescapable fact and to pose as an isolated observer of the drama is mere self-deception. It is also harmful; for to do so often serves to spread a whatever-wins-is-right type of opportunism in the name of 'impartial observation'. If a person professes to be a mere spectator of the

---

* Mannheim's sociology of knowledge represents in my mind the most penetrating investigation into the existentially bound character (*Seinsgebundenheit*) of social speculation.

all-out political struggle among the various types of *Welt-anschauungen*, he shows himself by that very fact to be unqualified as a political scientist.*

I have suggested that, like other scientists, a political scientist should depend only on truth in developing his thought. In this sense an attitude of 'abstinence' is necessary. But abstinence is meaningful only where desire is present. The keener the inner struggle against desire, the greater the moral value of 'abstinence'. If a person has lacked desire from the very beginning, then he is physiologically deformed. This applies no less to politics than to morals.

I have suggested that political science must not be the servant of a particular political force. This is not meant as a compliment to the adherent of 'desire-free objectivity', who evades clear political decisions. Political investigation both regulates and is regulated by its object of study. Therefore it is the 'original sin' of political theory to be markedly subjective and to take on an ideological cast. In so far as political science is a vocation, this is unmistakably a liability in truth value. Instead of simply resigning ourselves to the inevitability of 'original sin', we must aim at the highest level of objectivity and do our best to elimi-nate any distortion caused by ideological affiliations.

What is the best way to accomplish this—to close one's eyes to the stern fact that thinking is existentially bound, or humbly to recognize the existential limitations not only of others but also of oneself? The arrogant 'positivist' dislikes to pass value judge-ments and professes to stand for 'objectivity'. Though he makes a great show of his freedom from values, in the midst of his 'positivist' cognition value judgements are likely to creep inad-vertently into his 'objective observations'. On the other hand, a

* Max Weber's demand for value-free judgement is apt in Japan to become a disguise for the positivist 'onlooker'. But Weber himself thought that the separation of theoretical value relations from practical value judgements was an 'investigator's ideal', and that its perfect realization was even incompatible with the unity of the personality. See Marianne Weber, *Max Weber, Ein Lebensbild*, p. 330. In his *Die Objektivität der Sozialwissenschaftlichen Erkenntnissen* and his *Die Wissenschaft als Beruf* Weber sharply rejects any confusion of his theory with the attitude of the 'purely impartial observer' regarding value judgements on different *Weltanschauungen*, or with a neutral position *vis-à-vis* both the right and the left wings in politics. He claims that it is a scholar's duty as a citizen to state clearly his *Weltanschauung* and his political position. Both Marianne Weber and Jaspers recognize that Weber had an intensely active and practical personality. And this personality itself makes his view on value-free judgement all the more meaningful.

person who is deeply concerned with actual political trends and who sincerely desires to affect them will probably realize through self-examination that any speculation is existentially bound. In his perception of political reality he will be particularly conscious of the need to guard against any clouding of the cognitive process that arises from his own hopes and aspirations. Thus he is likely to attain a higher level of objectivity than the self-styled 'value-free' observer.* Here we find a relationship that suggests Shinran's paradox: the bad man stands closer than the good man to the saving grace of Amida Buddha.

In any case, the road to objectivity is never easy for the political scientist who has oriented himself to *Wirklichkeitswissenschaft* in the true sense of the word. In his innermost mind he must constantly experience the bitter struggle between the ideal of objectivity and the existential limitations of his cognitive process. The more he roots his scholarship in political reality, the more severe this tension will become. Unable to endure the strain the political scientist may throw himself directly into the excitement of actual politics and degrade his scholarship to the level of a pure 'ideology' that serves the ends of some specific political force. Or, on the contrary, he may close his eyes to concrete political situations and return to the old abstract ivory tower that Japanese political science occupied before the war.

If in the future Japanese political science takes either of these paths, it must resign itself to its former position as an outcast among the social sciences. But if political scientists are prepared to wrestle with this knotty problem, then, from the resultant 'purification through fire', they may be able to detect a glimmer of light that will lead them to a broader perspective. Only then will Japan have a political science that is not borrowed but rooted in Japanese soil.

POSTSCRIPT

In 1947 *Jimbun*, a journal published by the Education Ministry's Humanistic Science Committee, surveyed developments in each of the humanistic sciences (*Jimbun*, No. 2). I was

---

* Of course this is true only of those who desire to accomplish something in the field of scholarship. There is no question here of the 'political carnivore' (Spengler), whose sole concern is to push on like a cart-horse for political action.

assigned to cover the field of political science and on that occasion wrote this essay. The irritation I then felt towards the poverty and backwardness of Japanese political science was bound up in some curious way with the feeling of liberation I experienced after the war, a feeling that was not limited to me but ran high among social scientists in general. This is the reason for the plaintive tone of the present essay. Reading it over ten years later, I must confess that this tone rather embarrasses me. Nevertheless some distinguished colleagues were stimulated by my sweeping criticism of the traditional approaches of Japanese political science. It was one of the factors that shortly thereafter brought forth a brilliant work by Professor Rōyama Masamichi, *The Development of Modern Political Science in Japan*. This was an unexpected dividend.

Naturally the passage of ten years has greatly transformed conditions in this field. Formerly, political science was not even accorded full citizenship among the social sciences. Nowadays it has grown so big that it is being cautioned about the 'limits of modern politics' by investigators in adjacent fields and even by prominent leaders in the Marxist political parties. It was only natural that in the post-war period there should have been a great increase in the number of investigators working in disciplines that had just recently been introduced into Japan, social psychology and cultural anthropology, for example. Yet the tremendous multiplication of workers in the long-established field of political science has been astounding.

Those of us who are familiar with the pre-war situation of political science feel as if we were in another world. Talented young researchers are still rushing on to the scene and, with great energy and scholarly enthusiasm, bringing vast undeveloped areas under cultivation. The themes and trends of their research are so widely varied that it is difficult to keep up with all the recent developments, especially if, like myself, one is working both in political science and in Japanese intellectual history. The problem is aggravated by the extensive programme of international exchange.

In this sense the present essay can be regarded as a 'memento' of an old debate in Japanese political science. For instance, there has been a marked decline in the old tendency to waste time on methodology for methodology's sake and on definition for definition's sake. Though their viewpoints may differ, political scientists do come to grips with Japan's actual political processes. There has also been considerable acceptance of the attitude that even theory and research on foreign political systems should be developed with concrete problems in mind.

Some conditions of the past have continued into the present, while some new difficulties and problems have cropped up. For instance, there has been little, if any, progress in regard to communication between political scientists and practical politicians; on the contrary, the isolation of the two in certain respects is even more extreme than it was directly after the war. Secondly, research conditions vary greatly from region to region and from 'workshop' to 'workshop'. The distribution of researchers is also heavily concentrated in urban areas. Consequently students in the provinces are isolated, whereas in the large cities something like a 'consensus of opinion' is rapidly being developed through research meetings, group investigations, and other activities.

The problem that lies behind all this is in fact the pattern of modernization to be found in all areas of Japanese life since the Meiji Restoration, a pattern that to this day has not changed in the slightest. In such fields as political science, where it is still necessary to assimilate so much foreign research, this unbalanced development of research in urban and rural areas easily becomes pathological: 'the centre is the centre and the provinces are the provinces'.

Yet another problem is that there is still almost no exchange between political science and those neighbouring disciplines that have traditions: law, economics, history. As political science has developed, this lack of communication has tended to become worse rather than better. There are many reasons for this, but it can largely be attributed to the historical conditions that have prevailed in the social sciences. The academic autonomy of political science has always been the result of its emancipation from the legal approach of Law. In Europe and America, the more political science secured its independence from Law, the closer its relations with the other social sciences became. In Japan, however, either Marxism or the German school has traditionally been the chief influence in both economics and history. Thus, whenever political science tries an independent approach, it is likely to isolate itself not only from Law but from economics and history as well.

The terminology used in political science often encourages this trend. Leaving aside terms, such as those used by Lasswell, that have been received with perplexity even in their American homeland, we find that the Japanese social sciences are still unfamiliar with certain words and categories that are common terms in the Western academic world. When Japanese political scientists use such terms tentatively in their analyses, their colleagues in neighbouring fields frequently criticize them for creating incomprehensible ideographic compounds or accuse them of borrowing foreign words uncritically.

Of course one cannot exaggerate the necessity for taking precautions against the pedantry and the intellectual vanity that are apt to creep into new approaches. It is also a well-known social fact that isolation and *argot* mutually promote each other. On the other hand, I should like the reader to consider that the fairly special categories and terminology of Marxism, though translated into difficult ideographic compounds, have gained a certain popular currency.

This is not a proposal for the high-handed intrusion of political science terminology into other fields, nor is it a demand that Marxist terminology be discarded. It is an appeal for a tolerant attitude towards the difficulties Japanese political scientists are now facing.

In the long run 'time' will probably solve the problem. Meanwhile political scientists will have to go on using two techniques simultaneously: first, the 'from below' method, that is, refining a popular concept until it can be used for scholarly purposes; secondly, the 'from above' method, that is, attempting to popularize an academic term of fairly high effectiveness while constantly testing its applicability to concrete political situations.* Here I shall not go into details concerning the

* Incidentally, I should like to point out that when scholars in neighbouring fields, especially Marxists, use the term 'modern politics', they often assume it is a political version of modern economics. True, there are some schools of political science that consciously aim at using the same kind of quantification as economics. Furthermore, if we educe certain epistemological characteristics that are common not only to economics but even to such subjects as social psychology and semantics, then in contrast to Marxist social science we would probably place today's political science among the sciences that share those epistemological characteristics. However, I do not think that political science has ever had the same clear-cut boundaries

significance of the diverse methods used in political science, the differences and similarities between its approaches and those of neighbouring fields, or the main types of political science.* To do so would not be suitable since the main subject of this volume is contemporary political problems, not political science *per se*.

TRANSLATOR'S NOTES

1. The reader must remember that Professor Maruyama wrote this article in 1947 and is describing what were then contemporary events.
2. See Glossary: *House of assignation*.

as modern economics. Moreover, as things stand, it seems difficult even for Marxists to speak of 'Marxian political science' with the same kind of clarity that applies to Marxian economics. Marxism views things from the standpoint of a unified social science. Consequently it is natural that the varied approaches of political science should seem to the Marxists as really pieces of cloth from the same bolt. Still, I and probably most other '*bourgeois*' political scientists feel disturbed if a single approach in America is regarded as representing political science in general.

  * My general approach to political science is set forth in the appropriate section of *An Introduction to the Social Sciences* (Misuzu Shobō, 1949, rev. ed. 1956).

VIII. From Carnal Literature to Carnal Politics

TRANSLATED BY BARBARA RUCH

This essay was originally published in the magazine Tenbō, *October 1949*

TRANSLATOR'S NOTE

The dialogue in the Far East has a tradition not unlike that in the West. Confucius, like Socrates, explained the basic tenets of his philosophy in response to well-placed questions by eager disciples. But in both the Chinese and the Western traditions the *idea* has always preceded the discourse. It was, in fact, the excuse for the dialogue.

In Japan, however, the dialogue has taken several forms in the course of its evolution. It continues to be used in some circles as a medium for disguised didactics; in another form it now exists as a recognized literary genre for the exploration of new ideas that have not yet been fully developed. Writers who do not have the time for a thorough examination of every stimulating idea that occurs to them will tentatively pursue a particular insight by means of a loosely constructed colloquy. There is no intent to preach, or to press upon the reader, some well-rounded theory. Nor is there any pretence at sifting out internal inconsistencies. Ideas are submitted as they come to mind, for whatever they are worth, in the hope that the reader may carry the analysis one step further and gain some new insights for himself.

*   *   *

FROM CARNAL LITERATURE TO CARNAL POLITICS

A.   Quiet here, isn't it! You must be getting lots of work done.

B.   Yes, it's quiet. But I've just got here, you know, and it takes me a while to get warmed up. At least it's not like

Tokyo, where you've got to worry about visitors interrupting you at all hours of the day and night. Thank goodness I don't have that to contend with.

A.   And now, just when you've got away from it all, I come rushing in on you.

B.   Not at all. Man is a self-indulgent creature. In fact, now that I'm alone here like this, I've even been secretly hoping someone would drop in.

A.   I understand that writers often come to this hotel when they have important work to do.

B.   That's right. As a matter of fact, you know Mr. T, don't you—the man who caused such a scandal some time ago when he stabbed a friend of his? Well, they say he was staying here just the other day. It seems that while he was here he took another one of his overdoses of some drug—Adorm I think it was—and caused quite a commotion. Mr. S, who had come out here with him, took him back to Tokyo, but I understand that in the train on the way back he behaved outrageously towards the other passengers. It was quite an ordeal for everyone involved.

A.   Good heavens! Well, I must say he went to a lot of trouble coming all the way out here to go on a jag. He must be nicely hooked by now.

B.   Apparently when the drug takes effect he has all sorts of visual and auditory hallucinations and anyone from Dazai Osamu to the gas man may appear and carry on a conversation with him. So I'd say he's really had it.

A.   There have been a lot of Philopon and Adorm addicts cropping up among literary men lately, haven't there? I live the rather prosaic life of an office worker, and I must say, to a simple man like me this sort of thing is totally incomprehensible. Presumably they can't produce literature without leading that kind of off-beat existence. But really, if a man has to destroy himself in order to do his work, then I think he should reconsider the validity of his occupation. From the standpoint of ordinary people like myself, men in your line seem a good bit closer to the literary professions, so perhaps you can look at these writers with more sympathy than we can.

B.   No, I wouldn't say that. When it comes to being prosaic, my own special field could hold its own quite well with yours. Anyway, I still think literary men should be called to account, but not by men in my position. It's the public at large that should persistently be asking questions like yours.

But then from the very beginning the public has always assumed that literary men are some peculiar species of humanity, and this has had an adverse effect on them. In fact I get the feeling that they've taken advantage of this super-imposed image and have made themselves quite at home in the abnormal way of life we've just been talking about.

Of course there are many types of literary men and it's unfair to lump them all together in the same class with Philopon addicts. But in Japan at least, conditions may be such as to make creative work difficult within the atmosphere of ordinary life.

A.   Yes, I suppose external conditions do present a problem. But these writers don't even *try* to find their subject matter in the ordinary life of our society—in the everyday lives of ordinary citizens, if you will. They're ready and waiting, by nature as it were, to ferret out some unique circumstance or bizarre situation. So how can they help but inject abnormal 'experiments' into their own lives?

The other day I was reading through a special edition on fiction put out by some magazine, and I was amazed to find that in every one of the seven or eight stories included there was a scene in which a man and a woman went to bed together. When we reach this stage what's the use of having a special literary category like 'carnal literature'? I'm no puritan, I assure you. And I certainly don't think a writer is abnormal just because he's written a bedroom scene. But I must say I was really quite astonished to find that men who are regarded as fiction writers of the highest calibre have joined the ranks, and that every last one of them is describing the naked facts about what goes on between the sheets.

When I say this, people often argue that the state of post-war sex life itself is characterized by irresponsibility and that literature is only reflecting a real situation. Of course this might be true if we were considering only one segment of present-day society. But I don't for a moment believe that the whole nation has become as sexually obsessed as all that.

I really wonder what in the world the wild, reckless carrying-on you find in works labelled 'carnal literature' has to do with the everyday life of the people. As things stand now, isn't it possible that when future historians read some of these stories they'll assume they depict a fairly universal state of affairs in post-war Japan? Especially since this isn't just a question of the pulp magazines. At least it's not at all unlikely that people reading that special edition on fiction some hundred years, or even a few decades, from now will get the idea that in about 1949 the Japanese people had their heads filled constantly with the business of coitus.

B.   I doubt if things will come to that. Anyhow, most of the writers who grind out carnal or sex-obsessed brands of literature do so knowing full well that what they write doesn't spring from everyday events in the lives of ordinary people. And it's the same for the reader. Isn't it precisely because the circumstances depicted are remote from his actual life that he's so attracted? In other words, such literature constitutes a kind of 'symbol' of something he longs for.

A.   I think you're right. When you really stop to think about it, our day-to-day existence is so sterile, so totally devoid of poetry or dreams, that it simply doesn't provide the subject matter for creative writing. I suppose our standard of living hasn't risen high enough, and we don't have the material affluence needed to produce 'poetry'.

B.   Of course this problem has its roots in society. It's not something that novelists can solve just by their proficiency or goodwill. And yet, just look round. There's plenty of evidence that when our material requirements are met our inner resources don't automatically become enriched. As long as there isn't any inner working of the spirit that makes the creation of 'poetry' possible within the context of our lives, it's always going to be the same old story.

The Japanese are often criticized by foreigners for not

understanding sociability. But it seems to me that sociability doesn't lie in the act of getting together to consume
elaborate dinners and to dance. Rather, it's found in
making our conversations as universal as possible, and also
in having the kind of *rapport* that makes conversations
really fruitful. In this sense many European novels and
films show that in their part of the world 'sociability'
exists even in the lowest social classes.

The other day I saw Jean Cocteau's film, *Les Parents
Terribles*. Every single remark exchanged in that family,
even their most trivial repartee, was infused with such an
animated vitality that I was completely overwhelmed. If
I had understood French a little better no doubt I'd have
found it even more remarkable. I know you're going to
say it was just a theatre script and different from real
conversation. But let me ask you this. When are we ever
conscious of that much vitality during the household conversations in Japanese plays or films? I'm afraid I've come
to just one conclusion—that it all boils down to the discrepancy between the inner resources of the Europeans and
our own. To put it in exaggerated terms, I should almost
say that in Europe everyday life as such is already to a
certain extent a 'literary creation', that subject matter
itself has already been given form. It's precisely because
this is *not* the case in Japan that Japanese writers have been
reduced to fishing about for subject matter in peculiar
surroundings and bizarre events far removed from the
ordinary life of the common people.

A.   Well, in that case, how are we to interpret the 'autobiographical novel', which has practically become a national
tradition in Japan? I think it's related in some way to what
you've just said. And yet it sticks rather closely to everyday
experiences in the lives of average people. In that sense it
can be taken as the absolute antithesis of certain types of
war books and the topsy-turvy literature of the post-war
period in which the writer scours the landscape looking
for all sorts of abnormalities, and turns everyday moral
views on life upside down.

B.   As far as I can see, there's no radical difference between
these two types of literature, at least from the standpoint of

their ideas. To begin with, whether we're talking in terms of the abnormal or the normal, don't you agree that those writers in Japan who serve as photographic plates, who merely reflect what they see, are all cast pretty much in the same mould so far as their spirit is concerned? At best, only the scene portrayed and the technique employed differ to any noticeable extent. Carnal literature and war books may be far removed from ordinary situations, but so far as their spiritual dimensions are concerned these forms of writing aren't so very different from the realism of autobiographical writing. It's just that such literature takes the most sordid moments of our sensual experience, multiplies their number, and in doing so, magnifies them out of all proportion. An imagination capable of such exaggeration appears to be soaring away in unhampered freedom, but actually it's grubbing around on its hands and knees in quite a commonplace world.

A similar concern with the abnormal exists in both the East and the West, but don't you agree that we often find something demonic in European and Russian literature that differs constitutionally from everyday experience? When they do deal with carnal passion, the impression one gets is so entirely different from that created by Japanese novels that I don't think it's merely a question of the technique in handling the material.

Just to give you an example, I understand that in the West a writer of pornography is a 'specialist' in his field, and a sharp line of demarcation is drawn between him and the *littérateur*. Even the public, by general consent, makes a clear distinction between pornography and a work of art. But in Japan, from as far back as Tamenaga Shunsui to as recently as Nagai Kafū, the boundary line between the two has been exquisitely amorphous. For this reason Japanese pornographic works are actually much more 'artistic' than their counterparts in the West. The same analysis, I suppose, can be applied to the seventeenth- and eighteenth-century Japanese wood-block prints of the pleasure quarters.[1] So the problem lies in a discrepancy more fundamental than that of technique.

It might seem unreasonable to disregard the standards of

artistry that the autobiographical novel has already achieved, and to consider it along with today's carnal literature. But the minds of our writers cling like leeches to natural, sensual phenomena, and lack a really free flight of the imagination, so in one sense all of our literature is 'carnal'.

A. A remarkable point of view, I must say! But what about the autobiographical novels of someone like Shiga Naoya? They are considered to be the supreme achievement in that genre. Everyone says they're wonderful, they're great! Frankly, I find them a bit of a bore as novels. But I'm afraid if I were to say what I really think people would have a good laugh at my expense, and so, not having as much nerve as you have, I keep my honest impressions to myself. Nevertheless, can't we call this type of description 'realism'? You keep bringing up idealistic concepts like spirit or imagination, but . . .

B. Well, of course even imagination has its existential basis, you know. I mean, if to have imagination is just a matter of ignoring physical reality and floating about with one's head in the clouds, then the highest forms of art and culture are shuffling about in the wards of mental hospitals. I should have mentioned this before, but even realism is a method of creativity. It's not the faithful copying of a perceptible subject. It is precisely because the reality does not appear directly, but as a 'mediated reality' depending on the positive participation of the human spirit, that we can call it fiction. So the decisive factor lies in the integrating force of the spirit after all.

But in Japan the spirit is neither differentiated nor independent from perceptible nature—of course I include the human body as a part of nature—and so the mediating force of the spirit is weak. It fails to preserve the internal unity of fiction itself and in the end it's dragged off in all directions by separate, disjointed sensual experiences. As for the reader, since he can't enjoy fiction as fiction, he gets involved in speculations about the identity of the real-life counterparts of the characters. This sort of thing is always getting out of hand and causing one kind of scandal or another. I'm sure it's this uneasiness about 'made-up' stories that ultimately supports the 'true-story' journalism which is overrunning us now and which can certainly be considered the culmination of Japanese-style realism.

A.   You know, your conversation reminds me of one of those incendiary bombs I had the honour of meeting quite often during the air raids. You burst out from the point of contact and in a flash you've spread to the most unlikely places. It's rather disconcerting, to say the least. Actually I think I have a general idea of what you're trying to say. It's just that I can't agree with what you said about the separation of the spirit from nature, or something to that effect. I don't see how spirit, divorced from nature, could exist in the context of reality.

B.   When I make such a point of the independence of spiritual dimensions, or the separation of the spirit from perceptible nature, I'm talking about a *functional* independence. This has nothing to do with the metaphysics of whether or not the spirit, as an entity in itself, exists independent of the natural world. What I'm trying to say is that in Japan, when one speaks of spirit or of value, people immediately think in terms of concrete entities. As a result we have, on the one hand, materialists, who get hot under the collar just hearing an expression like 'independence of the spirit', and, on the other, existentialists, who come trooping out, speaking of nihilism or despair, and treasuring the spirit as if it were a 'thing'.

A.   What's the matter with you today, anyway? You're attacking everyone, left and right. I'd like to go back a little, if you don't mind, to the Japanese attitude towards fiction. You say we're uncomfortable about fiction, and so we try to push it in the direction of first-hand, sensual reality. Or I think you put it in more general terms when you said that the spirit is not functionally independent of nature. Well, don't you think this may be another ramification of the feudalistic nature of Japanese society?

B.   Honestly, it seems as if the word 'feudalistic' has become a standard epithet for Japan these days. Evidently people feel that by simply uttering the word they've made the essence of Japan infinitely clear. But at least there's one thing I'm sure of, and that is that the social foundation supporting this spirit we're talking about was built in pre-modern times.

A.   Would you elaborate on that point a little more concretely?

B.   Well, I'm not quite sure what to say. It's an enormous subject. If I were to give you an explanation I'd have to start with a general description of the development of modern society. And then I'd have to mention the Emperor system and the family system, which form a unique historic foundation for Japanese society. It would turn out to be quite an undertaking, you know. More than I can deal with. Well, all right, let's say I could do it. But at this moment if I had to condense the whole subject to its bare essentials—well, the best I could do would be to come out with a rather routine statement.

A.   I just asked a simple question. I had no intention of interrupting our conversation so that you could deliver a penetrating historical analysis. You're a brave one when you're lashing out with your arm-chair theories on literature. But the moment the problem moves within sight of your own field of study you pick up and run. They say that a scholar is a man who discusses his own speciality with a great deal of confidence and who keeps his mouth shut when it comes to things outside his field. I ventured to ask my question only because I had the feeling there was some correlation between the Japanese mentality we've been talking about and the way things are going in Japanese politics today.

B.   Well, after that dressing down, I'd better start talking—fast! But only on the condition that we keep the question of politics to a minimum, and that we limit ourselves to the history of social thought. So here goes.

The first question is why do people with the old-fashioned kind of social awareness feel uneasy about fiction? Or, to put it the other way round, why does the modern spirit believe in the value and use of fiction, and why does this spirit keep turning out fiction? There's no end of explanations for this, so let's analyse the word fiction etymologically. Look up the word in the dictionary and you'll see it comes from the Latin word *fingere*. It'll tell you that it originally meant 'to fashion', or 'to invent'. Then the connotation of the word changed, and it came to mean 'to imagine' or 'to pretend'. In other words, it originally referred, in a broad sense, to a human being having some purpose in mind, and *producing* something in line with his idea. So there's a specific attitude that underlies a belief in fiction. This attitude is one that evaluates man's intellectual productivity in the highest terms. And so it rates the product of intellectual activity much higher than natural realities.

Production is the processing of material in terms of some idea. So, when you look at this 'processing' from the standpoint of the material, it's 'matter *becoming* form'. But from the point of view of the producer it's *'making* matter into form'. There are different grades of the same type of product, though, and some have a more fictitious quality than others. The more we have of matter, the less we have of fiction. And it works the other way round too. The more form, the greater the fiction. The most fiction-like fiction completely dismisses natural, tangible realities. A man creates this kind of fiction entirely in his mind, according to a certain awareness of the ends involved. That's how we get such expressions as 'fictitious capital', when the value of stocks is artificially inflated on the basis of imaginary assets, and that's how the concept of a 'fictitious person' in the legal sense evolved.

But this idea that a fiction or fabrication exists outside the realm of reality ends up by giving fiction the bad connotation of 'falsehood'. And if we're going to say that falsehood or fact are defined in terms of their 'proximity' to the immediately perceptible circumstances, well then we might as well say the modern spirit sets greater store by falsehood than by fact. But actually this spirit sees 'mediated' reality as being on a higher level than 'immediate' reality.

A.   You know, somehow I get the feeling you're feeding me a 'false' philosophy. Is there any 'proximity' here to the main question of the formation of modern society?

B.   Now just be patient and listen. If I hadn't got at least this much said on the meaning of fiction you wouldn't be able to follow what I'm going to say next. Now then.

There are two phases to the formation of a modern society. First, there's the natural breakdown of the medieval social system, and then there's the founding of a new civic society on the ruins of the old order. But the point is that a certain consciousness must emerge before either of these things can be accomplished. First there has to be an awareness that the public order, institutions, *mores*, in short the whole social environment that encompasses mankind, is man-made, and can be changed by the force of man's intellect.

A.   Well, that's simply a matter of course, wouldn't you say?

B.   It's by no means a matter of course. That's the point. When people are *invested* with a place in life, when they get it by virtue of birth or social standing, when their role in society has been predetermined, then to these people, the social environment assumes the same kind of reality as the natural world. Even those institutions established for a specific purpose become mere given phenomena. In other words people see these institutions as natural formations and aren't aware that they're really man-made. And so they don't think to question the purposes for which they were set up. Well, such societies probably don't need to form well-defined institutions—but I'll get on to that subject a little later. Anyway, when people view their society as a *fait accompli* they don't just automatically start thinking in terms of fictions. And even if the thought occurred to them it wouldn't make much headway.

A.   From about what point in history would you say this fictional way of thinking began to take shape?

B.   Let's see, I suppose it was from about the time of the late scholastic philosophers, John Duns Scotus and William of Occam. You've heard of nominalism, I'm sure. Well, the nominalists were opposed to the orthodox views of Aquinas and others that universals do exist. They came out with the claim that universals are man-made concepts created for the sake of convenience, and that only individual things really exist. The Greek Sophists had already denied that social norms or institutions had any inherent binding power in a society. They regarded them as human 'fictions'. And the struggle between nominalism and realism has been with us ever since the beginning of the Middle Ages. But we are talking about what sort of connexion there is between this fiction-oriented attitude and the dissolution of the medieval social order. And in this regard I think the appearance of the late scholastic philosophers is most significant.

A.   And in what form did it develop after the Renaissance?

B.   Well, here again it would take for ever to go into details, but you know the theory of social contract that prevailed during the seventeenth and eighteenth centuries? That was nominalism's legal offspring, so to speak. Actually there are various theories of social contract. But there's one thing that clearly distinguishes a modern theory of social contract from the vertical ruler-subject contract of the Middle Ages and the ancient Far East. And that is, people were acting on a new appreciation of the individual as the only natural reality, and a realization that his role in society was entirely the conscious result of his individual choice. Later on, people began to complain that this atomistic theory of contract was non-historic or mechanistic. But it was precisely because it had gone so far in seeing man as completely divorced from his given environment that a kind of activating energy was born in this new type of man—an energy that severs the roots of deeply entrenched conventions and historic institutions.

On the other hand, of course, this liberated view of man could never have emerged if the medieval social order had not already been disintegrating. And then too we have to keep in mind the effect of the natural sciences and various other factors that might have set the wheels turning.

It was Rousseau and Kant who clearly recognized that a social contract is really a fiction rather than an historical event that actually took place. Until then the original social contracts had been considered a part of history. For this reason there was still no clear distinction between a fiction and what occurs naturally.

A.   There's something about this that bothers me. Recently I read a book that mentioned traditional Asian thought in some context or other and, as I recall, it said that the European approach to political thought emphasizes institutions over and above man, while Eastern thought maintains that the human being comes before institutions. Somehow this doesn't seem to square with what you just said about the modern European spirit. According to your definition, the modern spirit is one that denies the natural elements in an institution and emphasizes man as the agent creating it.

B.   I was about to mention that point. Just as you say, there was a 'humanism' in Asian thought from very early times. And even today in Japan we're always hearing people say: 'In the end, it's not the institution or the ideology, but it's a question of the man in charge.'

First of all, as soon as we examine ancient political thought in the East we see that there are practically no discussions on system or on organization such as you find in European thought. Instead it's mostly discussions on how a ruler can improve his virtuous character, or debates on the 'knack' of government. As far as the classics go, I suppose the *Four Books* and the *Five Classics* would represent the former approach, and the *Han Fei Tsu* and *Plots of the Warring States* would be examples of the latter. In either case these works deal only with immediate relationships between man and man. As long as social control is understood mainly in terms of direct and interpersonal relationships, it's not likely that considerations of systems and organizations will develop. Even in the West, if you look through the political writings of the Middle Ages, you'll find that there were very few discussions of systems, though granted, there's not as poor a showing as in Asia.

Well now, how does this pre-modern emphasis on 'humanism' differ from modern society's discovery of 'man'? Let's take this so-called 'humanism' first. Here the type of man exalted is one whose life is cluttered up with all sorts of 'relationships'. He's not thought of as an independent entity, but as part and parcel of his own concrete environment. For him morality and standards of behaviour hold good only in 'established' relationships with people. In these relationships he has a strong sense of honour, but at the same time he behaves disgracefully towards strangers or towards people with whom he has no 'defined' association. The strength of his control over, or influence on, another person depends on his position, status, family standing, or 'face'. In other words, it depends on an authority which is sanctioned by tradition. So all these things are a concrete expression of this first kind of 'humanism'. Here the true ruler isn't the sovereign, the feudal lord, or the family head. It's really Tradition. I don't have to tell you how restricted, as individuals, the leaders of various groups are in such a society. I'm sure you can see how every act of their daily life is bound up in social proprieties and customs.

But, precisely because the lives of these men have always been cluttered up with relationships, they can't see such relationships as something objective and abstract. In such a society there is no differentiation between laws and *mores*, and custom carries greater weight than positive law. This creates the illusion that individuals are having personal, first-hand associations without any mediating standards and without the intervention of any bothersome rules or systems at all. But actually all that has happened is that institutions of restraint and force have become so traditional that people are hardly aware of them.

In modern societies people have increasingly separated themselves from this kind of fixed environment. And so, when they are involved in widespread communication and have no predetermined social relationship to one another, then traditions or 'face', which were a determining factor in the context of set relationships, gradually lose their utility. Direct and tangible interpersonal relations are transformed more and more into relationships mediated by organizations, and objective systems and rules replace 'face'. In this sense we can say that modernization is the process of the *de-personalization* of *personal* relations. But at the same time people are waking up from their supine acceptance of old customs and conventions. And they're conscious of themselves as the agents that are devising these new rules and systems and setting them in motion. So in this sense the reverse is also true. Modernization becomes the *personalization* of *impersonal* relations. But these are really just two sides of the same coin.

A.   But surely traditions and customs are by their very nature man-made. So isn't it likely that so-called modern institutions and organizations will themselves some day become just like traditions and end up completely restricting the individual?

B.   No doubt they will. As I mentioned, the things that men 'make', whether they are made in the literal sense or not, are incorporated directly into man's environment, as things that have 'already been made'. So, while these things become permanently established as part of the environment, they are likely to adopt a position close to that of a natural reality. If we were to trace traditional manners and customs and so forth back to their very beginning, we would probably find that they started out as fictions. But as they moved closer to natural reality I suppose we could say they lost their meaning as fictions. Essentially a fiction isn't some kind of absolute with its own inherent values. It's always set up for the sake of some convenience or to carry out some kind of function. This is the reason why we have to keep on re-examining institutions and organizations in the light of their objectives and functions. If we don't keep re-examining them they solidify, so to speak, and end up simply as conventions. So the man who believes in fictions is just the opposite of the one who takes a 'ready-made' fiction and renders it absolute. Instead he's always trying to prevent a fiction from turning into an end in itself. He tries to keep a fiction relative, not absolute. A 'falsehood' has meaning when we recognize it as a falsehood, but once we mistake it for 'fact' it can't serve the function of falsehood any more. If we don't wake up to this simple phenomenon, then sooner or later falsehood turns into fact.

A.   You suggested earlier that the Japanese have a traditional way of regarding relationships as 'things', and it seems to me this is somehow related to what you're saying now.

B.   I'd say it's very closely related. As long as there's a tendency for people to take their social environment as a physical phenomenon, it's easy for fictions to solidify. Institutions or organizations are originally set up as 'means' to certain ends, but when they solidify they are no longer judged according to their utility. There's no mediation going on between ends and means, and so means quickly turn into ends in themselves. The Emperor system, of course, was typical of this kind of apotheosized institution. It was burdened with long-standing traditions and all our social values were based on it. To question its existence was taboo. But even our present political system is viewed in a similar way. It was transplanted to Japan from outside, handed down to us ready-made, so to speak, and so the people don't think of it as a fiction. They see it as a physical phenomenon in the same way that they viewed the old system which dominated their lives.

Let's take the parliamentary system. It's a good example of what I'm trying to say. This kind of system has a *functional* value. It's supposed to integrate the diverse interests of the people and to serve as a vehicle for articulating the national will. Theoretically there's no such thing as a parliamentary system without constant integrating activities of this kind. But it didn't work that way for the political parties and the Diet in Japan. They were just another solidified power-unit existing side by side with the military, the bureaucrats, and the Elder Statesmen. If this hadn't been the case in the 1940s, if the Diet had been functioning effectively as a vehicle of integration and articulation, then the Imperial Rule Assistance Association would never have appeared on the scene with such high-handed slogans as 'Reorganization of the Nation'.

From the moment it was first conceived, the Imperial Diet was handicapped. The principle of Imperial Prerogative incorporated into the Meiji Constitution undermined its position. But the principle of parliamentary sovereignty in the new Constitution doesn't automatically lead to a better functioning system. Instead I'm afraid this whole parliamentary-cabinet system may very well turn into nothing but a body with enormous autocratic power.

A.   At the same time there's the danger that elements in society that are not adequately represented in the Diet may explode irrationally because there's no outlet for their energies. The same thing happens when a pipe gets clogged. The water pressure bursts the pipe, you have water all over the place, and everything gets out of control.

B.   That's not a problem peculiar to the Diet. It can happen in other democratic institutions as well. Even the labour unions are no exception. As social specialization progresses in modern States, relations between people become less and less direct owing to the increased mediation of organizations. Interest and pressure groups of every description emerge in great numbers, all competing to articulate their special interests. And while this is going on there's also a functional division of labour taking place *within* each of these groups—secretariats, public relations officers, and so on. The difficulty occurs when the people's awareness of their own specialized function lags behind the growing rationalization of the whole system. Then one by one each organization, each department, begins to be apotheosized and its functional value is lost. Thus the division of labour results in rampant sectionalism and one's own specialization becomes one's private territory. If we take the trouble to look about us we see that in every single area of society functional or technological bureaucratization is turning into compartmentalization for its own sake. In such a situation, the more a society advances institutionally, the more anarchy takes root within it because each separate organization coagulates and loses its functional relationship with society as a whole. The danger is particularly great nowadays when various organizations grow to such mammoth proportions that they get beyond all human control and turn into Leviathans.

A.   This discussion is becoming more and more frightening, I must say. Didn't this same kind of development take place in Germany during the Wiemar Republic?

B.   Yes, that was the same sort of situation, I think. The Weimar Republic started out as a multi-party State, and some scholars say it forfeited its political unity because, one after another, each political party became a State in itself, creating any number of States within the State. But it wasn't just a problem of the parties. Every segment of society was suffering from a kind of hardening of the arteries, and it was this serious disorder that made Germany susceptible to the Nazi infection. As soon as the Nazis seized power, instead of a democratic kind of integration they imposed an authoritarian uniformity on society through their policy of *Gleichschaltung*, or synchronization, as they called it. The main reasons for their success were complicated, of course. But if the parties and labour unions and other such voluntary organizations had been functioning, as they should have been, as independent mediators between the political system and society instead of as ends in themselves, then such a state of affairs would probably never have occurred.

A.   Well then, are you saying that fascism was born when modern society had come to a dead end, and when people no longer believed in the significance of a fiction? In other words, that it's a child of the times?

B.   Yes, but it's a deformed child. It was an outgrowth of the structural specialization of modern society, to be sure. Yet it tried to overcome the difficulties by a return to 'immediate nature'—by a revival of the so-called principle of blood and soil. Scholars who supported the Nazis attacked the liberal democratic theories of 'representation' and 'majority rule', maintaining that both these concepts were mere 'fictions'—meaning falsehood, of course—not the 'true' expression of the people's will; that in contrast to this fraudulent kind of system it was actually their leader, Hitler, who represented the real will of the German people; that the tie between Hitler and the people was no lukewarm association filtered through a 'mechanical' system of counting heads at election time but that instead it was a more organic and emotional sense of unity; and that this unity was manifesting itself in such genuine forms as the 'acclamation' of the people; and so on and so forth. But the truth of the matter is that the German people, especially the unconsolidated masses, who had been driven to the wall during the economic crisis and who were in despair over the impotence of their parliamentary government, had lost confidence in the normal process of democratic integration. And so they sought a direct outlet for their frustrated desires and unsatisfied needs through an immediate identification with absolute authority.

Directly after the First World War, Georg Simmel wrote a small pamphlet called *The Conflict of Modern*

Culture and, if I remember correctly, he said something to the effect that during transitional periods in human history life is no longer compatible with the form in which it has previously expressed itself. The old form is discarded and a new pattern of culture is created which re-establishes the equilibrium between life and form. But today, he said, we are living in an age when men are not only discontented with the old forms but are in revolt against 'form' in general, and are trying to express themselves *directly* without any intermediation. Simmel cited various trends of expressionism and cubism in art as examples. Now in this situation he recognized the most serious crisis of the post-war period. When you line this up with what the Nazi scholars were contending you realize that the mentality which led to the sudden rise of Nazism was deeply rooted in modern intellectual history.

A. You said that the Nazis rebelled against a functional integration based on modern specialization. Yet surely there were very few systems in history capable of spreading out such a vast organized network as that of the Nazis, and which so effectively recruited modern science and technology to implement the organization of the masses.

B. That's the irony of it. No matter how much the Nazis admired the bold Teutonic life in the forests, no matter how much they called for a kind of primitive unity based on blood and soil, such simple naturalism wasn't feasible when it came to creating machinery for political control. Of course the Nazi State was armed to the teeth, and what the Nazis actually did was simply to break up the existing autonomous organizations and voluntary groups and re-mould the general public by means of gigantic official organizations based on the *Führer* principle. Thus there was an inherent contradiction between their primitivism and their reliance on organization. In order to conceal this contradiction, they settled on a myth. After modern fictions were demolished, myths appeared. But certainly in contrast to the myths of antiquity the 'twentieth century myth' was a horse of a different colour. It was 'fabricated' for the one and only purpose of political propaganda, and I doubt if there could have been a cruder 'production'.

A.   If you ask me, this conversation is getting a little too close to home. When the people are dissatisfied with mediated reality, and the country is overrun with a kind of 'true-story' mentality with everyone trying to immerse himself in raw first-hand sensations—well, then, that country had better watch its step.

B.   But the situation here in Japan is even more complicated than it was in Germany. When the Nazis appeared, the specialization of modern society had already reached a fairly high level. But in Japan, although we have modern specialization, pre-modern social relations are still deeply ingrained. So in this country we have more to worry about than just the danger of modern organizations or institutions becoming hypostatized and no longer performing their original function.

We've always had a vast arena in Japan where social co-ordination takes place without ever going through the channel of organizations. The things that go on in this arena are everything from naked violence, terror, and intimidation, down to the subtler pressures exerted by *oyabun* and other kinds of bosses. I suppose we can say that these are methods of solving the problem by means of *direct* human relations.

Even today these forces still have a firm grip on society and continue to hold back the process of functional differentiation and specialization. This means that our modern institutions are not yet firmly rooted in society. So if, at some time in the future, reactionary influences manage to mobilize these arena-forces in a time of crisis, voluntary organizations such as political parties, unions, and associations of various sorts could give little or no resistance and would be crushed. In any case these organizations are littered with false friends, even among the members themselves. These are the kind of people that quickly resort to *direct* action, rather than bother to go through the troublesome procedure of the organization itself.

In a country like Japan, democratic institutions such as the labour unions are walking along an almost impassable road through a swamp of pre-modern relationships. If they forget this even for a moment, I think they're lost. That road may be somewhat roundabout, but if they try to cut through the swamp they'll be swallowed up in the quicksand.

A.   You've been saying that the spirit is not separated from tangible nature, and by nature you said you meant the human body too. But as far as that's concerned, I don't imagine the *political* spirit is independent either, since it hasn't been able to free itself from a direct dependence on a 'body' made up of fist, 'face', and guts. So we have a state of *political* carnality as well. A little while ago you questioned the existence of sociability in the lives of the Japanese. But wouldn't you say that the spirit of social intercourse in private life is reflected in the spirit of deliberation in public affairs? You know, it's really shocking how even in the Diet, as soon as they have some disagreement, they immediately come to blows.

B.   Coming to blows is not a particularly *political* form of carnality. It's just carnality. But there's lots of evidence that the political spirit is not an independent one. Diet members often appeal to their constituents by promising to satisfy their individual private interests, or blatantly represent the concerns of certain business enterprises or influential local people. Political parties are said to represent class interests, but you should hear the inside story of the so-called *bourgeois* parties in Japan. The behaviour of party members is determined by personal connexions and often decided by financial backing. All of them belong to some clique, and each clique works completely at its own discretion. One often wonders how there can be even a semblance of party unity. And so, because of this lack of leadership, they hardly deserve to be called parties of the *bourgeois* class.

A.   You know, this corresponds exactly to the development of the so-called autobiographical novel in Japan. It's often nothing but a conglomeration of separate sensual experiences without the internal unity of fiction.

B.   Well, it looks as if you've caught the incendiary bomb disease from me. That was a flying leap if I ever saw one.

A.   And if you don't mind, I'll make another one. If I were to characterize the typical 'pre-modern' Japanese politician, I'd say he's probably a cross between the old-fashioned boss-type and the big-time gangster or racketeer-type. Neither of these types has an independent political spirit, and both are directly involved in special interests. So there's no fundamental difference between them on that score. But there's one way you can tell them apart. The boss-type prefers to set himself up within the limits of the relatively normal life of the *petit bourgeoisie*. The gangster-type, on the contrary, bases his life in the abnormal environment of so-called anti-social groups, and acts as if he owns the world. So actually the boss-type falls into the same category as the autobiographical novel, whereas the big-time gangster would probably be in a class with carnal literature. And that's not all. When you come right down to it, the abnormality of carnal literature has the same physiognomy as autobiographical normality. It's just that the 'private parts' of the normal are disproportionately magnified. The same can be said for the anti-social groups that big-time gangsters use as their base of operations. Their way of life and ours both spring from the same social sources, and have the same basic physiognomy. But don't you agree that after all's said and done the life of the big-time gangster is just a caricature of the traditional family system—the 'private parts' of Japanese society itself?

B.   Please stop right there, will you? If we go any further, we'll have Diet members *and* popular writers all down on our necks. Let me just say this. If we don't control carnal literature and carnal politics in one way or another, then it's senseless to talk about Japan as a democratic and cultured nation.

A.   You say 'control in one way or another'. But how in the world can we really control it?

I hesitate to suggest this, but—carnal literature, well, at least let's say carnal politics, is sort of a special concern of yours, wouldn't you say? Well, if you've got time to give private lectures to people like me when you're out here on a retreat, it seems to me you ought to find time to appeal to a somewhat broader audience when you get back to civilization. In times like these you might at least make some effort to rally the intelligentsia and give a good demonstration of that famous 'spontaneous spirit' of yours.

B.   You've got me this time. What can I say when you put it like that? But as far as rallying the intelligentsia is concerned—well, people are always calling for this sort of thing, and all kinds of meetings take place, but it never leads to any of the expected results. Of course one of the reasons that very little ever comes out of such meetings may be that the intellectuals themselves are too timid and indifferent. Still, I'm sure that's not the whole story. I think the real problem is the degree to which the intelligence of the so-called intelligentsia can function independently in spite of their attachment to particular groups. And that brings us back to our original theme. But I'm afraid this has turned out to be quite a long talk, so maybe we'd better leave it at that for today.

TRANSLATOR'S NOTE

1. See Glossary: *Ukiyoe.*

IX. Some Problems of Political Power

TRANSLATED BY DAVID SISSON

A revised and enlarged version of an essay originally written for the Dictionary of Political Science, *1953*

Power, while not the only category in political science, is certainly one of the most fundamental. Accordingly, to investigate thoroughly the problems associated with political power would mean dealing with almost every department and problem of political science. Naturally such a comprehensive treatment of power is not the purpose of the present essay. Here I have simply tried to indicate in general terms my own basic approach to the kind of questions that have become important in contemporary political science by doing point-duty, as it were, with several theories of political power. Since I have laid stress on clarifying certain particular angles from which one can study the problem of power, my analysis is bound to be one-sided and abstract. Yet, if it is of some use in helping non-specialists to understand that such problems exist, I shall be quite content.

SOCIAL POWER AND PHYSICAL LAWS

Political power is a type of social power; and social power, since it is an aspect of human behaviour, must be distinguished from the blind physical force that operates in the material world. Nevertheless, when we use mass observation to examine power relationships in human behaviour, we may sometimes apply the laws of mechanics derived from a study of the physical world—though of course only as a matter of probability. The process whereby the great stream of people emitted from the Marunouchi Building during the rush hour is separated and sucked in at the wickets of Tokyo Station is probably amenable to experiment using hundreds of balls from a pin-ball machine. It follows that, when we are examining social power, the functional relationships of physical force often provide us with valuable suggestions. Force is, after all, action opposing inertia and force is necessary when we move something that is at rest, or change the speed or direction of an already moving object. The same law of inertia seems to operate when revolutionary 'forces' act on social stagnation, or when repressive 'forces' act against sudden social change.

Force also means the quantity of mass and acceleration. Following this formula, traditional leaders have instinctively come to understand the efficacy of using springs and cushions, for example to avoid the action of sudden force when it is applied to a particular object. The laws regarding the equilibrium and parallelogram of forces are also largely applicable to social forces. Since it is difficult to maintain an equilibrium when the forces are polarized, the danger of disruption is great. Once a balance has been achieved, however, stability is high. When many forces are mixed together, they offset one another and equilibrium can be easily achieved. Yet a small change in the relationship of the forces can abruptly destroy it—i.e., the stability is low. Such laws, of course, are particularly applicable in situations where the power units are interacting on the same plane, as for instance in international politics.

The social physics approach, which arose in the middle of the nineteenth century from the rapid development of natural science and from the experience of radical social changes after the French Revolution, went to extremes with universal natural and social laws. Today, however, it is commonly accepted among social scientists that there are intrinsic limits to such universal application, and accordingly it may no longer be necessary, when applying the analogy of such laws of force to social phenomena, to stress the difference between social power and physical force. For even when we speak of 'means of *physical* coercion' we do so realizing that it is a concept depending on social, as distinct from physical, relationships.

THE SUBSTANTIVE AND FUNCTIONAL CONCEPTS OF POWER

If we can define the *substantive* concept of power as the view that sees power as a thing possessed by people or groups of people, i.e., the view that there is a substance, power itself, definite and unchanging, behind the various external appearances of specific exercises of power, then we may refer to the view that sees power in the interacting personal relationships in specific circumstances as the *relational* or *functional* concept. Until now philosophers and scholars have inclined to one or the other of these two approaches in their definitions of power. Yet it is difficult to catalogue them clearly within these two categories. For example, Friedrich* considers the Marxist concept of power as a model for the substantive concept. But, though it is quite true that Marxist methodology inclines towards the substantive view, Marx, Lenin, Mao Tse-tung, and others frequently base their arguments in specific political analysis on the relational concept of power.

What is important for us is, not to determine in the abstract which of the two is correct, but to investigate empirically what special features and trends in methods of thinking have arisen from the substantive and relational concepts in regard to understanding the phenomena of power, and what political ideologies each has come to be linked with historically. From such an analysis the strong points and weaknesses of each will become clear and we shall be able to deal more lucidly with those ideological biases to which they readily give rise.

If we view the question from an historical point of view, we find that in countries or periods in which a régime is rigidly established, and class or social mobility is lacking, the substantive concept of power generally prevails, and attitudes that stress (either supporting or opposing) autocracy and the violence of political power will have become linked to this concept. On the other hand, in countries or periods where the monopoly of social values by political power is relatively low, where the forms of communication are well developed, where social groups appear spontaneously and where the complex mutual checks between them (and between them and the State) operate vigorously, the relational concept of power is in the ascendant.

The relational concept stresses the psychological causes of submission and the reaction against the leaders or rulers by those who have submitted. Hence it has generally become associated with the ideologies of constitutionalism and democracy and has advanced in the countries of Western Europe where intellectual traditions of this kind prevail. It is no accident that the epoch-making work which presented the relational

* *Der Verfassungstaat der Neuzeit,* p. 24.

concept of power in epistemological terms was Locke's *An Essay Concerning Human Understanding.**

The strength of the substantive concept is that it seizes on the ineluctable fact that the forms of human behaviour will, by being socialized, become separated from mere mutual relations between individuals and become canalized in a definite objective pattern. When division of labour reaches a certain stage in its development, the control of human relations necessarily becomes organized and, to the extent that this organization develops, such control comes to be operated through a 'system' abstracted from individual processes of interaction. The appearance of social power always accompanies such abstraction, which constitutes the original form for the self-alienation of man.

Engels gives a classic description of the historical process whereby primitive community authority changed into rule-relationships and *puissance publique*. The reason that this description is still alive academically (though it requires a number of modifications as regards specific historical corroboration) is that it provides a formula showing how this sort of power is related to the phenomenon of alienation. The signs of organized power are the existence of: (i) rules that prescribe the outward forms of the exercise of power and the forms of behaviour of those over whom it is exercised, (ii) organs that undertake the various functions of power. As these rules and organs are perpetuated and expand their sphere of operation, power tends to be apotheosized and to become more and more of a 'substance'.

States, which are the archetype of systematized power, as well as other social organizations (economic, religious, public information, etc.), are today reaching mammoth proportions. Hence there is a constant tendency for their power relationships to be abstracted from individual interacting relationships and to become rigid, regardless of the extent to which their organization is democratized and their social values diversified. To the degree that the relational concept neglects this aspect, it becomes a sort of 'false consciousness' and, in the sense that it conceals reality, ideological.

On the other hand, the approach that treats power as the possession or essential attribute of that in which it resides has many weaknesses when we try to investigate the dynamics of

* Book 2, Chapter 21.

power empirically. Power does not always act with the same energy, but varies according to the nature and behaviour of those at whom it is directed. This can be conceded without too much difficulty when we are dealing with international politics or the power relationships of small circles. It is often forgotten, however, when we discuss the power of governments and power within large social groups. Neither leadership nor rule can exist except where they provide followers. Such factors as whether the followers actively co-operate, or resist passively, or give blind obedience, are not external circumstances, but govern the essential nature of power. The effectiveness of organized violence in the exercise of power must vary according to whether those over whom it is exercised worship armed might or, alternatively, give greater honour to money or intellect.

Thus there is a close relationship between the expressions of power and the scale of values accepted by those over whom it is exercised: it changes as they change. Moreover, both in international and in domestic politics, the image of power in the eyes of those over whom it is exerted, though it may not be a true image of the actual situation, helps nevertheless to determine the power relationships themselves.* This is the reason that loss of prestige often has a vital effect on power, even though the economic basis of that power and its military potential may not have changed in the slightest. If we take a microscopic view of power relations, we find that they involve an endless interaction between self-evaluation and evaluation of others among individuals or groups. Thus, with the development of communications and the enlargement of relations between social groups, the various social factors influencing this process become multiform and complicated. To this extent those who exercise power can no longer afford to rest complacently on the sustained identity of the system or of the organization. This applies not only to primary political power like governments but to the internal power relations and external force of political parties, trade unions, business firms, and similar associations; and of course it is connected with the increased role of public relations and of human relationships in the realms of social rule and leadership.

In examining the present amorphous state of the power

* Cf. H. Morgenthau, *Politics Among the Nations*, pp. 50–51.

situation in the United States, Riesman has applied the analogy of Heysenberg's principle that it is impossible to determine the position and the speed of an electron simultaneously: 'The point here is that power is not a commodity to be kept under lock and key but is founded, as is now widely realized, on interpersonal expectations and attitudes. If businessmen *feel* weak and dependent [towards trade unions], they *are* weak and dependent, no matter what material resources may be ascribed to them.'* Perhaps this involves carrying the functional interpretation of power too far. Nevertheless there is no denying that this observation of Riesman's (which is based on empirical research in political, business, military, and other fields) casts considerable light on certain aspects of power where mass society has developed to a high degree. But the real problem is this: should we recognize in such realities the trend towards the increased participation of the public in social power relationships, or should we, like C. Wright Mills,† concentrate on the tendency to organized irresponsibilities that attends the indistinctness of the agents of power? At this stage the answer depends very much on one's political ideology or *Parteitichkeit*.

As regards method, the substantive approach to power tends to get bogged down in theories of institutions and structures, while the functional approach becomes linked with noting the political processes of leadership, the strategy of organization, personality, and forms of behaviour. The traditional *Staatslehre* centres on the legal system and uses legal terminology when describing the functions and activities of the State. Hence a substantive approach naturally comes to prevail and, even when considering political processes other than governmental activities, emphasis is placed on formally organized social groups such as political parties or trade unions. Moreover such social groups tend to be treated as 'small States', and an analogy is drawn with the legal approach, which thinks in terms of the enactment and execution of law.

The Marxist theory of the State seeks to establish the connexion between production-relations and the political system, and aims at the total comprehension of the connexion between the class structure and the class struggle. Hence it goes further than the simple substantive approach to which we have referred

* *The Lonely Crowd* (Yale University Press), p. 250.   † *The Power Élite*, p. 342.

until now. Nevertheless, when it tries to explain the political system itself, it would appear from past Marxist writings that it is very close to the traditional approach centred on the formal system. It is not easy to say why this has come about, but the following factors seem to be relevant: (i) Europe in the middle of the nineteenth century, which produced Marxism, and Russia at the beginning of the twentieth century, in which Marxism developed into Leninism, were just at the stage of the 'eruption of classes' following the disintegration of the aristocracy; they had yet to experience the amorphous condition of mass society. This left a definite stamp on their categories of thought. (ii) The function of the State was at that time generally confined to the maintenance of order and to external defence—the police and the army; in other words, the level of its interaction with other social groups as well as the functional interchangeability between them were still low. (iii) The premise that all power is in the hands of the ruling enemy class derives partly from the ideological requirement that the revolutionary objective to over-throw the power of the State and seize political power be made visible and clear. (iv) In countries where Marxism became the orthodoxy of the régime any kind of consideration of the power process from a dynamic standpoint was avoided, because presumably there was no internal conflict within the State structure. The natural consequence of this is that authoritative descriptions by Marxists have concentrated on the legal system. (The theory of the Soviet state expounded by Vishinsky is a typical case.)

In revolutionary practice, on the other hand, the theory of organization inevitably concentrates on the functional links and on the mutual checks between the leaders and the led, and poses the question of how to turn against the régime those behaviour forms of the masses that have until this point been canalized behind it. For example, the works of Lenin, Stalin, and Mao Tse-tung contain many penetrating insights into the dynamics of the power process. They confine themselves, however, to particular situations, looking only at the strategic and tactical implications.

In fine, because the classical Marxist-Leninist theories of the State and of political processes have never been logically synthesized, their theory of power too reveals, on the one hand, a macroscopic understanding of the political system based on historical stages and, on the other, a politico-technical view of power not abstracted into theory, and these two exist side by side without any adequate correlation.

What we usually call an organization is a patterned process of human interactions which itself consists of the countless links of interpersonal relationships. This does not directly justify the nominalist theory that only individuals are real and that systems and organizations are abstract. Nor does it justify diagrams that put the State on one side and the individual, in opposition, on the other. The process whereby interaction of personalities is organized and power relationships arise is multi-dimensional. Qualitative differences in role and in meaning appear on the scene, depending on the dimension in which the organization process takes place. The power relations of a small group and those of a large group, those of a village and those of a State, differ structurally even when one has abstracted the particular values that they pursue. This is because of the difference in the level to which each has been organized. If, however, we confine our attention to formal organizations, then, in our attempt to separate what is inside and what is outside the organizations, we are liable to miss the communication process that is constantly going on both inside and outside, and between the inside and the outside. We are also likely to miss the informal organizing process that develops constantly within a formal organization.

This often produces an error that is fatal to the proper understanding of the complex stratification of power relationships such as exists at present. If we are to avoid such an error we must constantly dissolve the power *structure* so that it can be examined on the dynamic level of the power *process*, and we must investigate the latter in terms of the interpersonal relationships within a particular organization. This must be clearly separated from seeing the whole power structure as the quantitative sum total of the interpersonal process. As regards the functional relations between the whole and the individual in organization, the Gestalt theory offers many useful suggestions.*

THE POSTULATES OF THE POWER SITUATION

One advantage of analysing power from the standpoint of interpersonal relationships is that it makes clear the dynamics

* H. Heller, *Staatslehre* (Leyden, 1935), p. 63.

whereby human relations over a wide area change to power relations. This must not be confused with the question: how did power originate *historically* and how did it develop in human society? Though connected, they are not the same thing; for an analysis of political power in terms of interpersonal relations has as its immediate object the elucidation of the power process in all group relations, formal and informal, in the contemporary scene. An elucidation of this kind is particularly important in a situation like today's where the division between political control and non-political control (i.e., economic, religious, etc.) is ambivalent, and where the political function of non-political behaviour has become conspicuous. The basic postulate on which power relations come to intervene in human relations is that the social values which human beings pursue are diverse, yet scarce in proportion to human desires at a particular point of time and place. Power relations intervene decisively when, on the basis of this fundamental fact, human relations are controlled with the object of pursuing, winning, maintaining, increasing, or distributing values (including power itself), and when in exercising such control the power-carrier in the last resort uses the sanction of depriving others of the basic values they possess or pursue. This is the reason that power relations are correlated with the scale of values of the persons on whom power is being exercised.

The Chinese ancients expressed this logic in the simple phrase, 'the power over life, death, and property'. The physical safety of one's life has throughout the ages been the fundamental value that mankind cherishes. It follows that effective control of human action is in the last resort exerted by means of depriving people of this fundamental value, either in whole or in part, by murder, mutilation, imprisonment, or banishment. Thus the latent tendency of all power is to organize the physical means of coercion or violence. Yet even violence is thwarted when it is faced with those who stand on the firm conviction: 'Give me liberty or give me death.'

Similarly a minimum degree of wealth is a fundamental value both for maintaining physical life and for maintaining or gaining other social values. Hence the giving or depriving of economic value also occupies an important place as a means of traditional power-control, and will continue to do so in the future unless the production of economic value becomes as abundant as the air we breathe. But, when we examine the degree to which material recompense or deprivation can effectively control the forms of human behaviour, we find that the variation in effectiveness (depending on the individual, the rank, the race, and the era) is naturally wider than in the case of sanctions on mortal life. For a Roman Catholic, excommunication by the Pope, or for a communist, expulsion by the central party leadership, might mean a grave deprivation of respect, love, reputation, power, and other values. Hence the person or groups who are able to control such values are in a more favourable position to bring about a situation of power over those whom they wish to influence than are the people who can control their riches and, in some circumstances, even their lives.

On the premise of such a plurality of values Harold Lasswell makes a minute classification of power configurations by the cross-breeding of value types.* Some of these seem to be mere intellectual puzzles; but this approach undeniably reflects the diversification of people's concern for values, based on increasing social differentiations and communications. When, for example, Lasswell tries to distinguish between the base value of power and the value of power itself, he is dealing with the complex phenomena of today's power situations: the power over wealth (especially distribution of wealth) held by large trade unions that do not themselves have wealth; the power of sponsors and producers to control the fame of others although they lack fame themselves; or the multiple power relations, such as we see when A in terms of intellect and information, B in terms of wealth, and C in terms of esteem each has his respective power over the same individual, D. The strengthening of constitutional limitations on the exercise of governmental power has not automatically involved the enlargement of popular liberties in general. Rather, as we know, it has resulted in bringing to the surface power relations based on wealth. The collapse of nineteenth-century liberal optimism is symptomatic of its failure to understand such complex characteristics of power.

In gaining and increasing values, group co-operation is of course generally more effective than individual efforts. Hence

* *Power and Society*, p. 87.

the struggle for values tends to inspire greater group cohesiveness in proportion as a particular value is scarce and men's thirst for it strong. Since power itself is also a value and since it means control of human relationships, which include the deprivation of the values of other people or groups, power is highly effective as a basis for the pursuit of all other kinds of value. Thus disputes about values, to the extent that they are important to the people concerned, are liable to change quickly into power relations both between groups and within groups. It follows also that the organization of human relations by power control has an inherent tendency to go on enlarging its scale and to subsume within itself a pyramid of power relationships. This is not necessarily the result of the wickedness of the leaders and rulers; rather it arises from the specific dynamics of power that Hobbes has so perceptively analysed: 'The cause of this is not alwayes that . . . he cannot be content with a moderate power: but because he cannot assure the power . . . which he hath present without the acquisition of more.'*

Thus power relationships, which originally were aimed at the pursuit of other values, become objectives in and of themselves. Of course, this tendency manifests itself at a different tempo and in different forms depending on situations, on the culture, on the nature of power involved, and on the kind of group. It is especially evident where international relations are tense or where the situation is one of prolonged domestic unrest. In these cases important values (safety of life and the basic rights and interests of the people) are threatened, and people's concern for values becomes simplified and concentrated into one direction. Consequently power readily condenses in the hands of the people who can control these things. On the other hand, one often sees in history how unscrupulous forces or rulers, using these dynamics in reverse, maintain their own power by deliberately fomenting foreign tension or by constantly jeopardizing the important values of the group.

To understand the dynamics of the power situation it is also necessary to pay attention to the way in which institutionalized social values are distributed and to the potential power that arises from the direction and intensity of the concern for values. It is quite usual for people who are satisfied with the existing

* *Leviathan*, Part 1, Chapter 11.

power basis and who live peacefully under the *status quo* to forget to cultivate power, since they are wholly concerned with other values, and to lose their own power position. (This is another example of the 'tragedy of the third generation'.)[1] On the other hand, classes or races who have fallen into a nadir where they 'have nothing to lose but their chains' are confronted with two alternatives: either to escape completely from the power process or to arise with fearsome energy aiming at 'the whole world to win'.

In his youth Tokutomi Sohō accurately expressed this rule governing the power process:

It is not enough for people to know that wealth is might; they must realize that the desire for wealth is also might. They know that power is might, but not that the desire to get power is might ... Position is might, but the absence of position is also might because, if we fail to acquire it, we have nothing to lose and hence will act more resolutely. It is recognized that in politics wealth, power, education, and authority are capital. But one must recognize that the absence of such capital also constitutes capital. It is only the students and the youth of a country who have what one might call an infinite store of poverty.*

Until now we have been discussing the dynamics of power in general social relations, without paying attention to any particular political element in the power process. One of the reasons is that there are cases where rigid distinctions, such as those between political, economic, and cultural organizations, have a harmful influence on the investigation of political processes as they operate in practice. What then are the conditions under which the non-political process becomes political? Here the factor of policy first makes its appearance. By policy we mean an objective with regard to the acquisition, maintenance, or distribution of values and the means of realizing this objective. When the value relates to wealth we call it economic policy; when it relates to knowledge it is educational or cultural policy; and when the objective is the value known as power we may call it 'political' policy.

By the political process we simply mean the process whereby in the broad sense policies in general, and in the narrow sense political policies, are formed and implemented by means of the

* *Kokumin no Tomo* (The People's Friend), No. 6.

power process, that is to say, by the control of human relations using the deprivation of value as the means. Political power is *puissance publique.* We cannot call power political when it directly serves interests that are purely private (i.e., serves an individual or a primary group to which the individual belongs), even though such power may be organized for the pursuit of values. In this sense any policy implies an image of totality that transcends any individual or primary group. This does not mean that political power always serves the interests of the whole. Even if power is organized for economic exploitation, the leaders discharge a role that goes beyond their private and factional interests, and the exercise of power not based on this role is checked. Otherwise 'class rule', and other things besides, cannot be carried out.

In so far as it is *political* power, such policy necessarily includes consideration about which values are to be allocated and to what extent—not only to the ruling circles but to the governed classes and other social groups. Since totality is a relative category, it must differ according to the stage of history and the degree of development of communications. In the Middle Ages, for example, the power relations of the feudal lord, which then were those of *puissance publique*, lost their public nature with the establishment and development of the unified nation-states of the modern world. The readiness to adjust the distribution of values with other agents of *puissance publique* (i.e., diplomacy) is an effective test for determining the presence or absence of the image of totality.

The modern State is the most highly organized power relationship that the world has yet seen: within a defined territory it monopolizes violence and can exercise this violence as its *ultima ratio* to control secondary power relationships. Therefore anyone who succeeds in controlling the power of the State finds himself in a position to determine the distribution of values within its territory. This is why the political struggle in modern times, both international and domestic, develops round the acquisition, maintenance, distribution, and transformation of State power.

Today, owing to world-wide communications and other technical advances, the growing awareness of the evils of national egoism and war, and the heightened economic interdependence of the world, the image of totality is finally moving in the direction of transcending the symbols of the nation-state and of becoming identical with the dimension of humanity. Yet the organization of international society will have to advance much further if it is to slough off its addiction to the nation-state. Despite all the technological changes, the political power process still functions overwhelmingly in conjunction with the State.

Not all the activities of the government, however, constitute the political process—only those that are strictly relevant to the decision-making process regarding how power values will be increased and distributed. Only *führende Macht* (power that leads), not *ausführende Macht* (power that carries things out), is political power.* Yet, when circumstances lead soldiers and civil servants to exceed the mere execution of power laid down in legislation and to participate autonomously in deciding the distribution of power and other values, government by the military or the bureaucracy comes into being.

Although trade unions contain power relations within themselves, so long as their principal behaviour patterns concentrate on the maintenance or improvement of wages, they are not directly included in the political process. The support by a trade union of a particular political party at election time is its political policy, and in so far as it gives such support it participates *as an economic organization* in the political process. But, if a trade union goes further and seeks to destroy the government by resorting to a general strike, this means throwing all its activities into the political process: it has then changed into a political organization. Such a change may also occur in employers' associations. But generally big business can exert greater influence over the policy decisions of the government even when it is merely carrying out its traditional functions, and therefore it does not have to change into direct political organizations except under very special circumstances; it is already in a position where it can set the power situation of the State in motion.

It is clear from these examples that popular distinctions between political organizations and religious organizations have only a relative meaning in the actual political process. The important thing is to observe the role and the position that

* H. Heller, *Staatslehre*, p. 204.

each social group fulfils in the power situation and to relate these to the value that it pursues at a particular point of time.

In any given political situation it is not always easy to identify what kind of organ or group is in a position ultimately to determine the power relations of the State. One cannot find the source of such power in the constitutional provisions dealing with sovereignty or with the authorities of the various organs. The whereabouts of the supreme agent of political power, which in ordinary times is obscured, may in time of emergency (e.g., a large-scale purge, *coup d'état*, insurrection) become crystal clear. To this extent I agree with Carl Schmitt's proposition that 'Sovereign is he who decides things in an exceptional situation'.*

COMPOSITION OF POLITICAL POWER AND THE MEANS EMPLOYED

We may call the main organized bodies that participate constantly and as principals in the political power struggle the *power units* within that power situation. The State, supranational organizations (e.g. the Comintern), political parties, secret political societies, all are typical power units. Here I shall deal in general terms with the internal composition of such power units and the means they usually employ to organize people.†

Since organized power units normally involve stratified power relations, they appear as having a pyramidal structure. When we classify these broadly according to their concern for, and degree of, power participation, we get the following levels: (i) the central leadership (*Machtkern*), (ii) the *élite* or 'vanguard' that surrounds the leadership and directly assists it, (iii) the activists—those whom Alfred de Grazia calls 'politists' —who follow the *élite* and are constantly involved in the political process, (iv) the ordinary members, who participate in the power process only occasionally, for example when they attend the annual convention or vote in the elections held from time

---

* F. L. Neumann, 'Approaches to the Study of Political Power', *Political Science Quarterly*, June 1950, p. 178, later included in *The Democratic and Authoritarian State* (1957), p. 17.

† When we distinguish between, say, political and economic groups, we do so in terms of their social function, but in the case of power units we concentrate on the arena of political conflict and turn our attention to the principal actors.

to time. These divisions are of course not rigid; and the lower the mobility between these strata, the less their organizational output.

Regardless of the difference between democratic and undemocratic societies, a vital condition for the long-range maintenance of power relations is that men of (political) talent be constantly absorbed into the power apparatus from outside, and that they be promoted to suitable positions inside it.

The composition of political power can also be classified according to functional division of labour. The traditional differentiation focused on statute law—legislative, judiciary, executive—is not particularly helpful when it comes to analysing the amorphous dynamics of decision-making. It is more useful to regard the matter in terms of means of control. We then find the following main types: (i) people who are in charge of inventing or formulating symbols, myths, ideology, and policy, (ii) people who devise strategy and tactics in concrete situations, (iii) specialists in intelligence and propaganda, (iv) people engaged in raising contributions and funds, (v) people responsible for liaison, (vi) specialists in violence. These divisions too are fluid, and the nearer we come to the nucleus of the power unit, the more the various functions are combined. Again, the more harmoniously the various functions are carried out and the better the balance between them is maintained, the higher is the overall energy of the power unit. The implementation of these functions must depend on broad social, economic, cultural, and natural factors. Here lies the difficulty of correctly measuring the strength and intensity of political power.

The complexity of the power components is particularly notable when we come to State power. To underrate the complexity of political power by judging it in terms of only a single factor (for instance, physical force, such as armaments and police force, or economic strength) is one of the errors into which political leaders are most prone to fall, the other being the fetishism of power discussed earlier. It is a potent cause for failure in the international and the intranational power struggles.

The methods that the political power unit uses to control both subordinates and other power units widely overlap with the general methods of social control. The characteristic method in the case of political power is, as we have seen, the use of legitimate violence. The use of organized violence, however, represents an extreme in the function of political power; it is not the normal situation. As Talleyrand said, 'A man can do anything with a bayonet, except sit on it.' In this sense imprisonment or war simply indicate that all the resorts except the last one have been exhausted. From the standpoint of the 'economics of power' the *threat* of the exercise of force (for instance, in international politics, military mobilization or concentration in a particular area) is mightier than its actual exercise. Furthermore, indirect coercion, such as economic blockade or deprivation of honour, is a stronger method than threats of direct violence; and persuasion or consent are more effective than such coercion.

If we use the term 'naked power' to describe the situation in which the motive for submission is chiefly the fear of deprivation of values rather than sheer physical violence, then naked power represents the minimum spontaneity on the part of the governed, the maximum being represented by rational consent. On the other hand, the special nature of power control (as against control that does not depend on power relations) lies in the fact that it has as its background some kind of deprivation of value. Hence pure persuasion and consent cannot exist in power relationships: such terms as 'persuasion' by political power and 'government by consent' always contain a measure of fiction.

The provision of material or spiritual benefits, like reparations, preferment, and economic assistance, is an important means of control by political power. Yet here again there is the underlying threat, 'If you don't comply . . .'. There is no political power that relies purely on the whip; but similarly there is no power that uses only the carrot. In the control of human behaviour there are situations in which power units directly indicate and prescribe specific behaviour patterns, and others in which they do not directly indicate them but indirectly have the result of producing such behaviour. We call the latter 'manipulation', and it is these methods and their techniques that have developed to such a remarkable extent in the era of mass democracy.

A power unit, in order to achieve its political objectives, must arouse a sense of loyalty among the broad masses, either using traditional symbols or creating new ones. Flags, uniforms, songs, ceremonial, religious services, mass meetings, marches, myths, ideologies, all operate as such symbols, and their efficacy is greatly heightened by mass media. If extreme use is made of such means, it becomes tantamount to 'violence against the soul', and persuasion and consent become mere skeletons.

Yet those who possess political power are confronted with a dilemma when they use such means of control. To the extent that they succeed, the obedience of the masses becomes automatic and stereotyped; at the same time their spontaneity recedes, because their obedience has become habitual, and public concern is supplanted by private considerations—especially by the desire to enjoy a life of consumption. Again, under present technological conditions it is impossible, except in war or other extraordinary times, to limit communication to a one-way flow from those with power. Thus, no matter what kind of monopoly is enjoyed by the ruling group, there is a tendency for the 'auction' of opposing symbols that is carried on openly before the masses to destroy their own effect and to promote apathy. The law of diminishing returns applies in political power as well.

THE DEVELOPMENTAL TRENDS OF POLITICAL POWER

1. *The Relationship between Political Power and Other Social Power*

One of the characteristics distinguishing modern society from those of previous times is that political power in modern society has been differentiated from other kinds of social power and has become independent of them. In feudal society, for example, the economic relations of exploitation between the feudal lord and the peasants were straightforward political power relations; and the large landholder, by virtue of his position, was necessarily the holder of political power too. But, with the development of the modern State, political control has become abstracted and separated from economic relations, and political power has come to have its own independent organization and composition. The inseparable relationship between politics and economics has become concealed. In the image of the modern *bourgeoisie*, political power relationships have been absorbed into State power, while other dispositions of social forces have on the contrary faded into the private interaction of civil society (contractual relationships in a free market).

Thus the idea that ruler-subject relationships survive only in the political field, having disappeared in other areas (notably the economic), became the myth of modern liberalism, according to which the legal restraints of political power and the enlargement of the franchise are regarded as the alpha and omega of democratization. In actual fact this kind of democratization of political power has advanced since the end of the nineteenth century; yet the social pressure of capital based on the principle of private property has continued to grow, and the basic composition of productive relations has today steadily grown more oligarchical. The tension between these contradictory developments has become one major problem in the politics of the present century. In the face of such a split there are only two ways to deal with the problem: either to carry democratization to the inside of industrial organizations, or to rearrange political power so that it accommodates the oligarchical economic power in the country. To put the matter in sweeping terms, the various forms of socialism aim at the first solution, while the ultimate form of the second solution is fascism.

2. *The Tendency towards Concentration and Accumulation of Political Power*

Mass participation in political power relations has gradually been expanded. Nevertheless, as if to deride this process, the development of technology and the diversification of social functions have made the organization of the power units huge and bureaucratic and have resulted in a wide gap between the apex and the base. Spengler's ironic aphorism, 'As the franchise is enlarged the power of the individual voter proportionately declines',* has become most apposite.

Political power grows gigantic—in the number of persons it embraces, in the areas to which its control extends (the economy, education, etc.), and in its mobility. Moreover the tendency for the decision and execution of basic policy to concentrate at the nucleus is also manifest in State power. This is apparent in the expansion of leadership by presidents and prime ministers. It also emerges in other power units such as political parties. In

* *Der Staat*, p. 116.

the socialist and labour parties, which depend on mass organization and which represent the vanguard of democratization in modern times, this concentration of power in the executive is revealed to an ever higher degree.

The physiology of such a trend towards concentration differs only by a hair's breadth from its pathology because: (i) this tendency to oligarchy and the apathy at the base of the organization, promoted by the conditions of modern technology, are liable to form a vicious cycle; (ii) the power nucleus at the apex passes over or excludes the few 'activists', who have a comparatively strong concern with decision-making, and strengthens itself through the emotional support of the rank and file to whom it appeals directly (the tendency to plebiscite dictatorship); (iii) as the competition and struggle between power units become more intense, the necessity for maintaining secrecy in the realm of policy and tactics increases and the principle of 'advantage of small numbers' (Max Weber) operates.

There is a more troublesome problem, however: these questions, which formerly were recognized as an inherent danger to the Western European democratic system and which caused people to search for positive solutions, are today treated equivocally, so that the true points at issue are obscured. This is precisely the situation we have touched on earlier, namely, that in modern times the power situation has become amorphous. For example, to quote an American observer, 'The great decisions which influence the future of our people are decided in diplomatic reception rooms or inside the firmly closed doors of naval or military headquarters by people who have only limited responsibility.'* Furthermore, because the positions that constitute or basically control the power nucleus are increasingly occupied by what C. Wright Mills calls 'political outsiders' (military and business leaders in particular), and because the participation in decision-making by politicians, and indeed by the legislature itself, has become confined to decision-making on the middle level, the concept of 'checks and balances' has firmly taken root among the people. In terms of the total structure of the system, this may be a myth: but, because of the mutual checks by the numerous 'veto groups' (Riesman) at the

---

* Rear-Admiral E. M. Zacharias, quoted by H. H. Wilson in 'The Problem of Power', *Monthly Review*, June 1953.

middle and the bottom levels of the system, it is felt as reality in the everyday life of the people. In short, since 'big politics' and 'small politics', to borrow Nietzsche's terms, have been sharply differentiated, and since big politics increasingly concentrates at the summit while small politics is more and more diffused, the image of the distribution of power values is constantly being reproduced.

This trend in power relations corresponds to a similar phenomenon in business organization. As the standard of living rises, people become less concerned with the system and more interested in the secondary power situation at the middle and lower levels. Consequently they are less and less inclined to recognize, or to desire to recognize, the real state of the total power relationship. This is common to the Welfare States of Western Europe, though to different degrees. Furthermore, with the 'colossalization' of political, economic, and military organizations, and with the increase in the mutual interchange of personnel at the top, power tends to concentrate at the top level regardless of the legal apparatus of the State. At the same time there is a growing gap between the *actual* power and the *consciousness* of power enjoyed by the top leaders. Since their behaviour is not clearly differentiated from that of the masses, they fail to recognize the concentration of power for what it is. The 'system of irresponsibilities' in militarist Japan, described in an earlier essay,[2] is the product of interaction between these common characteristics of mass society and the peculiar power structure of Japan.

The communist line of thought originating with Lenin affirms bluntly and unequivocally the social necessity in the modern age of concentrating and accumulating political power. On the one hand, it fuses this with the 'consciousness of purpose' of a vanguard party; on the other, it tries to control this power by the 'mass line' and by the principle of democratic centralism. In the Soviet Union, where such an idea is institutionalized, the division between big and small politics is articulated in terms of the wide participation of the people in spheres closely linked with their daily life (co-operatives, trade unions, the local Soviets, etc.) and, at the top level, concentration of power in the hands of the Communist Party. Here, since the economic system and all departments of society are planned in an orderly fashion and led by a coherent goal-consciousness, they are free from the danger of self-deception and organized irresponsibilities, such as exists in capitalist countries. Top leadership tends to be assumed by 'philosopher kings' ('all-knowing men') rather than by 'massified' individuals. On the other hand, recent events in the communist world have revealed that, if this 'vanguard' leadership is corrupt, the nucleus of power becomes a caste and produces mammoth bureaucratization and autocracy.

Lord Acton said: 'Power tends to corrupt and absolute power corrupts absolutely.' If 'absolute power' means the concentration of power, this dictum is refuted by examples of concentrations of power in history that did *not* corrupt.* Just as we cannot solve the difficulties of monopoly capitalism by the deconcentration of enterprises, so we cannot solve today's complicated political problems merely by diffusing power and promoting rivalry. The problem now is whether we are able, on the one hand, to gear this concentrated power, which has emerged inevitably from the technical rationalization of modern society, to the welfare and autonomous participation of the people and, on the other, to prevent the frustration of social mobility that could result from bureaucratization. Yet, since the modern concentration of power has given rise to various pathological symptoms, and since this pathology involves many common dangers that go beyond any differences in social systems, Acton's dictum does contain a truth that transcends the historical context of liberalism. In all ages, in order to understand the reality of political power, we must have a clear eye and a detached, quiet courage that will allow us to recognize a disrobed emperor as naked. This will be achieved neither by a flight from 'things political', nor by any glib commitment to them.

* F. L. Neumann, op. cit.

TRANSLATOR'S NOTES

1. See Glossary: 'Third generation.'
2. 'Thought and Behaviour Patterns of Japan's Wartime Leaders.'

Glossary and Biographies

'*A Hundred Million Hearts Beating Like One*' (*Ichioku Isshin*). Famous maxim enunciated by Gen. Araki (q.v.). It was used as a poster slogan at the time of the China Incident; significantly, the characters were printed over a drawing of a distended ant, reminding people of the industry and co-operation of ants.

Abe Cabinet. The Cabinet under Gen. Abe Nobuyuki (1875–1953) lasted less than five months (1939–40) and was one of the most unsuccessful of the many governments that came and went during the turbulent years, 1939–41.

Adachi Kenzō (1864–1948). Served in the Ōkuma and Katō Cabinets and was Home Minister under Hamaguchi and Wakatsuki. He advocated the formation of a coalition Cabinet in 1931, bringing about the fall of the Wakatsuki Cabinet. Adachi was one of the more nationalist party politicians close to the Army.

Aizawa Incident (Aizawa Jiken). This refers to the murder on 12 August 1935 of Maj.-Gen. Nagata, Director of the Military Affairs Bureau and a leading member of the Army's Control Faction. The assassin, Lt.-Col. Aizawa Saburō, was an ultra-nationalist fanatic. His trial, during which he claimed that he had acted from patriotic motives, became a *cause célèbre*, and Aizawa attracted a good deal of sympathy. He was, however, executed in the aftermath of the February Incident.

Akamatsu Katsumaro (1894–1955). As an early member of the Japan Communist Party, he was associated with the present Socialist leader, Mr. Susuki Mosaburō, in an effort to dissolve the party in 1924. Thereafter he moved steadily in a right-wing direction. He was active in the Imperial Rule Assistance Association and as a result was purged after the war. Akamatsu was one of the more prominent right-wing writers after the war, being the author of an important, and surprisingly objective, history of the Japanese socialist movement. He was among the many former communists who turned to the extreme right.

Akao Bin (b. 1899). Professional agitator and one of the most vociferous anti-communists in the pre-war ultra-rightist movement. His fury has always been directed primarily against Soviet Russia.

Mr. Akao headed the National Founding Association (q.v.) and in 1942 was elected to the Diet. He is still active in rightist circles as president of the Great Japan Patriots' Party (Dai Nihon Aikoku Tō) and was an influence on the young assassin who in October 1960 killed Mr. Asanuma Inejirō, the Chairman of the Socialist Party.

Akiyama Teisuke (1868–1950). Nationalist writer who first made his name by attacking the government for the country's economic difficulties during the Russo-Japanese War. As a result his writings were banned and he was obliged to resign from the House of Representatives. Later he became active in the pre-war rightist movement.

All-Japan Patriots' Joint Struggle Council (Zen-Nihon Aikokusha Kyōdō Tōsō Kyōgi Kai). The first and most conspicuous of the right-wing unification attempts, the Council was formed in 1931 as a loose confederation of extremist groups with the immediate aim of organizing a united right-wing front to carry out the insurrection that was being planned at the time. This was later known as the March Incident and its failure was one of the reasons for the breakdown of the unification movement; the other principal reason was the perennial disagreement among the leaders.

Amano Tatsuo. Mr. Amano has had a long career of nationalist activity in pre-war and post-war Japan. As early as 1920 he was active in the Rising Nation Comrades' Association founded in that year by his teacher, Professor Uesugi Shinkichi (q.v.), of Tokyo Imperial University. He was Chairman of the Patriotic Labour Party founded in 1930. Mr. Amano was Inoue Nisshō's defending lawyer in the trial following the Blood Pledge Corps Incident of 1933 and he had a hand in the Heaven-Sent Soldiers' Unit Incident (q.v.). In June 1953 Mr. Amano took part in a regional right-wing unification rally.

Amur River Association (Kokuryū Kai). An aggressive nationalist organization. Founded in 1901 primarily by Uchida Ryōhei, and with the powerful backing of Tōyama Mitsuru, it continued until the end of the war. As the creature of the Dark Ocean Society, the Amur River Association gave more stress to the centrality of the Emperor and presented a more sharply defined anti-Westernism. The six-point programme of the Association emphasized Japan's leadership in Asia as harmonizer of Eastern and Western culture, foreign expansion, especially in Northern Manchuria, cultivation of the virtues of the Yamato race based upon national polity education and internal reform. The Association (which was revived in

1961 under the name of the Amur River Club) was popularly known in the West before the war as the 'Black Dragon Society'.

Anami Korechika (1887–1945). Vice-Minister for War in the Yonai Cabinet and War Minister at the time of Japan's defeat. He committed *hara-kiri* on the eve of the surrender in order, as he expressed it, 'to atone for his great sin'.

Anti-Red Corps (Sekka Bōshi Dan). Patriotic society formed in 1922 to combat socialist-communist groups and left-wing ideology.

Araki Sadao (b. 1877). An extreme militarist who played a prominent role in the 1930s as a general and member of the Imperial Way Faction of the Army. He served as War Minister on the Inukai and Saitō Cabinets and was an active supporter of the Manchurian Incident. After the February Incident he was placed on the inactive list. As Education Minister under Prince Konoe he had considerable influence in promoting ultra-nationalist education. Araki was tried as a Class A war criminal and sentenced to life imprisonment; he was released in 1955 owing to ill health.

Arima Yoriyasu (Rainei) (1884–1957). Count Arima was a member of the aristocratic group that was influential in Japanese politics in the 1930s. Of somewhat radical leanings in his youth, he came into a central political position with Konoe's first government. Later he became a prominent member of the Imperial Rule Assistance Association.

Asō Hisashi (1891–1940). At one time on the staff of the *Nichinichi*, a Tokyo newspaper, Asō was active from 1919 in labour organizations and in the labour union movement. A founder of the Labour-Peasant Party in 1926, he gained prominence as the real leader of the Social Masses Party from 1932 to 1940.

'Assistance' (yokusan). The term 'assist' was frequently used before 1945 to express the supporting function of the Japanese subject in relation to his sovereign. E.g., Imperial Rule Assistance Association (q.v.).

Atsumi Katsu (Masaru). A leader of a group calling itself the Nagoi anarchists which linked itself to the Association of Old Combatants (Rōsō Kai) in 1918. Elements of this group joined the Society of Those Who Yet Remain (q.v.) after 1919. Atsumi participated with Mr. Akao Bin in the creation of the National Founding Association in 1926 and was also involved in the establishment of the Imperial Flag Association in 1927.

Baba Eiichi (1879–1937). Finance Minister (March 1936–February 1937). Home Minister (June–December 1937). Doctor of Laws and member of the House of Peers.

Bakumatsu Period. The last part of the Tokugawa Period. See Chronology.

Bamboo spear principle (takeyari shugi). Principle of putting up a last-ditch stand with any resources at hand, rather than surrendering to the enemy. In 1945 instructions were sent down to local echelons and groups on measures for self-defence against an Allied invasion. Among such instructions was resistance with bamboo spears.

Blood Pledge Corps Incident (Ketsumei Dan Jiken), also translated as the *Blood Brotherhood League Incident.* An attempt in February 1932 by members of a fanatic agrarian radical society to remove the ruling clique, whom they considered to be responsible for agrarian suffering and national weakness. The plans called for the assassination of certain political and business leaders; about twenty prospective victims were listed and each one was assigned to a specific member of the Corps for disposal. Only two of the planned assassinations were actually carried out—those of the Finance Minister, Mr. Inoue Junnosuke, and of the director of the Mitsui Company, Baron Dan Takuma. Inoue Nisshō and other Corps members were sentenced to prison for their role in the incident, but they were all released before their terms expired.

Bungei Shunjū. The *Bungei Shunjū* magazine first appeared in 1923 as a literary journal dedicated to the task of introducing the best of modern Japanese literature to a wide reading audience, thus encouraging young and talented writers. Since the war, however, its policy has changed. It continues to print short fictional works by outstanding writers, but now also includes second-rate short stories, and its circulation has grown proportionately. *Bungei Shunjū* also publishes essays, reviews, etc. (see 'Composite magazine').

Chang Tso-lin (1876–1928). Warlord based in Manchuria who co-operated with the Japanese. As Chiang Kai-shek's northern expedition approached Peking, however, Chang Tso-lin abandoned resistance. On 4 June 1928 a railway carriage in which Chang was leaving Peking blew up and he was fatally injured. Young officers in the Japanese Army were responsible, but Premier Tanaka was unable to secure punishment of the culprits and was forced to resign.

Ch'en Po-ta (b. 1905). A member of the 8th Central Committee of the Chinese Communist Party. As a writer and theorist he is reputed to have ghosted many of Mao Tse-Tung's speeches and reports. Ch'en is also thought to be responsible for several of the important editorials in the Peking *People's Daily* since 1949.

Cherry Blossom Association (Sakura Kai). The most important of the radical rightist 'young officers' groups, it was organized in 1930 under the leadership of Col. Hashimoto Kingorō (q.v.) to 'reform the Army and nation'. The society, whose membership was limited to Army officers on the active list of the rank of lieutenant-colonel and below, was active in both the March and the October Incidents.

Chō Isamu (1894–1945). Joined the Cherry Blossom Association in 1930 and conspired with Col. Hashimoto (q.v.) in the abortive October (1931) plot. Lt.-Gen. Chō was a member of the garrison on Okinawa and committed suicide there in June 1945.

Clan clique (hambatsu). Refers to the fact that during most of the Meiji Period government was largely in the hands of men from certain areas corresponding to particular fiefs (notably the Satsuma and the Chōshū) that had helped to bring about the overthrow of the Tokugawa Shogunate and the restoration of the Emperor.

'Composite magazine' (sōgō zasshi). The generic name applied to non-specialized, but often highly academic, periodicals like *Chūō Kōron* and *Sekai*. Such magazines include essays and critical reviews in the fields of politics, economics, literature, philosophy, and the pure and social sciences, in addition to creative literature. With such diversified coverage, these magazines attract readers from a wide variety of fields and, by a policy of graded highbrowness, often maintain a good circulation. See Donald Keene, 'Literary and Intellectual Currents in Post-war Japan' in *Japan between East and West* (New York, 1957).

Control Faction (Tōsei Ha). See *Imperial Way Faction*.

Council for a Union of Patriotic Movements (Aikoku Undō Itchi Kyōgi Kai). One of the more ambitious federations of nationalist societies that were attempted in the 1930s. Formed in 1933, it included groups that were already amalgamated in the Joint Council for Solving the National Crisis and the Joint Association for the Defence of the National Polity. Despite its elaborate programme, the Council was no more successful than its predecessors in resolving the perennial disunity of the ultra-rightist camp.

Dark Ocean Society (Genyō Sha). The parent body of Japanese fascism, as it has been called, was founded in 1881 under Hiraoka Kōtarō (1851–1906). A native of Fukuoka, Hiraoka had supported Saigō

Takamori's rebellion of 1877, a major cause for which was Saigō's demand for an invasion of Korea. The Dark Ocean Society, founded by Saigō's sympathizers, made Japanese expansion on the Asian continent, specifically in Korea, its cardinal tenet.

Dazai Osamu (1909–1948). He was as well known for his dissipated life as for his short stories and novels. His most celebrated works were produced immediately after the war, and reflected not only the author's own nihilistic view of life, but also the confusion and despair of post-war Japan. After three suicide attempts in a period of eighteen years, he succeeded in taking his own life and that of his mistress in June 1948.

Doihara Kenji (1883–1948). Army officer stationed at Mukden at the time of the Manchurian Incident. Having played a leading role in Japan's aggressive policy at that time, he was sentenced to death as a war criminal and executed in 1948.

Education Rescript (Kyōiku Chokugo). The Imperial Rescript on Education, which until Japan's defeat in 1945 had the force of holy writ, was a statement (issued in 1890) enunciating traditional moral principles and stressing the Confucian virtues, such as filial piety and obedience, and also the need for loyalty and self-sacrifice in the service of the Emperor. The Rescript was regularly read aloud with great ceremony in schools and colleges. During the entire period of Japan's modernization it served to impress on the people that the State should exercise as absolute an authority over their 'internal' behaviour (thoughts, beliefs, etc.) as over their external actions.

Elder Statesman (Genrō). See *Senior Retainer*.

'Expel the Barbarians' (Jōi). See *'Revere the Emperor'*.

February Incident (Nigatsu or Niniroku Jiken). Carried out on 26 February 1936 in Tokyo, this was the most nearly successful of all the pre-war attempted *coups d'état*. It took the form of a major uprising by the militant Imperial Way Faction of the Army, with the aims of overcoming the Control Faction in the Army, destroying the ruling *élite*, and thus effecting a thorough reform of the national structure. After assassinating several important government leaders, the insurgents barricaded themselves in one part of the city; martial law was proclaimed, and after three days the rebels surrendered at the personal command of the Emperor. Subsequently thirteen Army officers and four civilians (including the national-socialist leader, Kita Ikki) were executed, and several leading military figures were removed from positions of authority. The incident failed to accomplish its specific objectives, but greatly encouraged the trend towards totalitarianism and Army control.

Five Classics: **Book of Changes, Book of History, Book of Odes, Book of Rites, Spring and Autumn Annals.** By the second century B.C. these five early Chinese classics had become the main course of study for cultivated Chinese. Together with the four books they represented the ultimate authority for all political and moral decisions.

Five Ministers' Conference. Type of inner Cabinet that was developed after 1932 for the formulation of important decisions. It consisted of the Prime Minister, Foreign Minister, Finance Minister, and the two Service Ministers.

Four Books: **Great Learning, Doctrine of the Mean, Analects, Mencius.** These four early Chinese philosophical works were considered by the Sung philosopher Chu Hsi (1130–1200) to be of primary importance to all educated people. Together they served as a kind of primer in Chinese education and until as late as 1905 they constituted the basis of all civil service examinations in China. They were also the staple texts of Japanese higher education during the Tokugawa Period.

Fujii Hitoshi (d. 1932). A lieutenant-commander on active duty, Fujii was a leading figure in inspiring young naval officers to become political activists. One of his disciples, Lt. Koga Kiyoshi, was a leader of the group that assassinated the Prime Minister, Mr. Inukai Tsuyoshi. Fujii himself was killed in action during the Shanghai military operations of 1932.

Fujita Tōko (1806–1855). A retainer and close adviser to Mito Nariaki towards the end of the Tokugawa period. He was an outstanding writer of the nationalist Mito school of thought.

Fukai Eigo (1871–1945). Started in newspaper work, but later became private secretary to the eminent Satsuma statesman, Marquis Matsukata. He turned to banking and was appointed Governor of the Bank of Japan in 1941. A member of the House of Peers and of the Privy Council, he was generally regarded as a liberal.

Fukuzawa Yukichi (1835–1901). Prominent educator and writer who played a leading role during the Meiji Period in introducing Western civilization to Japan. A firm believer in a responsible Cabinet system and in securing human rights, Fukuzawa was tireless in his attacks on feudal thinking in his country. He accompanied Japan's first delegation to the West in 1860. In 1868 he founded the famous

Keiō University in Tokyo and in 1882 he started the *Jiji Shimpō* newspaper. For further reading see *The Autobiography of Fukuzawa Yukichi* (Hokuseidō, Tokyo, 1950).

General Outline of Measures for the Reconstruction of Japan (Nihon Kaizō Hōan Taikō). Famous work by Kita Ikki (q.v.) in which he outlined his radical socialist utopia. It was first circulated in 1919 and, although it was barred by the government, it was widely read in the 1920s and early 1930s and exerted a great influence on the young officers and other nationalists. Kita's book called for an attack on the capitalist system and for vigorous expansion abroad. His domestic programme included the nationalization of major industries, an eight-hour working day, and land reform. He described Japan as a 'proletarian among the nations' and wrote that 'in the name of rational social democracy, Japan claims possession of Australia and Eastern Siberia'.

Golden Pheasant Academy (Kinkei Gakuin). Influential nationalist study group founded by Yasuoka Masaatsu in 1926 and attended by both civilian and military men. The group was named after the garden of a rich supporter, Count Sakai, where Yasuoka gave his lectures on Confucianism, the national polity, and related subjects. They were attended by ambitious civil servants, especially from the Home and Education Ministries, as well as by many of the young officers who took part in the incidents of the 1930s. The academy was included on the 1946 purge list.

Gondō Seikyō (Seikei) (1868–1937). A widely-travelled historian and right-wing activist, Mr. Gondō participated in the Chinese revolution of 1911 when he was in Shanghai. His father had been a samurai scholar of the Japanese classics. After returning to Tokyo in 1900 he wrote *The Principles of Autonomy Under the Emperor (Kōmin Jichi Hongi).* Foremost spokesman of a purely agrarian nationalism in the 1920s, he demanded a return to agrarian autonomy and an agrarian-centred economy. Gondō's thinking was influential among the younger officers. He was imprisoned on suspicion of having supported the Blood Pledge Corps Incident and the May 15 Incident, but was soon released.

Gotō Akinori. One of the activists in the May 15 Incident, in which the Prime Minister, Mr. Inukai, was assassinated.

Gotō Fumio (b. 1884). Minister of Agriculture and Forestry (May 1932–July 1934), Home Minister at the time of the Minobe Incident, Premier *ad interim* (February 1936), Minister of State (May 1943–July 1944), member of the National Foundation Society. In the 1920s, while in charge of the Home Ministry Police Bureau, he attended Yasuoka Masaatsu's lectures at the Golden Pheasant Academy. In the 1930s Gotō was associated with the Reform Faction (Kakushin Ha) of the bureaucracy, which co-operated with the military in advocating greater State control of the economy.

Great Japan National Essence Association (Dai Nihon Kokusui Kai). Founded in 1919 with the encouragement of the Home Minister and with the strong backing of Mr. Tōyama Mitsuru (q.v.). It was organized on paternalistic (*oyabun-kobun*) lines as a reaction to the growing influences of labour unions. Its most active members were builders' foremen and labour contractors, and its principal aim was to mobilize 'patriotic' elements in order to preserve industrial discipline. At its height the Association claimed to have a million members, but sixty thousand is probably closer to the actual number.

Great Japan Political Justice Corps (Dai Nihon Seigi Dan). Patriotic society organized in Osaka in 1925 by Mr. Sakai Eizō, a rich industrialist, who obliged all his employees to join. Membership rose to well over 100,000 in the early 1930s and the society was instrumental in settling many industrial disputes.

Great Japan Production Party (Dai Nihon Seisan Tō). In June 1931 the Great Japan Production Party was formed in an effort to unify all elements of the right-wing movement. It claimed a membership of 100,000 soon after its founding. One of its leading figures was Uchida Ryōhei, president of the Amur River Association, and it followed the tack set by that association, emphasizing in its programme a strong foreign policy under the banner of 'Greater Japan'. The party was also responsible for bringing or establishing labour unions and organizations within the rightist fold. It had only limited success, however, and declined as a political force after 1933.

Great Reform Association (Taika Kai). Minor nationalist society (named after the Great Reform that was carried out in the seventh century). It was formed in 1920 and managed to survive until the end of the war, when it was included on the list of purged organizations.

Greater Asia Society (Dai Ajiya Kyōkai). Established in 1933, it consisted mostly of retired officers and politicians. Its ideal was a league of Asiatic countries under Japan. The group is of particular interest because it illustrates how respectable men of the highest standing in public life came to be associated with professional nationalists (ref. Richard Storry, *The Double Patriots*, pp. 149–50).

Hamada Kunimatsu. In a speech in the Diet in January 1937, Hamada charged the Army with usurpation of political power. The War Minister, Gen. Terauchi, demanded an apology, but Hamada said he would disembowel himself if his charges could not be substantiated and called on Terauchi to do likewise if they could. Terauchi did not accept the challenge.

Hamaguchi Osachi (1870–1931). Hamaguchi held Cabinet posts under Katsura, Ōkuma, Katō, and Wakatsuki. He became head of the Minsei Tō upon its formation in 1927 and assumed the premiership two years later. Hamaguchi caused much resentment by his role in the London Conference and by his decision to abandon the gold standard. In 1930 he was shot by an assassin at Tokyo Station and died in the following year.

Han Fei Tzu. A lengthy work by the Chinese Legalist philosopher Han Fei Tzu (*d.* 233 B.C.). He completely rejected the interpersonal ethics taught by Confucius and advocated a hard-headed policy of absolute monarchy sustained by stringent laws, severe punishments, appropriate rewards, and expedient statecraft.

Harada Kumao (1888–1946). Long-time personal secretary to Prince Saionji, he kept a personal diary from March 1930 until November 1940, recording in considerable detail the political events in which the Prince was involved. The diary was published after the war in eight volumes under the title *Saionji Kō to Seikyoku.*

Hashimoto Kingorō (1890–1957). Army officer and leader of the Cherry Blossom Association (1930), the most famous of the young-officers' societies that sprang up in the early 1930s. Hashimoto took an active part in the abortive March and October (1931) Incidents, and was also privy to the February (1936) revolt. He was a militant xenophobe and was responsible for the shelling of H.M.S. *Ladybird* and U.S.S. *Panay* on the Yangtse in 1937. Hashimoto organized various ultra-nationalist societies in the late 1930s; in 1944 he was elected to the Diet. In 1948 he was sentenced to life imprisonment as a Class A war criminal. He was released in 1955, after which he stood as an independent in the 1956 Upper House elections. Although he received almost 200,000 votes, this was not quite sufficient to elect him.

Hashimoto Sanai (1834–1859). Executed by the Shōgun in 1859 for his part in requesting the Imperial Court to issue a message calling for reform in Shogunal administration.

Hashimoto Tetsuma (b. 1889). Founder and president of the Purple Cloud Pavilion (q.v.) and a writer of strong nationalist leanings.

Hata Bushirō (b. 1903). Politician and businessman, Mr. Hata has been elected to the House of Representatives five times since 1937. During part of the war he served in the Ministry of Transport and Communications. At present he heads the Hata Book Company.

Hata Shunroku (b. 1879). Prominent military leader. Commander-in-Chief of the Japanese forces in Shanghai (1938), War Minister in the Abe and Yonai Cabinets, Commander-in-Chief of the Japanese expeditionary forces in China (1941). Sentenced to life imprisonment by the I.M.T.F.E.

Hayashi Senjūrō (1876–1942). War Minister from January 1934 to September 1935. Prime Minister from February to June 1937, concurrently holding the Foreign and Education portfolios.

Heaven-Sent Soldiers' Unit Incident (Shimpei Tai Jiken), also translated as the *God-Sent Troops Incident*. An ambitious military-civilian attempt in 1933 to carry out the objectives of the May 15 Incident (q.v.) by assassinating a number of leading figures. The police heard about the plot and arrested the conspirators in time.

Higashikuni Naruhiko (b. 1887). Imperial Prince and Army officer, who rose to the rank of general. During the China crisis he was occasionally mentioned as a possible prime minister, but the plans of his supporters were abortive. After Japan's surrender he organized the first post-war Cabinet; it lasted for only fifty days.

Higher Ethics Association (Meirin Kai). Moderate nationalist society organized in 1932 (inaugurated in 1933) with the aim of stimulating political activity by retired officers. It built up close connexions with the War Ministry and included many senior officials among its members. The group survived until the general purge of 1946.

Hirano Rikizō (b. 1898). A peasants' union leader, associated with pre-war 'proletarian' parties. A right-wing socialist at first, Hirano became increasingly nationalistic, and by 1934 he had become permanent secretary of the Imperial Way Association. In 1947 he was appointed Minister of Agriculture and Forestry in the Katayama Cabinet, but was purged shortly thereafter. Reinstated in 1951, Hirano has continued to play an important role in the right wing of the Socialist movement.

Hiranuma Kiichirō (1867–1952). Minister of Justice in the second Yamamoto Cabinet; became Vice-President of the Privy Council in 1924 and served as President from 1936 to 1939. Headed the National Foundation Society (q.v.). Formed a Cabinet in 1939, which lasted for only eight months. Served in the second and third

Konoe Cabinets. Convicted as a Class A war criminal and given a life sentence, Baron Hiranuma died in prison.

Hirota Kōki (1878–1948). Diplomat-politician with extreme rightist leanings. Ambassador to the Soviet Union (1930), Foreign Minister (1933), Prime Minister (1936). Hirota was associated with the Dark Ocean Society. He was regarded as having considerable responsibility for the totalitarian trends in the late 1930s; after the war he was hanged as a Class A war criminal.

Honjō Shigeru (1876–1945). Commander-in-Chief of the Kwangtung Army at the time of the Manchurian Incident in September 1931. Gen. Honjō was apparently unaware of plans to create an 'incident', but he gave his approval for action taken subsequently by Japanese troops in Manchuria. He committed suicide in November 1945.

Hoshino Naoki (b. 1892). President of the Planning Board and Minister of State in the second Konoe Cabinet. He was associated with the Reform Faction (Kakushin Ha) of the bureaucracy, especially in its dealings with Manchuria (see *Gotō Fumio* above).

House of assignation (machiai). Sometimes incorrectly described as 'geisha houses', these are places traditionally used by a certain type of Japanese politician for behind-the-scene political dealings. 'Machiai politics', referring to political negotiations conducted in these houses, have a strong connotation of shadiness and corruption. Since the Meiji Period, geishas, who met their customers in these houses, frequently established close ties with Japan's political and military leaders, and some of the more intelligent ladies of this class were in a position to exert a good deal of influence.

Iimura Minoru (b. 1888). Military attaché in Turkey, Chief of Staff of the Kwangtung Army and (during the war) Chief of Staff of the South Pacific Army; later, chief of the Kempei Tai (*gendarmerie*).

Ikeda Seihin (1867–1950). Director of the Mitsui Bank and a leading figure in the vast Mitsui *Zaibatsu* complex. Although he gave help to extreme rightists, he was himself earmarked for assassination in 1932 as a member of the corrupt *bourgeoisie*. He served as Minister of Commerce and Industry during the war and was purged after the surrender.

Imperial Flag Incident (Kinki Jiken). Another name for the October Incident (q.v.).

Imperial Rule Assistance Association (Taisei Yokusan Kai). Formally organized in October 1940 after the dissolution of all political parties in the Diet, it sought to encompass all groups, promote national unity, and render the Diet co-operative. Among the aims of the association were: 1. to strengthen national defence, 2. to inculcate the Way of 'faithful loyal subjects', 3. to 'exalt the great Divine Way', and 4. to act as both the 'propelling force of the people' and as a medium for transmitting the wishes of the government to the people. Since the Association was joined by most former party leaders, it was plagued by factionalism, lack of responsibility, and weak popular appeal (see Robert A. Scalapino, *Democracy and the Party Movement in Prewar Japan*, pp. 388–9). The Association continued until the end of the war.

Imperial Rule Assistance Political Association (*Yokusan Seiji Kai*). Formed in 1942, in conjunction with the Imperial Rule Assistance Association, as the only legal political 'party'.

Imperial Rule Assistance Young Men's Corps (*Yokusan Sōnen Dan*). One of a nest of organizations created round the Imperial Rule Assistance Association (q.v.). (Others included a reorganized Great Japan Women's Association and similar bodies for farmers, traders, writers, etc.) The purpose of these groups was to provide additional channels for mobilizing the energies and enthusiasm of the people behind the Government's war effort. They were modelled in part on the totalitarian mass parties of the West, and yet continuous disputes arose within them over the extent to which they should be kept firmly under Home Ministry control, or alternatively be allowed some autonomy. The idea of a special Young Men's Corps for men between the ages of twenty and forty stems from the age-grading system traditional to villages in many parts of Japan.

Imperial Way Association (*Kōdō Kai*). Minor right-wing society, founded in 1933; not to be confused with the Imperial Way Principles Association (q.v.). One of its leaders was Hirano Rikizō (q.v.).

Imperial Way and Control Factions (*Kōdō Ha, Tōsei Ha*). In the early 1930s a factional group arose in the Army centred on Gens. Araki Sadao and Mazaki Junsaburō. These men advocated a forthright imperialistic policy based on the mystique of the Imperial Way, which attracted a number of idealistic young officers and civilian activists such as Kita Ikki. Other senior officers, led by Gen. Nagata Tetsuzan, opposed the growing influence of the Imperial Way Faction and sought to restore 'control' within the Army. The struggle between them was one of the factors leading to the mutiny of 26 February 1936, in which the Control Faction emerged the victor. The Imperial Way group advocated sweeping internal reforms and thus represented a more radical approach than the Control Faction. A clear strategic distinction between the two lay in the desire of the

Imperial Way Faction to move north against Russia while the Control Faction urged penetration south into China. Today, however, most scholars insist that the factional divisions in the Imperial Army were far more complex than the simple Imperial-Control dichotomy would suggest.

Imperial Way Principles Association (Kōdōgi Kai). Nationalist organization founded in 1918 by a group of Seiyū Kai politicians. Gen. Araki became its chief director; the society was patronized mainly by retired Army officers, who used it to spread their ultra-patriotic concept of the Imperial Way. The organization grew to a membership of some 40,000 and greatly helped to establish Araki's reputation as a militant patriot.

Inoue Junnosuke (1869–1932). After a long career in banking, Inoue was appointed Minister of Finance in 1923. In 1929, while occupying the same position in the Hamaguchi Cabinet, Inoue was largely responsible for removal of the gold embargo which, coinciding with the world-wide market crash, had a disastrous effect on Japan's economy. Resentment stemming from this resulted in his assassination by an ultra-nationalist youth in 1932.

Inoue Nisshō (Akira) (b. 1886). Nichiren priest of extreme rightist beliefs, who before turning to Buddhism had spent most of his life on the continent as a secret agent for the Japanese Army. On his return to Japan he organized several extreme nationalist societies. The most important of these was the Blood Pledge Corps, which was responsible for the killing in 1932 of the Finance Minister and of the director of Mitsui. As a result he was sentenced to life imprisonment; he was released in 1940 on a general amnesty. Inoue resumed political activity after 1952 and in collaboration with several former members of his Blood Pledge Corps he founded the extremist National Protection Corps (Gokoku Dan).

Itagaki Seishirō (1885–1948). While serving on the Staff of the Kwangtung Army he became involved in the Manchurian Incident (1931). Later he was appointed Vice-Chief of Staff in the Kwangtung Army. He was sent to China as divisional commander at the outbreak of the China Incident (1937). In 1938 he was appointed War Minister in the first Konoe Cabinet, and he continued in this post under the succeeding Hiranuma Cabinet. At the war crimes trials he was given the death penalty and hanged in 1948.

Itō Hirobumi (1841–1909). Leading statesman of the Meiji Period and the first Prime Minister of Japan (1885–8). He took the main part in framing the Meiji Constitution and in this task he was greatly influenced by the German model. When he was studying foreign constitutions, he spent more time in Germany than in any other foreign country. He met Bismarck frequently and was much impressed by the idea that the legislature should be tightly controlled by the executive, which would be responsible to the sovereign. The Bismarckian influence was also reflected in many aspects of Prince Itō's manner and appearance. Itō founded and became the first leader of the Seiyū Kai (q.v.). He was active in obtaining control of Korea for Japan and served as Resident-General in Korea from 1905 to 1909, in which year he was assassinated by a young Korean nationalist.

Itō Ritsu (b. 1913). Formerly a leader of the agrarian movement, Itō was a member of the Politburo of the Japan Communist Party after the war until his expulsion in 1953 for 'anti-party activities'.

Iwanami Publishing Company. One of the largest and most influential publishers in Japan today. It concentrates on academic books, reference works, and the best of Japanese literature, in addition to translations from almost all the world's greatest literature. Iwanami books are known for their high intellectual level and low prices, many of them appearing in pocket editions, and for this reason their readers are mostly scholars, professionals, and students. The political point of view supported editorially by the Iwanami Company is decidedly progressive. In general, therefore, the readers of Iwanami publications make up a special stratum of Japanese society—the articulate, progressive intelligentsia, which has, as it were, its own culture within a culture.

Japan Federation of Labour (Nihon Rōdō Sōdōmei), also translated as the *Japan General Federation of Labour.* First major amalgamation of trade unions; it was formed in 1919 and included about seventy unions with a membership of some 30,000. During the 1920s and early 1930s it suffered from successive splits and secessions; the federation was finally dissolved to merge into the Serve-the-State-through-Industry movement.

Japan National Council of Trade Unions (Nihon Rōdō Kumiai Zenkoku Hyōgi Kai), also translated as the *Council of Japanese Labour Unions.* The most militant left-wing labour union organization in the 1920s. It was formed in 1925 and the authorities correctly regarded it as being under Communist control. The Council was dissolved in 1928 on the grounds that its activities were 'harmful to peace and order' and violated the Peace Preservation Law.

Japan National Socialist Party (Nihon Kokka Shakai Tō), also translated as the *Japan State Socialist Party*. Radical rightist labour party organized in 1932 by Akamatsu Katsumaro (q.v.) after his split with the central groups of the labour movement.

Japan Peasants' Union (Nihon Nōmin Kumiai), also translated as the *Japan Farmers' Union*. Farmers' group organized in 1922 under moderate Christian socialist leaders. It suffered severe splits and defections; with reunification in 1928 it became the National Peasants' Union (Zenkoku Nōmin Kumiai).

Japan Proletariat Party (Nihon Musan Tō). A political party formed in 1937 which stressed a popular front against fascism. It was banned later in the same year for violation of the Peace Preservation Law.

Jimmu. According to official history (which until 1945 any scholar questioned at his peril), Jimmu, the traditional first Emperor of Japan, founded the Imperial dynasty in 660 B.C. The 2,600-year anniversary of the founding was celebrated with much fanfare in 1940. The present Emperor (Hirohito) was regarded as a direct descendant of Jimmu and accordingly of Jimmu's ancestress, the Sun Goddess.

Jimmu Association (Jimmu Kai). Rightist society organized in 1932 by Ōkawa Shūmei as a successor to his recently dissolved Activist Association. It was named after Emperor Jimmu, by tradition the first sovereign of Japan. The Association was active in the May 15 Incident and the failure of this *coup* virtually brought it to an end, though it was not officially disbanded until 1935.

Joint Association for the Defence of the National Polity (Kokutai Yōgo Rengō Kai). Right-wing unification movement organized in 1933, which included eighty patriotic societies, mostly of minor importance.

Joint Council for Solving the National Crisis (Kokunan Dakai Rengō Kyōgi Kai). One of the many rightist unification efforts in the early 1930s. It was a temporary amalgamation, organized in 1932, and included the Great Japan Production Party, the Jimmu Association, and the New Japan National League.

Kabayama Sukenori (1837–1922). Distinguished naval officer from Satsuma who served as Navy Minister in the first Yamagata and the Matsukata Cabinets; he fought in the Sino-Japanese War and was made Viscount; Governor-General of Formosa in 1895.

Kageyama Masaharu (b. 1906). A central executive of the Industrial Party, Kageyama was imprisoned for two and a half years for his participation in an extremist incident. He was the founder of the Greater Asia Society (q.v.).

Kaiten-shi Shi. A collection of reminiscences compiled by Fujita Tōko (q.v.) during a term of imprisonment in 1844. It became a great source of inspiration to patriots in the Bakumatsu Period.

Kamei Kanichirō (b. 1892). Right-wing socialist who became very nationalistic in the pre-war proletarian movement. He was a leader of the Social Mass Party in 1928 and since then has several times successfully stood for the House of Representatives. During the war Kamei was director of the East Asia Department of the Policy Bureau of the Imperial Rule Assistance Association. Since the war he has been active in the right wing of the Socialist Party.

K'ang Yu-wei (1858–1927). Chinese statesman and philosopher. Inspired the abortive Hundred Days of Reform in 1898, directed towards modernizing and strengthening the Empire. While advocating Confucianism as a State religion, he believed that technical knowledge from the West was indispensable for a strong China.

Kanin Sumihito (b. 1878). Imperial Prince and Field-Marshal of the Army. Appointed Chief of General Staff in 1931; urged an alliance with Germany and Italy in 1939.

Kanto National Essence Association (Kantō Kokusui Kai). Also known as the Kanto National Essence Headquarters (Kantō Kokusui Hombu), this organization was the result of a split in the Great Japan National Essence Association (q.v.). It consisted of members who had remained in Tokyo (in the Kanto area) after numerous dissenting elements had moved to Kyoto. The Kanto group was formed in 1921 with the backing of the Kensei Kai, one of the two major political parties.

Katayama Tetsu (b. 1887). Japan's only Prime Minister from the Socialist Party, May 1947 to June 1948, Mr. Katayama joined the Socialist Mass Party as secretary-general when it was formed in 1926. In the pre-war era he also served as director of the legal department of the Japan Federation of Labour and as legal adviser to farmers' associations. As a devout Christian, he has taken part in the affairs of the Young Men's Christian Association since 1919. After 1951 he served as adviser to the Right Socialist Party, and later he was active in the Democratic Socialist Party (Minshu Shakai Tō).

Kawakami Jōtarō (b. 1889). A Christian and a founder of the Labour-Peasant Party, Kawakami was later active in the pre-war proletarian party movement. But, since he helped to form the Imperial

Rule Assistance Association, he was purged during the Occupation. After his reinstatement, he became an influential Socialist leader; he was chairman of the Right Socialist Party 1951–5 and of the Socialist Party from 1961.

Kawakami Sōroku (1828–1899). A prominent military figure during the Restoration, he was later promoted to the rank of general and became Chief of Staff in 1898.

Kawasaki Misaburō (b. 1905). Kawasaki has published several works on post-war economic problems.

Kaya Okinori (b. 1889). Served as Finance Minister in the first Konoe Cabinet and held the same post during the early years of the Pacific War. He was imprisoned as a war criminal by the I.M.T.F.E. Following his release he was able to become Finance Minister again, in the Cabinet of his old associate, Mr. Kishi Nobusuke.

Kido Kōichi (b. 1889). Prominent statesman. After holding numerous Cabinet posts in the 1930s he was appointed Lord Keeper of the Privy Seal in 1940, and as the Emperor's closest adviser he played an extremely important role during the following crucial years. Marquis Kido was sentenced to life imprisonment by the I.M.T.F.E., but was released on parole in 1956.

Kita Ikki (1884–1937). Leading right-wing revolutionary and writer. He was a powerful advocate of national socialism and is frequently described as the founder of modern Japanese fascism. He demanded a radical change in Japanese society and the promotion of revolution in Asia under the aegis of Japan. Kita was executed after the failure of the February (1936) Incident, on which he was believed to have exerted great influence. Although his writings were suppressed, they circulated widely in the 1930s, especially among the young nationalist officers.

Kita Sōichirō (b. 1894). Graduated from Princeton University; was a professor at Waseda University and served in the Lower House of the Diet.

Kōda Kiyosada. An Army officer who was one of the activists in the February Incident.

Kōdan Sha. One of the leading publishing companies in Japan, founded by Noma Seiji (q.v.). In contrast to Iwanami (q.v.), it produces books and magazines of a popular nature geared to the interests of the general reading public. Just as the readers of Iwanami publications could be regarded as synonymous with the Japanese intelligentsia, so Kōdan Sha readers for the most part represented the 'pseudo-intelligentsia', that large proportion of Japanese who had an average education and enjoyed reading, but had neither the time nor the inclination for high-level study or intellectual involvement.

Koga Kiyoshi. Ringleader of the assassins in the May 15 Incident, he fatally wounded the Prime Minister, Mr. Inukai. Ōkawa Shūmei supplied Lt. Koga with pistols and ammunition for the incident. Between 1930 and 1932, Lt. Koga had attended right-wing lectures given at the Golden Pheasant Academy.

Koike Shirō (b. 1892). A founder of the Social Mass Party in 1926, he eventually followed Akamatsu Katsumaro out of the party and helped him to found the Japan National Socialist Party (q.v.) in 1932. In 1934 he became chairman of the short-lived League for Patriotic Politics (Aikoku Seiji Dōmei).

Koiso Kuniaki (1880–1950). An important military leader. Chief of Staff of the Kwangtung Army, Overseas Minister in the Hiranuma and Yonai Cabinets, and in 1942 Governor-General of Korea; Prime Minister 1944–5. Sentenced to life imprisonment by the I.M.T.F.E., he died in prison.

Kondō Eizō (b. 1883). After having graduated from California Polytechnic in 1908, he returned to Japan and became active in left-wing groups. Late in 1920 he founded the Association of Enlightened People (Gyōmin Kai), which was the predecessor of a formal Communist Party created in August 1921. Kondō is reported to have received funds from Comintern agents in Shanghai. After being arrested he became a violent anti-communist. Later he was involved in a nationalist labour federation organized by Akamatsu Katsumaro (q.v.).

Kōno Hironaka (1849–1923). A retainer of the Miharu Clan, who actively supported the pro-Imperial forces at the time of the Restoration. He helped to formulate plans for a parliamentary system and became a militant liberal politician whose outspoken opposition to authoritarianism led to imprisonment in 1883. He was associated with the Liberal Party from its inception, but left it in 1897 and in the following year helped to found a rival group. He became chairman of the new Imperial Diet and later he served in the second Ōkuma Cabinet as Minister of Agriculture and Commerce.

Konoe Fumimaro (1891–1945). A distinguished member of the Japanese aristocracy (he was a descendant of the great Fujiwara family which ruled Japan during much of the Heian period), Prince Konoe embarked on a political career on the advice of the eminent Elder Statesman, Prince Saionji. In his youth he was vaguely sympathetic to socialism, but he turned steadily to the right and was subsequently associated with members of the extreme right wing. He became President of the House of Peers in 1933 and Prime Minister on the eve of the China Incident. The Tripartite Pact was signed during his second Cabinet (1940), and in the same year the Imperial Rule Assistance Association was formed under his direction. Konoe's third Cabinet was formed in 1941 and collapsed two months before the outbreak of the Pacific War. Prince Konoe committed suicide by poison in 1945 when he was about to be arrested as a war crimes suspect.

Konuma Tadashi (b. 1912). A member of the Blood Pledge Corps, Konuma assassinated the ex-Minister of Finance, Mr. Inoue Junnosuke, on 9 February 1932. He was sentenced to life imprisonment in 1934 but was released at some time before 1940.

Kume Kunitake (1839–1931). Well-known historian and professor of Tokyo Imperial University. In 1893 Professor Kume was forced to resign his chair for having written that Shintō was a survival of a primitive form of sun worship.

Kumoi Tatsuo (1844–1870). Court official at Kyoto. When his plea to preserve the Shogunate was rejected he returned to the Yonezawa Clan to which he had been originally attached and attempted to rouse the northern clans against the Imperial Court. This failing, he returned to Edo (old Tokyo) and plotted to revive feudalism by overthrowing the government. He was executed when his plot was discovered.

Kuo Mo-jo (b. 1891). A distinguished novelist, poet, and archaeologist who has travelled extensively and has held numerous appointments under the Communist régime. He is at present the President of the Academy of Sciences and Vice-Chairman of the Standing Committee of the First National People's Congress.

Kuroda Kiyotaka (1840–1900). Prime Minister from April 1888 to December 1889. He also served as Minister of Agriculture and Commerce in Japan's first Cabinet under Itō Hirobumi. He was a retainer in the Satsuma Clan which, with the Chōshū Clan, provided most of the leadership in Meiji politics. Before his political career in the central government he had spent ten years in Hokkaidō as Vice-Governor of the Hokkaidō Development Board, in which post he made considerable improvements in land cultivation.

Kurusu Saburō (1886–1954). Pre-war diplomat who was dispatched to Washington on the eve of the Pacific War to help in the final abortive negotiations. From 1939 to 1940 he served for a short time as Ambassador to Germany during Ōshima's absence.

Kwangtung Army (Kantō Gun). During the 1930s the Kwangtung Army grew into a semi-autonomous military force which undertook the conquest and exploitation of Manchoukuo (Manchuria), pursuing a tough expansionist policy and presenting the home government with a series of *faits accomplis.*

Labour-Peasant Faction (Rōnō Ha), also translated as the *Labour-Farmer Faction.* A school of Marxist thinkers that emerged in 1927, concerning itself among other things with the nature of Japanese capitalism and of the revolution that Japan underwent at about the time of the Meiji Restoration.

Labour-Peasant Party (Rōnō Tō), also translated as the *Labour-Farmer Party.* Established in 1929 under the labour leader, Ōyama Ikuo, on the basis of remnants from the former militant Labour Peasant Party (Rōdō Nōmin Tō), which had been banned in 1928. This party moved to the right and joined with other proletarian parties in 1931 to form the National Labour-Peasant Mass Party.

Levelling Society (Suihei Sha). Organization founded in Kyoto in 1922 with the aim of improving the condition of the depressed 'special community' or Eta class. The emancipation movement spread throughout the country and was viewed with great suspicion by the authorities, who believed that it was tainted by anarchism. Though the members of the society were vigorously attacked by rightist groups such as the Great Japan National Essence Association (q.v.), the movement lasted through the war.

Liberal Party (Jiyū Tō). One of the two post-war conservative parties that merged in November 1955 to form the present Liberal Democratic Party (Jiyū Minshu Tō), which is now the majority party in the National Diet. The Liberal Party founded in 1881 under Itagaki Taisuke as its first president was the distant ancestor, through the lineage of the pre-war Seiyū Kai, of the post-war Liberal Party.

Liu T'iao River (Ryūjō Kō). Mentioned in this book in connexion with the Manchurian Incident, which broke out at the Liu T'iao River near Mukden on the night of 18/19 September 1931.

'Lobbyist' group (ingai dan). Non-parliamentary group, made up mainly of political bullies (sōshi) and used to ensure predetermined results in elections, to perform duty as bodyguards, strongmen, etc.

Although 'lobbyist group' is given in the dictionaries, 'extra-parliamentary strong-arm corps' would be a more accurate transla- tion.

Lu Ting-i (b. 1907). A member of the Central Committee of the Chinese Communist Party since 1945 who apparently has quite close ties with Mao Tse-tung. He often acts in the capacity of 'interpreter' of Mao's thoughts.

Maeda Torao. An extremist, connected with the Heaven-Sent Soldiers' Unit (q.v.); he was involved in an abortive attempt to assassinate the Premier and other leaders in 1940.

Makino Nobuaki (1861–1949). Son of the Meiji leader and Elder Statesman, Ōkubo Toshimichi, Count Makino was active in both diplomatic and domestic affairs, serving as Ambassador to Italy (1897), Minister of Education (1906–8), Minister of Agriculture and Commerce (1911–12), Minister of Foreign Affairs (1920), and Lord Keeper of the Privy Seal (1925–35). Count Makino, a friend and associate of Prince Saionji, was a close adviser to the Throne and one of the most influential leaders of the time.

March Incident (Sangatsu Jiken). Planned for March 1931, this was the first major attempt by military and civilian ultra-nationalists to organize a *coup d'état* at home in preparation for military action abroad. Col. Hashimoto Kingorō (q.v.) and other members of the Army's Cherry Blossom Association provided the driving force, but the main support came from certain senior officers. The uprising was also backed by Ōkawa Shūmei and other civilians. The plan aimed to overthrow civilian rule by violence and to substitute a military government under Gen. Ugaki. It was abandoned because of opposition from high Army circles, including Gen. Ugaki himself. The matter was officially hushed up and no punitive action was taken.

Marco Polo Bridge (Lukou Ch'iao). Famous as the place where the China Incident started on the night of 7 July 1937, when Chinese forces allegedly fired on a company of Japanese soldiers on night manoeu-vres near the bridge, which was on the Peiping-Tientsin railway.

Matsui Iwane (1878–1948). Served as military attaché in France and China. Supreme commander in the Shanghai region (1937). The outrages in Nanking took place during his term of responsibility. He was hanged as a war criminal.

Matsui Kūka. Pre-war civilian rightist, at one time associated with Marquis Kido.

Matsuoka Komakichi (1888–1958). Leader for a long time of the Japan Federation of Labour (q.v.), Matsuoka was associated with the Socialist Masses and the Social Democratic Parties in pre-war days. After the war he was prominent in the right wing of the Socialist Party and served for many years in the House of Representatives.

Matsuoka Yōsuke (1880–1946). Diplomat and politician fanatically opposed to the Western democracies. He attended university in America, thus providing a notable case in which first-hand experience of the West failed to inspire a sympathetic attitude. In 1933 as a Diet member he announced Japan's secession from the League of Nations. Later he resigned from the Diet and started a movement to dissolve all political parties. As Foreign Minister in the second Konoe Cabinet, he toured Europe and met Hitler, Mussolini, and Stalin. Matsuoka played an important role in persuading Japan to join the Tripartite Pact. He was arrested in 1945 as a Class A war criminal suspect, but became insane and died before the completion of his trial.

Matsutani Yojirō (1880–1937). Politician and lawyer. Joined the Labour-Peasant Party in 1936 when it was founded. Acted as mediator in the merger of five parties that in 1930 formed the National Labour-Peasant Mass Party, a social democratic party that survived only one year. Matsutani was elected to the House of Representatives in 1930 and in 1932. He was expelled from the party for demanding that it take a more nationalistic line after the Manchurian Incident. Gathering some right-wing supporters from the old party, he established his own group, the Workers' Federation (Kinrō Dōmei) in 1934.

May 15 Incident (Goichigo Jiken). An attempted *coup d'état* with the same general purpose as the Blood Pledge Corps Incident (q.v.) and carried out in 1932 by the same type of agrarian fanatics with the help of certain young officers. The plans were to assassinate political and business leaders, as well as certain statesmen close to the Throne; it was hoped that the Army would then take over and carry out the Showa Restoration (q.v.). The Prime Minister, Mr. Inukai, was killed, but the *coup* collapsed owing mainly to lack of support from the Army. Tachibana, Ōkawa, and other participants were sentenced to prison, but all were released before the end of their terms.

Mazaki Jinzaburō (1876–1956). Appointed Inspector-General of Military Education in 1934, Mazaki was one of the leading members of the Imperial Way Faction of the Army. Through the manoeuvring of the Control Faction, Gen. Mazaki was dismissed in 1935. The repercussions of this event led eventually to the February Incident.

Mikami Taku (*b. 1906*). A Navy officer who was one of the activists in the May 15 Incident. He was in the party that attacked the official residence of the Prime Minister, Mr. Inukai, and killed him. For his part in the Incident he was sentenced to ten years' imprisonment, but released before the end of his term. During the war Mikami was active in organizing rightist youth groups. His name reappeared in 1961 in connexion with a rightist plot to assassinate members of the Ikeda Cabinet.

Military Affairs Bureau (*Gummu Kyoku*). The Military and Naval Affairs Bureaux of the respective Ministries became especially important during the 1930s as the centres from which the 'middle-grade officers' (*chūken shōkō*) intruded increasingly on affairs of state. In particular the Director of the Military Bureau (Gummu Kyoku Chō) served as a link between the Chief of Staff and the War Minister, and had a major influence on forming Army, and thereby government, policy. Within the Military Affairs Bureau, policy functions were mainly handled by the Military Affairs Section (Gummu Ka). For details see Maxon, *Control of Japanese Foreign Policy*, p. 36.

Minami Jirō (*1874–1955*). Prominent military figure. War Minister (1931), Commander-in-Chief of the Kwangtung Army (1934), Governor-General of Korea (1936), member of the Privy Council (1942). Sentenced to life imprisonment by I.M.T.F.E., but released owing to ill health.

Minobe Tatsukichi (*1873–1948*). Prominent professor of Law at Tokyo Imperial University and one of Japan's most distinguished legal scholars since the Restoration. In 1935 Professor Minobe, then a member of the House of Peers, was violently attacked in the Diet because of his 'organ theory' (enunciated twenty-five years earlier), according to which the Emperor was one, though the highest, of the several organs of State. Professor Minobe was driven out of public and academic life and was also subject to personal assault.

Minoda Muneki. A former professor at Keiō University and a rightist scholar of the 1930s, Minoda led vigorous personal attacks against 'liberal' scholars, seeking to repudiate their opinions and to bring about their dismissals from prominent academic positions. Among his victims were Professors Takikawa Yukitatsu, Minobe Tatsukichi, and Kawai Eijirō.

Minsei Tō and Seiyū Kai. The two major political parties in the decade or so prior to the Second World War. The Seiyū Kai was established in 1900 with the Meiji statesman, Itō Hirobumi, as its first president.

The Minsei Tō came into being in 1927 through the amalgamation of two older parties. The parties were never able to establish the principle of party government and fought a losing battle with growing military authoritarianism in the 1930s. They were finally dissolved in 1940.

Mito School. Founded in 1657 by Tokugawa Mitsukuni with the purpose of writing a definitive history of Japan. *The History of Great Japan (Dai Nihon Shi)*, begun in that year, was not formally completed until 1906. The Mito School was especially active from 1829 to 1860, gaining a reputation for anti-foreignism and Imperial loyalism.

Mitsukawa Kametarō (1888–1936). Professor Mitsukawa was closely associated with Kita Ikki, Ōkawa Shūmei, and other nationalists in the years following the First World War. In 1918 he founded a group with Ōkawa which aimed at combating the pro-democratic forces centred on Professor Yoshino Sakuzō.

Miyake Setsurei (1860–1945). A pre-war journalist, Miyake was editor of the influential journal *Nihonjin* (later called *Nihon oyobi Nihonjin*). During the late Meiji period he was a severe critic of Japan's excessive Westernization and a strong advocate of nationalism.

Miyazawa Toshiyoshi (b. 1899). Recently retired from the Law Department of Tokyo University, Professor Miyazawa is considered the leading disciple of the late Professor Minobe Tatsukichi. He was an active proponent of the draft constitution as a member of the House of Peers in June–October 1946 and has since then been a strong advocate of the new constitutional order. His interpretation of the present constitution is based on the idea that inalienable human rights form the fixed basis of popular sovereignty, just as under the old constitution the inviolable and sacrosanct character of the Emperor had constituted the basis of Imperial sovereignty.

Mizuno Hironori (b. 1877). Naval captain; distinguished for his bravery in the Russo-Japanese War, but later attacked by the militarists for his 'liberal' views. During the post-war years he wrote commentaries on military affairs.

Mori Arinori (1847–1889). Statesman. A member of the Satsuma clan, Mori was sent to London to pursue his studies. On his return he became a prominent member of the Meiji Government. As the first Minister of Education (1885–9) he introduced many important reforms. Mori was assassinated for alleged irreverent conduct at Ise Shrine.

Mori Kaku (1883–1932). Influential politician closely associated with the Mitsui interests and with other groups concerned with investment in China. He joined the Seiyū Kai (one of the two leading conservative parties) in 1918 and later became secretary-general of the party. Mori typified the politicians who were connected with powerful business interests and who advocated co-operation with the military during their early rise to power.

Muramatsu Hisayoshi. Politician and businessman. Now affiliated with the Liberal Democratic (conservative) Party, he has served six times in the House of Representatives. Holds doctoral degrees in both law and economics. He was purged at the end of the war but reinstated shortly thereafter.

Muranaka Kōji (1903–1936). One of the young officer participants in the Officers' School Incident of 1934, Muranaka was released from active duty in punishment for his actions. In his 'retired' capacity he participated in the February Incident for which he was sentenced to death by court-martial and shot in August 1936.

Mutō Akira (1892–1948). Army officer. Studied in Germany after the First World War. Appointed Director of the Military Affairs Bureau in 1939. Served as Chief of Staff under Gen. Yamashita in the Philippines. Tried and convicted as a Class A war criminal for crimes against humanity and atrocities; hanged in 1948.

Nagai Kafū (1879–1959). One of Japan's most distinguished modern authors, Kafū was influenced by such writers as Zola, Verlaine, and Baudelaire. His best-known stories, written with much sensitivity and compassion, deal with the lives of geishas, street-walkers, dancers, and waitresses in the Asakusa district of Tokyo. They reflect a nostalgia for the days when sensual indulgence was accompanied by emotional sensibility, before the advent of modern debauchery with its cold and impersonal qualities.

Nagata Tetsuzan (1884–1935). Army officer noted for his exceptional administrative talent. After serving as Military Attaché in Germany and Scandinavia, he was appointed to a key position as Director of the Military Affairs Bureau. The acknowledged leader of the Control Faction, Nagata was murdered in his office by Lt.-Col. Aizawa (q.v.), a fanatic officer of the Imperial Way Faction.

Nakahashi Motoaki (1907–1936). After serving for half a year with the Imperial Army in Manchuria (1934), Nakahashi returned to his post with the Third Regiment of the Imperial Guards. He was executed in May 1936 for his part in the February Incident (q.v.).

Nakano Seigō (1886–1943). Prominent rightist politician, who founded the Tōhō Kai (Eastern Association) and other ultranationalist groups. In 1940 he became secretary-general of the Imperial Rule Assistance Association. He committed suicide following a clash with Gen. Tōjō.

National Foundation Society (Kokuhon Sha). Conservative nationalist group formed in 1924 under Baron Hiranuma with a wide range of membership, including high government officials, politicians, business leaders, and military men. Although by and large the society was a stronghold of traditional conservatism, it also had an extremist element. It had 170 branches with almost 200,000 members. The society was dissolved in 1936 when Hiranuma became President of the Privy Council.

National Founding Association (Kenkoku Kai), also translated as the *Society to Build the Country*. Rightist society founded in 1926 by Akao Bin (q.v.) and aimed at strengthening the State, 'restoring the national spirit', etc. At first it was backed by prominent figures like Baron Hiranuma, but many of them withdrew because of Akao's violent tactics. In the 1930s the society recouped its losses and it received considerable financial support from business interests.

National Labour-Peasant Mass Party (Zenkoku Rōnō Taishū Tō), also translated as the *National Labour-Farmer Masses' Party*. One of the several pre-war proletarian parties that were actually coalitions of factions. It lasted from 1931 to 1932, when it amalgamated with numerous other labour parties to form the Social Mass Party (q.v.).

National Police Reserve Forces (Keisatsu Yobi Tai). The reserve forces were formed in July 1950, with 75,000 men, to be the embryo of the new Japanese Army. Increased to 110,000 in 1952, they were renamed the National Security Forces. In 1954 the name was changed to the National Self-Defence Forces. The Maritime Safety Force is part of this self-defence arrangement, which has been steadily expanded since its formation.

National polity (kokutai). National polity, or national entity, is a vague and controversial concept which became a widely debated subject particularly after the war. Professor Miyazawa Toshiyoshi, former Dean of the Law Department of Tokyo University, has given three meanings for national polity as it was understood in pre-war Japanese law: 1. The orthodox theory, which defined the national polity as a distinction in the form of a State arising from the locus of sovereignty. 2. As defined by the Supreme Court in 1929, 'the condition whereby a line of Emperors unbroken for ages eternal deigns to reign over our Empire and to combine in itself the supreme right to rule . . .' 3. A political system in which an hereditary ruler serves at least as a symbol of national unity and as the concrete manifestation of moral righteousness. In the 1930s 'national polity' became an incantatory symbol to the nationalists, and 'failure to appreciate the national polity' was almost the gravest charge that could be levelled against an opponent.

National Prestige Maintenance Association (Kokui Kai). Nationalist society formed in 1932 by Yasuoka Masaatsu; its members were drawn from the higher bureaucracy leaders like Hirota and Konoe.

Navy Command Faction (Gunrei Ha). See *Navy Ministry Faction*.

Navy Ministry Faction (Gunsei Ha). The Navy Ministry and Navy Command Factions corresponded to the Navy Ministry and the Naval General Staff. A similar antagonism existed within the Japanese Army. At the London Conference the Navy Minister agreed to a ratio of warships that, according to the Naval General Staff, put Japan in a position of dangerous inferiority *vis-à-vis* the United States and Great Britain.

Nemoto Hiroshi. Together with Hashimoto Kingorō, Nemoto represented the extreme militaristic element in the Control Faction of the Army. He was a member of the Cherry Blossom Association and was involved in the abortive incident of October 1931.

New Japan National League (Shin Nihon Kokumin Dōmei), also translated as the *New Japan National Federation*. One of numerous nationalistic labour-oriented political groups. Organized in 1932 by Shimonaka Yasaburō after an argument with Akamatsu Katsumaro (q.v.).

New National Socialist Party Preparatory Committee (Kokkashakaishugi Shintō Jumbi Kai). Group of right-wing labour leaders organized by Akamatsu Katsumaro (q.v.) after his final split with the social democratic movement in 1932. Their activities led to the formation of the rightist Japan National Socialist Party (q.v.).

New Order Movement (Shin Taisei Undō). May 1940–July 1941. A movement to revamp the State along fascist lines that rallied round Prince Konoe. It got under way in May 1940 when Prince Konoe started a campaign for a one-party system, the new party movement *(shintō undō)*, that eventually led to the 'voluntary dissolution' of the political parties later in 1940. Having propelled Konoe into the Prime Minister's office in July 1940, the movement thereafter reflected more government control and pressure than popular participation and enthusiasm. In October 1940 the New Order

Movement gave birth to the Imperial Rule Assistance Association with the Prime Minister, Prince Konoe, as its first president.

Nire Kagenori (1831–1900). As a member of the Satsuma clan he participated in the unsuccessful engagement with the Allied fleet in 1863. After the Restoration he joined the Navy Ministry. He became Admiral, Privy Councillor, and Viscount.

Nishida Zei (1901–1937). Nishida was strongly influenced by the ideas of Kita Ikki and joined Kita in a number of extremist plots. He was either founder or member of many right-wing organizations and was one of the leaders of the February Incident. He was sentenced to death and executed in the following year for his part in the incident.

Noma Seiji (1878–1938). Prominent publisher of popular magazines and founder of the Kōdan Sha (q.v.). Mr. Noma had rightist leanings; his slogan was 'to serve the country by publishing magazines'.

Nomura Kichisaburō (b. 1877). Foreign Minister 1939–40; appointed as Ambassador to the United States in December 1940 and held the post during the crucial months before the Pearl Harbour attack. He had no public office after his repatriation to Japan in 1942. During the post-war period Nomura provided a focal point for activities of former officers of the Imperial Navy. After his release from purge restrictions he became associated as president or adviser of almost all the major organizations promoting the cause of Japanese re-armament. In 1954 he was elected to the Upper House with over a quarter of a million votes.

October Incident (Jūgatsu Jiken). Planned for October 1931, this was an attempt to carry out the so-called Shōwa Restoration and to install a government that would pursue a tougher policy in Manchuria. The plans were more concrete and violent than in the March Incident; few senior officers were involved. The plot was exposed to the authorities and the main participants were arrested. Although the plan had involved the assassination of the entire Cabinet, only mild 'administrative' punishment was given and the Army hushed up the incident.

Odaka Tomoo (1899–1956). Upon graduation from Tokyo Imperial University he was appointed professor at Seoul University and then at Tokyo Imperial University. Specialist in the philosophy of law.

Officers' School Incident (Shikan Gakkō Jiken), also translated as the *Military Academy Incident.* A military plot, planned for November 1934, to assassinate the Prime Minister and other high officials. The

War Ministry heard about the plot and arrested the ringleaders (mostly young Army officers) before they could do any damage. They were suspended from active duty, but not court-martialled.

Oikawa Koshirō (b. 1883). Navy Minister in the second and third Konoe Cabinets and later Chief of Naval Staff (1944–5). Appeared as a witness at the I.M.T.F.E.

Oka Takazumi (b. 1890). Prominent naval officer; sentenced to life imprisonment by the I.M.T.F.E. for war responsibility arising out of his position as Director of the Naval Affairs Bureau.

Okada Keisuke (1868–1952). Naval officer and politician. Promoted to rank of admiral in 1924; Navy Minister in the Saitō Cabinet; Prime Minister (1934); resigned after the February (1936) Incident, in which he narrowly escaped assassination.

Ōkawa Shūmei (1886–1957). A jurist, specialist in Oriental philosophy, and one of the most prominent civilians in the pre-war rightist movement. He maintained close connexions with high military and bureaucratic circles as well as with professional nationalists of the 'outlaw' variety, and founded many rightist societies. In the 1930s he was a prominent participant in several of the 'incidents'. In 1945 Ōkawa was arrested as a Class A war-criminal suspect, but he was declared insane and the case against him was dropped. He caused a sensation during the trial by slapping his fellow-defendant, Tōjō, on his bald pate as a sign of his disapproval. After 1952 Ōkawa was regarded as the doyen of the rightist movement, but he was not very active in any of the reconstituted societies. Shortly before his death he completed a translation of the *Koran* into Japanese.

Onozuka Kiheiji (1870–1944). Graduated from Tokyo Imperial University in 1895 and studied in Europe from 1897 to 1901. Appointed first professor of political science at Tokyo Imperial University in 1901 and became president of that university in 1928. He was also a member of the pre-war House of Peers.

Ōshima Hiroshi (b. 1886). Military Attaché in Berlin and a powerful advocate of close ties with Nazi Germany, General Ōshima was strongly opposed to the Western democracies and he is generally regarded as having played an important part in bringing about the Anti-Comintern and the Tripartite Pacts. He was sentenced to life imprisonment by the I.M.T.F.E., but released in 1955.

Ōsumi Mineo (1876–1941). Navy Minister in the successive Cabinets of Inukai, Saitō, and Okada. He was killed in an air accident while on an inspection tour of China in 1941.

Oyabun-kobun. 'The oyabun-kobun system is a particularistic pattern of social relationships based upon simulated patrimonial principles. In social groupings of this type, persons of authority assume obligations and manifest attitudes toward their subordinates much as if they were foster parents, and conversely the subordinates behave dutifully and hold feelings of great personal loyalty towards their superiors.' Ishino and Bennett, *The Japanese Labor Boss System* (The Ohio State University Research Foundation, 1952).

Ōyama Iwao (1842–1916). A loyalist during the Restoration and a leading military figure for half a century thereafter. Served in several Cabinets: Navy Minister (1885), Education Minister (1889), War Minister (1885–91); member of the Privy Council and one of the Elder Statesmen. Played an important part in the Sino-Japanese and Russo-Japanese Wars and was made a Prince. Lord Keeper of the Privy Seal under Emperor Taishō.

Ozaki Yukio (1858–1954). Well-known independent parliamentarian who was elected to the Lower House twenty-four consecutive times since 1890 and became known as the 'father of parliamentary politics'. In 1898 Mr. Ozaki, who was then Education Minister, made a speech in which he said: 'If you imagined that Japan adopted a republican form of government, a Mitsui or a Mitsubishi would immediately become a candidate for president.' Because of this audacious hypothesis the government of which he was a member had to resign.

Patriotic Labour Party (Aikoku Kinrō Tō). Founded in 1930 by former students of Professor Uesugi Shinkichi (q.v.). In 1932 Amano Tatsuo united the Patriotic Labour Party, of which he was chairman, with the New Japan National League.

Picture-story show (kamishibai). A form of entertainment, primarily for children, in which the audience watches a sequence of illustrations drawn on paper slides; the slides are manipulated by an operator, who tells the story.

Plots of the Warring States (Chan Kuo Ts'e). A collection of speeches by rulers and statesmen in various parts of China during the Period of the Warring States (403–221 B.C.). The work was probably completed at some time in the early years of the Han Dynasty (202 B.C.– A.D. 220). The compiler is unknown.

Politics and Learning Society (Seikyō Sha). Established in 1888 by Miyake Setsurei, it was a rightist society that stressed the need to reject Western influences and to promote a nationalist spirit. From

1907 until well into the Shōwa Period it published a magazine entitled *Japan and the Japanese* (*Nihon oyobi Nihonjin*).

Popular Rights Movement (*Minken Undō*). Upon the destruction of the Tokugawa authority and completion of the Meiji Restoration in 1868, a small group of ex-samurai assumed the power of State and established themselves as an exclusive oligarchy. Other ex-samurai attempted to gain participation in government through military rebellion and were defeated. Still others turned to the creed of Western liberalism and in 1873–4 began agitation for government by representative political parties. This Popular Rights Movement, also known as the Freedom and People's Rights Movement (Jiyū Minken Undō), culminated in the adoption of the Meiji Constitution in 1889. See Nobutaka Ike, *The Beginnings of Political Democracy in Japan* (Baltimore, 1959).

Portable shrine (*mikoshi*). A sacred palanquin containing the emblem of a Shinto deity, carried on the shoulders of devotees during shrine festivals.

Prerogative of supreme command (*tōsuiken*). Allegedly based on Article XI of the Meiji Constitution, which removed control of the armed forces from the general affairs of State and placed it directly in the hands of the Emperor. The prerogative of supreme command and its concomitants (such as the right of direct access to the Emperor) were more and more abused by the military, until in the early 1930s they succeeded in bringing about the virtual eclipse of civilian authority and the establishment of military control over the government.

'Pure literature' (*junsui bungaku*). The term is used in Japan, much as it is in the West, to describe literary works that have a decidedly aesthetic, rather than informational or recreational, value. It applies mainly to poetry, dramas, short stories, and novels that are written 'for art's sake'. 'Pure literature' has the additional connotation of being somewhat highbrow, and is used, therefore, in contrast to the type of literature popular with the general public. An overwhelming amount of recreational literature, often remarkably lacking in taste and devoid of aesthetic value, is published for the mass audience in Japan today. The existence of this type of literature has forced the Japanese to draw an even clearer line of demarcation between 'popular' and 'pure' literature than is usual in the West.

Purple Cloud Pavilion (*Shiun Sō*). Rightist society founded in 1924 by Hashimoto Tetsuma (q.v.). It had considerable financial support and inserted prominent advertisements in the newspapers to attack its enemies. Unlike most organizations of its type it took a pro-American stand and it was disbanded in 1941 under pressure from the military police (Kempei Tai). It was revived towards the end of the war and published a strongly anti-leftist magazine.

Restoration (Ishin). 'Restoration' in these translations invariably refers to the Meiji Restoration of 1868. ('Meiji' used as an adjective refers to the Meiji Period, see Chronology.)

'*Revere the Emperor, Expel the Barbarians*' (*Sōnnō Jōi*). Famous anti-Tokugawa slogan used by the loyalists prior to the Meiji Restoration.

Rōnin. Originally referred to disenfeoffed samurai (e.g. the Forty-Seven Rōnin), but later came to apply in general to adventurers, soldiers of fortune, and others who lived by their wits, courage, and readiness to break the law.

Rōyama Masamichi (b. 1895). Appointed assistant professor at Tokyo Imperial University in 1923 after having graduated from there in 1920. Resigned his professorship in 1939. Elected to the House of Representatives in 1942. Made president of Ochanomizu Women's University in 1954. One of Japan's foremost political scientists and a leading pre-war liberal.

Rule of the higher by the lower (gekokujō). Term used by Japanese historians to describe the phenomenon in which men who were lower in the social or military hierarchy were able to put pressure on their theoretical superiors and frequently, in the end, to supplant them. This was an outstanding aspect of the civil wars that were endemic in Japan from the fourteenth to the sixteenth centuries. More recently the term was used to describe the way in which colonels and other comparatively low-ranking officers succeeded during the 1930s in dictating to their superiors in Tokyo by ignoring their instructions and presenting them with *faits accomplis*. The term is discussed by Sansom (*History of Japan*, II, pp. 235–6), who translates it as 'the low oppress the high'.

Sagoya Tomeo (b. 1910). Member of the pre-war Patriotic Society (Aikoku Sha). Assassin of the Prime Minister, Mr. Hamaguchi, on 11 November 1930. Mr. Sagoya has been extremely active in post-war right-wing activities.

Sakomizu Hisatsune (b. 1902). Served before the war in the Finance Ministry, and later as the private secretary of the Prime Minister, Admiral Okada. He was Chief Secretary in the Suzuki Cabinet. After the war he entered politics, being elected to the Lower House in 1952 and to the Upper House in 1956.

Sakuma Shōzan (1811–1864). Assassinated by anti-foreign samurai. Having observed Commodore Perry's fleet in 1853, he sent recommendations to the Shōgun on weapons, forts, and a new military service. Both Hashimoto Sanai (q.v.) and Sakuma were representatives of the 'enlightened' class of lower samurai.

Sasai Itchō. Formerly of the Society to Carry Out Heaven's Way on Earth, Sasai became secretary-general of the New Japan National League (q.v.) when it was founded in 1932.

Satō Naotake (b. 1882). Foreign Minister in the Hayashi Cabinet (1937); he was appointed Ambassador to Moscow in 1942 and remained there until the end of the war. He has been a leading figure in the Conservative Party since the war.

Satō Tsūji (b. 1901). Specialist in German literature and philosophy; professor at Ajiya Daigaku (Asia University).

'Secretary' (kanji). The so-called secretaries consisted of, among others, the powerful Chiefs of the Military and Naval Affairs Bureaux and of the Chief Cabinet Secretary. They were responsible for preparing the agenda and, although they were not formally entitled to deliberate or vote, their influence on the course of the proceedings can hardly be exaggerated. For details see Y. C. Maxon, *Control of Japanese Foreign Policy*, pp. 152–3, and Richard Storry, *The Double Patriots*, p. 70.

Seiyū Kai. See *Minsei Tō*.

'Self-Government by the People' (Jichi Minpan). A work by Gondō Seikyō published in 1927 and calling for 'village autonomy' in a co-operative society through social reform and the initiative of the peasants.

Senior Retainer (Jūshin), also translated as *Senior Statesman*. One of an informal, extra-constitutional group of advisers to the Emperor which came into being in the 1930s to succeed the powerful Elder Statesmen (Genrō), another extra-constitutional advisory body which made most of the major political decisions between 1898 and 1918. Like its predecessor, the Jūshin group consisted of former Prime Ministers and high court officials; its senior member was Prince Saionji ('the last of the Genrō'). Though they never attained the prestige of the Genrō, the Jūshin exerted considerable influence until the military clique (gumbatsu) took over.

Serve-the-State-through-Industry Movement (Sangyō Hōkoku Undō), also translated as the *Industrial Patriotic Movement*. A labour movement founded in 1937 on the model of the Nazi *Arbeitsfront* to unite the efforts of Japanese labour behind the war effort. Branches were established in factories and plants throughout the country. When the war in China was prolonged, the government assumed control of the movement (April 1939), placing it under the Home and Welfare Ministries with prefectural mayors responsible on the local level. From April 1939 it became a purely government-controlled mechanism for forced labour.

Shiga Jūkō (Shigetaka). A conservative who deplored the extreme Westernization of Japan during the early Meiji Period, Shiga joined Miyake Setsurei and others to establish the Politics and Learning Society (q.v.).

Shiga Naoya (b. 1883). One of the most important writers of modern Japan, Shiga is famous for his delicate impressionistic style and for his realistic portraiture. But his greatest influence has been in the area of first-person novels (or 'I novels'), that is, fiction with auto-biographical undertones. His success attracted a wide range of writers to this genre, so much so that the autobiographical novel has become the most prevalent literary form of twentieth-century Japan.

Shimizu Gyōnosuke. A lesser figure among the ultra-nationalists of the 1920s and 1930s. A member of several groups led by such prominent activists as Kita, Ōkawa, and Nishida, he founded his own terrorist organization, the Great Deeds Society, in 1927.

Shinran (1173–1263). Founder of the Jōdo Shinshū branch of Japanese Buddhism. The cardinal tenet of this sect is that salvation is to be attained only through belief in the grace of Amida Buddha. Shinran believed that the good man, since he is apt to rely on his own virtue, is less likely to be saved than the sinner who throws himself entirely on the mercy of Amida.

Shiratori Toshio (1887–1949). Professional diplomat. He joined the Foreign Ministry in 1929 and was one of the ardent supporters of the occupation of Manchuria and of Japan's withdrawal from the League of Nations. Appointed Ambassador to Italy in 1938, he co-operated with Gen. Ōshima, the Ambassador to Germany, for the conclusion of the Tripartite Pact. With Gotō Fumio (q.v.), a member of the Reform Faction (Kakushin Ha) of the bureaucracy, he was appointed to the House of Peers in 1942. Tried as a Class A war criminal, he was given a life sentence and died in prison.

Shōwa Restoration (Shōwa Ishin). A term invented by the revolutionary right wing in the late 1920s signifying a plan of action to 'restore' the country to its ancient virtues under the authority of the Emperor and to eliminate the 'wicked advisers'—i.e., the party leaders, capitalist magnates, and weak-kneed bureaucrats. The term Shōwa Restoration is an obvious imitation of Meiji Restoration; the right wing felt that the Emperor had become imprisoned by his bad advisers, much as he had been under the Shōgun before 1868. The first major attempt at a Shōwa Restoration was the May 15 Incident of 1932. After the February Incident the term was less in vogue, having been supplanted by other slogans such as the 'New Order'. The last major attempt to effect a Shōwa Restoration was the July 15 Incident of 1940, which was quashed before the usual plans for violence were realized. The term has, however, gained currency in post-war right-wing circles. It means now, much as it did in the 1930s, a return to direct Imperial rule and an idyllic agrarian past by a thorough-going revolution in Japan's political structure.

Siberian Expedition. In July 1918 large Japanese forces were sent to Siberia as part of the Allied plan to aid the Czech troops in Russia. They remained there until 1925 and far outnumbered the other Allied troops in Siberia, with the result that during much of the time the Japanese effectively controlled the area. Numerous atrocities were ascribed to members of the Japanese expeditionary force at this time. See James Morley, *The Japanese Thrust into Siberia, 1918* (New York, 1957).

Social Mass Party (Shakai Minshū Tō), also translated as the *Social Democratic Party*. A moderate proletarian party formed in 1926 and opposing 'both the presently-established political parties which represent the privileged classes and the extremist parties which ignore the process of social evolution'. In 1932 its leadership split on the question of social democracy versus national socialism and many members, including its General Secretary, Akamatsu Katsumaro (q.v.), resigned to join the radical right. In 1932 the remainder of the party joined other proletarian groups to form the Social Masses Party (q.v.).

Social Masses Party (Shakai Taishū Tō), also translated as the *Socialist Masses Party)*. Amalgamation of several moderate proletarian parties formed in 1932 with a programme of opposing capitalism, communism, and fascism. It gradually lost some leaders as it moved towards the right; in 1940 it voluntarily disbanded to make way for the formation of the Imperial Rule Assistance Association.

Society of Those Who Yet Remain (Yūzon Sha), also translated as the *Society to Preserve the National Essence*. Small ultra-nationalist group founded in 1920 by Kita Ikki and Ōkawa Shūmei (q.v.) to establish the 'revolutionary Empire of Japan'. It broke up shortly after Ōkawa's resignation in 1923 but gave rise to a long line of rightist societies associated with the Shōwa Restoration movement.

Society to Carry Out Heaven's Way on Earth (Gyōji Sha or Kōchi Sha), also translated as the *Activist Society)*. Influential rightist society established in 1924 by Ōkawa Shūmei (q.v.) which aimed at building a 'Restoration Japan'. The society attempted to combine the agrarian and the national-socialist strains in the rightist movement, and built up a working relationship between civilian nationalists and young officers in the Army. It was dissolved in 1932 and revived under the name of the Jimmu Association (q.v.).

Sohō. See *Tokutomi Iichirō*.

Statesmanship League (Keirin Gakumei). Influential though short-lived society founded in 1919; it combined the national-socialist strain in the rightist movement (represented here by Takabatake) with the conservative 'Japanist' strain (represented by Uesugi). The fundamental incompatibility between these two approaches soon led to the society's dissolution.

Suetsugu Nobumasa (1880–1944). Admiral, appointed Commander-in-Chief of the Combined Fleet (1933); later served as Home Minister in the first Konoe Cabinet. Noted as an advocate of submarine warfare.

Sugiyama Gen (1880–1945). Prominent Army officer who in 1943 was appointed Field-Marshal and put in charge of the Mainland Defence Forces. He was Vice-Minister of War in the second Wakatsuki Cabinet and War Minister in the Hayashi and first Konoe Cabinets. After 1936 Gen. Sugiyama took strong action to restore discipline within the Army and to prevent political action by lower officers. He and his wife committed *hara-kiri* after Japan's surrender.

Suzuki Kantarō (1868–1948). Naval officer who distinguished himself in the Russo-Japanese War. In 1923 he became an admiral and Chief of General Staff. Later he served as Grand Chamberlain and Privy Councillor. He was seriously wounded in the February Incident. On 7 April 1945, shortly before the end of the war, he became Prime Minister in the so-called Surrender Cabinet, which lasted until 17 August.

Suzuki Kisaburō (1867–1940). Justice Minister (January–June 1924) and Home Minister (April 1927–May 1928, March–May 1932). Became president of the Seiyū Kai Party in 1932 just after the May

15 Incident. Mr. Suzuki was also a member of the right-wing National Foundation Society.

Suzuki Teiichi (Sadaichi) (b. 1888). A prominent member of the military bureaucracy, he was Minister of State and Director of the Cabinet Planning Board in the third Konoe and in the Tōjō Cabinets. Tried as a war criminal and sentenced to life imprisonment; released in 1956.

Suzuki Zenichi (b. 1904). Former member of the Central Executive Committee of the Great Japan Production Party. At the time of the Heaven-Sent Soldiers' Unit Incident he was head of the youth section of the Great Japan Production Party. He was 'chief of staff' for the above Incident. Suzuki was also involved in a short-lived attempt at union of the right-wing groups in March 1936.

Tachibana Kōsaburō (b. 1893). A native of the economically depressed area to the north-east of Tokyo, Tachibana was an important figure in the agrarian movement of the early 1930s. He was involved in the plots surrounding the assassination of the Prime Minister, Mr. Inukai, on 15 May 1932. Sentenced to life imprisonment, Tachibana was released in 1940.

Taishō Sincerity League (Taishō Sekishin Dan). Anti-leftist patriotic society organized in 1918.

Takabatake Motoyuki (1886–1928). A socialist thinker associated with many left-wing magazines and organizations; he translated *Das Kapital* into Japanese. In the 1920s he became interested in national socialism and joined Uesugi Shinkichi, a well-known rightist scholar, in founding the Statesmanship League. This is an interesting example of the mixing of right and left during that period.

Takuya Dempu. Minor right-wing agitator active in the 1920s.

Tamenaga Shunsui (d. 1842). The best-known writer of the early nineteenth-century *ninjō-bon* or 'sentiment books'. His stories deal primarily with prostitutes and derelict samurai, and his sympathetic treatment of their all-too-human lives was deplored by the rigidly Confucian Tokugawa Shogunate. *Ninjō-bon* were eventually banned by the government as having a disruptive effect on public morals.

Tanaka Giichi (1863–1929). Baron and General, War Minister (September 1918–June 1921, September 1923–January 1924), Prime Minister and concurrently Foreign Minister (April 1927–July 1929). President of the Seiyū Kai Party (1925). Alleged author of the Tanaka Memorial, a master plan for the conquest of Asia, which was published in 1927 by the Chinese.

Tanaka Kunishige (1869–1941). One-time commander of the Imperial Guards. President of the Higher Ethics Association (1932). Served as military attaché to the Japanese Embassies in Great Britain and in the United States.

Tatekawa Yoshitsugu (1880–1945). Gen. Tatekawa's military career involved mostly staff and diplomatic assignments. He had served as military attaché in China and in India, as a member of the Japanese delegation to the disarmament conference of August 1932, and as an instructor at Army colleges. After his retirement in 1936, the Konoe Cabinet called upon him to serve as Ambassador to the Soviet Union (September 1940). Tatekawa was also active in right-wing affairs. He was one of the founders of the Golden Pheasant Academy (q.v.); in about 1927 he organized a group of reserve officers into a right-wing society; in 1929 he formed a more broadly based reserve officers' group.

Terauchi Hisaichi (1879–1946). War Minister (March 1936–February 1937). As War Minister, Gen. Terauchi had considerable influence in determining both the composition of the Cabinet and its policies. He was known for his dislike of 'liberals' in government and of 'interference' by the political parties in the operations of government. During the Pacific War he was Supreme Commander of the Southern Army and was elevated to the ranks of Marshal and Count.

The Road to Success and Prosperity (Sakaeyuku Michi). The title of a best-seller by Mr. Noma Seiji (q.v.).

The True Meaning of Japan's Political Reformation (Nihon Aikoku Kakushin Hongi). Published in 1932, this work by Tachibana Kōsaburō discussed the way of salvation for Japan, the absolute nature of Japan's patriotic reformation, and the fundamental source of Japanese solidarity.

The Way of the Subject (Shimmin no Michi). Textbook prepared by the Education Ministry in 1941 'to contribute to the destruction of self-centred and utilitarian ideas that have seeped into Japan from the West'. As explained in this widely disseminated primer, the way of the subject is based above all on service to the State.

'*Third generation*' (*sandaime*). There is a Japanese proverb to the effect that the first generation establishes the family's prosperity, the second squanders it, and the third lives in poverty.

Tōgō Shigenori (1882–1950). Prominent diplomat who was serving as Foreign Minister at the outbreak of the Pacific War. He resigned in 1942, but entered the Suzuki Cabinet as Foreign Minister and was active in persuading the government to accept the Allied terms of surrender. He was sentenced to twenty years' imprisonment by the I.M.T.F.E. and died while serving his sentence. His memoirs have been translated into English under the title *The Cause of Japan* (New York, 1956).

Tōjō Assistance Election (Tōjō Yokusan Senkyo), 30 April 1942. Under the strict surveillance of Tōjō's Imperial Rule Assistance Association the electorate gave his officially endorsed candidates a smashing victory. Thereafter Tōjō's programme met with no difficulties in the Diet.

Tōjō Hideki (1884–1948). Prime Minister of Japan and virtual dictator during the Second World War. After graduating from the Military Staff College in 1915, he rose steadily in the military hierarchy, becoming Chief of Staff of the Kwangtung Army in 1937. He served as War Minister in the second and third Konoe Cabinets and succeeded Konoe as Prime Minister on the eve of the Pacific War; concurrently he held the post of War Minister. He resigned in 1944 after the fall of Saipan. Tōjō was found guilty of war crimes by the I.M.T.F.E. and was hanged in 1948. For a specialized study see Robert Butow, *Tōjō and the Coming of the War* (Princetown, 1961).

Tokugawa Period. 1603–1867 (see Chronology), when Japan was under the rule of an hereditary line of Shōguns belonging to the Tokugawa family.

Tokutomi Iichirō (Sohō) (1863–1957). Critic, journalist, and author. At one time both a Christian and a democrat, he turned against Western democracy after the Sino-Japanese War (1895), and in the 1930s he was co-operating with the militarists and ultra-nationalists in favour of Emperor-centred nationalism. His best-known work is entitled *Modern Japanese History*.

Tōyama Mitsuru (1855–1944). One of the most dynamic and influential of the ultra-nationalists. He was a leading organizer of the Dark Ocean Society (q.v.) and other nationalist groups and took an active part in shaping Japan's aggressive policy towards Korea and China. During the Shōwa period he enjoyed great prestige and respect as the doyen of the ultra-nationalist movement and he maintained close connexions with many of the government leaders.

Toyoda Teijirō (b. 1885). Admiral, politician, and businessman; he served as Foreign Minister in the third Konoe Cabinet.

Treatise on Rural Self-Help (Nōson Jikyū Ron). An idealization of ancient village life, in which the author, Gondō Seikyō (q.v.), envisages rural self-government in a decentralized society.

Tseng Kuo-fan (1811–1872). Leader of government forces which put down the T'aip'ing Rebellion (1850–64) in China. Advocated peace with foreign countries and worked 'towards an adjustment with the West while protecting Chinese tradition'. See Mary C. Wright, *The Last Stand of Chinese Conservatism* (Standard University Press, 1957), pp. 73–75.

Tsinan Incident. In May 1928 Chiang Kai-shek's Army on its famous Northern Expedition entered the city of Tsinan on the Shantung peninsula. On 3 May fighting broke out between Chinese and Japanese troops, the latter being there ostensibly to protect Japanese nationals residing in Shantung. In this clash between Chinese nationalism and Japanese imperialism the Chinese were forced to respect Japanese interests in Shantung.

Tsuda Sōkichi (1873–1961). An authority on early Japanese and Chinese history, particularly intellectual history; professor emeritus, Waseda University.

Tsukui Tatsuo (b. 1901). A prominent national-socialist writer. He was active in numerous right-wing groups in the 1920s and 1930s. Since the war he has worked in the rightist unification movement. Mr. Tsukui has written several books (including one on China) which are of a much higher level than those usually associated with rightist authors.

Uehara Yūsaku (1856–1933). Served in the Sino-Japanese and Russo-Japanese Wars; War Minister in the third Katsura Cabinet, Inspector-General of Military Education (1914), Chief of General Staff (1915), member of Supreme War Council (1924); promoted to ranks of Field-Marshal and Viscount.

Uesugi Shinkichi (1878–1929). A noted professor of law at Tokyo Imperial University, who lectured on the Constitution at the Military and Naval Academies for many years. His constitutional theory, that the Emperor was the State, was the foundation of the pre-war orthodox school of constitutional thought. His major opponent was his colleague at Tokyo Imperial University, Professor Minobe Tatsukichi (q.v.), whose 'organ theory' of the Emperor was branded by Uesugi as contrary to the 'national polity' when it first appeared in 1911. The debate between the two polarized Japanese constitutional thought in the 1930s. Professor Uesugi was also active in right-wing intellectual groups; in 1926 he became president of the National Founding Association (q.v.).

Ugaki Kazushige or *Kazunari* (*1868–1956*). Officer-politician who became a general in 1925. He was War Minister in several Cabinets and also served as Governor-General of Korea. He was resented by the militarists for his moderate views, and the Army prevented him from becoming Prime Minister by its usual method of refusing to appoint a War Minister to serve under him. Gen. Ugaki served as Foreign Minister in the first Konoe Cabinet. In post-war elections he was one of the most successful ex-military candidates.

Ukiyoe. The Japanese wood block print of the Tokugawa Period is a familiar art form in the West; in fact the finest collections of these prints are now found in the Western hemisphere. Yet a large part of the collections are never shown to the public, owing to the highly erotic nature of many of the pictures. Along with his purely aesthetic creations, almost every wood print artist produced his share of startlingly frank representations of sex. Some are outstanding works of art in their own right, while others are simply crude pornography.

Umezu Yoshijirō (*1882–1949*). Commander of Japanese forces in China (1934). Vice-Minister of the Army in the Hirota, Hayashi, and first Konoe Cabinets. Prominent leader of the Control Faction; Chief of the General Staff in 1944. Gen. Umezu died in prison while serving a life sentence imposed by the I.M.T.F.E.

Yamaguchi Saburō. Brother of Inoue Nisshō. He was assigned the task of bombing the Prime Minister's residence as his part in the attempted *coup* planned for July 1933, the Heaven-Sent Soldiers' Unit Incident. Commander Yamaguchi died while in custody of the military police after the Incident.

Yamanashi Katsunoshin (*b. 1877*). Promoted to rank of admiral in 1932; served as Vice-Minister of Navy. He was attacked for his conciliatory attitude at the time of the London Naval Conference, and in 1933 he was transferred to the reserve.

Yanagawa Heisuke (*1879–1945*). A member of the Imperial Way Faction, Yanagawa rose to high rank with the backing of Gen. Araki Sadao. He was Assistant Minister of the Army at the time of the February Incident and was subsequently transferred to reserve status. He later served as Justice Minister in the second Konoe Cabinet and Minister of State in the third Konoe Cabinet.

Yasuda Masaru (*1912–1936*). He and three other young officers were assigned to assassinate Viscount Saitō, Lord Keeper of the Privy Seal, on 26 February 1936. After Yasuda and his group had murdered the Viscount, he led a group to the residence of Gen. Watanabe

Jōtarō, Inspector-General of Military Education, and killed him. Yasuda was executed in July 1936 together with the other ringleaders of the February Incident.

Yasuda Tetsunosuke. Lieutenant-Colonel in charge of funds for the Heaven-Sent Soldiers' Unit Incident and other plans.

Yasukuni Jinja. Huge Shinto shrine in Tokyo, founded in 1869 as the central gathering-place for the deified spirits of all those who have died for the 'peace of the land' (*yasukuni*), that is, for the Imperial cause. It is a traditional rendezvous for right-wing nationalists.

Yasuoka Masaatsu (Masahiro) (b. 1898). One of Japan's most respected intellectuals in the pre-war nationalist movement. Yasuoka's primary concern was with spiritual education rather than political intrigue. After associating with several right-wing societies such as Kita's Society of Those Who Yet Remain (q.v.), he founded in 1926 the Golden Pheasant Academy, a group patronized by both civilian and military men. Though he was active in various pre-war nationalistic societies, Yasuoka's approach has been that of an independent scholar.

Yonai Mitsumasa (1880–1948). Naval officer who entered politics and became Prime Minister in 1940. Later he served as Navy Minister in the Koiso and Suzuki Cabinets, and in 1945 he used his influence to help to bring the war to an end. He was viewed askance by the militarists for being too moderate and for having opposed the Tripartite Pact. Admiral Yonai was an important witness at the I.M.T.F.E.

Yoshino Sakuzō (1878–1933). Graduated from Tokyo Imperial University in 1906 and was appointed assistant professor there in 1909. Studied in Europe and America from 1910 to 1913. Resigned his professorship in 1924. Probably the most important intellectual leader in the moderate wing of the Japanese democratic socialist movement in the 1920s. Helped to found the Social Mass Party in 1926.

Yūki Toyotarō (1877–1951). Finance Minister (February–June 1937). Governor of the Bank of Japan. In the 1920s attended lectures by Yasuoka Masaatsu at the Golden Pheasant Academy. Mr. Yūki was also a member of the National Foundation Society (q.v.).

Chronology

Periods in Modern Japanese and Chinese History

JAPAN Tokugawa (Edo) 1603–1867 (of which the final years are known as Bakumatsu).
Meiji 1868–1912.
Taishō 1912–1926.
Shōwa 1926–present.

CHINA Ch'ing (Manchu) 1644–1912.
Republic of China 1912–present (on Taiwan since 1949).
Chinese People's Republic 1949–present.

Principal Events Mentioned in the Essays

1868		Meiji Restoration.
1872		Korean problem placed before Council of State; Saigō Takamori starts a campaign in favour of invading Korea.
1874		Punitive expedition to Formosa.
1889		Meiji Constitution promulgated.
1890	(Oct.)	Imperial Rescript on Education.
1890	(Nov.)	First Imperial Diet convened.
1894–5		Sino-Japanese War.
1904–5		Russo-Japanese War.
1918–21		Japanese expeditionary force to Siberia.
1923		Great Kantō Earthquake.
1930		London Naval Treaty.
1931	(Mar.)	March Incident.
1931	(Sept.)	Manchurian Incident.
1931	(Oct.)	October (Imperial Flag) Incident.
1932	(Jan.)	Shanghai Incident.
1932	(Feb.–Mar.)	Blood Pledge Corps Incident.
1932	(May)	May 15 Incident.
1933	(Mar.)	Japan secedes from the League of Nations.
1933	(July)	Heaven-Sent Soldiers' Unit Incident.
1934		Officers' School Incident.

1935		Minobe case.
1936	(Feb.)	February 26 Incident.
1936	(Nov.)	Anti-Comintern Pact (Germany-Japan).
1937	(July)	Outbreak of China Incident (Marco Polo Bridge).
1937	(Aug.)	Expeditionary force to Shanghai.
1937	(Dec.)	'Rape of Nanking.'
1940	(May)	New Order Movement (political parties and labour unions dissolved).
1940	(Sept.)	Tripartite Pact (Germany, Italy, Japan).
1940	(Oct.)	Imperial Rule Assistance Association inaugurated.
1941	(Apr.)	Non-Aggression Pact with U.S.S.R.
1941	(Dec.)	Japan attacks Pearl Harbour.
1941–5		Pacific War.
1945	(Aug. 15)	Japan accepts the Potsdam Declaration.
1945	(Sept.)	Imperial Rescript of Surrender.
1946	(Jan.)	Imperial Rescript denying the divinity of the Emperor.
1946	(Nov.)	New Constitution promulgated.
1946–8		International Military Tribunal for the Far East.
1950	(Jan.)	Cominform attack on the Japan Communist Party.
1952		Peace Treaty comes into effect: Japanese sovereignty restored.

Cabinets *1885–1957*

1.	1885	First Itō	30.	1931	Inukai
2.	1888	Kuroda	31.	1932	Saitō
3.	1889	First Yamagata	32.	1934	Okada
4.	1891	First Matsukata	33.	1936	Hirota
5.	1892	Second Itō	34.	1937	Hayashi
6.	1896	Second Matsukata	35.	1937	First Konoe
7.	1898	Third Itō	36.	1939	Hiranuma
8.	1898	First Ōkuma	37.	1939	Abe
9.	1898	Second Yamagata	38.	1940	Yonai
10.	1900	Fourth Itō	39.	1940	Second Konoe
11.	1901	First Katsura	40.	1941	Third Konoe
12.	1906	First Saionji	41.	1941	Tōjō
13.	1908	Second Katsura	42.	1944	Koiso
14.	1911	Second Saionji	43.	1945	Suzuki
15.	1912	Third Katsura	44.	1945	Higashikuni
16.	1913	First Yamamoto	45.	1945	Shidehara
17.	1914	Second Ōkuma	46.	1946	First Yoshida
18.	1916	Terauchi	47.	1947	Katayama
19.	1918	Hara	48.	1948	Ashida
20.	1921	Takahashi	49.	1948	Second Yoshida
21.	1922	Katō Tomosaburō	50.	1949	Third Yoshida
22.	1923	Second Yamamoto	51.	1952	Fourth Yoshida
23.	1924	Kiyoura	52.	1953	Fifth Yoshida
24.	1924	First Katō Takaaki	53.	1954	First Hatoyama
25.	1925	Second Katō Takaaki	54.	1955	Second Hatoyama
26.	1926	First Wakatsuki	55.	1955	Third Hatoyama
27.	1927	Tanaka	56.	1956	Ishibashi
28.	1929	Hamaguchi	57.	1957	First Kishi
29.	1931	Second Wakatsuki	58.	1957	Second Kishi

Suggested Reading

Readers of Professor Maruyama's essays may find the following books in English useful:

Brown, Delmer M. *Nationalism in Japan: an Introductory Historical Analysis.* Berkeley, Calif., 1955.

Burks, Ardath W. *The Government of Japan.* New York, 1961.

Butow, Robert. *Tōjō and the Coming of the War.* Princeton, 1961.

Cole, Allan. *Japanese Society and Politics; the Impact of Social Stratification and Mobility on Politics.* Boston, Mass., 1956.

De Bary, William Theodore. *Sources of the Japanese Tradition.* New York, 1958.*

Dore, R. P. *City Life in Japan.* London, 1958.

Holtom, D. C. *Modern Japan and Shinto Nationalism.* Chicago, 1947.

Jansen, Marius. *The Japanese and Sun Yat-sen.* Cambridge, Mass., 1954.

Japan, Ministry of Education. *Kokutai no Hongi* (Cardinal Principles of the National Entity of Japan), trs. by J. O. Gauntlett, ed. by R. K. Hall. Cambridge, Mass., 1949.

Maxon, Y. C. *Control of Japanese Foreign Policy: a Study of Civil-Military Rivalry, 1930–1945.* Berkeley, Calif., 1957.

Morris, Ivan. *Nationalism and the Right Wing in Japan: a Study of Post-War Trends.* London, 1960.

Norman, E. H. *Japan's Emergence as a Modern State.* New York, 1940.

Sansom, Sir George. *The Western World and Japan.* New York, 1950.

Scalapino, Robert. *Democracy and the Party Movement in Pre-War Japan.* Berkeley, Calif., 1953.

Storry, Richard. *A History of Modern Japan.* London, 1960.

Storry, Richard. *The Double Patriots: a Study of Japanese Nationalism.* London, 1957.

Yanaga, Chitoshi. *Japanese People and Politics.* New York, 1956.

* Part V of this work (pp. 589–906) contains a valuable set of translations of modern Japanese writings about the development of the country, the majority being concerned with political trends since the Meiji Restoration.

Index

(Figures in bold type refer to the Glossary)

'A Hundred Million Hearts Beating Like One' (Ichioku Isshin), 123, **290**

Abe Cabinet, 72, 111, **290**

Adachi Kenzō, 65, 81, **290**

Aikoku Kinro Tō, *see* Patriotic Labour Party

Aikoku Undō Itchi Kyogi Kai, *see* Council for a Union of Patriotic Movements

Aizawa Incident (Aizawa Jiken), 26, 66, 68, **290**

Akamatsu Katsumaro, 31, 82, 92 n., **290**

Akao Bin, 28, 75, **290-1**

Akiyama Teisuke, 92 n., **291**

All-Japan National Socialist Council (Nihon Kokkashakaishugi Zenkoku Kyōgi Kai), 32

All-Japan Patriots' Joint Struggle Council (Zen-Nihon Aikokusha Kyōdō Tōsō Kyōgi Kai), 30, 31, 32, **291**

Amano Tatsuo, 28, 31, 54, **291**

Amur River Association (Kokuryū Kai), 27, 31, 51 n., 143, **291-2**

Anami Korechika, 99, **292**

Anti-Red Corps (Sekka Bōshi Dan), 27, **292**

Araki Sadao, **292**; views on armed forces, 14; Imperial Way, 22, 94; his own responsibility, 121; role in May 15 Incident, 54, 67; agrarian movement, 66; Imperial Way Faction, 66 and n.; February Incident, 70 n.; October Incident, 110

Arima Yoriyasu, 168 n., **292**

Asahi Shimbun, 61 n.

Asia Development League (Kōa Dōmei), 74

Asō Hisashi, 32, 82, **292**

Assignation house, *see* House of Assignation

'Assistance' (yokusan), 7, 20, **292**

Assistance Association, *see* Imperial Rule Assistance Association

Assistance Election, *see* Tōjō Assistance Election

Atrocities, *see* Prisoners of war

Atsumi Katsu (Masaru), 28, **292**

Baba Eiichi, 71, **293**

Bakumatsu Period, 56, 79, 80, 137, 139, **293**

Bamboo spear principle (takeyari shugi), 64, **293**

Blood Pledge Corps Incident (Ketsumei Dan Jiken), 26, 29, 32, 45, 53, **293**

Bungei Shunjū, 63 n., **293**

Central Co-operative Assembly (Chūō Kyōryoku Kai), 73-74

Chang Tso-lin, 81, **293**

Ch'en Po-ta, 220, **293-4**

Cherry Blossom Association (Sakura Kai), 29 and n., 68, **294**

Chō Isamu, 110 n., **294**

Christianity, 5-6, 140

Chūō Kyōryoku Kai, *see* Central Co-operative Assembly

Clan clique (hambatsu), 13, 41, 126, **294**

Communist Party, 29, 135, 188, 190, 195-6

'Composite magazine' (sōgō zasshi), 63 and n., **294**

Conscription, 147-8

Control Faction (Tōsei Ha), **294**; criticized by young officers, 56, 69; identity, 66 n.; struggle with Imperial Way Faction, 66, 68-69; role of Nagata, 70 n.; dissolution, 74

Council for a Union of Patriotic Movements (Aikoku Undō Itchi Kyōgi Kai), 32-33, **294**

Dai Ajiya Kyōkai, *see* Greater Asia Society

Dai Nihon Kokusui Kai, *see* Great Japan National Essence Association

338 *Index*

Dai Nihon Sangyō Hōkoku Kai, *see* Serve-the-State-through-Industry Association
Dai Nihon Seigi Dan, *see* Great Japan Political Justice Corps
Dai Nihon Seisan Tō, *see* Great Japan Production Party
Dai Nihon Yokusan Sōnen Dan, *see* Great Japan Imperial Rule Assistance Youth League
Dai Tōa Kyōei Ken, *see* Greater East Asia Co-Prosperity Sphere
Dark Ocean Society (Genyō Sha), 27, 30, 51 n., 79, 143, **294-5**
Doihara Kenji, 91 n., **295**

Education Ministry (Mombu Shō), 10
Education Rescript (Kyōiku Chokugo), 5-6, 9, 20, **295**
'Eight Corners of the World under One Roof' (Hakkō Ichiu), 1, 2, 88, 103, 148
Elder Statesmen (Genrō), 232, 260, **295**
Emperor, role of, 19-20, 123-8
'Expel the Barbarians' (Jōi), 5, 139, **295**

February Incident (Nigatsu Jiken), **295-6**; general significance as a turning-point, 26, 33, 34 n., 66 and n., 70, 71; role of Kita Ikki, 28; right-wing groups, 32; Araki Sadao, 70 n.; objectives, 55-56, 56 n., 69, 70 n.; punishments, 68 and n.; financial backing, 92 n.; threat of repetition, 111
Feudalism, 15, 252
Five Classics, 257, **296**
Five Ministers' Conference, 104, 120 and n., **296**
Four Books, 257, **296**
Freedom and People's Rights Movement (Jiyū Minken Undō), *see* Popular Rights Movement
Fujii Hitoshi, 29 n., 54, **296**
Fujita Tōko, 55-56, **296**
Fukai Eigo, 109 n., **296**
Fukuzawa Yukichi, 18, 146, 209, **296-7**

Gekokujō, *see* Rule of the higher by the lower
General Outline of Measures for the Re-construction of Japan (Nihon Kaizō Hōan Taikō), 28, 37, 42, 55, **297**
Genrō, *see* Elder Statesmen
Genyō Sha, *see* Dark Ocean Society
Germany, *see* Nazi Germany
Goichigo Jiken, *see* May 15 Incident
Golden Pheasant Academy (Kinkei Gakuin), 32, **297**
Gondō Seikyō (Seikei), 31, 38-40, 40 n., 42, 43, 53, **297**
Göring, Hermann, 12, 91 n., 100-1
Gotō Akinori, 45, 67, **297**
Gotō Fumio, 66, **297-8**
Great Deeds Association (Taikō Sha), 168 n.
Great East Asia Co-Prosperity Sphere (Dai Toa Kyoei Ken), 51, 88
Great Japan National Essence Association (Dai Nihon Kokusui Kai), 27, 28, **298**
Great Japan Political Justice Corps (Dai Nihon Seigi Dan), 27, 28, **298**
Great Japan Production Party (Dai Nihon Seisan Tō), 30-31, 44, 54, 143, **298**
Great Japan Serve-the-State-through-Industry Association (Dai Nihon Sangyō Hōkoku Kai), *see* Serve-the-State-through-Industry Movement
Great Reform Association (Taika Kai), 29, **298**
Greater Asia Society (Dai Ajiya Kyōkai), 95, **298**
Grew, Joseph, 95-96, 98-99, 106, 114 n.
Gunmu Kyoku, *see* Military Affairs Bureau
Gunrei Ha, *see* Navy Command Faction
Gunsei Ha, *see* Navy Ministry Faction
Gyōji Sha, *see* Society to Carry Out Heaven's Way on Earth

Hakkō Ichiu, *see* 'Eight Corners of the World under One Roof'
Hamada Kunimatsu, 70, **299**
Hamaguchi Osachi, 29, 81, **299**
Hambatsu, *see* Clan clique
Han Fei Tsu, 257, **299**
Harada Kumao, 111 n., 112 n., 120 n., **299**
Hashimoto Kingorō, 29 n., 91 n., 110 n., **299**
Hashimoto Sanai, 140-1, 149, **299**

Hashimoto Tetsuma, 92 n., 129 n., **299**
Hata Bushirō, 47, **300**
Hata Shunroku, 99–100, 111, 133, **300**
Hayashi Senjūrō, 61, 72, **300**
Heavenly Sword Party (Tenken Tō), 29 n.
Heaven-Sent Soldiers' Unit Incident (Shimpei Tai Jiken), 26, 28, 31, 32, 54–55, 65, **300**
Heimu Koku, *see* Military Service Bureau
Higashikuni Naruhiko, 88 n., **300**
Higher Ethics Association (Meirin Kai), 32, **300**
Himmler, Heinrich, 91 n., 94
Hirano Rikizō, 31, 32, **300**
Hiranuma Kiichirō, 28, 32, 72, 112 n., 120, **300–1**
Hirota Kōki, 66, 71, 120, **301**
Hitler, Adolf, 37, 57, 74, 79, 91 n., 93, 107, 262
Honjō Shigeru, 56 n., **301**
Hoshino Naoki, 115, 122, **301**
House of assignation (machiai), 80, 110 n., 129, 232, **301**

Ichioku Isshin, *see* 'A Hundred Million Hearts Beating Like One'
Iimura Minoru, 122 n., **301**
Ikeda Seihin, 92 n., 111, **301**
Imperial Flag Incident (Kinki Jiken), *another name for the* October Incident, *q.v.*
Imperial Rescript on Education, *see* Education Rescript
Imperial Rule Assistance Association (Taisei Yokusan Kai), **301–2**; general significance as turning-point, 34 n., 172; limitations, 59; change in character, 70 n., 73, 97 n.; inauguration, 34 n., 72; absorption of right-wing groups and political parties, 74, 80, 172; criticism by Akao Bin, 75; propaganda, 147–8; function, 260
Imperial Rule Assistance Political Association (Yokusan Seiji Kai), 73, **302**
Imperial Rule Assistance Young Men's Corps (Yokusan Sōnen Dan), 73, 167, **302**
Imperial Warriors' Association (Ōshi Kai), 29 n.

Imperial Way Association (Kōdō Kai), 32, **302**
Imperial Way Faction (Kōdō Ha), **302–3**; identity, 66 n.; struggle with Control Faction, 66, 68–69; ideology, 69, 70 n.; dissolution, 74; post-war reappearance, 68, 75–76
Imperial Way Principles Association (Kōdōgi Kai), 27, **303**
Industrial Service Movement (Sanpō Undō), *see* Serve-the-State-through-Industry Movement
Ingai dan, *see* 'Lobbyist' group
Inoue Junnosuke, 45, **303**
Inoue Nisshō, 53, 92 n., 97, 129 n., **303**
Ishiwara Hiroichirō, 30
Ishizeki Sakae, 54
Itagaki Seishirō, 91 n., 120 and n., **303**
Itō Hirobumi, 127, **303–4**
Itō Ritsu, 194, **304**
Iwanami Publishing Company, 63, **304**
Iwata Fumio, 29, 92 n.

Japan Economic League (Nihon Keizai Remmei), 71
Japan Federation of Labour (Nihon Rōdō Sōdōmei), 72, **304**
Japan National Council of Trade Unions (Nihon Rōdō Kumiai Zenkoku Hyōgi Kai) 29, **304**
Japan National Socialist Party (Nihon Kokka Shakai Tō), 31, **305**
Japan Peasants' Union (Nihon Nōmin Kumiai), 32, **305**
Japan Proletariat Party (Nihon Musan Tō), 72, **305**
Japan Village Government League (Nihon Sonji Ha Dōmei), 37
Jichi Mimpan, see *Self-Government by the People*
Jimmu, 20, **305**
Jimmu Association (Jimmu Kai), 30, **305**
Jimmu Kai, *see* Jimmu Association
Jiyū Minken Undō, *see* Popular Rights Movement
Jiyū Tō, *see* Liberal Party
Jōi, *see* 'Expel the Barbarians'
Joint Association for the Defence of the National Polity (Kokutai Yōgo Rengō Kai), 32, **305**

Joint Council for Rural Policy (Nōson Taisaku Rengō Kyōgi Kai), 65–66, **305**
Joint Council for Solving the National Crisis (Kokunan Dakai Rengō Kyōgi Kai), 32, **305**
Jūgatsu Jiken, *see* October Incident
Junsui bungaku, *see* 'Pure literature'
Jushin, *see* Senior Retainers

Kabayama Sukenori, 127, **305**
Kageyama Masaharu, 54, **305–6**
Kaiten-Shi Shi, 55, **306**
Kamei Kanichirō, 32, 82, **306**
Kamishibai, *see* Picture-story show
K'ang Yu-wei, 141, **306**
Kanin Sumihito, 99, **306**
Kanji, *see* 'Secretary'
Kanokogi Kazunobu, 31
Kantō Gun, *see* Kwangtung Army
Kantō Kokusui Kai, *see* Kanto National Essence Association
Kanto National Essence Association (Kantō Kokusui Kai), 27, **306**
Katayama Tetsu, 31, **306**
Kawakami Jōtarō, 49, **306–7**
Kawakami Sōroku, 127, **307**
Kawasaki Misaburō, 201 n., **307**
Kaya Okinori, 115, 120, **307**
Keirin Gakumei, *see* Statesmanship League
Keisatsu Yobitai, *see* National Police Reserve Force
Kenkoku Kai, *see* National Founding Association
Ketsumei Dan Jiken, *see* Blood Pledge Corps Incident
Kido Kōichi, **307**; comments on Konoe, 97; relations between Suzuki and Yonai, 108 n.; October Incident, 110, 111 n.; March Incident, 168 and n.; attitude to his own responsibility, 104–5, 121; relations with rightists, 129
Kinkei Gakuin, *see* Golden Pheasant Academy
Kinki Jiken, *see* Imperial Flag Incident
Kita Ikki, **307**; founds the Society of Those Who Yet Remain, 28; describes Japan as a family, 37; breaks with Ōkawa, 38; his reform programme and its exceptionality in Japan, 42; influence on February

Incident, 55, 68, 69; significance of his execution, 67, 68 n.; financial backing, 92 n.
Kita Sōichirō, 17, **307**
Kōa Dōmei, *see* Asia Development League
Kōchi Sha, *see* Society to Carry Out Heaven's Way on Earth
Kōda Kiyosada, 68, **307**
Kōdan Sha, 63, **307–8**
Kōdō Ha, *see* Imperial Way Faction
Kōdōgi Kai, *see* Imperial Way Principles Association
Kōdō Kai, *see* Imperial Way Association
Koga Kiyoshi, 53–54, 67, **308**
Koike Shirō, 31, **308**
Koiso Kuniaki, 29, 66, 105–6, 112 n., **308**
Kokkashakaishugi Shintō Jumbi Kai, *see* New National Socialist Party Preparatory Committee
Kokuhon Sha, *see* National Foundation Society
Kokui Kai, *see* National Prestige Maintenance Association
Kokunan Dakai Rengo Kyōgi Kai, *see* Joint Council for Solving the National Crisis
Kokuryū Kai, *see* Amur River Association
Kokutai, *see* National polity
Kokutai no Hongi, see *Principles of National Polity*
Kokutai Yōgo Rengō Kai, *see* Joint Association for the Defence of the National Polity
Kondō Eizō, 31, **308**
Kōno Hironaka, **308**; *see* **308**
Konoe Fumimaro, **308–9**; New Order Movement, 33 and n., 72–73; attitude on eve of Pacific War, 88 n.; weak spirit, 97–98, 132; discussion with Hata (1940), 111; relations with rightists, 129 n.
Konuma Tadashi, 45, **309**
Kume Kunitake, 9, **309**
Kumoi Tatsuo, 56, **309**
Kuo Mo-jo, 216, **309**
Kuroda Kiyotaka, 41, **309**
Kurusu Saburō, 87, 99, 112, **310**
Kwangtung Army (Kantō Gun), 70 n., 109, **310**
Kyoiku Chokugo, *see* Education Rescript

Labour-Peasant Faction (Rōnō Ha), 72, **310**
Labour-Peasant Party (Rōnō Tō), 29, 82, **310**
League of Nations, Japanese withdrawal, 10, 30
Levelling Society (Suihei Sha), 27, **310**
Liberal Party (Jiyū Tō), 4, **310**
Liu T'iao River (Ryūjō Kō), 109, **310**
'Lobbyist group' (ingai dan), 27, 82, **310–11**
London Naval Conference and Disarmament Treaty, 81, 123
Lu Ting-i, 216, 220, 222, **311**

Machiai, *see* House of assignation
Maeda Torao, 28, 54, **311**
Makino Nobuaki, 53, 54, 55, **311**
March Incident (Sangatsu Jiken), 26, 29, 56, 70 n., 110, 168, **311**
Marco Polo Bridge (Lukou Ch'iao), 109, **311**
Matsui Iwane, 95, 112–13, 117–18, 132, **311**
Matsui Kūka, 92 n., 129 n., **311**
Matsukata Cabinet, 127, 133
Matsuoka Komakichi, 31, **312**
Matsuoka Yōsuke, 91, 106–7, **312**
Matsutani Yojirō, 31, **312**
May 15 Incident (Goichigo Jiken), **312**; participants, 32; role of Gondō Seikyō, 38; official report, 48; plan and objectives, 53; effect, 65; punishments, 67, 68 n.
Mazaki Jinzaburō, 66, **312**
Meiji Constitution, 20, 118–19, 122, 133, 229
Meirin Kai, *see* Higher Ethics Association
Mikami Taku, 67, **313**
Mikoshi, *see* Portable shrine
Military Affairs Bureau (Gummu Kyoku), 99, 108, 119–20, 124, **313**
Military Service Bureau (Heimu Kyoku), 124
Minami Jirō, 94–95, 110, **313**
Minken Undō, *see* Popular Rights Movement
Minobe Tatsukichi, 9, 32, 61–62, **313**
Minoda Muneki, 62, **313**
Minsei Tō, 53, 55, 81, **313–14**
Mitamura Takeo, 75
Mito School, 139, **314**

Mitsukawa Kametarō, 28, **314**
Miyake Setsurei, 41, **314**
Miyazawa Toshiyoshi, 56, **314**
Mizuno Hironori, 123, **314**
Mombu Shō, *see* Education Ministry
Mori Arinori, 145, **314**
Mori Kaku, 130 n., **315**
Muramatsu Hisayoshi, 46, **315**
Muranaka Kōji, 49, 55, **315**
Mutō Akira, 108, 116–17, 119, **315**

Nagai Kafū, 250, **315**
Nagata Tetsuzan, 29, 56, 68, 70 n., 110, **315**
Nakahashi Motoaki, 70 n., **315**
Nakano Seigō, 75, 92 n., **316**
Nanking, *see* 'Rape of Nanking'
National Council of Trade Unions (Zenhyō), 72
National Foundation Society (Kokuhon Sha), 32, **316**
National Founding Association (Kenkoku Kai), 28–29, **316**
National Labour-Peasant Mass Party (Zenkoku Rōnō Taishū Tō), 31, **316**
National Police Reserve Force (Keisatsu Yobitai), 153, **316**
National polity (Kokutai), **316–17**; comprehensiveness, 6; source of political conflict, 9; used as a political weapon by various opposing groups, 10, 36 n., 37, 68, 69, 70 n., 78 n., 81; effect of defeat, 21, 148, 149; sacrosanctity, 61, 229; use as a unifying slogan, 72; education, 145–6; effect on Communist Party, 190
National Prestige Maintenance Association (Kokui Kai), 32, **317**
Natsume Sōseki, 7
Naval Affairs Bureau, *see* Military Affairs Bureau
Navy Command Faction (Gunrei Ha), 123, **317**
Navy Ministry Faction (Gunsei Ha), 123, **317**
Nazi Germany, comparison with Japan, attitude of war criminals, 12; treatment of prisoners, 12; popular organization and revolution from below, 33, 74, 76, 82; absence of family concept of State, 37; concentration on industrial workers, 48–49, 76; democratic influence and

Nazi Germany—*cont.*
 trappings, 50–51, 56–57, 76; reliance
 on civilian support, 52; support by
 intelligentsia, 59, 63; superior orga-
 nization, 79–80; eradication of all
 other political forces, 80; leadership,
 90–103 passim; acceptance of re-
 sponsibility, 107
Nemoto Hiroshi, 29 n., **317**
New Japan National League (Shin
 Nihon Kokumin Dōmei), 31, **317**
New National Socialist Party Prepara-
 tory Committee (Kokkashakaishugi
 Shintō Jumbi Kai), 31
New Order Movement (Shin Taisei
 Undō), 33 and n., 72–73, **317–18**
Nichimu, *abbreviation of* Nihon Musan
 Tō, *q.v.*
Nigatsu Jiken, *see* February Incident
*Nihon Aikoku Kakushin Hongi, see True
 Meaning of Japan's Political Reforma-
 tion*
*Nihon Kaizō Hōan Taikō see General
 Outline of Measures for the Reconstruc-
 tion of Japan*
Nihon Keizai Remmei, *see* Japan
 Economic League
Nihon Kokkashakaishugi Zenkoku
 Kyōgi Kai, *see* All-Japan National
 Socialist Council
Nihon Kokka Shakai Tō, *see* Japan
 National Socialist Party
Nihon Musan Tō, *see* Japan
 Proletariat Party
Nihon Nōmin Kumiai, *see* Japan
 Peasants' Union
Nihon Rōdō Kumiai Zenkoku Hyōgi
 Kai, *see* Japan National Council of
 Trade Unions
Nihon Rōdō Sōdōmei, *see* Japan
 Federation of Labour
Nihon Sonji Ha Dōmei, *see* Japan
 Village Government League
Nire Kagenori, 127, **318**
Nishida Zei, 28, 29 n., 67, 68 n., **318**
Noma Seiji, 7 n., **318**
Nomura Kichisaburō, 99, **318**
*Nōson Jikyū Ron, see Treatise on Rural
 Self-Help*
Nōson Jikyū Undō, *see* Rural Self-
 Help Movement
Nōson Taisaku Rengō Kyōgi Kai, *see*
 Joint Council for Rural Policy

Obata Torikichi, 66, 70 n.
October Incident, 26, 56, 65, 70 n.,
 110–11, 110 n., **318**
Odaka Tomoo, 231 n., 236 n., **318**
Officers' School Incident (Shikan
 Gakkō Jiken), 26, 66, **318–19**
Ogura Hirokatsu, 220
Oikawa Koshirō, 88 n., **319**
Oka Takazumi, 115–16, **319**
Okada Keisuke, 61, 124 n., **319**
Ōkawa Shūmei, **319**; founds the Society
 of Those Who Yet Remain, 28,
 Jimmu Association, 30, Society to
 Carry Out Heaven's Way on Earth,
 28, 38, 91; role in March Incident, 29,
 168 and n.; estimate of capitalism
 and socialism, 35, 38; psychopathic
 character, 91
Onozuka Kiheiji, 230 n.–231 n., **319**
Ōshi Kai, *see* Imperial Warriors'
 Association
Ōshima Hiroshi, 101–2, 104, 115, **319**
Ōsumi Mineo, 61, 67, **319**
Oyabun-kobun, 60, 79, 150, 264, **320**
Ōyama Iwao, 127, **320**
Ozaki Yukio, 9, 128, **320**

Patriotic Labour Party (Aikoku
 Kinrō Tō), 54, **320**
Pearl Harbour, Japanese attack on,
 16, 84–85, 98–99
Picture-story show (kamishibai), 147,
 320
Plots of the Warring States, 257, **320**
Politics and Learning Society (Seikyō
 Sha), 129 n., **320–1**
Popular Rights Movement (Minken
 Undō), 13, 51, 145, 229, **321**
Portable shrine (mikoshi), 128–30, **321**
Prerogative of supreme command
 (tōsuiken), 13, 119
Prisoners of war, treatment of, and
 atrocities, 11–12, 19, 119 n.
'Pure literature' (junsui bungaku),
 63, **321**
Purple Cloud Pavilion (Shiun Sō),
 129 n., **321–2**

'Revere the Emperor, Expel the
 Barbarians' (Sonnō Jōi), 5, **322**
Ribbentrop, Joachim von, 84 n., 87, 101
Road to Success and Prosperity, The
 (*Sakaeyuku Michi*), 7, **328**

Rōnin, 31, 79, 91 and n., 92, 107, **322**
Rōnō Ha, *see* Labour-Peasant Faction
Rōnō Tō, *see* Labour-Peasant Party
Rōyama Masamichi, 241, **322**
Rule of the higher by the lower
(gekokujō), 109–10, 113–14, **322**
Rural Self-Help Movement (Nōson
Jikyū Undō), 38–39, 40 n.
Ryūjō Kō, *see* Liu T'iao River

Sagoya Tomeo, 29, **322**
Saigō Takamori, 24
Sakaeyuku Michi, see *Road to Success
and Prosperity*
Sakomizu Hisatsune, 123, **322**
Sakuma Shōzan, 141, **323**
Sakura Kai, *see* Cherry Blossom
Association
Sampō Undō, *abbreviation of* Sangyō
Hōkoku Undō, *q.v.*
Sangatsu Jiken, *see* March Incident
Sangyō Hōkoku Undō, *see* Serve-the-
State-through-Industry Movement
Sasai Itchō, 31, **323**
Satō Naotake, 87, **323**
Satō Tsūji, 21 n., **323**
'Secretary' (kanji), 108, **323**
Seikyō Sha, *see* Politics and Learning
Society
Seiyū Kai, 53, 55, 62, 81–82
Sekka Bōshi Dan, *see* Anti-Red Corps
*Self-Government by the People (Jichi
Mimpan)*, 38–40
Senior Retainer(s) (Jūshin), **323**; role
during 1936–45, 27; relations with
Control Faction, 70 n.; inadequate
rapport, 108 n.; inability to control
army units, 109; ideology and objec-
tives, 109 n., 124 and n.; policy
towards the military, 111 n., the
Emperor, 128
Serve - the - State - through - Industry
Movement (Sangyō Hōkoku Undō),
34 n., 50, 72, **323–4**
Shakai Minshū Tō, *see* Social Mass
Party
Shakai Taishū Tō, ·*see* Social Masses
Party
Shanghai Incident, 30
Shiga Jūkō, 41, **324**
Shiga Naoya, 251, **324**
Shikan Gakko Jiken, *see* Officers'
School Incident

Shimmin no Michi, see *Way of the
Subject*
Shimizu Gyōnosuke, 168 n., **324**
Shimonaka Yasaburō, 31
Shimpei Tai Jiken, *see* Heaven-Sent
Soldiers' Unit Incident
Shin Nihon Kokumin Dōmei, *see*
New Japan National League
Shin Taisei Undō, *see* New Order
Movement
Shinran, 240, **324**
Shiratori Toshio, 91, 103–4, 111 n., **324**
Shiun Sō, *see* Purple Cloud Pavilion
Shōwa Ishin, *see* Shōwa Restoration
Shōwa Restoration (Shōwa Ishin), 49,
55, 68, **324–5**
Siberian Expedition, 116, **325**
Since Then (Sore Kara), 7
Social Mass Party (Shakai Minshū
Tō), 31, 82, **325**
Social Masses Party (Shakai Taishū
Tō), 32, 55, 72, **325**
Society of Those Who Yet Remain
(Yūzon Sha), 28, 30, **325–6**
Society to Carry Out Heaven's Way on
Earth (Gyōji Sha *or* Kōchi Sha), 28,
38, **326**
Sōgō zasshi, *see* 'Composite magazine'
Sohō, *see* Tokutomi Iichirō
Sonnō Jōi, *see* Revere the Emperor,
Expel the Barbarians
Sore Kara, see *Since Then*
Sōryokusen Kenkyūjo, *see* Total War
Research Institute
Sōseki, *see* Natsume Sōseki
'Spreading the Emperor's Mission to
Every Corner of the Earth' (Tenkyō
Kaikō), 1
Statesmanship League (Keirin
Gakumei), 29, 30, **326**
Suetsugu Nobumasa, 123, **326**
Sugiyama Gen, 66, 110, **326**
Suihei Sha, *see* Levelling Society
Suzuki Kantarō, 108 n., **326**
Suzuki Teiichi, 88 n., **327**
Suzuki Zenichi, 54, 97, **327**

Tachibana Kōsaburō, 42–43, 52,
68 n., **327**
Taika Kai, *see* Great Reform
Association
Taikō Sha, *see* Great Deeds
Association

344

Index

Taisei Yokusan Kai, *see* Imperial Rule Assistance Association
Taishō Sekinshin Dan, *see* Taishō Sincerity League
Taishō Sincerity League (Taishō Sekishin Dan), 27, **327**
Takabatake Motoyuki, 29, **327**
Takeyari shugi, *see* Bamboo spear principle
Takuya Dempu, 129 n., **327**
Tamenaga Shunsui, 250, **327**
Tanaka Giichi, 81, **327**
Tanaka Kunishige, 32, **328**
Tatekawa Yoshitsugu, 29, **328**
Tengyō Kaikō, *see* 'Spreading the Emperor's Mission to Every Corner of the Earth'
Tenken Tō, *see* Heavenly Sword Party
Terauchi Hisaichi, 46–47, 66–67, 68, 69, 70, **328**
'Third generation', 128, 279, **328**
Tōgō Shigenori, 53, 98, 104–5, 105 n., **328–9**
Tōjō Assistance Election, 33, 34 n., 73, **329**
Tōjō Hideki, **329**; representative Japanese politician, 11, 17; denial of dictatorship, 17; significance of his dictatorship, 33–34; attitude to farmers and factory workers, 47, 49–50; opposed by young officers, etc., 56, 68, 76; formation of his dictatorship, 72; acquires hegemony, 74; criticism of his dictatorship, 75; ignorance, 85 and n.; attitude on eve of Pacific War, 88 n., 112; comparison with Hitler, 91 n.
Tokutomi Iichiro (Sohō), 46, 147, 279, **329**
Tōsei Ha, *see* Control Faction
Tōsuiken, *see* Prerogative of supreme command
Total War Research Institute (Sōryokusen Kenkyūjo), 121–3
Tōyama Mitsuru, 28, 79, 130 n., **329**
Toyoda Teijirō, 88 n., **329**
Treatise on Rural Self-Help (*Nōson Jikyū Ron*), 38–40, **329**
Tripartite Pact, 33; effects on Japanese politics, 34 n., 99; role of Ōshima, 101–2, Kido, 104, Tōgō, 104–5, Koiso, 112 n.

True Meaning of Japan's Political Reformation, The (*Nihon Aikoku Kakushin Hongi*), 42–43, **328**
Tseng Kuo-fan, 141, **330**
Tsinan Incident, 81, **330**
Tsuda Kōzō, 37
Tsuda Sōkichi, 23, **330**
Tsukui Tatsuo, 28, 92 n., **330**

Uehara Yūsaku, 127, 133–4, **330**
Uesugi Shinkichi, 28, 29, **330**
Ugaki Kazushige, 29, 111, **331**
Umezu Yoshijirō, 66, **331**

War crimes trials, 12, 83–123 passim (esp. 89 n., 101)
Way of the Subject, The (*Shimmin no Michi*), 7, 10, **328**

Yamada Takao, 21
Yamaguchi Saburō, 54, **331**
Yamakawa Hitoshi, 40 n.
Yamanashi Katsunoshin, 123, **331**
Yanagawa Heisuke, 66, 70 n., **331**
Yasuda Masaru, 58 n., **331–2**
Yasuda Tetsunosuke, 54, **332**
Yasukuni Jinja, 112, **332**
Yasuoka Masaatsu (Masahiro), 28, 32, **332**
Yokusan, *see* 'Assistance'
Yokusan Seiji Kai, *see* Imperial Rule Assistance Political Association
Yokusan Sōnen Dan, *see* Imperial Rule Assistance Young Men's Corps
Yonai Mitsumasa, 72, 99, 101, 108 n., 133, **332**
Yosano Akiko, 147, 154–6
Yoshino Sakuzō, 227 n., **332**
Yūki Toyotarō, 71, **332**
Yūzon Sha, *see* Society of Those Who Yet Remain

Zenhyō, *see* National Council of Trade Unions
Zenkoku Rōnō Taishū Tō, *see* National Labour-Peasant Mass Party
Zen-Nihon Aikoku Kyōdō Tōsō Kyōgi Kai, *see* All-Japan Patriots' Joint Struggle Council

Masao Maruyama was born in Osaka in 1914, graduated from Tokyo University in 1937, and was appointed Assistant Professor in the same University in 1940. In 1950 he was appointed Professor of Political Theory. From October 1961 to June 1962 he was Visiting Professor at Harvard University and in October 1962 was appointed Visiting Professor at St Antony's College, Oxford, returning to Tokyo in the spring of 1963. He was called up for military service in the last war and was stationed at Hiroshima in August 1945, being only three miles from the centre of the city when the atomic bomb fell. He was at that time Private First Class; his officers included a number of his former pupils.